NAZISM AND GERMAN SOCIETY, 1933–1945

"David Crew's selection is outstanding. He includes richly detailed and very nuanced articles as well as provocative think pieces painted in broad strokes. . . . The book abounds in significant conflicts, contending voices, and a sense of scholarly responsibility."

Rudy Koshar, *University of Wisconsin*

"An excellent introduction. . . . The volume brings together some of the most interesting recent research on the Third Reich. . . . It is an invitation to think critically about how to conceptualize the Third Reich. . . . A valuable teaching tool."

Robert Moeller, *The Woodrow Wilson International Center*

The "totalitarian" image of the Third Reich has been thoroughly displaced during the past two decades by new research on the social history of the Nazi years which reveals the variety and complexity of the relationships between the Nazi regime and the German people. The articles in *Nazism and German Society* focus the issues. This textbook:

- addresses the key debates;
- includes the most recent revisionist and challenging interpretations;
- raises important methodological and theoretical questions;
- contains several German authors not easily available in English;
- provides a lucid, informative and thought-provoking introduction;
- encompasses many viewpoints in a coherent structure.

David F. Crew is Associate Professor of History at the University of Texas at Austin.

REWRITING HISTORIES
Series editor: Jack R. Censer

Already published

ATLANTIC AMERICAN SOCIETIES
From Columbus through Abolition 1492–1888
Edited by Alan L. Karras and J. R. McNeill

DIVERSITY AND UNITY IN EARLY NORTH
AMERICA
Edited by Philip D. Morgan

GENDER AND AMERICAN HISTORY SINCE 1890
Edited by Barbara Melosh

THE INDUSTRIAL REVOLUTION AND WORK IN
NINETEENTH-CENTURY EUROPE
Edited by Lenard R. Berlanstein

ORIGINS OF THE COLD WAR
An International History
Edited by Melvyn P. Leffler and David S. Painter

SOCIETY AND CULTURE IN THE SLAVE SOUTH
Edited by J. William Harris

Forthcoming

REFORMATION TO REVOLUTION
Edited by Margo Todd

SEGREGATION AND APARTHEID IN
TWENTIETH-CENTURY SOUTH AFRICA
Edited by William Beinart and Saul Dubow

NAZISM AND GERMAN SOCIETY, 1933–1945

Edited by David F. Crew

London and New York

First published 1994
by Routledge
11 New Fetter Lane, London EC4P 4EE

Simultaneously published in the USA and Canada
by Routledge
29 West 35th Street, New York, NY 10001

Phototypeset in Palatino by
Intype, London

Printed and bound in Great Britain by
Mackays of Chatham PLC, Chatham, Kent

British Library Cataloguing in Publication Data
A catalogue record for this book is available from the British Library.

Library of Congress Cataloging in Publication Data
A catalog record for this book is available from the Library of
Congress.

ISBN 0–415–08239–0 (hbk)
ISBN 0–415–08240–4 (pbk)

CONTENTS

List of tables   vii
Editor's preface   ix

GENERAL INTRODUCTION   1
David F. Crew

**Part I   "Victims" or "perpetrators?" The German people and
the Nazi regime**

1 THE MISSING YEARS: GERMAN WORKERS,
GERMAN SOLDIERS   41
Omer Bartov

2 THE "HONOR OF LABOR": INDUSTRIAL WORKERS
AND THE POWER OF SYMBOLS UNDER NATIONAL
SOCIALISM   67
Alf Lüdtke

3 ANTINATALISM, MATERNITY AND PATERNITY
IN NATIONAL SOCIALIST RACISM   110
Gisela Bock

4 VICTIMS OR PERPETRATORS? CONTROVERSIES
ABOUT THE ROLE OF WOMEN IN THE NAZI
STATE   141
Adelheid von Saldern

5 OMNISCIENT, OMNIPOTENT, OMNIPRESENT?
GESTAPO, SOCIETY AND RESISTANCE   166
Klaus-Michael Mallmann and Gerhard Paul

CONTENTS

6 THE "HITLER MYTH": IMAGE AND REALITY IN
THE THIRD REICH 197
Ian Kershaw

Part II The "racial community" and its enemies

7 LABOR AS SPOILS OF CONQUEST, 1933–1945 219
Ulrich Herbert

8 THE GENESIS OF THE "FINAL SOLUTION" FROM
THE SPIRIT OF SCIENCE 274
Detlev J. K. Peukert

9 ONE DAY IN JOZEFOW: INITIATION TO MASS
MURDER 300
Christopher R. Browning

Suggestions for further reading 316

TABLES

1 Female employment in Germany during World War II (in millions) 231

2 Productivity levels of foreign workers and POWs in the Rhineland and Westphalia, mid-1943, in comparison with the average productivity of German workers in the same job (in percentage) 231

3 Escapes by foreign workers, 1943 262

EDITOR'S PREFACE

Rewriting history, or revisionism, has always followed closely in the tow of history writing. In their efforts to reevaluate the past, professional as well as amateur scholars have followed many approaches, most commonly as empiricists, uncovering new information to challenge earlier accounts. Historians have also revised previous versions by adopting new perspectives, usually fortified by new research, which overturn received views.

Even though rewriting is constantly taking place, historians' attitudes toward using new interpretations have been anything but settled. For most, the validity of revisionism lies in providing a stronger, more convincing account that better captures the objective truth of the matter. Although such historians might agree that we never finally arrive at the "truth," they believe it exists and over time may be better and better approximated. At the other extreme stand scholars who believe that each generation or even each cultural group or subgroup necessarily regards the past differently, each creating for itself a more usable history. Although these latter scholars do not reject the possibility of demonstrating empirically that some contentions are better than others, they focus upon generating new views based upon different life experience. Different truths exist for different groups. Surely such an understanding, by emphasizing subjectivity, further encourages rewriting history. Between these two groups are those historians who wish to borrow from both sides. This third group, while accepting that every congeries of individuals sees matters differently, still wishes somewhat contradictorily to fashion a broader history that incorporates both of these particular visions. Revisionists who stress empiricism fall into the first of the three camps, while others spread out across the board.

Today the rewriting of history seems to have accelerated to a blinding speed, as a consequence of the evolution of revisionism. A variety of approaches has emerged. A major factor in this process has been the enormous increase in the number of researchers. This explosion has reinforced and enabled the re-testing of many assertions. Significant ideological shifts have also played a major part in the growth of revisionism. First, the crisis of Marxism, culminating in the events in Eastern Europe in 1989, has given rise to doubts about explicitly Marxist accounts. Such doubts have spilled over into the entire field of social history, which has been a dominant subfield of the discipline for several decades. Focusing on society and its class divisions implies that these are the most important elements in historical analysis. Because Marxism was built on the same claim, the whole basis of social history has been questioned, despite the very many students that had little directly to do with Marxism. Disillusionment with social history simultaneously opened the door to cultural and linguistic approaches largely developed in anthropology and literature. Multicultural-ism and feminism further generated revisionism. By claiming that scholars had, wittingly or not, operated from a white European/American male point of view, newer researches argued other approaches had been neglected or misunderstood. Not surprisingly, these last historians are the most likely to envision each subgroup rewriting its own usable history, while other scholars incline toward revisionism as part of the search for some stable truth.

Rewriting Histories will make these new approaches available to the student population. Often new scholarly debates take place in the scattered issues of journals which are sometimes difficult to find. Furthermore, in these first interactions, his-torians tend to address one another, leaving out the evidence that would make their arguments more accessible to the unin-itiated. This series of books will collect in one place a strong group of the major articles in selected fields, adding notes and introductions conducive to improved understanding. Editors will select articles containing substantial historical data, so that students – at the least those who approach the subject as an objective phenomenon – can advance not only their comprehension of debated points, but also their grasp of substantive aspects of the subject.

While interest in the Third Reich has not lessened, distance from the events has permitted much reconsideration, including changing the focus from Hitler alone. As this volume clearly indicates, this revisionism propelled scholars to reduce further the notion of a Germany locked in the vise-like grip of one party and its leader. Instead, historians see enough room for maneuver that for non-Jewish Germans the division between victim and perpetrator has become clouded. Many, though oppressed, also acted as oppressors. A fascinating debate in this volume over women highlights just this problem. Through this specific case and others, David Crew presents here a far more complex view of German society, but without neglecting the ultimate horror of the Nazi regime.

Jack R. Censer

GENERAL INTRODUCTION

David F. Crew

In the 1950s and 1960s, Hannah Arendt, Carl Friedrich and Karl Dietrich Bracher constructed a remarkably long-lived description of Nazi Germany as a "totalitarian" state and society. In a popularized Orwellian rendition – the monolithic state presiding over the brainwashed, fanatical masses – this "totalitarian" image of the Third Reich retains a tenacious grip on the imaginations of university students as well as the general public. The totalitarian model was derived from the Nazi regime's own ideological self-representations rather than from any close analysis of German society under National Socialism. David Schoenbaum's pioneering book on *Hitler's Social Revolution* published in 1966, proposed a new agenda for research on Nazi society, but it was not until the 1980s that German, British and American historians began to penetrate deep inside Nazi Germany. In the past ten years, a growing body of research on the social history of the Nazi years has made possible a new understanding of the Third Reich. This volume introduces readers to this new social-historical research and to the interpretive issues it raises.[1]

For many years after 1945, discussion of the popular experience of German fascism seldom went beyond vague assertions of "collective guilt" or equally simplistic attempts to differentiate between the "victims" and the "perpetrators." Recent research shows, however, that the realities of everyday life in Nazi German will simply not submit to black and white description. Most social historians would now present a more complex and disturbing picture of "the multiple everyday ambiguities of 'ordinary people' making their choices among the various greys of active consent, accommodation and non-conformity."[2]

Social historians have also uncovered the continuities that link

1

the Third Reich to the more "normal" periods of German history which both preceded and followed it. The most provocative formulation of this relationship has been proposed by Detlev Peukert who suggests that the Third Reich was a pathological variant of the "normal" modernity which preceded and in important ways produced the National Socialist phenomenon. His approach calls for a "sceptical de-coupling of modernity and progress" which would allow historians to pay closer attention to the "dark side" of modernity and to "raise questions about the pathologies and seismic fractures within modernity itself, and about the implicit destructive tendencies of industrial class society, which National Socialism made explicit and which it elevated into mass destruction."[3]

WORKERS UNDER NAZISM

Class conflict in the Third Reich?

Our knowledge of German society under Nazism owes a great deal to social historians' intensive investigation of the position, attitudes, and behavior of German workers. More than two decades of research have produced clearly opposed interpretations. In a highly influential thesis formulated in the 1960s, Tim Mason claimed that the Nazis failed to integrate workers into the Nazi regime or suppress class conflict between workers and employers and between workers and the state. By the early 1980s, Mason's argument had almost attained the status of orthodoxy. As one of his students put it:

> the essential starting point for any examination of Nazi society and economy as a whole, is the acknowledgement of the persistence of what it is convenient to label "class conflict", albeit in forms which are often hard to track down and evaluate.[4]

But the research of the past decade has increasingly cast doubt upon this "class conflict" paradigm and has tended "to place greater emphasis upon the elements of consensus, integration and approval, in contrast with the arguments about non-conformity, opposition and resistance."[5]

In the last years of the Weimar Republic, the Nazis piled up astounding electoral victories, constructing a larger, more diverse base of voters than any other single party in German history. But the German working class remained far more immune to Nazi political influence than any other social group or political milieu in Weimar Germany. After the Nazi "seizure of power," the new regime attempted to coerce and persuade all racially pure Germans to cast off their old loyalties – class, political and religious – and to immerse themselves in a new collective identity, the *Volksgemeinschaft* or "racial community." In the spring of 1933, the Nazis destroyed the trade unions and working-class parties. German socialists and Communists hoped, however, to preserve "class consciousness" in the "half-public" working-class milieux of neighborhood and factory, as the socialist movement had done during Bismarck's anti-socialist law. But the Nazis managed to penetrate even the informal structures of "everyday life" with intimidation and terror. Hunted by the Gestapo, the small minority of political activists who continued, after the first few years of the Third Reich, to offer resistance to the Nazi dictatorship found they were increasingly isolated from their working-class base.[6] But Mason thought he could detect clear signs, among these ordinary workers, of "opposition," if not political "resistance," to the regime.[7] Mason claimed that from the mid-1930s full employment increasingly afforded German workers the opportunity to engage in

> spontaneous work-stoppages . . . collective pressure upon employers and Nazi institutions, in various sorts of insubordination against work-rules and state regulations, in "go-slow" actions, in missing work, in reporting sick, in various other manifestations of their discontent.[8]

Mason did not claim that these actions were politically motivated or, for that matter, that they were even formally organized. None the less, he detected in this behavior a collective "refusal of the working-class, to submit fully to the National Socialist system of domination."[9] Mason claimed that this "worker's opposition" threatened the Nazis' economic preparations for war and presented a substantial challenge to the Hitler regime.[10] He even suggested that Hitler's decision to go to war in 1939 was significantly influenced by the social and economic conflicts between workers and the regime that the rearmament boom had unleashed.[11] Although this particular hypothesis has not

3

gained wide acceptance, Mason's fundamental argument, namely that "even under extremely unfavorable circumstances, class-struggle reproduced itself in a variety of forms,"[12] has unquestionably structured the debate on the working class in the Third Reich for the past two decades.

Recent research has, however, begun to offer a different picture of the effects of economics upon working-class consciousness and behavior during the 1930s. Full employment, at least in the armaments sector of industry, encouraged workers to exploit their newfound position of economic advantage – but as workers generally bargained individually, not collectively, with employers these wage negotiations should be seen as a symptom of the decomposition, rather than of the continuation of "class conflict." In his recent important book, Rüdiger Hachtmann concludes, for example:

> Workers had at their disposal no institution or organisation that would have allowed them to articulate and to satisfy their interests collectively. . . . Demands for the improvement of their income could only be presented and achieved – if at all – on an individual basis. For this reason, the pressure which workers could exert upon wages was relatively weak.[13]

Contrary to Mason's original assessment, full employment appears to have made German workers less, not more resistant to Nazi propaganda.[14] Having a secure job, even at reduced wage rates, became the top priority for many workers and a powerful influence upon their attitudes toward the Nazi regime. As a Social Democrat in the Ruhr mining community of Hochlarmark put it: "They had four, five, even six years of unemployment behind them – they would have hired on with Satan himself."[15]

This "politics of the full-wage packet" certainly did not convert every worker into a Hitler enthusiast.[16] Higher incomes were achieved largely by working longer hours and workers still had to endure significant shortages, especially in housing. Various more or less disguised new forms of Nazi "taxation" also took a substantial bite out of workers' increased earnings.[17] The Nazi economic "miracle" did, however, convince many workers that things were getting better, especially as, for most of them, the

4

point of reference was not the best years of the Weimar Republic but the more recent depths of the Depression.[18]

Hachtmann also suggests that even in the pursuit of individual economic interest – the quintessence of the "worker's opposition" so far as Mason is concerned – worker's abilities to resist the demands of the regime were increasingly diminished by the modernization and rationalization of German industry in the 1930s, processes that the Nazis had by no means discovered, but whose potential, not only in preparing for modern war, but also in constructing and stabilizing their dictatorship, they seemed to understand only too well. Hachtmann argues that the spread of the assembly line, the introduction of modern forms of wage payment and wage measurement based upon individual productivity such as the Refa-Verfahren, the German version of Taylorism, made the preferred form of the "worker's opposition" – restriction of output – increasingly more difficult.[19] A repressive system of "factory medicine," which "was increasingly converted from an instrument of preventive and remedial care into a means of control,"[20] also made it more and more dangerous to resist the demands of Nazi labor discipline by feigning sickness.[21] In other words, the Nazi legal and political system had given German employers a much greater real control over the labor process which National Socialism was in turn able to use as "the basis for a tyranny . . . without parallel in the twentieth century."[22]

The Nazi economic mobilization for war also uprooted millions of Germans both physically and psychologically. The effects were most extreme in the new centers of war production, such as the Bremen aircraft industry or the Herman Goering *Reichswerke* in Salzgitter, which recruited labor from all over Europe as well as Germany, even before the war. Here a new workforce was assembled which disposed of few, if any, common traditions, or social and cultural institutions.[23] In the Saar, a relatively backward economic region, the "modernization processes" set in motion by Nazi rearmament,

> strengthened the (existing) trend towards social and geographic mobility, forced the process of urbanization forward, and altered the composition of classes and social milieux. Productivity incentives and new methods of wage payment promoted the segmentation of the working class.

5

Firm integration into traditional socio-cultural milieux was shaken, as was identification with inherited occupational and gender roles and with easily surveyed social and geographic spaces. The complex task of reorienting oneself and of finding new, reliable points of identification in everyday life absorbed a great deal of energy . . . this preoccupation with the problems of everyday life probably made it difficult for people to engage in oppositional behavior.[24]

Under the Nazis, German workers may have continued to represent a "class" in sociological terms, but they were either encouraged or forced to act and increasingly to see themselves in individualistic or other non-class collective terms (i.e. worker in a specific branch of industry, or even a specific plant; male worker versus female worker, etc.).

This fragmentation of interests and identities was also promoted by the destruction of the collective legal guarantees of wages, working conditions and social insurance benefits provided by the Weimar welfare state. The bankruptcy of the state welfare system during the Depression had already allowed the initiative in social policy to pass from the hands of the state into those of individual employers.[25] Company social policy continued to play an important role after 1933, especially as employers used social benefits to attract and retain workers when the demands of the Nazi rearmament boom began to produce labor shortages. But the German Labor Front increasingly attempted to interfere in the development and administration of company social policies, transforming them in the process from social to racial policies. German historians have only recently begun to see the importance of this specifically Nazi fusion of social with racial policy, in which the goal of "race hygiene" was pursued by both "positive" and "negative" means.[26] Workers whose social behavior and work performance showed the Nazis that they possessed "biological value" could expect improved housing, living and working conditions. They would also be encouraged to expand the "valuable substance" of the collective racial body by producing more children.[27] But the Nazis likewise intended to eliminate the biologically "inferior" from the workforce because their inefficiency threatened the German "racial community's" ability to win the

6

international struggle for survival against the world's other races. Ulrich Herbert thus concludes that

> to grasp the specifically National Socialist component of the development of labor and social policy during the "Third Reich", both elements – support and exclusion, "social policy" and eradication – have to be understood as inseparable components and expressions of one and the same ideological plan.[28]

The full force of this Nazi "social racism," as Detlev Peukert has termed it, was directed initially against marginal lower-class groups – vagrants and the homeless, for example, as well as casual laborers or prostitutes.[29] But "social racism" eventually put enormous pressure on *all* workers to conform to the required standards of productivity and labor discipline. For if the price of absenteeism or the failure to meet production norms before 1933 was low wages or unemployment, in the Third Reich such breaches of labor discipline were now read as symptoms of biological "inferiority" requiring confinement in a labor camp.[30] Here a short, sharp shock was administered which would either quickly rehabilitate the worker for "useful labor," or show the authorities that they had on their hands one of those "community aliens" or "anti-social elements" (*Asozialen*) that Nazi racial policy dictated should be segregated from the "healthy" body of the *Volk*, or perhaps even annihilated. During the war, the majority of the inmates of these "work/re-education camps" (*Arbeitserziehungslager*) were foreigners, but a significant minority were German workers. Although German workers did not generally have to fear the same kinds of extreme mistreatment, even death, that often awaited German Jews or foreign workers in these camps, the propagandistic effect was none the less substantial:

> the Gestapo did not punish every disobedient act, but workers had certainly heard rumors about what could happen to them if they fell into Gestapo hands ... employers used the threat of the Gestapo to intimidate their workers.[31]

It is not an exaggeration to suggest that the persecution of German workers under the heading of "racial hygiene"

7

increasingly became as important a threat as the persecution of political opposition.[32]

But the Third Reich also attempted to present a "sunny side" to German workers in the attempt not merely to neutralize them but also to integrate them into the Nazi system.[33] Until recently, this side of Nazi labor policy has been seen as scarcely more than a form of meaningless window-dressing, the substitution, as one of Mason's students put it, of "status for material improvements."[34] But in an important reconsideration of his own original arguments, Mason acknowledged that he had perhaps focussed too exclusively upon workers' "opposition" to Nazism[35] and that future research would have to pay more attention to the variety of ways in which German workers may also have become (at least partially) reconciled to, even integrated into, the Nazi regime.[36]

The Nazis held out the prospect of a new mass consumerism which would spread the material benefits of industrial society (and, after 1939, of German imperialism) far beyond the narrow confines of the middle classes which had previously monopolized them. German workers would have paid vacations, go on trips to the mountains or on ocean cruises sponsored by the Nazi "Strength through Joy" organization. German workers would also have a "people's car" which they could drive along the new super highways (Autobahnen), Hitler's engineering marvel. German cities would be rebuilt and workers would no longer have to live in overcrowded slums. In their new homes, working-class families would have modern conveniences, including the "people's radio receiver." That most German workers never even saw most of these wonders of modern consumer society, except in Nazi propaganda, until the 1950s did not necessarily diminish their impact. Especially among the younger generation of workers who had not been socialized in the Weimar labor movement, Nazism stimulated what one historian calls Ausbruchshoffnung – the hope that it might for the first time be possible to escape, or at the very least to expand the traditionally narrow economic, social and cultural horizons of working-class life.[37] In solidly proletarian districts, like the Ruhr, such hopes might be aroused by even relatively modest changes – in Hochlarmark, for example, the spread of cheap radios put miners' families in touch with the outside world, and miners' sons were offered new opportunities to receive technical training or went off to work at higher wages in the armaments industry.[38] Nazi youth organizations gave working-class girls, as well as boys, the chance to contest parental authority and to escape the family. Especially for the young, then, the 1930s seemed, under the Nazis, a time of new possibilities.

But Nazi appeals to German workers were by no means limited to these material inducements to passivity. In his contribution to this volume, Alf Lüdtke explores the effects of the Nazi regime's "symbolic offerings" to the German working class. Lüdtke suggests that even workers who supported the Social Democrats or Communists during the Weimar Republic displayed ambivalent attitudes toward the Nazi regime after 1933. The Nazis attempted to exploit this "sceptical acquiescence" by calling for recognition of the "honor of labor" (Ehre der Arbeit) and by insisting upon the importance of "German quality work" (Deutsche Qualitätsarbeit). These were resonant and enduring "cultural icons" in German society which could engage the sympathies of a wide range of ordinary Germans, from factory engineer to skilled worker, regardless of their former political persuasions.

Non-class identities and interests

Like their non-working-class fellow Germans, workers were also motivated by interests that are difficult to equate with those of any specific class. So, for example, though many workers who were socialists and trade unionists before 1933 may well have maintained a critical distance from the Nazi movement, they could none the less approve of Hitler's foreign policy successes, thus participating in the construction of a "Hitler myth" (discussed in Ian Kershaw's contribution to this volume) which was the most important integrative mechanism in the Third Reich. In his research on the miners of Hochlarmark, Zimmerman has confirmed what Ian Kershaw discovered in his earlier study:

> Next to the transition from unemployment to full employment, the most important influences encouraging a reduction of the miner's distrust of the Nazi regime were the integrative role played by Hitler, who, as "Führer", seemed to be enthroned somewhere above the petty

9

quarrels of everyday life, and the foreign policy successes of the regime – "bringing home" the Saar to the *Reich* in 1935, the reoccupation of the Rhineland in 1936, and the annexation of Austria and the Sudetenland in 1938.[39]

On the other hand, a worker who was a Catholic might, like other German Catholics, become progressively alienated from the regime because of its campaign against the Catholic church in Germany. Catholics and other Christians were also outraged by certain aspects of Nazi racism, such as the Euthanasia Campaign.[40] Non-class identities and interests thus overlaid and intersected with the already complicated and contradictory perspectives on the Nazi regime constructed from workers' experiences in the factories and working-class neighborhoods.

Workers at war

The great bulk of research on the social history of Nazi Germany concentrates on the years before 1939; yet some of the deepest, most rapid changes affecting the structure, behavior and consciousness of German workers occurred during the war. After the war began, the face of racism in the Third Reich assumed an even more contradictory complexion. During the war, German workers were, if anything, persecuted even more severely than before 1939 for any signs of alleged biological "inferiority"; but, at the same time, the massive importation of "racially inferior" foreign workers to meet the needs of the German war economy gave "Aryan" German workers a *de facto* position of privilege. In his contribution to this volume, Ulrich Herbert shows that the conditions under which the largely forced labor of foreigners was performed during the Second World War were extremely brutal. Some German workers displayed sympathy for the sufferings of foreign workers, but these seldom went beyond small acts of kindness, such as illegally passing a foreign worker a piece of bread. Other German workers flagrantly mistreated foreign workers. But the behavior and attitudes of the majority of German workers towards the foreigners appear to have been characterized more by

> a sort of indifference and disinterest which made the presence of foreign labor simply a fact of life, not to be questioned. These attitudes became ever more deeply

entrenched as the war dragged on and as the German population's own cares and problems increased. Germans found the oppression of Poles and Russians no more unusual than their own position of privilege.[41]

A great deal remains to be learned about the exploitation of foreign labor and about the relationships between foreign and German workers in different industrial sectors, in different regions of Germany and in different phases of the war.[42] But it is unlikely that future research will significantly revise the general picture we now have of the restructuring of the working class in Germany that was produced by Nazi racism: "the process of creating an under-class, set in motion by the the presence of foreign forced labor, permitted [German workers] unprecedented possibilities for social advancement."[43]

In addition to the massive importation of foreign labor, at least two other subjects deserve attention; first, the experiences of the millions of young, male workers who were conscripted into the German army, especially those sent to the Eastern Front.[44] Josef Mooser points out that,

at least two generations of workers were stamped with the experience of being soldiers. . . . Their experience of the extremely violent social processes of the twentieth century – war, mass murder, deportation, totalitarian repression – continues to evade effective communication. But it is important to grasp the fact that workers were implicated in these processes, not only as victims but also as perpetrators.[45]

Second, we need to pay more attention to the experiences of the workers who remained at home, among whom the progressive worsening of living and working conditions, caused by Allied bombing raids and the mounting threat of Soviet invasion, produced a widespread "defeatism" and a myopic focus upon the day-to-day struggle for survival. The war and in particular the worsening of conditions and prospects on both the fighting and home fronts after 1942–3 produced an important rupture in German workers' experiences and memories of the Third Reich.[46] The few existing studies of the "homefront" suggest that during the war the material living conditions of German workers ceased to provide a reliable guide to working-class

11

experience. Any collective identity that may have survived the 1930s could only have been further fragmented by the war experience:[47]

> during at least the last third of the war, the development of the working class could, in fact, not be differentiated precisely from the situation of other groups in the population. . . . The criteria which determined the fate of individuals and shaped their experiences were such things as being drafted into the army or being deferred from the draft, being sent to the western or to the eastern front, being wounded or being spared injury. Whether a family lived in a small town or an industrial region, on the edge of a city, or in an inner-city neighborhood threatened by the bombs, whether it was bombed out or not, whether the children were evacuated; whether one had to take in bombed-out or refugee families or whether one was forced oneself to seek shelter with strangers, whether one lived in the west of Germany or in the east and was forced to take flight – all these factors weakened the tie to the collective experience of the class to which one belonged and began to reduce its significance. In the place of "class identities", "communities of fate" took shape. Their welfare depended upon geographic, military, and political factors and, not least, upon sheer chance.[48]

Perhaps only the individual factory, provider of work, sometimes of food, and certainly of what little meaning there was to be found in the increasing chaos of wartime Germany, offered any sort of stable reference point, a function it continued to perform in the first post-war years as well.[49] The destruction of Germany's industrial cities by allied bombing combined with the defeat at Stalingrad to deprive the "Hitler myth" of its vital integrative function.[50] In the last war years, the balance of Nazi policy toward the German working class had to shift heavily in the direction of massive coercion.

In conclusion, we can suggest that most workers' experiences of Nazism cannot be pigeon-holed into simple black and white categories. A Ruhr mine-worker who opposed the Nazis in 1933, might have become a "racially privileged" foreman supervising "sub-human" Russian prisoners of war by 1943. A Hamburg Social Democrat could end up killing Jews as a member of an "order police" (*Ordnungspolizei*) unit in occupied Poland, as Christopher Browning demonstrates in his contribution to this volume. And even workers far less tainted by their experience of National Socialism were still aware that simply by continuing to do their job until the "bitter end" they, too, had helped sustain the dictatorship; at the MAN factory in Nuremberg, for example, post-war de-Nazification ran aground on the recognition that

> in the final analysis, even if they might be formally innocent, people had nonetheless been intimately involved in the Nazi system; [they] had ensured its survival long enough through their passivity and their labor power.[51]

During the twelve years of the Third Reich, the "structure, self-consciousness and perspective of the German working class . . . had undergone a deep transformation".[52] Many historians would now support Detlev Peukert's suggestion that

> the Nazis' destruction of the old structures of solidarity in the labour movement paved the way for a new, more individualistic, more achievement-oriented, "sceptical" type of worker, of the sort described by sociologists in the 1950s.[53]

WOMEN IN THE THIRD REICH

While the history of the German working class under Nazism has increasingly shown just how difficult it is to draw clear-cut lines between the "victims" and the "accomplices" in the Third Reich, women's history has, until recently, been far less nuanced; German women seem so obviously to have been the victims of Nazism. Indeed, one of the aims with which the Nazi movement came to power was the removal of women from all areas of public life, both economic and political; "Emancipation from emancipation" was the Nazi slogan and for women this meant, at least in the purity of Nazi ideology, that women must be confined to the "separate sphere" prescribed by the unique qualities of their own biological "nature," namely the home and the family. It has been argued that women were treated primarily as "objects" in the Nazi regime, reduced to those functions of their bodies which could serve the Nazis' racial goals. Denied even the most elementary autonomy required to assume the role of an active subject in Germany, women could scarcely, so this interpretation runs, be responsible for any of the Nazi regime's enormous crimes. Only men could assume this guilt, because under the Nazis, only men were allowed, in any meaningful sense, to be historical actors. The Third Reich was a "male" dictatorship which oppressed all women.[54] Anti-Semitism and racism were "male" ideologies, alien to women's "caring", "feminine" nature.[55] Diametrically opposed to this view, which has been advanced most adamantly by Gisela Bock, is the position taken by Claudia Koonz in her book, *Mothers in the Fatherland*. Koonz suggests that, far from being the victims of National Socialism, many women were "accomplices" of Nazism because the "emotional work" they performed within the "private" sphere of the family contributed to the reproduction and stability of the Nazi system.

Women's historians have, however, begun to realize that most women in the Third Reich cannot simply be cast in the role of "victim" or "perpetrator." Early discussions of women's position under Nazism failed to recognize the complexities of Nazi policy toward women. Eve Rosenhaft observes, for example, that

it is no longer possible to assert simply that National Socialism pursued a conservative (or reactionary) policy of returning women to the home. On the contrary, within the context of a general determination to subordinate women to institutionalized male power, the Nazi system identified a place for women at work as well as in the family. What was peculiar to National Socialism was its intention to rationalize the process of deciding which women should perform which functions.[56]

After 1933, women were expelled from positions of influence in the state administration. In the Third Reich, women were either barred altogether from state employment or else permitted only a very limited access. But even in the public sector, Nazi efforts at "masculinizing" employment were by no means thorough or complete. Ursula Nienhaus' research shows, for example, that significant numbers of women continued to work in the Postal Service after 1933. Some 250 of these women, all active National Socialists, even managed to achieve higher level positions where they exercised considerable authority over other women, including the female forced laborers who did the heavy lifting and carrying during the war.[57] The thousands of women who worked in the Postal Service, which also controlled the German telephone system, helped to ensure the performance of communications functions that were vital to the German war effort. Some even helped the Gestapo by listening in on telephone conversations between individuals who were under police surveillance. In short, these women actively "worked for" the Nazi regime.[58]

The Nazis could not exercise the same direct influence over female employment in private industry. The system of marriage loans introduced in 1933 tried to draw women out of the workforce, but the economic needs of employers as well as of hard-pressed working-class families, still coping with the effects of mass unemployment proved more decisive. During the 1930s, not only did the numbers of married women working in industry and commerce *not* decline but the numbers of married women working actually increased between 1933 and 1939.[59] The rationalization of German industry in the 1930s and 40s demanded an adequate supply of unskilled or semi-skilled assembly-line labor. Nazi officials and industrial managers argued that women's physical and mental characteristics made them ideal candidates for the boring, monotonous repetition of assembly-line labor.[60] And women's assembly-line work appeared to pose no serious threat to women's health or reproductive capacities, so long as it was flanked by maternal welfare schemes which would ensure that German women continued to produce healthy Aryan children as well as industrial goods. In 1942, the German Labour Front (DAF) even supported a plan for a national maternity law (*Mutterschutzgesetz*).[61]

But Aryan women's bodies could be protected from extreme physical exploitation because large numbers of non-Aryan females were forced to slave in German war industry with no regard to their physical well-being or even their survival.[62] Most industrialists were prepared to support maternal welfare programs for Aryan working mothers "as long as National Socialist racial policy . . . procured a sufficient work force, composed of both men and women, to whom considerations of population policy did not apply."[63]

Despite the obvious racial privileges enjoyed by Aryan women, Gisela Bock still insists that *all* women, Aryan as well as non-Aryan, were victimized by the "sexist-racist" Nazi regime. "Racially inferior" women were certainly worked to death (*Vernichtung durch Arbeit*) or simply exterminated.[64] But even Aryan women judged by the Nazis to be biologically "unworthy" were subjected to forced sterilization (which, Bock argues, was far more traumatic, physically and psychologically, for women than for men). And Bock argues that the harsh penalties for abortion or the use of birth control victimized even the women judged to be biologically "worthy" by forcing them into "compulsory motherhood."[65]

Adelheid von Saldern's contribution to this volume shows, however, that Bock fails to recognize important distinctions between different categories of women. A middle-class German woman denied access by Nazi population policies to abortion or birth control was hardly the same kind of "victim" of Nazi racism as a Jewish woman murdered in an extermination camp.[66] And while Nazi racial policies may have been formulated largely by men, women frequently implemented them. The women who continued to function as social workers and health-care professionals after 1933 were increasingly caught up in the Nazis' use of the health and welfare services for eugenic screening and regulation.[67] These women became active participants in the Nazi killing machine.[68] It would appear, then, that at least some women cannot claim the "blessing of having been born female" so far as responsibility for the crimes of the Nazi regime is concerned.[69]

Yet even the acknowledgment that certain women were "perpetrators" as well as "victims," that "in the concentration and death camps, some women treated other women with particular cruelty" still leaves us with an incomplete picture of women under Nazism.[70] The position of women who were not the explicit victims of biological and racial persecution must be seen as complex and contradictory, a "site of contradictions" (*Gemengelage*) where subordination and oppression were often mixed together with new possibilities and hopes.

In her study of the League of German Girls (BdM), for example, Dagmar Reese has discovered that the Nazi regime's invasion of the most intimate reaches of private family "space" supported young women's own desires for escape from parental and familial controls.[71] The women she interviewed remembered their years in the BdM as a time of personal growth and achievement over which Nazi sexism seems to have cast hardly a shadow. In the League of German Girls, young women were able to make careers for themselves as group leaders, not because of their ideological enthusiasm but as a result of their organizational capacities and leadership skills; indeed, their experiences in the BdM prepared some of these women to become socially and politically active in the post-war years.[72] Reese concludes that the Nazi regime was able to instrumentalize these young girls' desires in the expansion of its own power; at the same time, these young women became "willing accomplices" (*willigen Komplizinnen*) of the Nazi regime, actively, if unconsciously, participating in the construction of Nazi domination by fulfilling their own personal needs.[73]

The most recent work in women's history has thus begun to produce a differentiated description of women's complicated and contradictory relationships with Nazism, which will no longer allow us to speak of "women" as if they possessed a homogeneous collective identity. However, "women's history" has not yet managed to negotiate the difficult passage to "gender history." Certainly, references to Nazism as a particularly sexist "gender regime" abound in current discussions of women in the Third Reich. Yet a comprehensive history of gender relations in the Third Reich, examining Nazi representations of both "masculinity" and "femininity," their interactions and mutual exclusions, has not yet emerged from the new women's history.[74]

A PARADISE FOR THE LOWER MIDDLE CLASS? ARTISANS, PEASANTS AND SHOPKEEPERS IN THE THIRD REICH

Since the 1930s, orthodox Marxists have seen National Socialism as an instrument of "monopoly capital" which provided a brutal, authoritarian resolution of the economic, social and political crisis caused by the Great Depression. This argument, presented most insistently by East German historians (until 1989, when their country collapsed) claimed that Nazism preserved and promoted the interests of German big business by destroying the organized labor movement and by offering new opportunities for the economic exploitation of conquered territories, particularly in the east.

17

This interpretation has been made the target of withering attacks by western non- and neo-Marxists alike.[75] Henry Turner has, for instance, failed to find any convincing evidence that big business brought Hitler to power in 1933.[76] And Timothy Mason, an English Marxist, has argued that, far from being the tool of "monopoly capital," the Third Reich was an "exceptional" form of the modern state, which achieved an unusual degree of autonomy from capitalist economic forces and interests.[77]

Western European and American research has, in general, paid more attention to the voters and supporters who made Nazism a mass movement than to the industrial elites who allegedly helped Hitler into power. In response to the question "Who voted for Hitler?," there seemed, until recently, to be remarkably little disagreement:

> virtually every analysis of Nazi support produced between 1930 and 1980 concluded that the social bases of the NSDAP were to be located almost exclusively in elements of the German *Kleinbürgertum* or petty bourgeoisie. . . . Driven by intense economic distress, especially after the onset of the Great Depression in 1929, and desperately afraid of "proletarianisation", these small shopkeepers, independent craftsmen, white-collar workers, low-ranking civil servants and small farmers of the lower middle class deserted the traditional parties of the bourgeois centre and right after 1928 for the radical NSDAP.[78]

The research of the past decade has increasingly challenged this conventional wisdom. Employing sophisticated statistical techniques, electoral studies have shown that Nazism was a broadly based political movement, drawing from a wide range of German voters.[79] At the peak of its electoral strength in the summer of 1932, the NSDAP "could make at least a plausible claim to be a socially heterogeneous people's party (*Volkspartei*)[80] an achievement unmatched by any other German political party until after the Second World War.

But even though Nazism before 1933 can no longer be seen as a distinctly middle and especially lower middle-class political movement, it cannot be denied that the disaffected peasants, artisans, retailers and white-collar workers who voted for Hitler expected the Third Reich to pay particular attention to their interests, needs and desires; the Nazi *Volksgemeinschaft* would be a petty bourgeois "paradise" governed by the material interests and moral values of the *Mittelstand*.[81]

Historians have tended to see the German *Mittelstand* as a "backward" pre-industrial class intent upon halting the forward march of industrialization and modernization. According to this interpretation, the Nazis gained *Mittelstand* votes before 1933 by promising to turn back the clock. Heinrich August Winkler has, however, argued that after 1933 the "old lower middle class" – peasants, artisans and shopkeepers – quickly, became "Der entbehrliche Stand" (the disposable estate), because continued modernization and industrialization were the indispensable prerequisites of Nazi plans for world domination.[82] The Nazi regime failed to redeem most of its election promises to the *Mittelstand*; department stores and consumer co-ops, traditional *Mittelstand* enemies, were not immediately closed down after 1933 because this would only have increased the numbers of unemployed. The regime did respond to some longstanding *Mittelstand* demands – for example, the so-called *"Grosse Befähigungsnachweis"* in 1935, which made the master's certificate a precondition for opening a craft workshop. But Winkler argues that shopkeepers and artisans did not benefit as much as big business from the Nazi armaments boom and that many craft workshops were hurt by the labor shortage while others were closed down by the government because they were not considered vital to the war effort.[83]

Adelheid von Saldern argues, however, that the Third Reich did not have a uniform effect upon all members of the *Mittelstand*:

> the entire artisanate did not become a "disposable estate"; on the contrary, a section of the artisanate in a sense advanced – to put it in an exaggerated formulation – to the status of an "indispensable estate", whereas another part was indeed "put on half pay."[84]

The Nazis promoted the most productive sections of the *Mittelstand* at the expense of its more marginal elements. The "modernization" of the German economy that rearmament required set definite constraints upon Nazi policy toward the *Mittelstand* but it did not completely prevent the Nazis from responding to at least some of the demands of important sections of the *Mittelstand*. For example, the "combing out action" of 1939, along with other subsequent closures of artisan enterprises, freed labor for the war industry, but it also reduced the overcrowding and extreme competition that artisan producers had been complaining about for many years.[85] In the early 1930s, the Nazi "Trustees of Labour" also permitted artisan employers to cut their costs by significantly lowering their workers' wages.[86] Nazi anti-Semitism and imperialism offered artisans new economic opportunities; the "Aryanization" of the German economy got rid of Jewish competitors, while expansion to the east promised new markets and raw materials for artisan producers as well as for big business.[87] Although the restricted supply of raw materials and the labor shortage produced by the rearmament drive undoubtedly hurt artisan interests, some handicraft producers also benefitted from lucrative war contracts as suppliers for the big armaments firms or for the military.[88] Nor should the effects of the Nazis' "symbolic offerings" to the German *Mittelstand* be overlooked or underestimated; under no other regime since Bismarck had the German *Mittelstand* enjoyed as high a degree of public prestige even if this "symbolic capital" did not always translate into concrete material advantages.[89] Von Saldern concludes that important sections of the artisanate continued to support the Nazis until as late as 1942–3 when they became increasingly disheartened by allied bombing raids, by the transition to a "total war" economy and by the receding prospects of a "final victory."[90]

Recent research also shows that it is impossible to speak of an artisanate with uniformly anti-modern interests and identities.[91] Von Saldern argues that the artisans who voted for Hitler had no real interest in returning to an imagined pre-industrial past. Realizing that they must come to terms with, not resist, economic modernization, what they really wanted was corporatist protection *within* the industrial capitalist order. Artisan producers also understood that only the economically efficient sectors of handicraft production could expect to survive and prosper in the future. Viewed from this perspective, Nazism's "modernizing" tendencies appear to have been a good deal less antithetical to *Mittelstand* interests than earlier historians had supposed.

The relationship between German peasants and the Nazi regime was shaped by somewhat different factors, but above all by the extensive state controls imposed upon agriculture by the

"Reich Food Estate" (*Reichsnährstand*) which removed peasant production from the economic market-place.[92] Whereas artisan producers could blame their troubles upon market forces and welcome the attempts (however limited and hypocritical) of the Nazi regime to "protect" them from "unfair competition," peasants had no choice but to see the Nazi state as the cause of their economic difficulties. In his study of Bavaria, for example, Ian Kershaw shows that peasants resented government controls upon agricultural production which they saw as a revival of the hated "coercive economy" to which they had been subjected during the First World War and the early Weimar Republic.[93]

Even Nazi measures that specifically protected the economic and social position of the peasantry – such as the Reich Entail Law, designed to prevent peasant indebtedness and the loss of family farms – contributed to peasant discontent.[94] Gustavo Corni concludes that German farmers were not prepared to accept

> [Nazi agrarian policy chief Walter] Darré's project for a static, immutable, subsistence economy ... the project of the Minister and theoretician of *Blut und Boden* ["blood and soil" ideology], whose utopian vision was very far from the concrete real-life needs of the peasant economy, was a failure.[95]

Peasants made large numbers of appeals against the strict application of the Entail Law.[96] Furthermore, the special courts set up to adjudicate these cases (*Anerbengerichte*) frequently permitted the sale and transfer of land which the law was supposed to prevent.[97]

Kershaw also shows that Bavarian peasants did not respond to Nazi racial appeals to stop doing business with Jewish cattle dealers who paid better prices than their "Aryan" competitors.[98] And, like other Catholics in Bavaria, peasants were also estranged by the Nazi regime's conflicts with the Catholic church.[99] Yet Kershaw concludes that although

> criticism of the regime was at its most vehement among the peasantry and the *Mittelstand* ... this produced few outward signs of opposition. ... The peasantry and the middle-class groups posed no threat to the regime. If disenchanted, querulous, angered, and frustrated, such groups

were not totally alienated by Nazism. Their grievances in one direction were so frequently overcome by integration in another. They could identify with and approve of much that Nazism stood for and could offer them.[100]

Although historians have begun to reconstruct the economic and political history of the *Mittelstand* under National Socialism, we are still relatively ill-informed about the culture and "everyday lives" of artisans, shopkeepers or peasants during the Third Reich. In what ways did Nazism affect the cultural practices of peasant communities or artisan families? To historians and anthropologists, the cultural patterns of the village have seemed peculiarly resistant to change.[101] Did the cultural "rules" of the peasant *Heimat* emerge from the Third Reich, basically intact, to be dissolved only by the "economic miracle" of the Federal Republic?[102] Or had the cultural disintegration of the peasant community already begun under Hitler's rule? In his study of Korle in Hesse, Gerhard Wilke has discovered that the Nazi takeover introduced generational conflict into the village; the younger generation who became active in the Nazi movement challenged the authority of their elders. Indeed, villagers describe this as the period of "war in every household."[103] The Nazi regime also brought important changes to women's lives. Various Nazi organizations gave the village's women and girls the opportunity to become active in public life, to travel beyond the village and to meet women from other social classes.[104] During the war, women had to shoulder additional burdens, often being left to run the family farm while their husbands and brothers were conscripted into the army.[105] The war also forced large numbers of outsiders upon the village as each household had to take in evacuees from the cities that were being bombed by the allies.[106] Many of the village's men were killed or wounded during the war. Wilke concludes that by May 1945,

> the social and political composition of the village had changed for good. . . . Far from ensuring that a German rural way of life based on *"Blut und Boden"* . . . would endure, the Nazis had unleashed forces which effectively destroyed the "traditional" structure of village life.[107]

"MODERNIZATION" OR THE "PATHOLOGIES OF MODERNITY"?

In his influential study, *Society and Democracy in Germany*, Ralf Dahrendorf proposed the ironic thesis that it was the Nazis who finally cleared the path for democracy in Germany by destroying the social bases of authoritarian government and by dissolving the family, class, religious and regional identities that had fractured German society before 1933.[108] David Schoenbaum's important study, *Hitler's Social Revolution*, presented a more complex and, in several respects, more contradictory assessment of Nazism's effects but, like Dahrendorf, Schoenbaum concluded that the Third Reich had a revolutionary impact upon German society.[109]

The "modernity" of Nazism has recently been reconsidered in a collection of essays edited by Michael Prinz and Rainer Zitelman, although some of the contributors are concerned more with the aims than with the actual effects of the Third Reich. In his introduction to the volume, Prinz suggests that closer attention should be paid to the social ideas of the leading Nazi figures – Hitler, but also Robert Ley, Fritz Todt, Albert Speer, Joseph Goebbels, etc. – who "had at their disposal comparatively modern conceptions of the future of German society after the war."[110] Far from envisaging a "Great German Reich" in which most Germans would be peasant-soldiers, these Nazi leaders looked to the Soviet Union and to the USA for models of Germany's future.[111] The other essays in this volume explore subjects as diverse as "Americanism," architecture, the "social planning" of the German Labour Front and "reform" psychiatry; the contributors do not arrive at a single definition of modernity, but they seem to agree

that secularisation, the dismantling of *traditional* forms of social inequality, the improvement of chances for social ascent, technical progress, the institutionalisation of science, the rule of the expert, economic growth, rationalisation and mass production, a rational-instrumental attitude towards tradition, all represent central elements of modernisation, with reference to which a measure of the reality of the Third Reich is to be taken.[112]

In his own sweeping essay, Prinz concludes that Nazi economic, social and cultural policies promoted rationalization, efficiency, productivity, social mobility and the welfare state.[113]

A wide variety of professionals and technical experts found the Third Reich's version of "modernity" extremely attractive. [The Nazi regime gave architects, engineers, city planners, doctors, social workers, the criminal police and other "modern" experts the opportunity to put "social engineering" projects into practice, unhampered by the democratic political and financial constraints that had often frustrated their ambitions during the Weimar Republic.[114] The Nazi regime was also able to profit from popular fascination with modern technology and machinery.[115] The "people's car" and the new super highways were sensations. Pilots, race-car drivers and motorcycle riders became popular heroes.[116] Workers in the aircraft industry were proud to be involved in the construction of such distinctly "modern" machines.[117] And although the Nazis had condemned the influence of the "degenerate Jewish-Bolshevik" *Bauhaus*, the radios, electrical appliances, chairs, sofas and beds that furnished middle-class and white-collar households in the 1930s bore the unmistakable imprint of "modern" design.[118] [Modern forms of mass entertainment and communication – such as radio and film – also became widespread during the Third Reich.[119]]

But the Third Reich's "modernity" cannot be viewed in isolation from the racial and political purposes it was meant to serve. Nazi Germany reminds us that modernity can have a barbarous as well as a "progressive" face.[120] Economic modernization and industrial rationalization were the necessary prerequisites of a modern mechanized war of racial conquest. The Nazis used social policy, modern mass media and the prospect (if not the reality) of modern mass consumerism to construct a broad basis of popular support for their regime. But the "biological unworthy" and the "racially inferior" were excluded from these benefits; they saw only the dark side of Nazi "modernity." The implementation of the Nazis' inhuman racial "projects" and, above all, the "Final Solution" would not have been possible without the technical and organizational "assistance" of a wide range of modern professionals.[121] An army of "racial experts" used their "scientific" knowledge to legitimate the segregation and destruction of "racial enemies" and "community aliens," "burdensome existences" and "useless eaters."[122] Hitler's "wonder weapons," the V1 and V2 rockets, designed by

24

German scientists but built with slave labor, provide a particularly striking example of the peculiar Nazi synthesis of "modernity" with barbarism.[123] Prinz cautions that we can no longer assume "modernity" to be inherently progressive. But by detaching the modernization promoted by the Third Reich from the inhuman racial goals which were the essence of Hitler's regime, the essays in Prinz and Zitelmann's book certainly run the risk of normalizing the Nazi regime and downplaying its barbarity.[124]

The pathological character of Nazism as "a distinct mode of dealing with and instrumentalizing modernity"[125] emerges much more clearly from Detlev Peukert's recent work. Peukert argued that Nazism was "modernity's most fatal developmental possibility."[126] Whereas supporters of the *Sonderweg* interpretation located the origins of Nazism in the persistence of "pre-industrial traditions," Peukert argued that Germany had already been introduced to "classical modernity" by the Wilhelmine Empire (1890–1918). The Third Reich was the result of Weimar's failure to resolve the multiple crises of Germany's "classical modernity" within the political framework of bourgeois democracy: "The NSDAP was at once a symptom, and a solution, of the crisis."[127]

The Nazis certainly did not disdain the use of an archaic "anti-modernist" rhetoric, but their response to the crises of classical modernity in the Weimar Republic was by no means simply "backward-looking". The *Volksgemeinschaft* ("national community") promised not so much an impossible return to the pre-industrial past, as a society free of the contradictions and "irritations" of everyday life in the epoch of "classical modernity."[128] Yet beneath the ideological representations of the smoothly functioning, monolithic *Volksgemeinschaft*, the real contradictions of modern industrial society remained:

> The much-heralded *Volksgemeinschaft* of the National Socialists in no way abolished the real contradictions of a modern industrial society; rather, these were inadvertently aggravated by the use of highly modern industrial and propaganda techniques for achieving war-readiness.[129]

The Nazi failure to construct the promised *Volksgemeinschaft* intensified the regime's hunt for internal and external "enemies."[130] Unable to produce the material and psychological "paradise" promised Nazi supporters before 1933, the Nazis gave

25

the *Volksgemeinschaft* an increasingly negative definition, turning ever more viciously against new "threats" to the imaginary unity and purity of Nazi society. Indeed the *Volksgemeinschaft* needed restlessly to manufacture enemies which it could then persecute. The fate of European Jewry remains central to any discussion of Nazism, but recent research has also drawn attention to the other, "forgotten victims" of Nazi genocide – the aged, the physically and mentally handicapped, Sinti and Roma (Gypsies), Jehovah's Witnesses, homosexuals and all those whose "deviant" social behavior made them "genetically deficient" in Nazi eyes.[131] The dynamic of this negative project for the progressive eradication of all deviance, difference and non-conformity increasingly moved the trajectory of mass violence from the periphery to the very center of German society, eventually exposing even Aryan Germans to the threat of persecution.

But racism had its attractions; racial membership in the *Volksgemeinschaft* promised status and economic rewards at the expense of the racially or biologically "unfit" in Germany and in occupied Europe. And National Socialist racism could corrupt even those who resisted its cruder manifestations. Nazi depersonalization of the Jews and other "community aliens" made the Holocaust possible. As Kershaw puts it: "The road to Auschwitz was built by hate, but paved with indifference."[132]

The Nazis had no substantial aims beyond creating a constant sense of movement toward some unspecified goal; as Peukert observes, "It was more important to travel hopefully than to arrive."[133] The Nazis' violent "answers" to the "contradictions of modernity" could not construct a stable social order; Nazi dynamism was primarily negative and "The Nazi 'solution' to the crisis was headed for disintegration from the start."[134]

By describing National Socialism as a pathological variant of "normal" modernity, Peukert certainly had no intention of "relativizing" Nazi genocide, of trivializing the significance of the Third Reich, or of relieving German historians of the responsibility for providing explanations of Nazism. Peukert's work does, however, issue a challenge to begin radically rethinking the history of the twentieth century. By offering "a warning against the fallacious notion that the normality of industrial society is harmless,"[135] Peukert's research encourages historians to pay closer attention to the "dark side" of modernity in more "normal" western industrial nations and to ask why these other countries managed to pass through their "crisis years' of "classical modernity" without succumbing to the "seductions of totalitarianism":[136]

> The view that National Socialism was . . . one of the pathological development forms of modernity does not imply that barbarism is the inevitable logical outcome of modernisation. The point, rather, is that we should not analyse away the tensions between progressive and aberrant features by making a glib opposition between modernity and tradition: we should call attention to the rifts and danger-zones which result from the modern civilizing process itself, so that the opportunities for human emancipation which it simultaneously creates can be the more thoroughly charted. The challenge of Nazism shows that the evolution of modernity is not a one-way trip to freedom.[137]

* * *

The essays which follow are divided into two major parts. In Part I, I have grouped together six essays which examine the relationships between different groups of ordinary Germans and the Nazi regime. With the exception of Omer Bartov's and Gisela Bock's articles, all of these essays draw attention to the "multi-layered, contradictory and complex" realities of everyday life in the Third Reich.[138] They show that the attitudes and behavior of any single individual, at any given point in the history of the Third Reich, might combine different degrees of active consent, accommodation and nonconformity. Most of the articles in this section also show that many ordinary Germans actively participated in the construction of Nazi rule, not because they had been converted to Nazi ideology, but because, under Nazism, the satisfaction of quite ordinary needs and desires could contribute to the extension and reproduction of Nazi power. This conclusion emerges brutally from the article by Mallmann and Paul on the Gestapo. The Germans who deluged the Gestapo offices with a veritable "flood" of denunciations were, for the most part, not avid Nazis but angry or greedy private citizens seeking to use the police state to settle scores with neighbors or relatives. The Nazi regime was constructed in a similar, if less immediately murderous fashion, by the workers who took pride in the fighter planes they built for the Nazi airforce, or by women who saw in the Nazi women's organizations new opportunities to escape the claustrophobic confines of the household.

The last three articles in the book take up the important theme of racism as a specifically Nazi response to the "contradictions of modernity." Racism pervaded everyday life in the Third Reich but its effects were contradictory. The articles by Herbert and Browning show that racism constructed new collective identities and interests. The Nazis gave the German people a perverse "social contract" which offered *all* Aryan Germans *some* advantage and benefit at the expense of all other "races." For those fortunate enough to be classed as members of the "master race," even if they were workers, there were new positions of privilege over those doomed by the Nazis to be slaves and victims. But Detlev Peukert's article makes it clear that the relentless compulsion of Nazi racism to divide humanity into those who were biologically "valuable" and those considered genetically "inferior," extended even into the ranks of the otherwise racially "superior" Aryan Germans, exposing them as well to the threat of racial persecution.

NOTES

1 Research on the social history of Nazi Germany, has increasingly turned toward the history of "everyday life" (*Alltagsgeschichte*). Two major research projects have made vital contributions to this new departure, the "Bavaria project," headed by the late Martin Broszat, and the Ruhr oral history project (*LUSIR*), directed by Lutz Niethammer; see Martin Broszat *et al.* (eds), *Bayern in der NS-Zeit*, Vols I–IV (München/Wien, 1977–83); Lutz Niethammer (ed.), *"Die Jahre weiss man nicht, wo man die heute hinsetzen soll." Faschismuserfahrungen im Ruhrgebiet* (Berlin/Bonn: Dietz, 1983); Lutz Niethammer (ed.), *"Hinterher merkt man dass es richtig war, dass es schiefgegangen ist." Nachkriegserfahrungen im Ruhrgebiet* (Berlin/Bonn: Dietz Verlag, 1983). On *Alltagsgeschichte* more generally, see David F. Crew, *"Alltagsgeschichte*: A new social history 'from below'?," *Central European History*, Vol. 22, Nos 3/4. September/December 1989, pp. 394–407.

2 Detlev Peukert, *Inside Nazi Germany. Conformity, Opposition and Racism in Everyday Life* (New Haven/London: Yale University Press, 1987), p. 243.

3 Ibid., p. 16.

4 Stephen Salter, "Class harmony or class conflict? The industrial working class and the National Socialist regime, 1933–1945" in Jeremy Noakes (ed.), *Government, Party and People in Nazi Germany* (Exeter: Exeter Studies in History No. 2., 1980), p. 96.

5 Ulrich Herbert, "Arbeiterschaft im 'Dritten Reich'. Zwischenbilanz und offene Fragen," *Geschichte und Gesellschaft*, vol. 15, 1989, p. 358.

6 Ulrich Herbert, "Arbeiterschaft unter der NS-Diktatur" in Lutz Niethammer *et al.*, *Bürgerliche Gesellschaft in Deutschland. Historische Einblicke, Fragen, Perspektiven* (Frankfurt am Main: Fischer Taschenbuch Verlag, 1990), p. 448. See also Timothy W. Mason, "Die Bändigung der Arbeiterklasse in nationalsozialistischen Deutschland" in Carola Sachse, Tilla Siegel, Hasso Spode and Wolfgang Spohn, *Angst, Belohnung, Zucht und Ordnung. Herrschaftsmechanismen im Nationalsozialismus* (Opladen, 1982), p. 22.

7 Ibid., p. 293.

8 Ibid., p. 293.

9 Ibid., p. 293.

10 Ibid., p. 303.

11 See Timothy W. Mason, "Some origins of the Second World War," *Past and Present*, Vol. 29, December 1964, pp. 67–87; "Innere Krise und Angriffskriege, 1938/1939" in Friedrich Forstmeier and Hans-Erich Volkmann (eds), *Wirtschaft und Rüstung am Vorabend des Zweiten Weltkrieges* (Düsseldorf, 1975); and, most recently, "The domestic dynamics of Nazi conquests: A response to critics" in Thomas Childers and Jane Caplan (eds), *Reevaluating the Third Reich* (New York and London: Holmes & Meier, 1993), pp. 161–89.

12 Mason, "Die Bändigung der Arbeiterklasse im nationalsozialistischen Deutschland," p. 17.

13 Rüdiger Hachtmann, *Industriearbeit im "Dritten Reich". Untersuchungen zu den Lohn- und Arbeitbedingungen in Deutschland 1933–1945* (Göttingen: Vandenhoeck & Ruprecht, 1989), p. 131.

14 See Ulrich Herbert, "Good times, bad times" in Richard Bessel (ed.), *Life in the Third Reich* (Oxford: Oxford University Press, 1987) and Klaus-Michael Mallmann and Gerhard Paul (unter Mitarbeit von Hans-Henning Kramer), *Herrschaft und Alltag. Ein Industrierevier im Dritten Reich. Widerstand und Verweigerung im Saarland 1935–1945*, Vol. 2 (Bonn: Verlag J. H. W. Dietz Nachf., 1991).

15 Michael Zimmermann, *Schachtanlage und Zechenkolonie. Leben, Arbeit und Politik in einer Arbeitersiedlung 1880–1980* (Essen: Klartext, 1987), p. 191.

16 Mallmann and Paul, *Herrschaft und Alltag. Ein Industrierevier im Dritten Reich*, pp. 76–80.

17 Dieter Pfliegensdorfer, ' "Ich war mit Herz und Seele dabei, und so, dass mir das gar nichts ausmachte' – Bremer Flugzeugbauer im Nationalsozialismus," *1999. Zeitschrift für Sozialgeschichte des 20. und 21. Jahrhunderts*, Vol. 3, January 1988, p. 74.

18 Wolfgang Franz Werner, *"Bleib übrig". Deutsche Arbeiter in der Nationalsozialistische Kriegswirtschaft* (Düsseldorf: Schwann Verlag, 1983), p. 19.

19 Hachtmann, *Industriearbeit im "Dritten Reich,"* p. 302.
20 Dieter Pfliegensdörfer, "Ich war mit Herz und Seele dabei . . . ,"
   p. 80; see also Hachtmann, *Industriearbeit im "Dritten Reich."*
21 Hachtmann, *Industriearbeit im "Dritten Reich,"* p. 307.
22 Ibid., p. 302.
23 Gerd Wysocki, *Arbeit für den Krieg. Herrschaftsmechanismen in der Rüstungsindustrie des "Dritten Reiches". Arbeitseinsatz, Sozialpolitik und Staatspolizeiliche Repression bei den Reichswerken "Hermann Goering" im Salzgitter-Gebiet 1937/8 bis 1945* (Braunschweig: Steinweg Verlag, 1992), pp. 458–9.
24 Mallmann and Paul, *Herrschaft und Alltag. Ein Industrierevier im Dritten Reich,* pp. 417–18.
25 Carola Sachse, *Siemens, der Nationalsozialismus und die moderne Familie. Eine Untersuchung zur sozialen Rationalisierung in Deutschland im 20. Jahrhundert* (Hamburg: Rasch und Röhring, 1990), pp. 54–9.
26 Herbert, "Arbeiterschaft im 'Dritten Reich'," pp. 333–6 and p. 358.
27 Ibid., p. 334.
28 Ibid., p. 334.
29 See Klaus Scherer, *"Asozial" im Dritten Reich. Die vergessenen Verfolgten* (Münster: Votum Verlag, 1990) and also Wolfgang Ayass, *Das Arbeitshaus Breitenau. Bettler, Landstreicher, Prostituierte, Zuhalter und Fürsorgeempfänger in der Korrektions- und Landarmenanstalt Breitenau (1874–1949)* (Diss. Gesamthochschule Kassel, 1992), pp. 262–328.
30 See, for example, Wysocki, *Arbeit für den Krieg,* pp. 312–59 and Gudrun Schwarz, *Die nationalsozialistichen Lager* (Frankfurt/New York: Campus Verlag, 1990), pp. 82–3.
31 Wysocki, *Arbeit für den Krieg,* p. 461.
32 Herbert, "Arbeiterschaft im 'Dritten Reich'," p. 334.
33 Peter Reichel, *Der schöne Schein des Dritten Reiches. Faszination und Gewalt des Faschismus* (München/Wien: Carl Hanser Verlag, 1991).
34 Salter, "Class harmony or class conflict?," p. 83.
35 Mason, "Die Bändigung der Arbeiterklasse," p. 35.
36 Ibid., p. 39.
37 Michael Zimmermann, "Ausbruchschoffnung. Junge Bergleute in den Dreissiger Jahren" in Lutz Niethammer (ed.), *Die Jahre weiss man nicht, wo man die heute hinsetzen soll. Faschismuserfahrungen im Ruhrgebiet* (Bonn: Dietz, 1983), pp. 97–132.
38 Zimmermann, *Schachtanlage und Zechenkolonie,* p. 192.
39 Michael Zimmermann, *Schachtanlage und Zechenkolonie,* p. 192.
40 See, especially, Ian Kershaw, *Popular Opinion and Political Dissent in the Third Reich: Bavaria, 1933–1945* (Oxford, 1983), pp. 334–40.
41 Herbert, "Arbeiterschaft im 'Dritten Reich'," p. 352.
42 Hans-Ulrich Ludewig, "Zwangsarbeit im Zweiten Weltkrieg: Forschungsstand und Ergebnisse regionaler und lokaler Fallstudien," *Archiv für Sozialgeschichte,* Vol. 31, 1991, pp. 558–77.
43 Herbert, "Arbeiterschaft im 'Dritten Reich'," p. 352.
44 See in this volume the essay by Omer Bartov, pp. 41–66.
45 Josef Mooser, "Einleitung und Auswertung: Kontinuität und Dis-

kontinuität in der Arbeitergeschichte des 20. Jahrhunderts" in Klaus Tenfelde (ed.), *Arbeiter im 20. Jahrhundert* (Stuttgart: Klett-Cotta, 1991), p. 663.

46 See Herbert, "Good times, bad times."

47 Herbert, "Arbeiterschaft im 'Dritten Reich,' " p. 360. ·

48 Ibid., p. 356.

49 Ibid., p. 357.

50 Ibid., p. 355. By the end of the war, Allied bombing raids had made approximately every fifth dwelling in Germany uninhabitable; but in some of the larger urban centers, which were subjected to massive air-raids, the damage was much greater. Allied bombs destroyed almost half of Berlin's housing and 60 to 70 per cent of the housing in Cologne, Dortmund, Duisburg and Kassel; see Marie-Luise Recker, "Wohnen und Bombardierung im Zweiten Weltkrieg" in Lutz Niethammer (ed.), *Wohnen im Wandel. Beiträge zur Geschichte des Alltags in der bürgerlichen Gesellschaft* (Wuppertal, 1979), pp. 410–11. See also Jeffrey M. Diefendorf, *In the Wake of War. The Reconstruction of German Cities after World War II* (New York/Oxford, 1993), pp. 3–18. In addition to the difficulties of finding shelter, Germans also had to deal with growing food shortages which persisted during the immediate post-war years; see Michael Wildt, *Der Traum vom Sattwerden. Hunger und Protest. Schwarzmarkt und Selbsthilfe in Hamburg 1945–1948* (Hamurg, 1986) and Rainer Gries, *Die Rationengesellschaft. Versorgungskampf und Vergleichsmentalität. Leipzig, München und Köln nach dem Kriege* (Münster, 1991).

51 Paul Erker, "Die Arbeiter bei MAN 1945–1950" in Tenfelde (ed.), *Arbeiter im 20. Jahrhundert*, p. 553.

52 Ibid., p. 359.

53 Detlev J. K. Peukert, *Inside Nazi Germany. Conformity, Opposition and Racism in Everyday Life* (New Haven/London: Yale University Press, 1987), p. 117.

54 Dorothea Schmidt, "Die peinliche Verwandtschaften – Frauenforschung zum Nationalsozialismus" in Heide Gerstenberger and Dorothea Schmidt (eds), *Normalität oder Normalisierung. Geschichtswerkstätten und Faschismusanalyse* (Münster: Westfälisches Dampfboot, 1987), pp. 50–3.

55 Ibid., p. 57.

56 Eve Rosenhaft, "Women in modern Germany" in Gordon Martel (ed.), *Modern Germany Reconsidered 1870–1945* (London: Routledge, 1992), p. 142.

57 Ursula Nienhaus, "Von der (Ohn) Macht der Frauen. Postbeamtinnen 1933–1945" in Lerke Gravenhorst and Carmen Taschmurat (eds), *Töchterfragen. NS-Frauen Geschichte* (Kore: Verlag Traute Hensch, 1990), pp. 209–10.

58 Ibid., p. 210.

59 Rosenhaft, "Women in modern Germany," p. 143.

60 Annemarie Tröger, "The creation of a female assembly-line proletariat" in R. Bridenthal, A. Grossmann and M. Kaplan (eds),

When Biology Became Destiny: Women in Weimar and Nazi Germany (New York: Monthly Review Press, 1984), pp. 237–70.

61 Carola Sachse, *Siemens, der Nationalsozialismus und die moderne Familie*, p. 52. The *Mutterschutzgesetz* was, however, by no means exclusively National Socialist in origin. Proposals for the legal "protection of motherhood" had been formulated by bourgeois feminists, both in Germany and in other European countries, since the late nineteenth century; see, for example, Ann Taylor Allen, *Feminism and Motherhood in Germany, 1800–1914* (New Brunswick, 1991) and Seth Koven and Sonya Michel (eds), *Mothers of a New World. Maternalist Politics and the Origins of Welfare States* (New York and London, 1993). After 1945, the "protection of motherhood" continued to be an important issue in social policy discussions; see Robert G. Moeller, *Protecting Motherhood: Women and the Family in the Politics of Postwar West Germany* (Berkeley, 1993).

62 Ibid., p. 52.

63 Ibid., p. 53

64 Gisela Bock, "Motherhood, compulsory sterilization and the state" in Renate Bridenthal, Grossmann and Kaplan (eds), *When Biology Became Destiny*, pp. 271–96 and also Bock's article in this volume pp. 110–40. See also Dagmar Reese and Carola Sachse, "Frauenforschung zum Nationalsozialismus. Eine Bilanz" in Lerke Gravenhorst and Carmen Taschmurat (eds) *Töchterfragen. NS-Frauen Geschichte* (Kore: Verlag Traute Hensch, 1990), pp. 86–98.

65 On forced sterilization, see Gisela Bock, *Zwangssterilization im Nationalsozialismus: Studien zur Rassenpolitik und Frauenpolitik* (Opladen: Westdeutscher Verlag, 1986).

66 On the experiences of Jewish women before the war, see Marion A. Kaplan, "Jewish women in Nazi Germany: daily life, daily struggles, 1933–1939," *Feminist Studies*, Vol. 16, 1990, pp. 579–606.

67 Stefan Schnurr, "Die nationalsozialistiche Funktionalisierung sozialer Arbeit. Zur Kontinuität und Diskontinuität der Praxis sozialer Berufe" in Hans-Uwe Otto and Heinz Sünker (eds), *Politische Formierung und soziale Erziehung im Nationalsozialismus* (Frankfurt: Suhrkamp, 1991), pp. 106–40.

68 See especially Angela Ebbinghaus (ed.), *Opfer und Täterinnen. Frauenbiographien des Nationalsozialismus* (Nördlingen: Verlag Franz Greno, 1987).

69 Karin Windaus-Walser, "Gnade der weiblichen Geburt? Zum Umgang der Frauenforschung mit Nationalsozialismus und Antisemitismus" in *Feministische Studien*, Vol. 6, No. 1, 1988, pp. 102–15.

70 Quoted in Gudrun Brockhaus, "Opfer, Täterin, Mitbeteiligte. Zur Diskussion um die Rolle der Frauen im Nationalsozialismus" in Gravenhorst and Taschmurat (eds), *Töchterfragen. NS-Frauen Geschichte*, p. 120.

71 Dagmar Reese, "Emanzipation oder Vergellschaftung: Mädchen im 'Bund Deutscher Mädel'' in Hans-Uwe Otto and Heinz Sünker (eds), *Politische Formierung und soziale Erziehung im Nationalsozialismus* (Frankfurt: Suhrkamp, 1991), pp. 203–25.

72 See, for example, Anne-Katrin Einfeldt, "Zwischen alten Werten und neuen Chancen. Häusliche Arbeit von Bergarbeiterfamilien in den fünfziger Jahren" in Lutz Niethammer (ed.), *"Hinterher merkt man dass es richtig war, dass es schiefgegangen ist"*. *Nachkriegserfahrungen im Ruhrgebiet* (Berlin/Bonn: Dietz Verlag, 1983), pp. 149–90.

73 Dagmar Reese, "Emanzipation oder Vergellschaftung," pp. 222–3. On the ambiguous consequences of the BdM experience, see also Christa Wolf, *Kindheitsmuster* (Darmstadt, 1977).

74 The history of gender in the Third Reich would have to incorporate the valuable insights offered by both Theweleit's psycho-historical study of the *Freikorps* and Balistier's research on the SA, but also to extend this analysis beyond 1933; see Klaus Theweleit, *Männerphantasien*, 2 vols (Frankfurt am Main, 1977/8) (translated into English as *Male Fantasies* (Minneapolis, 1987/9)) and Thomas Balistier, *Gewalt und Ordnung: Kalkül und Faszination der SA* (Münster, 1989).

75 See Anson Rabinbach, "Toward a Marxist theory of Fascism and National Socialism: A report on developments in West Germany," *New German Critique*, Vol. 1, No. 3, Fall 1974, pp. 127–53 and Jane Caplan, "Theories of Fascism: Nicos Poulantzas as historian," *History Workshop*, pp. 83–100.

76 Henry Ashby Turner, Jr, *German Big Business and the Rise of Hitler* (New York: Oxford University Press, 1985); see also the excellent discussion by Dick Geary "The industrial elite and the Nazis in the Weimar Republic" in Peter Stachura (ed.), *The Nazi Machtergreifung* (London: George Allen & Unwin, 1983), pp. 85–100.

77 Timothy W. Mason, "The primacy of politics – Politics and economics in National Socialist Germany" in S. J. Woolf (ed.), *The Nature of Fascism* (New York: Vintage Books, 1969), pp. 165–95.

78 Thomas Childers, "The middle classes and National Socialism" in David Blackbourn and Richard J. Evans (eds), *The German Bourgeoisie. Essays on the Social History of the German Middle Class from the Late Eighteenth to the Early Twentieth Century* (London/New York: Routledge, 1991), p. 318.

79 Thomas Childers, *The Nazi Voter. The Social Foundations of Fascism in Germany, 1919–1933* (Chapel Hill, 1983); Jurgen W. Falter, *Hitler's Wähler* (München, 1991).

80 Childers, "The middle classes and National Socialism," p. 319.

81 *Mittelstand* is a collective social but often also political designation for the "lower middle class" with strong corporatist and conservative overtones. Peasants, artisans and shopkeepers were considered to be members of the "old" *Mittelstand*, whereas white-collar workers formed a so-called "new" *Mittelstand*. In the following discussion, I am dealing primarily with the "old" *Mittelstand*. For an excellent introduction, see David Blackbourn, "The *Mittelstand* in German society and politics 1871–1914," *Social History*, Vol. 2, 1977, pp. 409–33.

82 Heinrich August Winkler, "Der entbehrliche Stand: Zur Mittelstandspolitik im 'Dritten Reich' " in Heinrich August Winkler, *Zwi-*

schen Marx und Monopolen. Der deutsche Mittelstand vom Kaiserreich zur Bundesrepublik Deutschland (Frankfurt am Main: Fischer Verlag, 1991), pp. 52–98.

83 Heinrich August Winkler, *Zwischen Marx und Monopolen. Der deutsche Mittelstand vom Kaiserreich zur Bundesrepublik Deutschland* (Frankfurt am Main: Fischer Verlag, 1991), pp. 13–14.

84 Adelheid von Saldern, " 'Alter Mittelstand' im 'Dritten Reich'. Anmerkungen zu einer Kontroverse," *Geschichte und Gesellschaft*, Vol. 12, 1986, p. 237; see also Adelheid von Saldern, *Mittelstand im "Dritten Reich". Handwerker-Einzelhändler-Bauern* (Frankfurt/New York: Campus Verlag, 1985).

85 von Saldern, " 'Alter Mittelstand' im 'Dritten Reich,' " pp. 238–9; see also Adelheid von Saldern, "The old *Mittelstand* 1890–1939. How 'backward' were the Artisans?," *Central European History*, Vol. 25, No. 1, 1993, pp. 27–51.

86 Hachtmann, *Industriearbeit im "Dritten Reich"*, p. 304.

87 von Saldern, " 'Alter Mittelstand' im 'Dritten Reich'," p. 241.

88 von Saldern, "The old *Mittelstand*, 1890–1939: How 'backward' were the artisans?," *Central European History*, Vol. 25, No. 1, 1993, p. 43.

89 von Saldern, " 'Alter Mittelstand' im 'Dritten Reich'," p. 241.

90 Ibid., p. 240; for Winkler's rebuttal of von Saldern's critique, see Heinrich August Winkler, "Ein neuer Mythos vom alten Mittelstand. Antwort auf eine Antikritik," *Geschichte und Gesellschaft*, Vol. 12, 1986, pp. 548–57.

91 David Blackbourn, "The *Mittelstand* in German society."

92 von Saldern, *Mittelstand im "Dritten Reich,"* pp. 243–4 and also Gustavo Corni, *Hitler and the Peasants. Agrarian Policy in the Third Reich, 1930–1939* (New York/Oxford/Munich: Berg, 1990) and Daniela Munkel, *Bauern und Nationalsozialismus. Der Landkreis Celle im Dritten Reich* (Bielefeld, 1991).

93 See, for example, Kershaw, *Popular Opinion*, pp. 33–65; Robert G. Moeller, *German Peasants and Agrarian Politics, 1914–1924. The Rhineland and Westphalia* (Chapel Hill, 1986), pp. 43–67.

94 Kershaw, *Popular Opinion*, pp. 41–5, 48–9, 51–3.

95 Corni, *Hitler and the Peasants*, p. 152.

96 Ibid., p. 151.

97 Munkel, *Bauern und Nationalsozialismus*.

98 Kershaw, *Popular Opinion*, p. 242.

99 Ibid., pp. 185–223.

100 Ibid., pp. 374–5.

101 See, for example, Walter Rinderle and Bernard Norling, *The Nazi Impact on a German Village* (Lexington: University of Kentucky Press, 1993). For a critical discussion of recent research on the history of German peasants before 1933, see David Crew, "Why can't a peasant be more like a worker?: Social historians and German peasants," *Journal of Social History*, Vol. 22, No. 3, Spring 1989, pp. 531–40.

102 See, for example, Gerhard Wilke, "The sins of the fathers: Village

society and social control in the Weimar Republic" and Wolfgang Kaschuba, "Peasants and others: The historical contours of village class society" in Richard J. Evans and W. R. Lee (eds), *The German Peasantry. Conflict and Community in Rural Society from the Eighteenth to the Twentieth Centuries* (London/Sydney: Croom Helm, 1986), pp. 174–204 and 25–64.

103 Gerhard 'Village life in Nazi Germany" in Richard Bessel (ed.), *Life in the Third Reich* (Oxford, 1987), p. 21.

104 Ibid., p. 22.

105 Ibid., p. 23; see also Sigrid Jacobeit, " ' . . . dem Mann Gehilfin und Knecht. Sie ist Magd und Mutter . . .' Klein- und Mittelbäuerinnen im faschistischen Deutschland" in Johanna Werckmeister (ed.), *Land-Frauen-Alltag. Hundert Jahre Lebens- und Arbeitsbedingungen der Frauen im ländlichen Raum* (Marburg: Jonas Verlag, 1989), pp. 66–90.

106 Wilke, "Village life in Nazi Germany," p. 23.

107 Ibid., p. 24.

108 Ralf Dahrendorf, *Society and Democracy in Germany* (New York, 1967).

109 David Schoenbaum, *Hitler's Social Revolution. Class and Status in Nazi Germany 1933–1939* (New York, 1966).

110 Ibid., p. ix.

111 Ibid., p. ix.

112 Ibid., pp. ix-x.

113 Michael Prinz, "Die soziale Funktion moderner Elemente in der Gesellschaftspolitik des Nationalsozialismus" in Prinz and Zitelmann (eds), *Nationalsozialismus und Modernisierung*, pp. 297–327.

114 See, for example, "Architektur und Stadtplanung im Dritten Reich" in Prinz and Zitelmann, (eds), *Nationalsozialismus und Modernisierung*, pp. 139–171; Alf Lüdtke, "Funktionseliten: Täter, Mit-Täter, Opfer? Zu den Bedingungen des deutschen Faschismus" in Alf Lüdtke (ed.), *Herrschaft als Soziale Praxis. Historische und sozialanthropologische Studien* (Göttingen: Vandenhoeck & Ruprecht, 1991), pp. 559–90; see also Stefan Schnurr, "Die nationalsozialistische Funktionalisierung sozialer Arbeit. Zur Kontinuität und Diskontinuität der Praxis sozialer Berufe" in Hans-Uwe Otto and Heinz Sünker (eds), *Politische Formierung und Soziale Erziehung im Nationalsozialismus*; Patrick Wagner, "Feindbild 'Berufsverbrecher'. Die Kriminalpolizei im Übergang von der Weimarer Republik zum Nationalsozialismus" in Frank Bajohr, Werner Johe and Uwe Lohalm (eds), *Zivilisation und Barbarei. Die Widersprüchlichen Potentiale der Moderne. Detlev Peukert zum Gedenken* (Hamburg, 1991), pp. 226–52; Michael Zimmermann, *Verfolgt. Vertrieben. Vernichtet. Die Nationalsozialistische Vernichtungspolitik gegen Sinti und Roma* (Essen: Klartext, 1989), pp. 11–32.

115 Zimmermann, *Schachtanlage und Zechenkolonie*, pp. 184–5.

116 Peter Reichel, *Der schöne Schein des Dritten Reiches*, pp. 275–311; Rainer Stommer (ed.), *Reichsautobahnen/Pyramiden des Dritten Reiches* (Marburg: Jonas Verlag, 1982); Peter Fritzsche, *A Nation of Fliers. German Aviation and the Popular Imagination* (Cambridge,

Mass.: Harvard University Press, 1992); Adelheid von Saldern, "Cultural conflicts, popular mass culture, and the question of Nazi success: The Eilenriede motorcycle races, 1924–1939," *German Studies Review*, Vol. XV, No. 2, May 1992, pp. 317–38.
117 See Alf Lüdtke's contribution to this volume (pp. 67–109) and Dieter Pfliegensdörfer ' "Ich war mit Herz und Seele dabei . . .,' " p. 99.
118 Reichel, *Der schöne Schein des Dritten Reiches*, pp. 312–20.
119 Ibid., pp. 157–207 and Stephen Lowry, *Pathos und Politik. Ideologie in Spielfilmen des Nationalsozialismus* (Tübingen: Max Niemeyer Verlag 1991).
120 See Detlev J. K. Peukert, *Max Webers Diagnose der Moderne* (Göttingen, 1989) and also Bajohr, Johe and Lohalm (eds), *Zivilisation und Barbarei*.
121 Lüdtke, "Funktionseliten: Täter, Mit-Täter, Opfer?," pp. 559–90; see also Ulrich Herbert, "Rassismus und rationales Kalkül. Zum Stellenwert utilitarische verbrämter Legitimationsstrategien in der nationalsozialistischen 'Weltanschauung' " in Wolfgang Schneider (ed.), *"Vernichtungspolitik". Eine Debatte über den Zusammenhang von Sozialpolitik und Genozid im Nationalsozialistischen Deutschland* (Hamburg: Junius Verlag, 1991), pp. 25–36 and Christopher Browning, "Bureaucracy and mass murder: The German administrator's comprehension of the Final Solution" in Christopher Browning, *The Path to Genocide. Essays on Launching the Final Solution* (Cambridge, 1992), pp. 125–44.
122 See, for example, Michael Zimmermann, " 'Zigeunerforschung' im Nationalsozialismus," in "Mit-Täter: Gesellschaft im Nationalsozialismus," *SOWI/Sozialwissenschaftliche Informationen*, No. 2/91, pp. 104–10 and also Zimmermann, *Verfolgt. Vertrieben. Vernichtet*; Detlev J. K. Peukert, "Racialism as social policy" in *Inside Nazi Germany*, pp. 208–35; Klaus Scherer, *"Asozial" im Dritten Reich. Die vergessenen Verfolgten* (Münster, 1990).
123 Rainer Eisfeld, "Vom Raumfahrtpionieren und Menschenschindern. Ein verdrängtes Kapitel der Technikentwicklung im Dritten Reich" in Rainer Eisfeld and Ingo Muller (eds), *Gegen Barbarei. Essays Robert M. W. Kempner zu Ehren* (Frankfurt am Main: Athenaum Verlag, 1989), pp. 206–38.
124 See Michael Burleigh and Wolfgang Wippermann, *The Racial State. Germany 1933–1945* (Cambridge, 1991) and Wolfgang Schneider (ed.), *"Vernichtungspolitik"* (Hamburg: Junius Verlag, 1991).
125 Thomas Saunders, "Nazism and Social Revolution" in Gordon Martel (ed.), *Modern Germany Reconsidered, 1870–1945* (London/ New York: Routledge, 1992), p. 164.
126 Peukert, *Max Webers Diagnose der Moderne*, p. 82.
127 Peukert, *Inside Nazi Germany*, p. 42.
128 Ibid., p. 245.
129 Ibid., p. 246.
130 Ibid., p. 76.
131 Research on the Nazi persecution of gay men, as well as on the

general issue of homosexuality (both male and female), under the Nazis has expanded considerably in recent years; see, in particular, Burkhard Jellonek, *Homosexuelle unter dem Hakenkreuz: Die Verfolgung von Homosexuellen im Dritten Reich* (Paderborn, 1990) and Claudia Schoppmann, *Nationalsozialistische Sexualpolitik und weibliche Homosexualität im Dritten Reich* (Pfaffenweiler, 1991). Also of interest are: Gunter Grau (ed.) *Homosexualität in der NS-Zeit: Dokumente einer Diskriminierung und Verfolgung* (Frankfurt am Main, 1993); Rüdiger Lautmann, "Categorization in concentration camps as a collective fate: A comparison of homosexuals, Jehovah's Witnesses and political prisoners," *Journal of Homosexuality*, Vol. 19, 1990, pp. 67–88; Lautmann, "The Pink Triangle: The persecution of homosexual males in concentration camps in Nazi Germany," *Journal of Homosexuality*, Vol. 6, 1980–1, pp. 141–60; and Erwin J. Haeberle, "Swastika, Pink Triangle and Yellow Star: The destruction of sexology and the persecution of homosexuals in Nazi Germany" in Martin Bauml Duberman, Martha Vicinus and George Chauncey, Jr (eds), *Hidden From History: Reclaiming the Gay and Lesbian Past* (New York, 1989).

132 Kershaw, *Popular Opinion*, p. 277.
133 Peukert, *Inside Nazi Germany*, p. 245.
134 Ibid., p. 44.
135 Detlev J. K. Peukert, "The Weimar Republic – old and new perspectives," *German History. The Journal of the German History Society*, Vol. VI, No. 2, 1988, p. 137.
136 See, for example David Garland, *Punishment and Welfare. A History of Penal Strategies* (Brookfield, Vermont: Gower, 1985).
137 Peukert, *Inside Nazi Germany*, p. 249.
138 Rolf Schörken, *Jugend 1945. Politisches Denken und Lebensgeschichte* (Opladen, 1990), p. 19.

Part I

"VICTIMS" OR "PERPETRATORS?"

The German people and the Nazi regime

1

THE MISSING YEARS
German workers, German soldiers

Omer Bartov

More research has been devoted to the working class than to almost any other social group in the Third Reich. Yet historians have generally failed to follow workers from the shopfloor to the frontline, even though millions of young, male workers were conscripted for military service in "Hitler's Army." Despite the claims of German generals after 1945 that the army was innocent of Hitler's crimes, many ordinary soldiers participated in the barbarities of racial war in the Soviet Union. The fact that large numbers of German workers were also soldiers must clearly influence the way that we think about the role of German workers in Nazi society.

In the following article, Omer Bartov argues that after over a decade of Nazi indoctrination many young workers came to their military service prepared to embrace the racist goals of the Nazi regime. Their admiration for the Führer, their pride in Germany's military power and their own racial prejudices turned these young recruits into the "tenacious, increasingly brutalized and fanaticized soldiers" (p. 46) who made possible the implementation of Hitler's murderous policies in the east.

Bartov's article demonstrates the value of paying much closer attention to the war years than most social historians have been prepared to do until now.* Readers may, however, want to ask whether Bartov's broad generalizations about the mentalities of millions of German

* See also, more recently, Alf Lüdtke, "The appeal of exterminating 'others': German workers and the limits of resistance," *Journal of Modern History*, Vol. 64, December 1992, pp. 46–67.

soldiers in "Hitler's Army" can be adequately sustained by the limited range of individual memoirs and autobiographies which he cites.†

* * *

I

Though conveniently well-defined chronologically, the Third Reich has never ceased to present scholars and laymen alike with disturbing questions of definition. Indeed, it has proved excessively difficult to fit the "Hitler State" into an historical context. While the search for the roots of National Socialism has encumbered German (and to some extent European) historiography as a whole with the burden of hindsight, on the one hand, the attempt to "come to terms with the past" in the post-Nazi era has left deep marks of disconcerting amnesia and empty rhetoric, on the other hand. Just as many of the "ideas" enthusiastically propagated and ruthlessly put into practice by the Nazis predate Hitler's "seizure of power" and even the founding of the NSDAP, so too Germany's *Stunde Null* has failed to erase the past and allow the two new republics which had emerged out of the debris of the Reich to set off on their diametrically opposed *Neubeginnen* as if nothing had happened. Too many people who had experienced Hitler's twelve-year rule were still alive, too many minds were still filled to the brim with terrible (though for some also pleasant) memories, for that era of great hopes and deep disillusions, vast conquests and bitter defeats simply to vanish. A glimpse at the dust-jacket biographies of books published in the Federal Republic, for instance, will easily demonstrate the glaring absence of the years 1933–45 from the lives of Germany's literati.[1]

The question of continuity and discontinuity has thus remained at the core of German history ever since the "catastrophe" of 1945, with the Third Reich, its actual brief tenure notwithstanding, stubbornly casting a long shadow over periods both preceding its conception and stretching far beyond its

---

† Bartov presents a more sustained and fully documented argument in his recent book, *Hitler's Army. Soldiers, Nazis, and War in the Third Reich* (New York/Oxford, 1992). See also the collection of captured letters home from the front in Soviet archives edited by Anatoly Golovchansky, Valentin Osipov, Anatoly Prokopenko, Ute Daniel and Jürgen Reulecke, *"Ich will raus aus diesen Wahnsinn": Deutsche Briefe von der Ostfront 1941–1945. Aus Sowjetischen Archiven* (Wuppertal, 1991).

demise. The view of Nazism as an aberration, a society inexplicably gone mad, or taken over by a "criminal clique" against its will, has not been corroborated by the historical evidence.[2] Moreover, rather like the claim regarding the "uniqueness" of the Holocaust, it has always suffered from being entirely ahistorical, in that it attempted to lift a significant chunk of history out of the general stream of events and to discard it as not belonging to the "real" Germany, a monstrous Mr Hyde who has fortunately been forced back into the test-tube whence he had sprung. A characteristic example of what such artificial detachment from recent events can lead to is to be found in the East Berlin Museum for German History where, for instance, the caption under the photograph of a *Wehrmacht* officer, killed in front of the Reichstag building in May 1945, describes him as a "dead fascist soldier." Apparently, whereas those (communist workers) who opposed Hitler were German, those (other classes) who fought for him were merely "fascists," though once they changed into *Volksheer* uniforms (or joined the *Bundeswehr* in the case of the FRG), they inevitably regained their national identity.

Conversely, it has generally been acknowledged that excavating the roots of Nazism far into the Dark Ages has had a major distorting effect on historiography, often obscuring other social, political, religious, and cultural currents which had contributed to making European civilization what it is today, for better or worse. Consequently, some scholars have recently proposed to "normalize" the historical position of the Third Reich by locating it within a wider context, and at the same time to "historicize" the writing of its history by doing away with the hitherto almost obligatory rhetoric and examining its various aspects with the proper mixture of objectivity and empathy. Indeed, it has been said that instead of concentrating mainly on the criminality of the rulers, the suffering of the victims, and the heroism of the resisters, more attention should be given to contemporary social phenomena relatively unrelated to the regime, as well as for instance to legislative and organizational initiatives which, though carried out at the time, have since made an impact on post-Nazi society, not all of it necessarily negative.[3]

Attempts to point out that in its foreign relations the Third Reich behaved quite "normally," both in comparison with other powers and as far as its own predecessors and successors were concerned, have, however, proved far from uncontroversial.[4]

Similarly, on the domestic front too, it has been aptly pointed out that what may have seemed to many good German citizens a "normalization" of their society under Nazism, following a period of political and economic crisis, was actually achieved by ruthlessly "uprooting" the representatives of "abnormality." With the disappearance of the insane, beggars, handicapped, Gypsies, Jews, and so forth, and the enforcement of strict order and discipline, many an average "Aryan" must have felt that the situation had indeed been pleasantly "normalized," at least as far as her or his own, often self-willed narrow view was concerned.[5] Moreover, once Nazi rule was over, its memory too had to be "normalized." Thus we should not simply speak of "missing years," but rather of a period in the lives of people in whose memory much was repressed, and much else given a "normalizing" interpretation, enabling them to live with its recollection and even cherish some of its more enjoyable moments, particularly as it had all happened when they were young, healthy, and for a while also relatively well-off and members of a great power ruling over vast territories. Only in this manner can both individual and national history follow their uninterrupted course, so necessary if one is to make some sense out of the chaos of events.[6] This, it will be argued below, applies not only to those small-town, white-collar, Protestant Germans who are said to have constituted Hitler's strongest supporters,[7] but also, though not precisely in the same sense, to the working class, generally considered to have remained least susceptible to Nazism.

II

In recent years it has been convincingly shown that far from conforming to the totalitarian image it strove to project, the "Hitler State" was in fact made up of a chaotic conglomeration of competing, overlapping, and often superfluous institutions, with only the Führer, himself described by some historians as a "weak dictator" with limited powers, to divide and rule over it.[8] Moreover, the Nazi ideal of establishing a so-called "*Volksgemeinschaft*" is also said to have failed miserably, with German society, though submitting to a terroristic police state, remaining riven by conflicting class interests.[9] Similarly, while the "Hitler Myth" retained its hold as a unifying concept for a growing proportion of the German population until very late in the war, the NSDAP, which in any case had never achieved even a simple majority, lost much of its popularity in the early years following the "seizure of power."[10]

The German working class is probably the most significant case in point as regards the Nazi regime's failure – or unwillingness – to break down those very class barriers against which the party had allegedly fought and whose disappearance in an idyllic *Volksgemeinschaft* should have legitimized the replacement of the Weimar Republic by a ruthless dictatorship. Extensive research into this issue has indeed demonstrated that quite apart from outright resistance to the regime, mostly by former socialist and communist activists, workers had shown a surprising degree of opposition to attempts by the employers and the state to limit their gains, made following the rapid shift in the 1930s from unemployment to manpower shortage as a result of massive rearmament. The workers' struggle, involving an array of industrial actions such as strikes, go-slows, frequent changes of work-places, and lowered productivity, has been presented as a clear sign of the regime's failure to create a totalitarian "people's community," based not just on fear and suppression, but also on acceptance of the new political system and creed. Social structures inherited from pre-Nazi times are thus said to have persisted under Hitler's rule and to have evolved gradually only after the fall of the Third Reich, owing both to the terrible destruction of the war and the political upheavals which followed it.[11] Nevertheless, while on the one hand it may astonish us that there actually was such interest-group pressure from the working class under the Nazi dictatorship, on the other hand there is also room to inquire why this domestic tension rarely transformed itself into political resistance, and why the regime, though making a few temporary concessions to the workers (as it also did to the churches), does not seem to have been seriously threatened by the working class at any time, and could by and large pursue expansionist policies with no hindrance from within, indeed, with a great measure of support.[12]

Findings regarding industrial unrest in Germany in the late 1930s have significantly influenced views on some major issues of the period, such as the debate over the origins of the Second World War, the inquiry into the deeper causes and wider implications of the *Blitzkrieg* strategy, as well as the historical value of earlier theories of fascism and totalitarianism.[13] At the same time, it has also become necessary to define more precisely the meaning and applicability of such terms as "resistance" and "opposition," both as regards the working class, and in the case of other groups hovering between collaboration and resistance, such as the churches, the military, and the traditional liberal-conservative elites.[14]

Yet precisely because of the centrality of this issue and the wide range of its implications, it may be of some interest to stress one of its aspects which does not seem to have received appropriate attention hitherto. The point is that in September 1939 Germany launched what turned out to be a world war, and although initially its people marched to battle without much enthusiasm, and its resources were not totally mobilized, as of winter 1941 Hitler's Reich found itself up to its neck in a vast military confrontation, fielding millions of soldiers, and straining both its physical and its mental capacities to the limit. Ultimately, the mass of Germany's population became involved in one way or another in the war, and a growing proportion of its men, young, middle-aged, and old, workers, bourgeois, and aristocrats, Nazis and former socialists and communists, were recruited and sent to the front, turning miraculously into Europe's toughest and most determined troops, mostly fighting with extraordinary cohesion almost until the bitter end. For throughout the war, combat morale in the *Wehrmacht* generally remained extremely high, mutinies were almost unknown, and an excellent system of manpower organization, draconian punishment, and extensive indoctrination combined to hold combat units tightly together, while a series of astonishing victories made it easier to withstand even greater defeats in the hope of fortune's wheel turning once more in Germany's favour.[15]

The question to be asked is thus, how did it come about that men who had been recruited from the mines and factories, who had demonstrated their capacity to oppose at least the social and economic policies of the regime, and some of whom may well have still remembered their former trade-union, SPD, or KPD affiliations, could within a matter of months be transformed into Hitler's tenacious, increasingly brutalized and fanaticized soldiers, spearheading his expanding Reich and executing or making possible the execution of his murderous

46

policies? Indeed, what light does this shed on the greater or lesser susceptibility of various social strata to Nazism, on the extent, aims, and nature of opposition, on the degree to which it actually threatened the regime, and on the Third Reich's capacity to mobilize the mass of German society, *"Volksgemeinschaft"* or not?

Put differently, it seems that we should clearly distinguish between the Nazi regime's evident failure to realize its proclaimed aim of establishing a *"Volksgemeinschaft"* free of intersocial tensions, on the one hand, and the willingness of large sectors of the population to accept that same regime as the embodiment of the nation, and to sacrifice themselves for it at a time of war and crisis, on the other hand. The great patriotic surge of August 1914, when German, British, and French workers went off to slaughter each other in defence of their respective class-ridden societies, had already demonstrated that a just, classless society is not a necessary precondition for total mobilization. Furthermore, we now know that even in Wilhelmine Germany, for instance, the renowned workers' "sub-culture" was anything but free from a widespread penetration of bourgeois values and norms, tastes, manners, and ambitions.[16] It took four years of unprecedented blood-letting and suffering, almost culminating in victory over materially stronger foes, for the nightmare of the *Kaiserreich's* ruling elites, namely that its working-class recruits would refuse to die for king and country, but rather would ferment a social revolution, to become reality.[17] Meanwhile, and this is the crucial point, the trenches of the Great War turned out to have been the breeding ground of the myth of the *"Kampfgemeinschaft,"* that community of warriors in which all social and material distinctions had allegedly disappeared under the impact of a shared *Fronterlebnis*. Thus the prewar dream of replacing existing society, riven as it was by class struggles and competing interest groups, by a harmonious community, was realized, at least in some men's minds, in the bloody fields of Flanders. And as Hitler's idyllic *"Volksgemeinschaft"* was in fact a warring community, eternally engaged in a struggle for survival, it was only natural that it should strive to return to those very battlefields where it had achieved such perfection.[18] Indeed, the spell seems to have worked once more, and men who only yesterday had confronted each other in that imperfect "people's community," suddenly joined together and, in the name of that Nazi regime so many of them were supposed to oppose, fought shoulder to shoulder against those they had been persuaded to believe were their common enemies.

Is this merely the Nazi regime's propagandistic description of the *"Kampfgemeinschaft"* in action? Did those workers who as civilians had demonstrated their dissatisfaction with at least some aspects of Hitler's regime, in fact show less enthusiasm also as soldiers, fight with less resilience, tend more towards indiscipline and subversion? And, if not, was this simply because they had been cut off from their familiar social and economic context and plunged into a radically different environment, where old interests and loyalties were no longer relevant, while new ones assumed the utmost existential importance? Or does this phenomenon actually indicate that their own civilian environment had also been increasingly permeated with Nazi ideas and organizations? That such questions have not been posed in this manner hitherto, is due not least to the wide gap which seems to have appeared between the social and military history of the Third Reich. For, while social historians have probed into civilian society, military historians have concerned themselves mainly with tactics, strategy and generals. Although it has of course long been recognized that in modern conscript armies the borderline between civilians and soldiers is extremely blurred, the army was treated as a separate institution, maintaining its own particular relationship with the state. If the social background of soldiers was considered at all, it was mainly that of the older, senior ranks, or of that tiny group of resisters, likewise quite highly placed in the military hierarchy.[19] Consequently, once conscripted, the social historians' protagonists were passed over to the military historians who, as far as the rank-and-file and junior officers were concerned, treated them as part of a vast, faceless mass of field-grey uniforms devoid of any civilian past. Conversely, once the war was over, those soldiers who had survived it were, so to speak, delivered back into the hands of the social historians, only to continue their civilian existence with very little reference to the fact that for years they had served as soldiers – just as in dust-jacket biographies, or in that recent film saga, *Heimat*, the workers too went off somewhere for a few years, and then some of them returned. What happened in between was a matter for soldiers' stories.

48

III

Yet what happened in between is precisely what one would like to know in order to put the experience of German workers into the context not only of the failed *Volksgemeinschaft*, but also of Hitler's devoted army. Now in order to do this, a number of fundamental questions have to be raised. First, we would like to know how many soldiers actually came from a working-class background; secondly, we should ask to what extent the *Wehrmacht*'s soldiers were supportive of the regime, its ideology, and its war aims; thirdly, it would be crucial to find out how much the men's attitudes were in fact influenced by their social stratum, and how much they had to do with other, though not entirely unrelated, categories, such as age, family, and educational background, as well as membership of premilitary or paramilitary organizations. The experience of the war itself would also presumably have played a significant role in moulding the soldiers' attitudes.

Whereas regarding civilians it is relatively simply to determine their class affiliation, once they become soldiers we are faced with a serious problem of identifying their social background. Straightforward documentary evidence on this question is almost impossible to come by, and consequently there are also hardly any secondary works on this issue, particularly as far as the rank-and-file are concerned, whereas, its egalitarian rhetoric notwithstanding, most of the *Wehrmacht*'s officers came from the middle, upper-middle, and upper classes.[20] Nevertheless, I would like to suggest here a few ways of tackling this problem, albeit mostly indirectly, so as to enhance our knowledge regarding worker-soldiers' attitudes in the Third Reich.

First, it may be useful to point out that although during the initial stages of the war the regime had in fact exempted vast numbers of able-bodied workers from service, both because of economic needs, and because of its fears that by mass recruitment from the working class it might hasten another "1918 crisis," by autumn 1941 the tremendous casualties already inflicted upon the *Wehrmacht* by the Red Army made it unavoidable to conscript a growing number of industrial workers, eventually replacing them with millions of forced-labourers from the Reich's expanding empire. Thus as of the winter crisis of 1941–2 an ever larger proportion of Germany's troops came from the working class.[21] This means that when we speak of the *Wehrmacht*, and especially of the rank-and-file, we have to take it for granted that a significant proportion of its men were workers. Although we normally cannot say how these workers were distributed among the units (except in individual cases to be noted below), this point has to be taken into account when we speak in more general terms of the soldiers' attitudes and conduct.

Secondly, a number of negative and positive inferences have to be made regarding the behaviour of the *Wehrmacht*'s rank-and-file in the war. Negatively it can be said that no convincing evidence could be found to show that workers performed less well in battle, were proportionately more involved in breaches of discipline, or indeed demonstrated any opposition to the army's criminal activities in the East. In fact, there is very little evidence to show that there was opposition from any lower-ranking soldiers, workers or not. Thus, such opposition as there was came mostly from higher-ranking officers, and had initially to do mainly with the possible effects of the "criminal orders" on soldiers' morale and the enemy's resistance, and later on with hopes for a political arrangement with the Allies in the face of an approaching catastrophe. Moreover, the revision of the "Barbarossa" directives in spring 1942, due mostly to the growing need for foreign labour in the Reich (following the conscription of the workers), actually failed to impress the troops at the front who kept up with the old habit of indiscriminate shootings.[22]

More positive evidence regarding soldiers' attitudes towards the war is in fact quite abundant, coming from a variety of sources and indicating that by and large, at least until the last few months of the war, the *Wehrmacht*'s troops were among the regime's strongest supporters, no matter where they had come from and what their opinions had been before the war. This is not to say, of course, that they were all Nazis in the strict sense of the word (which is in any case extremely difficult to define); rather, it indicates that they supported Hitler's rule, agreed with his policies as far as they concerned them, and were mostly willing to fight, die, and commit an array of criminal acts in his service, accepting the regime's view of Germany's mission in the world and its perception of the Reich's enemies as consisting mostly of inferior beings unworthy of life.

Thus, for instance, two major studies of morale in the Third Reich have pointed out that the front-line troops remained in much higher spirits than the population in the rear until very late in the war. Indeed, it is claimed that "periods of buoyancy [in the rear] were triggered mostly by the confidence and attitude of the front-line soldiers," who were "the staunchest supporters of Hitler and the regime," to the extent that by spring 1943 "Mobilization of officers and soldiers to raise the public mood ... had long since been introduced."[23] Similarly, SD reports in June 1943 led another historian to conclude that "The 'Führer myth' remained relatively strong ... [among] ordinary Front soldiers."[24] Moreover, following the attempted assassination of Hitler in July 1944, once more various reports showed that a vast majority of the troops "believed" in the Führer.[25] The bomb plot also justified viewing military setbacks as merely the result of a conspiracy. As another report pointed out, "today [people] think that for some time the traitors have sabotaged the Führer's objectives and orders. This opinion is primarily due to an increase in the written and oral reports by soldiers from the Eastern Front who declare that they are now discovering the reasons for the absence of reinforcements and the often senseless shifting of units and exposure of the front."[26] Hitler's popularity among German POWs captured by the Americans stood at 69 per cent in August 1944, 42 per cent in mid October, and 64 per cent again in late November.[27] A military report dated 15 December 1944 maintained that there was little defeatist talk among the troops, and "There is a firm conviction that the tremendous military efforts of our people will lead us to victory."[28] Indeed, strong signs of disintegration were noted only towards March 1945.[29] Yet even then a large proportion of the soldiers were said to have retained their courage and willingness to fight, especially the old fighters and the "marvellous youth," though by this stage there were also many tired and apathetic soldiers, as well as some cowards and deserters.[30]

Other sources give the same impression of widespread support for the regime, as embodied by Hitler, among the soldiers, and of the manner in which "his" war was being conducted. Thus on 4 July 1941 Goebbels could write in his diary that "our soldiers at the [Eastern] front are now completely convinced of the necessity of this war,"[31] and repeated four days later that "Morale of our men at the front [is] very good. The soldiers now realize that this campaign was necessary."[32] Even as late as March 1945 Goebbels quoted Allied sources as maintaining that "our men have been fighting like savage fanatics."[33] Indeed, he wrote that "The effect of the Führer's visit [to I Corps on the Eastern Front] both on officers and men was enormous,"[34] adding later that "The general officers put on a good show and the soldiers cheered the Führer."[35] Although morale among the troops was evidently sinking at this last, desperate stage of the war,[36] Goebbels insisted that the men were "resisting at all costs – to the extent that the situation and their equipment permit."[37] Depending on the commanders, some units still retained a good fighting spirit. Summarizing his visit to Colonel-General Schörner's troops, Goebbels wrote that "there is not the smallest sign of defeatism here,"[38] but, quite to the contrary, he had observed "that faith in victory and in the Führer is prevalent among these men."[39] Thus, although he admitted that "German fighting morale has reached its nadir," Goebbels was encouraged by enemy reports, according to which "our prisoners still maintain the view that Germany must definitely win the war," and that they "have an almost mystical faith in Hitler. This is the reason," he concluded, "why we are still on our feet and fighting."[40] Goebbels also realized that "the present level of morale must not be confused with definite defeatism. The people will continue to do their duty and the front-soldier will defend himself as far as he has a possibility of doing so." The problem was that "These possibilities are becoming increasingly limited."[41] Thus the sinking morale "is evidenced not by any revolutionary symptoms" (that is, by opposition to the regime as such) "but by the general attitude of lethargy now prevalent among both officers and men."[42]

The Minister of Propaganda of course had his own reasons for describing the Wehrmacht's troops as fanatically supportive of the regime, even when confiding these remarks to the privacy of his diary. The Generals had other reasons for saying the same. Yet it cannot be ignored that in their memoirs they repeatedly point out the fact that the army, and particularly the rank-and-file and junior officer corps, were National Socialist through and through, especially as at the same time they tried to present the Wehrmacht as a professional organization quite indifferent to ideology. Von Manstein, for example, wrote that "The preconditions for a coup d'état would have been ... the following of the whole *Wehrmacht* and the agreement of the majority of the population. Both did not exist during the years of peace in the Third Reich as well as during the war (with the exception perhaps of the very last months)."[43] Heinz Guderian too had no doubts as to his soldiers' faith in the Führer. As he wrote in his memoirs, following Hitler's "seizure of power," "as one year succeeded the next, the opposition within the Army was continually weakened, since the new age groups that were now called to the colours had already served in the Hitler Youth, and in the National Labour Service or the Party, and had thus already sworn allegiance to Hitler. The Corps of Officers, too, became year by year more impregnated with young National Socialists"[44] – including, of course, Guderian himself. Indeed, as he adds elsewhere, "When National-Socialism, with its new, nationalistic slogans, appeared upon the scene the younger elements of the Officer Corps were soon inflamed by the patriotic theories propounded by Hitler and his followers."[45]

The conspirators against Hitler knew well enough that the majority of the soldiers and civilians would see the assassination as an act of treason – as indeed they did following its failure.[46] Simply finding a single military unit whose men could be depended upon proved impossible, as Johnnie von Herwarth wrote, the reason being, as he says elsewhere in his book, that "the soldiers ... were naturally under the influence of Nazi propaganda,"[47] where this had to do with their attitudes towards the Russians and Jews, or with their support of Hitler. "It would have been difficult in any circumstances to identify among the tens of thousands of troops those upon whom we could count," he writes. "The task of locating them became more vexatious as we realized that few, if any, were likely to fit that category. . . . We never had any troops upon which we could rely one hundred per cent."[48] Planning the *Putsch*, the conspirators realized that almost everyone was against them, not against Hitler. In fact, the very reasoning behind the decision to kill the Führer was "the general conviction that German troops would never be willing to accept a different command as long as Hitler lived, but that news of his death would instantly bring about the collapse of the myth that surrounded his name. Hence there was no way of gaining the support of large numbers of German troops without eliminating Hitler."[49] This was clearly correct, as was shown less than a year later, following Hitler's suicide.

Coming closer to the soldiers themselves, there is little doubt that their letters home may be quite instructive regarding what they thought about the regime, the enemy, and the war. Here too we are hampered by the fact that it is usually impossible to tell the social background of these men. Nevertheless, just as in the cases quoted above, considering the fact that a growing proportion of the troops were recruited from the working class, one may be allowed to assume that a fair number of the letters were written by former workers, especially in the case of non-commissioned ranks. Now from the available evidence, and it is admittedly only a minute sample of the vast wartime correspondence,[50] there does seem to have existed a great deal of agreement among the soldiers as regards the regime's views of its enemies and the sort of treatment they deserved, as well as a widespread admiration of the Führer. Indeed, it is quite striking to find the troops describing Russians, communists, and Jews in terms obviously lifted directly from propaganda sheets, orders of the day, newspapers and radio broadcasts, betraying the effects of years of ideological training as civilians and soldiers alike by their distorted perception of reality.[51] This impression is confirmed both by the demands made by the front-line units to be supplied with even greater amounts of propaganda material, particularly at times of crisis,[52] as well as by the above-quoted surveys conducted among German POWs during the war, indicating that almost until the very end a majority of the men went on "believing" in Hitler and, by implication, consciously or not, in much of what he stood for.[53]

A few representative quotes from soldiers' letters must suffice to illustrate this point. In November 1940 one soldier belonging to the 16 Army wrote that "We are all burning to be allowed to present those who are guilty of this great war with the last reckoning" (referring to Britain and its "Jewish plutocrats"), and added that as regards occupied France,

we have had more than enough of the moral, ethical decay, which appears to us here again and again.... Here one can see for the first time how beautiful Germany is, and how proud we should be of being German, and thankful to our Führer, who has spared our people the misery which we now see daily.[54]

Drawing on the Buchbender and Stertz collection, we find that less than two weeks after the invasion of the Soviet Union, Lance-Corporal F. of the 125th Infantry Division wrote from the East that "Here one sees evidence of Jewish, Bolshevik atrocities, the likes of which I have hardly believed possible.... You can well imagine that this cries out for revenge, which we certainly also take."[55] Another NCO exclaimed on 19 July 1941: "The German people owes a great debt to our Führer, for had these beasts, who are our enemies here, come to Germany, such murders would have taken place, which the world has never seen before.... And when one reads the *Stürmer* and looks at the pictures, that is only a tiny fraction of what we see here and the crimes committed here by the Jews."[56] One private wrote on 1 August that the Russians are "a people which needs long and good training in order to become human,"[57] and another expressed the same view on the 20th, rejoicing that "these uncultivated, multi-raced men ... have been thwarted from plundering and pillaging our homeland."[58] While the NCO H.B. of the 125th Infantry Division stressed that "for us the Führer's words are gospel," and went on to describe the Soviet prisoners as "animal-like,"[59] an NCO of the 183rd Infantry Division maintained that the Russians "are no longer human beings, but wild hordes and beasts, who have been bred by Bolshevism during the last 20 years," and thus "one may not allow oneself to feel any compassion for these people, because they are all very cowardly and perfidious."[60] Similarly, an NCO of the 251st Infantry Division wrote in mid November 1941 that "Had these cannibalized heaps of soldiers fallen upon Germany, everything which is German would have been done with."[61] And yet, one should keep in mind that there was no need for men writing private letters home to express themselves in this manner, as censorship concerned itself with negative, rather than with the absence of positive, remarks.[62]

Another means of gauging the attitudes of the *Wehrmacht*'s troops brings us to the third question posed at the beginning of this section, namely, how important class affiliation actually was in determining the men's opinions and conduct, and how much it had to do with other categories. Memoirs of former soldiers, rather than high ranking generals, may help us to understand the psychology of the Third Reich's youth and soldiers. Alfons Heck's autobiography begins in 1933, when he was 6 years old. Raised in a small Catholic Rhineland town, he soon became a devout *HJ* leader and a self-proclaimed fanatical supporter of Hitler, though his family showed no strong inclination towards Nazism. His book is a detached, apparently accurate description of the manner in which young boys in the Third Reich were made into Nazis, first and foremost by the Hitler Youth, while both school and family retreated well into the background. Heck had been to a Nuremberg rally, and hearing Hitler's speech left an everlasting impression on him. Like many others of his generation, he was eager to fight for Führer and *Volk*, and prepared to denounce anyone who expressed other views (though, again like many others, he apparently relented from denouncing a close friend). However, his "Nazism" vanished very quickly following the capitulation.[63]

Rolf Schörken has analysed a number of memoirs of this kind. His first case, Dieter Borkowski, grew up in Berlin. His father dead, his mother wielding little influence on him, his character was moulded mainly by the *HJ*, films such as *Jud Süss*, and the National Socialist *Wochenschauen*. On 2 May 1945, this 16-year-old boy was on the great anti-aircraft tower of the capital, when he heard of Hitler's suicide. "These words make me feel sick, as if I would have to vomit. I think that my life has no sense any more. What was this battle for, what were the deaths of so many people for? Life has apparently become worthless, for if Hitler has shot himself, the Russians will have finally won. . . . Has the Führer not betrayed his *Volk* then after all?"[64] It is interesting to note that Hans Ulrich Rudel, the ace Stuka pilot, son of a Silesian village pastor, who was 29 when he heard of Hitler's death, wrote that "The shock of the news . . . has a stunning effect upon the troops. But . . . we must fight on. We shall only lay down our arms when our leaders give the order."[65] Indeed, the need to go on believing in something so as not to admit the senselessness of the struggle was also reflected in soldiers' letters from Stalingrad. As one man wrote shortly before the surrender: "The Führer has promised to get us out of here. . . . I still believe it today, because I simply must believe in something. If it isn't true, what is there left for me to believe in? . . . If what we were promised is not true, then Germany will be lost, for no other promises can be kept after that."[66]

Schörken's second case, Karl Hillenbrand, tells in his memoirs of his idyllic childhood in a Siegerland village, where he had hardly known anything of the Nazis or the war almost until the very end, and even when war came to his doorstep, by which time he was 16 years old, he experienced it mainly from the technical point of view through his fascination with weapons. Yet when his father beats him, his instinctive reaction is to denounce him for listening to a foreign radio broadcast. Though he ultimately relents, this boy too, much as he had seemed untouched by events, in fact comes to realize the destructive potential the regime had put into his hands.[67]

Even the 12-year-old Jochen Ziem, Schörken's third example, almost denounces his parents, though in this case, considering both his age and the approaching end of the war, the mutual fear awakened in both sides draws him finally closer to his family.[68] The fourth case, Eugen Oker, on the other hand, raised in a Bavarian village, becomes an ardent HJ follower in 1933 at the age of 14. Thus, Schörken rightly remarks, these autobiographies demonstrate that the "social stratum" of such boys had little to do with their development. The parents were all "little people", some mildly opposed to the regime, others quite indifferent or filled with a sense of helplessness. This did not have a consistent effect on the boys, but especially those who were about 14 years old in 1933–4 – that is, the Third Reich's future soldiers – were highly likely to come under the influence of the regime and to react against their parents' opinions. Moreover, whenever neither the home nor the peer group exercised a political influence on the boys, the Nazi propaganda picture tended to take over, mainly via the HJ.[69] As Heinrich Böll's autobiography demonstrates, however, if the family united in strong, articulate opposition to the regime, it could have a major impact on the boy, whatever social class he belonged to.[70]

Hannsferdinand Döbler, Schörken's last example, is a particularly interesting case, for this young man, 26 years old in 1945, though describing himself as a "150 per cent idealistic-believing officer" who kept fighting even after the capitulation, was not a Nazi in the strict sense of the word. Rather, he conformed to the ideal type of the Wehrmacht officer, totally internalizing the regime's value system without considering himself ideologically a party member. Indeed, in contradiction to the recent theories concerning the manifestations of resistance in a daily life of nonconformity and passivity, here we have the daily manifestations of collaboration expressed in a will to conform and act, so characteristic of the Third Reich's youth, whatever their social background. Raised by his mother in a petit-bourgeois family, Döbler's main wish was "to belong" and "to be there." The pastor who tried to divert him from this course was perceived by him as pathetic, his friendship with a half-Jewish girl had no impact on his anti-Semitic views, and his ideal model, as for so many others of his generation, was a tough, exemplary company commander, quite reminiscent, for instance, of Guy Sajer's own company commander, whose idealistic-nihilistic speech to his men he quotes at length in his autobiography. "His obvious and passionate sincerity affected even the most hesitant," Sajer concludes, "we loved him and felt we had a true leader, as well as a friend on whom we could count."[71] Döbler too was moulded in a constantly military environment, where there was neither need nor time for questions. He was driven by a sense of responsibility for "his men" and by a burning desire to be at the front, notwithstanding numerous injuries (which paradoxically, was also the case of Böll, in spite of his very different upbringing).[72] In Döbler we have an outstanding example of the type manufactured by that powerful combination of the Nazi regime's ideology, the *Wehrmacht*'s system of values, and the reality of the war, enhanced by the youthfulness of the soldiers, the manifest weakness of family and school in the face of totalitarian rule, and the tremendous impact of a highly appealing youth movement, which deliberately mobilized the rebellious spirits of the young against their parents and teachers, providing them instead with military trappings, power over their elders, and an opportunity to sacrifice themselves for a "good cause."[73] Indeed, all one can ask is, how could anyone have turned out differently under such circumstances?

Finally, we can consider a few examples of workers who served as soldiers during the war. Some oral testimonies given after the war by men of working-class origin have already been analysed and published,[74] while a significant amount of such collected evidence is still awaiting examination.[75] Drawing conclusions from interviews conducted long after the event of course presents numerous difficulties, particularly as regards the experience of the Third Reich, much of which will have been either repressed or reinterpreted in people's minds under the influence of all that has been said and written about it since 1945.[76] Nevertheless, properly treated, it may tell us a great deal about what individuals felt, thought, and did at the time, questions which more conventional historical evidence can rarely answer, especially regarding the lower strata of society. Furthermore, in this manner we can also learn something of the impact such experiences may have had on these men once the regime had collapsed and they returned to their old workplaces or found new employment. Four such interviews, as analysed by Lutz Niethammer, are of particular interest for this article.

Fritz Harenberg, a zinc miner, considered his army service as the most important junction in his life. "At the time," he said, "one didn't have the guts to go against it all. Today one sees it all differently, because those were all years lost for nothing, which one misses today." And yet, he added, "as far as the barracks were concerned, not what came afterwards – I liked them better than the time in the Labour Service. . . . We got very good food." Indeed, as an occupation soldier in France too, "we lived well. . . . Near Nancy. And in the evenings . . . one went to a pub . . . and there were the soldiers' cinemas and soldiers' homes," while "inside the city . . . they had meanwhile set up brothels." Whilst in Sarayevo, Harenberg remembered buying himself chocolate and a watch, as well as presents for his wife, and claimed to have "got along well, very well with the population." Simultaneously he recalled that "there was there . . . a Jewish cemetery. . . . And then the Gestapo were told that in the Jewish cemetery so much had been buried, good money and good things. Yes, the Gestapo rounded up the Jews, had to dig them up."[77]

Josef Paul, who had lost his leg in the war and whose father and grandfather had both been SPD members, remembered his father saying to him in 1945 that "because of the party I had almost lost my work. And if you join a party here, then I'll box your ears right and left. Because a party is a filthy affair."[78] Gustav Köppke, however, though both his father and stepfather had been miners and communists before 1933, became an ardent member of the *HJ*. He could clearly remember watching *Kristallnacht* as a 9-year-old: "It was terribly impressive, when the SA marched. . . . I was on the side of the strong guys; the Jews, they were the others." Indeed, he reported, "Our workers' suburb and the *HJ* were in no way contradictory . . . this idea of the *HJ* versus the people, you shouldn't see it as if we young lads had to decide for something or against something; there was nothing else ... and whoever wanted to become something belonged to it.... The *HJ* uniform was something positive in our childhood." For Köppke the partisans were *Untermenschen*, and he too came close to denouncing his parents. In 1944, aged 16, he volunteered for the SS *HJ*-Division, and was filled with bitterness following the capitulation: "I was raised then, in the National Socialist time and had seen the world just as they had shown it to us.... And suddenly nothing made sense any more." But, tending towards extremes, he soon joined the communist party.[79]

The locksmith Gisberg Pohl, after the war a trade-union and SPD official, already held a senior position in the *HJ* when he volunteered in 1943 for the *Waffen*-SS at the age of 18. He did basic training in Buchenwald. Observing those scenes, he said, "For me a whole world came apart then," particularly, as he explained, because "I was then ... quite earnest," and "Although they naturally tried to explain to us ... that these were *Untermenschen*, Russian POWS, Jews, I don't know who they rounded up there." Yet, he hastened to add, "I naturally made too much of it then, right, and one has made too much of it later." Pohl also participated in the suppression of the Warsaw rising: "I had ... a strong conviction, not this way, I mean: 'Does the Führer know this then?' or rather, if you like, well, this is after all not right, I thought." But again he qualified himself, explaining that "being a young man one easily made too much of it. We had after all gone to Russia, we wanted [to go] there, [to destroy?] subhumanity – I was, that is, strongly convinced of my task, that I was right. And once it goes that far, then you don't think about it much, then only one thing remains, then you know very well, either him or me." Only while in a POW camp after the wear, Pohl found "that I actually knew nothing of the world," and some time later he joined the SPD.[80]

IV

It would thus seem that by stressing the close connection between the Third Reich's civilian population and its soldiers, and by realizing that, though of course biased in favour of certain social and age (let alone gender and "racial") categories, the *Wehrmacht* increasingly reflected the society from which its

[handwritten margin note: German soliers reflect German society; wide-spread indoctrination of National Socialism.]

troops were recruited, our underst
duct, and more generally of confor
Germany on the whole, can be su
the point of view of the military
succeeded beyond all expectation:
recruits into well-disciplined and
whatever their social origins and political traditions. Quite apart
from its policy of harsh punishments,[81] the *Wehrmacht* managed
to persuade a high proportion of its men that, headed by "the
greatest *Feldherr* of all time," they were fighting for the right
"cause" against an infernal host of political and biological enemies. Yet this could not have succeeded without first penetrating
wide-ranging sectors of civilian society and indoctrinating sol-
diers-to-be into believing the central tenets of National Socialism. This process is of particular significance in the case of the
working class, that social stratum said to have been most resistant to Nazi propaganda. For, examining what worker-soldiers
thought, wrote, and carried out, one may well find it worthwhile
to reconsider the nature and reasoning behind their opposition
to the regime, and ask whether it actually stemmed from politi-
cal/ideological, or rather from economic/interest-group
motivation.

The limited evidence presented here seems to suggest that
Nazi ideas had indeed had an impact upon the German working
class, and particularly upon the younger generation, as they had
on German youth on the whole. This in no way means that
those same workers did not hope to improve their economic
condition, or protect those gains they had already made. But it
does indicate that there was a large pool of nationalist phobias
and racial prejudices among the working class on which the
regime could draw, just as there is evidence of quite a powerful
admiration for the Führer, whatever may have been thought of
the party.[82] It is also quite likely that especially some of the
younger men were attracted to the prospect of exchanging their
dreary work-places for what seemed to be an invincible army,
in which, moreover, owing mostly to the tremendous casualties,
one could hope for relatively rapid promotion with diminishing
consideration of social and educational qualfications, even if in
reality this was not often the case.[83] The *Volksgemeinschaft* may
well have turned out to be an illusion, but perhaps precisely
because of that the longing for a real *Kampfgemeinschaft* actually

61

increased, especially when facing, and initially smashing, enemies allegedly determined to destroy the Reich. Finally, it is also possible that particularly men stemming from the lower strata of German society felt a certain attraction to the idea of ruling over other peoples as the proud representatives of the Aryan *"Herrenvolk."*

How would the experience of fighting an exceedingly brutal war for many years have influenced the views of the average worker? Could these men simply return to their work-places as if nothing had happened, while their minds were still fresh with the memories of treating whole populations as so many insignificant *"Untermenschen"*? Some may have reacted like Paul, concluding that all parties were "filthy" and refraining from all political activity, while others may have decided like Köppke to join precisely the other political extreme. But can one really speak of continuity in the history of the working class in Germany once we realize where they spent those "missing years" and what they did there? For although there are certainly no simple answers to these questions, it is perhaps by constantly posing them that we may see a little more clearly what it was that supplied the Third Reich with such tremendous destructive energy, and to what extent the experience of participating in "Hitler's war" has retained its influence upon post-war German society.

NOTES

Reprinted from *German History*, Vol. 8, No. 1, 1990, pp. 46–65.

1 There is another interesting trend. See, e.g., the biographical note in S. Lenz, *Deutschstunde*, 13th edn (Hamburg, 1968), which does not mention his military service at all, though significantly, just like his main protagonist's brother, he too had deserted from the navy. In his *Meistererzählungen* (Hamburg, n.d.), on the other hand, we are simply told that "Als Abiturient trat er kurz vor Kriegsende noch in die Marine ein."

2 See, e.g., K. D. Bracher, *The German Dictatorship* (New York, 1970).

3 See particularly M. Broszat, "Plädoyer für eine Historisierung des Nationalsozialismus," *Merkur*, Vol. 39, 1985, pp. 373–85.

4 See, e.g., the debate over A. J. P. Taylor, *The Origins of the Second World War* (London, 1963), in E. M. Robertson (ed.), *The Origins of the Second World War*, 5th edn (London, 1979).

5 D. J. K. Peukert, "Alltag and Barbarei. Zur Normalität des Dritten

Reiches" in D. Diner (ed.), *Ist der Nationalsozialismus Geschichte?* (Frankfurt/M., 1987), pp. 51–61.

6 This is, of course, one of the main bones of contention in the current *Historikerstreit*. See, e.g., numerous articles in Diner, *Nationalsozialismus*; and *Historikerstreit*, 3rd edn (Piper: Munich, 1987). Also contrast E. Nolte, *Das Vergehen der Vergangenheit* (Berlin, 1987); H.-U. Wehler, *Entsorgung der deutschen Vergangenheit?* (Munich, 1988); and C. S. Maier, *The Unmasterable Past* (Cambridge, Mass./London, 1988).

7 See mainly T. Childers, *The Nazi Voter* (Chapel Hill, N.C., 1983); R. F. Hamilton, *Who Voted for Hitler?* (Princeton, N.J., 1982); M. H. Kater, *The Nazi Party* (Oxford, 1983).

8 H. Mommsen, "National Socialism: continuity and change," in W. Laqueur (ed.), *Fascism, A Reader's Guide* (Harmondsworth, 1979), pp. 151–92; E. N. Peterson, *The Limits of Hitler's Power* (Princeton, N.J., 1969).

9 T. Mason, *Sozialpolitik im Dritten Reich* (Opladen, 1977); S. Salter, "Class harmony or class conflict?" in J. Noakes (ed.), *Government, Party and People in Nazi Germany* (Exeter, 1980), pp. 76–97.

10 I. Kershaw, *The "Hitler Myth"* (Oxford, 1987); and id., *Popular Opinion and Political Dissent in the Third Reich* (Oxford, 1983).

11 T. Mason, "The workers' opposition in Nazi Germany," *History Workshop Journal*, Vol. 11, 1981, 120–37; I. Kershaw, *The Nazi Dictatorship* (London, 1985), p. 143. The opposite view in R. Dahrendorf, *Society and Democracy in Germany* (London, 1968); D. Schoenbaum, *Hitler's Social Revolution* (London, 1966).

12 This question is in fact posed by Mason himself in his "Workers' opposition."

13 T. Mason, "The primacy of politics," in H. A. Turner (ed.), *Nazism and the Third Reich* (New York, 1972), pp. 175–200; and id., "Some origins of the Second World War", in Robertson, *The Origins*, pp. 105–35; A. Milward, "Fascism and the economy," in Laqueur, *Fascism*, pp. 409–53; a different view in R. J. Overy, "Hitler's war and the German economy," *Economic History Review*, Vol. 35, 1982, pp. 272–91. Also see, Institut für Zeitgeschichte (ed.), *Totalitarismus und Faschismus* (Munich, 1980).

14 Mason, "Workers' opposition"; Kershaw, *Dictatorship*, pp. 14 (n. 38 for further literature), 34. See also, e.g., H. Graml *et al.*, *The German Resistance to Hitler* (London, 1970); K.-J. Müller, *Armee, Politik und Gesellschaft in Deutschland, 1933–45* (Paderborn, 1979); J. Conway, *The Nazi Persecution of the Churches, 1933–1945* (London, 1968); K. Kwiet and H. Eschwege, *Selbstbehauptung und Widerstand* (Hamburg, 1984).

15 Emphasis on indoctrination in O. Bartov, *The Eastern Front, 1941–45* (London, 1985); and M. Messerschmidt, *Die Wehrmacht im NS-Staat* (Hamburg, 1969). Outline of disciplinary measures in M. Messerschmidt, "German military law in the Second World War", in W. Deist (ed.), *The German Military in the Age of Total War* (Leamington Spa and New Hampshire, 1985), pp. 323–35.

Emphasis on organization in M. van Creveld, *Fighting Power* (Westport, 1982); E. A. Shils and M. Janowitz, "Cohesion and Disintegration in the Wehrmacht in World War II," *Public Opinion Quarterly*, Vol. 12 (1948), pp. 280–315.

16 See, e.g., P. Nettl, "The German Social Democratic Party as a political model," *Past and Present*, Vol. 30 (1965), pp. 65–95; G. Roth, *The Social Democrats of Imperial Germany* (Totowa, 1961); V. R. Berghahn, *Modern Germany* (Cambridge, 1982), pp. 25–6.

17 V. R. Berghahn, *Germany and the Approach of War in 1914*, 4th edn (London, 1979), pp. 5–24.

18 See, e.g., E. J. Leed, *No Man's Land* (Cambridge, 1979); B. Hüppauf, "Langemarck, Verdun and the myth of a new man in Germany after the First World War," *War and Society*, Vol. 6, 1988, pp. 70–103; R. Wohl, *The Generation of 1914* (Cambridge, Mass., 1979), pp. 42–84.

19 See, e.g., on the army as an institution, K.-J. Müller, *Das Heer und Hitler* (Stuttgart, 1969); R. J. O'Neill, *The German Army and the Nazi Party, 1933–39* (London, 1966). On senior ranks and resisters, K.-J. Müller, *General Ludwig Beck* (Boppard am Rhein, 1980); J. Kramarz, *Stauffenberg* (Frankfurt/M., 1965). Some initial work on junior officers in Bartov, *Eastern Front*, pp. 40–67; I. Welcker *et al.*, *Qualifikation zum Offizier?* (Frankfurt/M., 1982); D. Bald, *Der deutsche Offizier* (Munich, 1982).

20 Bartov, *Eastern Front*, pp. 43–7.

21 B. Kroener, "Die Personelle Ressourcen des Dritten Reiches im Spannungsfeld zwischen, Wehrmacht, Bürokratie und Kriegswirtschaft 1939–1942", in Militärgeschichtliches Forschungsamt (ed.), *Das deutsche Reich und der Zweite Weltkrieg*, Vol. VI (Stuttgart, 1988), pp. 871–989. R. Absolon, "Die personelle Ergänzung der Wehrmacht im Frieden und im Kriege," typescript of an article issued by the Bundesarchiv-Zentralnachweisstelle (Kornelimünster, 1972); U. Herbert, *Fremdarbeiter*, 2nd edn (Berlin, 1986).

22 C. Streit, *Keine Kameraden* (Stuttgart, 1978); Bartov, *Eastern Front*, pp. 107–19.

23 M. G. Steinert, *Hitler's War and the Germans* (Athens, Ohio, 1977), p. 196. See also V. R. Berghahn, "Meinungsforschung im 'Dritten Reich'," *Militärgeschichtliche Mitteilungen*, Vol. 1, 1967, pp. 82–119.

24 Kershaw, "Hitler Myth," p. 209.

25 Steinert, *Hitler's War*, pp. 264–73; Kershaw, "Hitler Myth," pp. 217–18.

26 Steinert, *Hitler's War*, p. 272.

27 Ibid., pp. 282–3.

28 Ibid., p. 289.

29 Ibid., pp. 298–300.

30 Ibid., pp. 301–2, where reports of the Reich propaganda office from late February 1945 are also cited, contrasting the "profound lethargy" of the "so-called middle classes" with "the working class in large factories, which continues to fulfil its responsibilities in an exemplary manner."

31 *The Goebbels Diaries 1939–1941*, trans. and ed. by F. Taylor, 2nd edn (Harmondsworth, 1984), p. 446.
32 Ibid., pp. 452–3.
33 *The Goebbels Diaries: The Last Days*, ed. by H. Trevor-Roper, 2nd edn (London and Sydney, 1979), p. 21.
34 Ibid., p. 34.
35 Ibid., p. 40.
36 Ibid., pp. 72–3, 78, 94, 265, 276, 304. Here the claim is constantly made that the poor morale of disintegrating *Wehrmacht* units is badly affecting the civilian population.
37 Ibid., p. 75.
38 *The Goebbels Diaries: The Last Days*, ed. by Trevor-Roper, 2nd edn (London and Sydney, 1979), p. 80.
39 Ibid., p. 82.
40 Ibid., pp. 89, 95.
41 Ibid., p. 113.
42 Ibid., p. 143.
43 E. von Manstein, *Aus einem Soldatenleben* (Bonn, 1958), pp. 353–4.
44 H. Guderian, *Panzer Leader*, 4th edn (London, 1977), p. 436.
45 Ibid., p. 462.
46 Graml, *German Resistance*, pp. 195–7, 232–3; Steinert, *Hitler's War*, p. 267.
47 J. von Herwarth, *Against Two Evils* (London, 1981), pp. 203ff. Even the diary entries and letters collected in H. Meier-Welcker, *Aufzeichnungen eines Generalstabsoffiziers 1939–42* (Freiburg, 1982), pp. 128–9, 148, 150, etc., betray his and his troops' astonishment at gradually discovering that the Russian *Untermenschen* were actually human beings.
48 Herwarth, *Two Evils*, p. 255.
49 Ibid., p. 254.
50 Some 40 milliard letters were exchanged between the German front and rear during the Second World War. See O. Buchbender and R. Sterz (eds), *Das andere Gesicht des Krieges* (Munich, 1982), p. 9.
51 See further on this in my article, "Daily life and motivation in war," *The Journal of Strategic Studies*, Vol. 12, 1989, pp. 200–14; and in my book, *Hitler's Army. Soldiers, Nazis, and War in the Third Reich* (New York/Oxford: Oxford University Press, 1991).
52 Bartov, *Eastern Front*, pp. 92–100; V. R. Berghahn, "NSDAP und 'Geistige Führung' der Wehrmacht 1939–45," *Vierteljahrshefte für Zeitgeschichte*, Vol. 17, 1969, pp. 17–71.
53 Further in M. I. Gurfein and M. Janowitz, "Trends in Wehrmacht Morale" in D. Lerner (ed.), *Propaganda in War and Crisis* (New York, 1951), pp. 200–8; Shils/Janowitz, "Cohesion and Disintegration," p. 304.
54 Bundesarchiv-Militärarchiv, Freiburg: RH26-12/238, 26.11.40, p. 7.
55 Buchbender/Sterz, *Gesicht*, pp. 72–3. letter 101.
56 Ibid., p. 74, letter 104.
57 Ibid., p. 76, letter 108.
58 Ibid., p. 78, letter 116.

59 Ibid., p. 84, letter 134.
60 Ibid., p. 85, letter 139.
61 Ibid., pp. 86–7, letter 143.
62 Ibid., pp. 13–25.
63 A. Heck, *A Child of Hitler*, 3rd edn (Toronto, New York, and London, 1986).
64 R. Schörken, "Jugendalltag im Dritten Reich", in K. Bergmann and R. Schörken (eds), *Geschichte im Alltag – Alltag in der Geschichte* (Düsseldorf, 1982), pp. 238–9.
65 H.-U. Rudel, *Stuka Pilot*, 3rd edn (Maidstone, 1973), pp. 1, 189.
66 *Last Letters from Stalingrad* (London, 1956), pp. 27–8.
67 Schörken, "Jugendalltag," pp. 239–40.
68 Ibid., p. 240.
69 Ibid., pp. 240–1.
70 H. Böll, *Was soll aus dem Jungen bloss werden?* (Bornheim, 1981).
71 G. Sajer, *The Forgotten Soldier*, 2nd edn (London, 1977), pp. 263–7.
72 Schörken, "Jugendalltag," pp. 242–4. See also H. Böll, *Der Zug war pünktlich*, 12th edn (Munich, 1980).
73 See, e.g., H. Scholtz, *Erziehung und Unterricht unterm Hakenkreuz* (Göttingen, 1985); G. Platner (ed.), *Schule im Dritten Reich*, 2nd edn (Munich, 1984); N. A. Huebsch, "The 'wolf cubs' of the new order: The indoctrination and training of the Hitler Youth," in O. C. Mitchell, *Nazism and the Common Man* (Washington D.C., 1981), pp. 93–114; D. J. K. Peukert, *Inside Nazi Germany* (London, 1987), pp. 145–74.
74 L. Niethammer, "Heimat und Front. Versuch, zehn Kriegserinnerungen aus der Arbeiterklasse des Ruhrgebietes zu verstehen," in L. Niethammer (ed.), *Die Jahre weiss man nicht, wo man die heute hinsetzen soll* (Berlin, 1983), pp. 163–232.
75 I would like to thank Dr Ulrich Herbert for bringing this collection to my attention and for his instructive remarks on this issue as an active participant in the Ruhr industrial area oral history project.
76 See, e.g., L. Niethammer, "Fragen – Antworten – Fragen. Methodische Erfahrungen und Erwägungen zur Oral History," paper delivered at the Wiener Library Seminar, Tel-Aviv University, 1987.
77 Niethammer, "Heimat und Front," pp. 167–75.
78 Ibid., pp. 195–9.
79 Ibid., pp. 209–13.
80 Ibid., pp. 213–18.
81 See n. 15 above. A good example in Goebbels, *The Last Days*, p. 80.
82 Kershaw, "*Hitler Myth*," pp. 65–6, 71, 86–7, 90–3, 126–8, 132, 215.
83 On changes in promotion policy, see G. Papke, "Offizierkorps und Anciennität," in H. Meier-Welcker (ed.), *Untersuchungen zur Geschichte des Offizierkorps* (Stuttgart, 1962), pp. 177–206.

2

THE "HONOR OF LABOR"

Industrial workers and the power of symbols under National Socialism

Alf Lüdtke

In the following article Alf Lüdtke demonstrates the importance of "symbolic practice" in the Third Reich, an aspect of Nazism that earlier social historians were inclined to dismiss as superficial and meaningless rhetoric meant to disguise the "real" economic and political interests that Nazism served. Walter Benjamin had drawn attention, in the mid–1930s, to the Nazis' "aesthetization of politics" in the form of huge meetings and marches, or mass sporting events. But Lüdtke suggests that these mass spectacles should not obscure the power of the less dramatic, everyday use of symbols by the Nazis. Lüdtke focusses in particular upon the rich symbolism surrounding and representing manual work. He contends that even workers who had supported the Social Democrats or Communists during the Weimar Republic displayed ambivalent attitudes toward the Nazi regime after 1933. The Nazis attempted to exploit this "sceptical acquiescence" with a "symbolic offering" in the form, for example, of Nazi insistence on the importance of "German quality work" and "the honor of labor," enduring "cultural icons" in German society that could engage the sympathies of a wide range of ordinary Germans, from factory engineers to skilled workers, regardless of their former political persuasions.

In support of this argument, Lüdtke digs deeply into the many, sometimes ambiguous and contradictory, layers of meaning that German workers themselves attached to industrial work. He shows that the identities of male German workers were intimately connected with the sights, sounds, smells, textures, symbols and images that surrounded and represented industrial work. Lüdtke suggests that the Nazi language of labor expressed meanings attached by ordinary workers to work that the Marxist language of class did not. German socialists recognized that manual labor was a source of pride and dignity for the German labor movement. But in Marxist theory, "alienated" manual labor was the undeniable sign of the oppression and exploitation of the German working class under capitalism, which only a socialist revolution could abolish. National Socialism was the first political regime to commit itself publicly to promoting the "honor of labor" within the framework of the existing economic system. The Nazis praised "German quality work" and "national labor;" they promised "joy in work," a "factory community" (Werksgemeinschaft) and a "national community." Yet these ideas and images were by no means the unique invention of the Nazis; well before 1933, an array of nationalist conservatives, efficiency experts and industrial managers had already developed a language of labor that incorporated these central terms of the Nazi regime.

What the Nazis said about industrial work thus appears to have been more a particular expression of a long tradition than a hypocritical attempt to camouflage the real political and economic losses inflicted upon German workers by Hitler's seizure of power in 1933. The Nazi regime did not remove class barriers but it did offer German workers new forms of recognition, new status, new opportunities and new hopes which facilitated workers' acceptance of and participation in the construction of the murderous Nazi regime. At the very least, the Nazis' commitment to the "honor of labor" improved workers' survival chances and allowed workers the physical and symbolic space within which they could engage in small acts of daily self-assertion (Eigen-Sinn).

The Nazis frequently used the written or spoken word to communicate their image of the "honor of labor", but they also mobilized nonverbal, sensual, visual images – for example, photographs of laboring bodies – which, as Walter Benjamin recognized, could be infinitely replicated and circulated to a mass audience. The "readers" for whom these words and images were intended were, however, primarily men. As Lüdtke points out, the labor which the Nazis attempted to dignify and through which industrial workers constructed their own identities and self-esteem was paid wage-labor performed by the skilled, strong bodies of German men, and not the unpaid housework of German women.

* * *

LEY: "I GAVE THEM MY HAND"

The German Labor Front (DAF) was supposed, once and for all, to put an end to conflicts of interest and thus to "class conflict" in manufacturing and industrial enterprises. This Nazi organization was founded on 10 May 1933, a few days after the acts of violence and the spectacular staging of 1 and 2 May: the "Day of National Labor" and the dissolution of the trade unions. . . . This occupation of the free labor movement's forms of organization and expression marked one of the first high points of massive Nazi terror which raged, at all levels, against "black" as well as against "red" workers, against the "commune" (KPD) and the "proles."[1] The "Reich organization leader" of the Nazi party, Robert Ley, was installed as "Führer" (from 1934, director) of the DAF.[2] In November 1933, as the preparations for the reconstruction of labor law proceeded under great pressure, the DAF managed to have itself declared the single organization of *all* employees in industry and commerce. And in the corresponding "Law for the Protection of National Labor," the so-called "Law for the Organization of Labor" (AOG) of 20 January 1934, the "factory leader" and his "retinue" were obliged to construct and to cultivate the "community of the enterprise."[3] But the law also required that "social honor" be safeguarded – henceforth the "malicious exploitation of labor power" could be prosecuted in a court of honor, although not upon the direct petition of the plaintiff.[4]

The assertions of the National Socialist leaders, that they were the first in German history to appreciate "the dignity of labor" and energetically to promote its recognition, characterized the high point of the Nazi "seizure of power," the celebration of the "Day of National Labour" on 1 May 1933. Nazi efforts went beyond demonstrative performances and the taking of ritual oaths to the "people's community" (*Volksgemeinschaft*), which was supposed already to have begun to overcome class division. In a less inflated manner, gestures and ceremonies were meant to demonstrate that the Nazis intended to be serious about the "honor of labour." This included a practice about which Robert Ley, above all, repeatedly boasted, "I gave my hand to the men."[5]

Ley referred to numerous (but not precisely enumerated) factory visits, which he claimed to have undertaken since the summer of 1933. Admittedly, "giving his hand" could have been "a great danger" since he might easily have made himself a laughing stock! In the "old days" it would have been quite unthinkable to "go into the factories, without offering the men any sort of material advantage." And what could he have brought them? He could "only give them . . . his hand." He claimed to have gone "from work bench to work bench," asking the men "how things were going, whether they had worries and concerns." His goal, he claimed, was to speak with "people," "to be able to engage them in conversation, to forge a connection with them." And, once more: "I assembled all my energies, I focussed on every single individual, I grasped his hand, I did not relent." Even later, looking back on it, the effect seemed astonishing to him. He claimed that at first (only a few) individuals gave him their hands, although not without some hesitation; but then others gathered around him, finally he was encircled, "and eventually they raised me up on their shoulders." Looking back on it, what counted as the real victory was the fact that "The battle was joined."

This story of "I gave the men my hand" had already been part of a speech by Ley on 1 May 1934, which he delivered at a reception given for the diplomatic corps by Alfred Rosenberg. There, Ley described the "giving of hands" as his "new method."[6] After the phase of mass parades . . . it became a question of "winning these people's hearts". . . . "It was wonderful to observe how timidity, downheartedness, yes, even to some extent oppositional hatred and rage, were overcome." The medium of this purported miracle was a physical gesture (body-language), a demonstration of respect between equals: a hand-shake, or rather, a "simple hand-shake of two *men*."

The repeated, insistent reference suggests that this was meant to appear and to be valued, as a unique gesture. The story played insistently upon conversion experiences. Seeking out, greeting and addressing – as if in no time at all skeptics became enthusiastic believers. But a second theme was also addressed here: Ley presented himself as a member of the inner circle of power in a "movement" that would bring a completely new beginning in politics and society, through the impetus of the "national revolution" to which the Nazis laid claim.[7] Rituals of popular homage-giving formed a part of the coronation ritual of new rulers, asserting a connection between "investiture" and mass approval.[8] The "masses" thereby moved toward the center of power, passing in review before the leaders. The (people) gave evidence of their obedience and approval there, where the new rulers specified their center of power.

Ley claimed to have reversed such rituals; he had not waited, but had gone instead to the workers themselves. He claimed to have sought out the people he wanted to win over, there, in the workplace, one of the centers of their lives. Rather than summoning others to his presence, Ley had gone out and asked the nameless workers, who lacked the necessary confidence or simply thought it impossible to speak directly to a "leader," about their hopes and fears. He claimed thereby to have renounced all hierarchical distance, even to have overcome it. Indeed this important figure of the Third Reich went without hesitation to the ordinary people. And even when he talked with women, the claim to a free exchange of thought . . . necessitated the formula that he had spoken "man to man." This was complemented by the "simple hand-shake," which he had offered to as many as possible. Ley presented himself as a "Führer," who at the same time claimed to be one among many "soldiers of (manual) labor. . . ."

SYMBOLS AND THE PRACTICE OF DOMINATION

In the following section, Lüdtke argues that "symbolic practice" is an integral part of normal, everyday life, even in advanced industrial societies. "Symbolic practices" are the activities and social interactions through which workers construct and express the meanings they attach to the "real world" of industrial work. These "symbolic practices" may assume an exceptional, ritualistic form, such as the celebration of a birthday or a company anniversary; but they can also be quite prosaic, such as the daily handling of tools. Following a more general, theoretical discussion, Lüdtke examines in detail how symbolic practices operated in a variety of circumstances. He shows that the meanings of industrial work produced and expressed by German workers were multi-layered and often contradictory, making it difficult for the Nazis to impose a single, desired meaning "from above" by their own "symbolic practices." Unable simply to manipulate workers with their appeals to the "honor of labour," the Nazis had to find points of contact with the meanings that workers themselves attached to industrial work and to employ symbols which had the power to draw workers into active participation in the Nazi regime.

* * *

In the informal catalogue of epithets with which the behavior of many Nazi power-brokers was caricatured – but to a certain extent also made cosy and familiar – Ley counted as the Reich drunk.[9] But quite independent of his habits (and addictions) as well as his political poses, Ley did not manage in the long run to assume a strategic position in the "polycratic" [fragmented, multi-centred] field of power exercised by the Nazi ruling groups. From about 1938 onward, he was no longer able to expand the beginnings of his general political influence.[10]

Yet references to the dominating personalities and structures of power do not really get at the effects of the Nazi movement upon the masses, which can also be detected among male and female industrial workers and their families. So far as mass acceptance of and participation in the regime in the years after the Nazi accession to power is concerned, it was German fascism's *practice* of domination that was decisive. But what were the forms and the effects of the forms in which the "will" and the "commands" of the leading functionaries of the party and the state were supposed to be put into practice?[11] In this context, what was the significance of references to the "honor of labor?" What do symbolic practices, such as seeking the workers out in the workplace, which in his presentation Ley tried to make "significant," really show us?[12] Or to put it another way: by what symbols and everyday practices did (industrial) workers allow themselves to be addressed; which ones did they share, whether in agreement or rejection?

Symbols by no means refer to mythical worlds, withdrawn from the historical context and process. Rather, symbols relate to meanings that are always multi-layered. This multiplicity of meanings is, however, bound up with the way in which the symbols are presented and used, hence reinterpreted. Their actual attraction, and thus their power to have an effect, lies in the fact that symbols simultaneously invite what appear to be incompatible constructions of meaning; indeed they "entice" and accentuate these (different meanings). A variety of hopes and also fears become quite concrete and "real," at least for the moment. Victor Turner has made us aware that symbols bring together "normative" with "emotive" polarities.[13] The latter are distinguished especially by their "sensory" qualities. They speak directly to the senses, through, for example, sounds, pictures, smells. We can think here of the photographs or statues, aimed at the visual sense, that were supposed to (re)present the "quality worker." Such icons simultaneously evoked a self-portrait and (cultural) representations of the good, the valuable quality worker.

Symbols were experienced in ritual practices, in interactions, which were laden, in specific ways, with the representations and expectations of all involved. For the participants, they were "heavy with meaning." So for machine-building workers the handling of tools was joined with the experience of their own manual skill. Simultaneously, the expectations and the prodding of their overseers and their colleagues – as well as their own individual "self-assertion" (Eigen-Sinn)[14] – shaped their interaction with each other as well as with the tools; so the work tools became everyday symbols of this mixture of opportunities for and limits to action, symbols of satisfactions and failures, which "colored" survival in the work-place.[15] In male work-teams looking after the tools was connected with valuing an indispensable aid. . . . With this were bound together pictures of a practice, which, because it dealt predominantly with metal raw materials and machines, counted as (particularly) "manly."

Symbolic practice also revealed itself in transgressions of labor discipline in the workshop and at the machines which were both purposeful and tolerated. The connection of collegiality with the factory hierarchy became physically "tangible" in the rituals with which birthdays and company jubilees were celebrated;[16] here hierarchy was relativized (if not suspended) at least for a short period of time. In the longer view, however, the momentary experience of "being together" only served once again to renew the inequalities between the members of a work team and lead-hands, on the one side, masters, or even engineers and company directors, on the other. In this demonstrative conviviality – expressed in stopping work, eating and in drinking (of alcohol) – on the actual site where these activities normally were forbidden, everyone thronged around the celebrant. For the participants and those who came after them, this was immortalized in the jubilee photograph. In the presence of overseers a reduction of hierarchical distance became clear. At the same time, the person honored by the celebration might appear especially cherished and respected. But on the next shift this earlier loosening of the hierarchy actually made it possible to intone even more strongly the distance between the overseers and their subordinates, where possible to demand it with even less restraint. These kinds of celebrations had an additional significance. They drew a line dividing the participants from "all the others," other colleagues as well as the "higher ranks" in the factory, the members of other work-teams and workshops, and, indeed, all outsiders, whether they were or were not workers. . . .

HITLER: "THERE IS NO DISHONOR IN MANUAL LABOR"

The "honor of labour" was one of the key points in Hitler's speech at the 1933 May Day celebrations, an appeal to the *Volksgemeinschaft* (transmitted by radio all over Germany); "Spirit, brain and fist, worker, farmer and citizen,"[17] all belonged together. Each had his own honor; each should respect that of the other. But the highest measure was manual labor. According to Hitler, the "labor service" would teach everyone that "manual labor neither pollutes, nor dishonors." Manual labor would be dignified, above all, when "it was filled with loyal and honest meaning." Loud applause can be heard on the tape-recording when Hitler added that "we want to lead everyone at least once in his life to manual labor." The voices of workers on the "Day of National Labor" which were transmitted earlier by the radio had already emphasized that the true voice of the people should be that of the working men; their hearts were in the right place and they (knew how to) roll up their sleeves and get the job done.

In a speech a few days later, in which he celebrated the foundation of the DAF, Hitler presented himself as a worker: he claimed to have worked on a building site and "earned his own keep."[18] And as an ordinary soldier he knew the life of the "broad masses" much better than many who were born into "those classes." Likewise, an "ABC of National Socialism", that appeared in six editions totaling 40,000 copies between January and the summer of 1933, depicted Hitler as someone who knew precisely what he was talking about: in Vienna before 1914 he had survived "by means of heavy physical labor" as a "concrete mixer and building worker," before he became a draftsman and "artistic painter for architects."[19]

Leading National Socialists frequently talked about the "honor of (manual) labor." This way of talking had at least three aims. It harnessed (popular) animosity toward the party-political business of the Republic; by deriding the allegedly lazy "(party) bosses" it was able to exploit a widespread distrust of professional politicians and functionaries.[20] Second, despite all the rhetorical-ritual estimation of manual labor (also in the metaphor of the "hand" or the "fist"), a strict subordination in the work-relationship itself appeared indispensable. It was taken for granted that the manual worker was supposed to "obey" not only the contract, but also the overseers. Similarly, it was his own knowledge of manual labor that permitted the overseer "more easily to command." "Work" was depicted as the "battle of labor," a struggle requiring obedience.[21] The "competition" inside the factory, among the workers and the work-teams, and even the "struggle" between factories was one form of this battle. But productive labor would also allow the economic independence which would bring victory to the Nazi state in the (international) "struggle" of peoples and races.[22]

But it went beyond this exhortation to obey and to fight. Connected, but none the less still distinct, was a third aspect – the reverence for diligence and for "doing one's duty," a reference to the internal dimension of labor-"discipline." "Diligence" and "duty" were invoked in many different forms – as the obverse of the middle-class "thriftiness" which served to maintain the individual, but also as a consequence of those preconceptions of "progress" and growth, shared by "right" and "left" alike, which aimed at the expansion of industrial production. Orderliness and deftness of hand were the distinguishing characteristics; order must reign in the work-place; deft hands ensured that at the very point of production itself, the job orders and technical drawings would become the desired, "precise," good product.

"DIGNITY OF LABOR": THE HORIZONS OF MEANING

In the following section, Lüdtke traces the development before 1933, and particularly during the Weimar Republic, of the central terms, "German quality work," "joy in work" and the "factory community," which the Nazis later incorporated into their own language of labor. But Lüdtke does more than simply examine the ways in which the dominant groups in German society constructed notions of the "honor of labor." He also attempts to show how workers themselves gave this central concept their own particular meanings. To signal the difference between these two levels and types of meaning, a different translation of the central German term (Ehre der Arbeit) is employed in the following section; whereas the "honor of labor" refers to the first level and type of meaning, produced "from above," "dignity of labor" refers to the ways in which workers themselves appropriated, negotiated, or otherwise gave their own meanings to the concept of Ehre der Arbeit.

* * *

Here we need to excavate in a number of stages. Only a reconstruction of the longer-term configurations in which the "honor of labor" was invoked and alluded to will make it possible, more precisely, to sketch out the extent of the symbols connected with this image.

1   Orderliness and physical dexterity had class-specific as well as cross-class meanings and horizons. Within the working class, "orderliness" was the cardinal division separating those who aspired to be seen as the "respectable working class" (i.e. "honorable" workers) from the – not inconsiderable – remainder. In spectacular but also in daily interactions the signs were eloquent; clear divisions in the neighborhoods, as well as in the work-place, between the unskilled laborers on the one side, the semi-skilled and skilled workers on the other.

To the outside observer, from other classes and milieux, orderliness at work remained invisible. That made forms of (re)presentation to the outside world all the more important. So, for example, "orderly" processions in May Day demonstrations, counted as more than just a tactical concession to the middle classes. In the *Kaiserreich*, when workers appeared in military-style formation, they won praise in the social-democratic papers as well as in the bourgeois press.[23]

Year after year, before 1914, Social Democratic May Day posters called for their followers to understand that emancipation "from their chains," overcoming need, drudgery and want, required not the abolition but the expansion of industrial labor.[24] Pictures of orderliness dominated, linked in part with stereotyped visions of an emancipated world; allegorical maidens that admittedly resembled the agile "Marianne" more than the full-bodied "Germania." By their side stood proletarians whose bodies exuded strength. These muscular young men leaned upon hammers and anvils: craftwork and manual labor, but not the domination of machinery, was on display.[25] And even though the female figure clearly represented no real person, this was less apparent with the male symbols. In any case, it was certainly only men that functioned as icons of work.

2   The suggestiveness of the symbol remained undisturbed by changes in life situation, by social ascent and descent; on this point the semi-skilled met on common ground with many outside the working class and its political "camp." In the work process, manual dexterity combined with sharp eyes, physical strength and "toughness' with "hard labor." This "work" was essential for daily survival. Housework was, to be sure, omitted from this representation – work with tools, at machines and in workshops, was suffused with ideals of "male" appropriation of "the world." This work was more than just a means to an end. Instrumental orientations were mixed together with meanings, in which work showed itself to be an exhausting but fascinating "metabolism with nature."[26] Especially dangerous, resistant work situations could only be endured by demonstrating "self-assertiveness" (*Eigen-Sinn*), even if that meant no more than not having the starch knocked out of you, for example, in the "fiery-workshops" of heavy industry, or in cleaning the salt pans in a refinery, in roadworks or at the pit-face in mining.

"Good work" meant the successful product of wage-labor. Housework was not included. Order and performance dominated in the workplace, in the work-team. Even in specialized, subdivided jobs, for example, the (relatively few) work-places on the assembly line, it was stimulating to be able to get a grip (*"ein Griff herauszuholen"*). There were two possibilities: building up an extra buffer of time and demonstrating your superiority over the machinery and over the engineers who organized the work process.

Proper work meant the capacity for organization; it signaled and demanded unceasing application to a given task.[27] Such men would master the present and secure the future! The other side – individual suffering under the pressures of work, but also the fate of being unemployed (likewise crossing class and political lines) – was experienced either as personal failure or blamed upon the political "system." But in either case the basic valuation of "work," whether manual or machine, remained undisturbed. And in either of these two forms, "work" was indispensable for daily survival. This experience, which did not need to be stated in explicit terms, shaped the expectations of colleagues, of neighbors, of relatives.

3   A horizon of meaning may have been suggested in the "dignity of labor" which was marginalized by the labor movement and also in the public discourse of the parties and Parliament during both the Wilhelmine Empire and the Weimar Republic. Demands for the "full' or "just" return of labor, for "justice" had been a fundamental canon of belief in the producers' co-operatives of the 1860s and 1870s.[28] But in the political program which, at least rhetorically, from the 1870s onwards oriented itself increasingly toward the Marxist critique of capitalism, "justice" became thinkable only after the complete revolutionary upheaval.[29]

In the mass organizations which after the end of the century turned to individual reforms of society, there was likewise no reawakening or renewal of interest in "dignity" and "justice." The "dignity of labor" counted for no more than an empty formula in the trade unions, if it did not produce the organization of interest group representation. According to this view, it was only the collective (and collective legal) guarantees and the improvement of wages that could create the material precon-ditions, which would permit an adequate standard of living – and thereby restore "dignity." Experience of changing employ-ment cycles . . . sharpened distrust of references to one's own significance that could not be grasped in terms of marks and pennies. If manual labor was so decorative, why, then, did not everyone apply themselves to it? How could one explain that,

even with so many improvements,[30] manual work still paid
so little, so that living and surviving continued to be such a
struggle?[31]

In only a few regions or branches of industry did the working-
class organizations manage to retain as members a majority of
those they seriously sought to reach.[32] Outside the Socialist Party
congresses or the columns of the party press, among the
ordinary members, demands for "just" treatment could none
the less be heard. Adolf Levenstein, who in 1910 surveyed the
opinions of approximately 6,000 mine, textile and machine-
building workers who were trade union members in several
different regions, published a list of these kinds of statements.[33]
"I will not be degraded to the status of a machine," protested
one metal presser (*Metalldrucker*), or, from a coal-cutter:
"humanity is becoming disgraceful." Certainly, these statements
were not uniform; to some degree, machine work was felt to be
a relief from the burden of labor, even a type of emancipation
(not least, because then one was "more equally exploited"). But
there were clearly numerous complaints about not being treated
as a "human being"; respect for the "worth" of the individual
was demanded, even when the precise words were not explicitly
pronounced.

4   Appeals for the "honor of labor" and of the worker increased
under other headings as well. Parallel with the tones of cultural
pessimism, in which simple manual labor became an emblem
of anti-industrial Utopia – as in the writings of Wilhelm Heinrich
Riehl or Gustav Freytag from the 1850s and 1860s – there
developed a rhetoric of "national labor."[34] Alongside the class-
specific models in which the "honor of labor" was represented,
there developed a specifically *national* (and *völkisch*) pattern.
"National Labor" harmonized especially in literary middle-class
circles with a previously unknown estimation of the "man of
work". This did not mean, however, real workers; quite the
opposite – the proletarians appeared, by contrast, as the "all too
many," if not quite as "beasts" (K.-M. Bogdal).[35] What was being
applauded here was an abstraction.

However, "national labor" did not remain the exclusive preserve of bourgeois groups or authors. It was to be found again
in the poems with which authors, such as Paul Lersch and Karl
Broger, who had both been manual workers, sang the praises

of the soldier's sacrifice after 1914. Broger's dictum, that "in Germany's greatest danger her poorest sons (had shown themselves to be) the most loyal" fell upon receptive ears. "National labor" promoted and confirmed understanding between the classes and the political camps.[36] In the war propaganda of 1914-18, the representation of "national labor" was emphatically connected with the image of "quality work." In books and in (illustrated) magazines and newspapers one could find, for example, such statements as:

> Is there a more diligent, more apt, more dexterous, better trained, more reliable, more productive but also better paid worker than the German? Who keeps his workplace, his machine and his tools cleaner than the German? I state explicitly *his* workplace, *his* machine, because the German worker loves his labor and takes good care of his equipment, as if it were his own personal property. In no way does he feel himself to be a slave to mechanized production, no, he is the master of his machine.[37]

Certainly the social democratic press generally commented sceptically and critically about the party's (SPD) support of the war;[38] but there were doubtless many who were supporters of the SPD or had voted for the party among the soldiers, who nevertheless "participated" at the front as in the armaments industry.

Naturally during the war years, male and female workers learned each day what real drudgery meant, especially in the war industries, and increased exertion by no means led to corresponding wage increases or even secure earnings. Above all, prices for the basic foodstuffs exploded; everyday life was characterized by hunger, misery and the death of close relatives.[39] Nevertheless, the self-understanding of workers complied in many respects with the picture of "national labor" that also served the purposes of war propaganda. The complaints of the "nameless" (like the Pohlands in Bremen) about the extensive "participation" of even organized workers reflected only the considerable extent of this conformity. The strikes in January 1917 or those of 1918 remained confined to the centers of war production, where a predominantly "young" workforce was concentrated. But for the most part, factory work could clearly not be reduced just to wages, products or their appropriation by others. The worsening living and working conditions did not get rid of industrial work as a way of life, as self-assertion and "everyday culture," the actual execution of the work, the direct interaction with the raw materials and machines, with male and female colleagues. Quite the opposite: the appropriation of work became even more important as the fixed point of attempts to survive.

5   The national hue of the representations and pictures of "labor" by no means disappeared in the 1920s. The predominantly social-democratic orientated trade union confederation (ADGB) differed in this respect very little from the industrial interest groups. Indeed in both their rhetoric and in their industrial practices the trade unions combined class-specific "quality work" with "national labor." In "German quality work," both sides clearly saw an acceptable standard of measurement.[40] The national impulse belonged once again – or, perhaps, still – to the essence of at least the leading functionaries' political perspective in the General German Trade Union (ADGB). The mass strike movement of 1919 permanently terminated neither the co-operation with the employers in the Central Working Partnership (*Zentralarbeitsgemeinschaft*) of November 1918, nor the domestic political truce (*Burgfriedenspolitik*) of the war years. The trade unions were just as much concerned as most of the local workers' councils (*Arbeiterräte*) with securing workers' survival needs. After the end of the mass movement, it was above all in the "Ruhr Struggle" of 1923 [against the French and Belgian occupation] that national identity once again cut through class divisions, probably even within the factory itself. The heads of the trade unions clearly saw only the opportunity for a new foothold provided by a national intonation, not least because not a few such voices were to be found in the ranks of their own members.[41]

But within the factories in the post-war period, the cultivation of "skill" and "dexterity" dominated; they became bench-marks for the "rationalizers" in both the company boardrooms and the factory councils.[42] The factory practitioners saw this as an explicit alternative to Taylorism, the kernel of "American mass production." But the rhetorical as well as the financial-organizational efforts concerning "adroitness" were not just anchored in the interests of the ruling class. At the same time, they followed, probably above all, the demands of industrial management

81

calculations. Because, despite all of the rage for "rationaliz-ation," a survey undertaken by trade union representatives in 1931 reported that in 84 per cent of the large and mid-sized enterprises there was no "flow production" and in 95 per cent of the cases, no "assembly line." But in three-quarters of the factories, new machines had been installed.[43] Workers had to master the running of several machines at the same time and at a faster pace much more often than a few years before: the old transport problems remained, compounded, perhaps, by new ones. As a safety net within the factory "a feel for the work" therefore increased considerably in importance. Thus the production increases from "rationalization, which not only the managers and engineers but also the workers themselves hoped for, were made possible not by re-tooling the machines, or by the preparation of the work, but by the worker's day-to-day "adaptation" of work methods and tools. Moreover, new functional elites were being trained and cultivated within the factory. In the 1920s and then once again during the armaments boom from the middle of the 1930s, the segregation of the unskilled and the de-qualification of skilled craftworkers gave the "semi-skilled" (*Angelernten*) wholly unexpected chances which corresponded with the beginnings of a new hierarchy within the workforce.[44]

The safeguarding of "quality work" became the motif and justification for considerable scientific activity and publicity funded by both public and private industrial money.[45] One field was work physiology and "fatigue studies" (Edgar Atzler);[46] another was concerned with psychological formation (*Formierung*) or "psycho-physics" (Freitz Giese),[47] "job training" and, beyond this, the promotion of the "factory community" (*Werksgemeinschaft*). In 1929, Albert Vogler, the general director of the United Steelworks (*Vereinigte Stahlwerke*), wrote in a greet-ing for the "German Institute for Technical Job Training" (DINTA, founded 1925; after 1933 taken over by the Nazi German Labor Front), which was financed by industry, that the goal must be to teach and to learn "work through work."[48]

6 The "dignity of labor" advertised a claim. In its light the reality of work appeared to many observers as "alienation from work" (Goetz Briefs). That made it all the more important to awaken a sense of "joy in work and a feeling of responsibility"

which would set free the worker's purportedly "original direct emotional involvement with his work."[49] Along with the purely instrumental proposals we can also recognize considerations which sought – at least from the perspective of the drawing board – not simply to increase the usefulness of the male worker (and the female worker who was clearly always implicitly included). One of these concepts was "team production." With this form of the organization of work, the individual workers were supposed to experience their own worth in an expanded work-group which was dependent upon each individual.

The psychologist Willy Hellpach was involved in this scheme, along with Richard Lang, one of the directors of the Daimler Automobile Company.[50] At Daimler, Lang had set up such a production group, for the construction of (motor) housings. Various groups of workers were brought together – turners, drill operators, fitters; on a co-operative basis, they were supposed to prepare the various parts that fit together. Admittedly, the authors did not try to hide how difficult it was to discern whether they had been successful. Because "in the expressions, the posture, indeed, the entire behavior, of those in the factory who participated there was no sign of enthusiasm"; the "peculiar dullness in the average physiognomy of our skilled worker" did not recede. But the practitioner knew that this could just as well be "a conscious disguise." It therefore continued to be indispensable to "approach the worker with esteem, to respect the 'human' in him. . . ."[51]

More important than the details of this proposal was the fact that monotony and deadening in the work-place did not appear as just the expression of group-specific deficits or technical failures, of "psycho-physical fatigue."[52] An altered organization of work would, more importantly, permit recognition of the workers and, at the same time, the profitable productivity of their activity. In contrast to a primarily instrumental orientation, here respect for the "personality" of the worker was called for; it should receive recognition for its own "value."

The demand for proper treatment is a decisive element in the study, "The Struggle for Joy in Work," which the lecturer at the Frankfurt Academy of Work, Hendrik de Man, submitted in 1927.[53] The study is shaped by great skepticism concerning the class perspective. De Man interviewed seventy-eight manual and white-collar workers who visited the Academy in 1925–6.

According to this survey, the organization of work, work experiences, but also wage conditions were shaped by a basic perception of subordination: "The worker is normally dominated by the feeling that he is under the control of a superior, enemy force."

This subordination was not just experienced "in general"; it was felt not only in the multiple uncertainties, experienced, in particular, by workers on piece-rates, but was also revealed in daily confrontations with overseers. De Man confirmed a series of (earlier) results by Levenstein, when he came to the conclusion that "The worker feels that the overseer, and not just the machine is his worst enemy." This meant not so much the factory director or even the owner. Dislike, even feelings of hatred, were directed above all at the immediate overseers, against the "masters," the "minders," the "drivers," the "intriguers," the "time-keepers": in sum, all those "who bowed down to those above them and stepped on those beneath them." According to De Man, workers felt they were subjected to excessive claims to control and subordination, which went beyond the generally accepted normal discipline required in industrial production.

The same tone characterizes a study which an American work psychologist made of three railway repair shops between the fall of 1932 and the summer of 1933.[54] The author, Rex Hersey, investigated the labor process, or, more precisely, the reactions and emotions of several dozen workers. From interviews and participant observation (the results of which were compared with an earlier study in an American workshop), Hersey showed how unfairness "produced not only a decline in production and depression of feelings" but might also "generate a crisis in the relationship of the worker to his family." Above all, being goaded by a lead-hand or a master enraged the person affected: "When you are yelled at, it does not matter whether you are lucky and you get the job done quickly, or you have to work against all the odds. . . ." The feeling of being treated arbitrarily and unjustly, can clearly be traced back to these oft-repeated disappointments and injuries; being driven by others, having to endure yells and loud rebukes. Hersey's study appeared in German in 1935. It was prefaced with a short, but emphatic word of praise from Robert Ley.

7   The concepts of "group manufacture" and "joy in work" as a means of "overcoming the distance" between workers and the "objectified factory" (Ernst Michel)[55] found only a limited scientific resonance. These ideas remained without any real effect as instructions for behavior in the everyday life of the factory. The works councils and trade unionists also saw no chance of exercising any real influence over the extent or the tempo of "rationalization."[56]

In contrast, proposals for the promotion of the "factory community" (*Werksgemeinschaft*) did meet with some interest (although only among entrepreneurs and "employers" or the business directors of industrial interest groups (syndici)). The development of an *esprit de corps*, parallel to and in tune with measures for the development and cultivation of a "core workforce," was also a central element of the company paternalism of Krupp or Stumm-Halberg [leading German industrialists]. But now it was a question not only of creating an atmosphere, which would do everything possible to avoid "frictions" in individual plants, but also engaging in a comprehensive, concerted campaign, across whole regions and branches of industry. The "factory community" had a twofold thrust. Above all, the community of interests of everyone who participated at the factory level as well as in the macro-economic "working partnership" of industrial production, was supposed to bring back to life, in a new form, the anti-strike politics of the economically peaceful "company unions.". . . . Second, the idea of an industrial community of interests was aimed at all of those fellow employers who, for example, sought to evade expanded legal wage controls and thereby weaken their own trade associations.

The "factory community" was thus meant to reach considerably beyond the individual work-place. In contrast with the ideas of Lang and Hellpach, the actual labor process itself was left completely out of the picture. Much more attention was paid to forming a comprehensive connection with the workers and their families, at the "edge" of the factory, in their "free time." In this respect, *Kindergarten* places and household and sewing courses for the wives and daughters were just as important as financial support for gardening clubs, convalescent homes and rest cures. Reinforcing these material benefits was a verifying publicity: a company magazine which, not infrequently, was technically advanced as well as "modern" in design and layout.

Its photographs utilized the stylistic suggestions of a "documentary" presentation of a many-sided and "successful" organism. By setting individual workers into visual relief – as celebrants of an anniversary with the company or in reports about individual sections of the factory or workshop – the individual was always brought into a direct relationship with the "whole."

This ensemble of allowances and inspections, of monetary benefits and binding symbols which excluded third parties, naturally exceeded the resources of small and mid-sized enterprises. Here everything revolved around the leadership style of the employer or manager and his middle-men; flanking measures were absent. But here as well the critical question in the workplace addressed itself, above all, to the issue of how far at least a certain measure of "fairness" for male and female workers could be made evident.

8   Pride in "quality work" was not reserved for directors and engineers alone. When the magazine for works councils published by the German Metalworkers' Union wrote that in the USA every detail had to be "foolproof," then both the editor and the reader could think contentedly about the fact that in German factories, successful products depended upon the knowledge and ability of experienced workers, that among one's colleagues the assortment of head-scratching and testing counted not as a burdensome evil, but rather as an indication of qualified work.

Here we can detect a peculiar fixation, especially within the labor movement: the motifs and symbols which presented "work" revolved around the image of a competence saturated with experience. This "feel for the work" was admittedly reserved for those who engaged in "trained" activities (even when they were actually only semi-skilled). So, for example, a photograph of a (repair) turner was printed as the cover picture for the communist-oriented but also commercially successful *Workers' Illustrated Newspaper* (*Arbeiter-Illustrierte Zeitung*). This manly worker radiated a controlled calm; the perspective and the way the picture is framed emphasized his concentration on the tools, on the materials and on the task at hand; both orderliness and deftness were signaled.[57] The picture of the confident, experienced machine tender was a citation of the ideal skilled worker.... [58]

A typical example of this "picture" of the worker is the turner Melmster in Willi Bredel's autobiographical novel *Maschinenfabrik N & K.*[59] Bredel, himself a lathe operator, then a "worker-author," described how his mastery of a bank of lathes, drawing on knowledge derived from experience, allowed him to foil the attempt of a time-study man and his foreman, to prove that it was possible to achieve a faster cutting speed (and thus establish new piece-rates). The direct producer triumphed because *he* alone had insight into the nuances of the raw materials and the tools, *he* alone controlled the labor process at the individual machine, or should we rather say, at *his* machine. "Capital's junior officers" (Marx) were powerless in doubtful cases; they ran the risk of making themselves figures of fun. The figure of the lathe operator Melmster also shows that class-conscious proletarians were at the same time knowledgeable masters of the machines.

Knowledge of raw materials, of the characteristics of machines, of various tricks – for instance, the preparations for the removal of metal chips – were not only indispensable in order to achieve recognition by one's colleagues: these qualities went much beyond everyday life inside the factory; being experienced at work counted as the basis upon which colleagues could become "comrades." Certainly, the social composition of the Communist Party (KPD) conformed much less to this picture of qualified work (skilled or semi-skilled) than the membership of the Social Democrats (SPD). But this text by a communist author showed how much the image of industrial work was shaped by conceptions of "manual dexterity" saturated with experience among the workers themselves.

It was politically consequential that factory practitioners, such as industrial engineers and directors, had a more precise picture of industrial labor processes than many labor movement functionaries whose images and symbols of work were oriented more toward the presentation of a political fighter. For the labor movement, it was precisely the "careless" expedients and numerous ways of "getting-by" which were incompatible with the image of the class-conscious proletarian. The labor process was at best a burdensome preparation for actual politics. By contrast, in order to promote the flow of work and labor productivity, the authorities within the factory had at least to tolerate, perhaps even to encourage, such expedients which at the same time transmitted to individual workers an increased sense of their own capabilities.

9   Forms of communication and domination played the decisive role in these proposals for the organization of work and the "factory community." But the material side of industrial work scarcely figured in these ideas even though it could hardly be ignored in the work-place itself. It began with the plethora of sensual impressions and influences, the noises but also the smells. It included, above all, the constant struggle with tools and raw materials, the metal handles, the cloth or wood parts and implements. Moulding, stretching, hammering and smithing, stamping and drilling, turning on a lathe and milling – hard and soft, often uncommonly heavy objects, but also splinters, chips and fibers, which could only too easily cause injuries – all these determined everyday life in the factory. There was a connectedness of experience learned by doing and of physical activity, in which the resistance of the materials, the tools, but also of the colleagues, continued to be felt permanently and everywhere.

But the tool was more than just an instrument of work. Everyone had to have the appropriate tools immediately ready at hand and ready for use. Therefore, careful handling of one's own tools, but also respect for other workers' tools, was one of the fundamental expectations between colleagues in the workplace. De Man observed that it was essential not only to skilled workers, such as fitters or carpenters, but even to warehouse workers or window-dressers that "the objects used . . . always be seen as one's property."[60] And it was not really important whether the tools were actually one's own or had been provided by the factory; however, what was important was a work situation in which the execution of the work should be respected by colleagues as well as overseers and not be experienced by the worker himself as unusually burdensome. Parallel to this "desire for ownership," a certain "desire for power" might also be recognized; "Frequently one had to deal with a feeling (towards tools or machines) that was colored with lust." Workers talked about their "love" of their tools; cigarette sorting machines were said to possess a "soul," a locomotive was patted verbally like a "horse."[61] The use and misuse of tools, of pet-names and swearwords showed that the individual, almost always emphatic, claims of the owners and users were taken seriously.

Knowing what was what in the use of raw materials and tools, the ability to get along with, but also keep one's distance from, fellow workers was, of course, not confined in industrial everyday life to a certain circle of "qualified" tasks or male workers (or the much fewer female workers). Workers' remembrances show that a wide-ranging ability to improvise and test was required on a day-to-day basis even when it came to highly subdivided, carefully defined tasks on the assembly line; one could "squeeze out a few handholds."[62] The attraction of "being tested and testing oneself" is evident.

At the same time, such memories also show that as "quality work" factory labor always had a material equivalent. One's experiences were not just "incorporated" in one's eyes and hands. They were also imprinted in a variety of forms; they showed themselves in one's demeanor and gestures; they were preserved, for example, in one's own discrete notes. Such secretive drawings, concerning, for example, the degree of adjustment for sheet metal shears, mirrored conflicts with overseers. But they also showed how expertise and ability nourished one's own sense of esteem (or the estimation of colleagues). And, finally, because such (impermissible) aids to memory were indispensable for building up reserves of time, they could conserve or even increase one's own labor power.

Such drawings demonstrate, moreover, that alongside or "beneath" the official nomenclature of "quality work" there was also a significant unofficial one which needs attention. Whereas in the official rhetoric the successfully finished product supplied the crucial gauge to which other measurable quantities – such as the "time required" or the "waste produced" – might be added, the unofficial discourse took as its measure the amount of effort the job had required and the burden felt by the worker. Nevertheless these two meanings overlaid one another: they found a common ground in the focus upon ability, a knowledge dense with experience and dexterity in the work-place.

THE DRIVE FOR RATIONALIZATION
AFTER 1935–6 – A MYTH?

In the section which follows, Lüdtke contends that the apparently dramatic changes in the organization of the labor process, promoted

by the Nazis to build up their war machine (which Rüdiger Hacht-
mann has described as a new phase of "modernization" and "rationali-
zation" in German industry), did not qualitatively change many
workers' daily experiences of work. ⌉ *Lüdtke argues that even during*
the armaments boom it is difficult to discern a uniform, thoroughgoing
transition to mass production which would have deprived the notion
of German "quality work" of any real significance, making Nazi
appeals to the "honor of labor" meaningless.

* * *

Demands for the "rationalization" of industrial labor were certainly no discovery of Nazi industrial managers, bureaucrats in
the Four-year Plan or work-science specialists serving the
German Labor Front (DAF), especially as the debate about
rationalization or the failure to rationalize had met with a
serious reception in both the industrial interest associations and
the trade unions, from 1924, at the latest. None the less, even
trade union investigations, which were certainly not interested
in downplaying the extent of rationalization showed that up to
1931, flow production, subdivision of work tasks, multiple
machine tending as well as increasing the running speed of
machines were utilized in only a small number of factories or
only in specific sections of factories.

It continues to be difficult to decide whether there actually
was a "modernization of productive facilities . . . in large parts"
of the manufacturing industries after 1935–6 and whether "from
about 1935–6 a "drive for rationalization" began to have an
effect.[63] But there is, in any case, some evidence that differences
between industrial branches and regions became deeper.
Workers who were employed in completely new enterprises (the
aircraft industry, for example) experienced more intensely the
changes which were felt in all industries connected with rearmament; "new" work-places in new factory buildings and also at
new machines. They worked on a product which could not just
function when it left the factory halls, all polished and shining.
Airplanes stood as unparalleled symbols of that "modernity"
which would overcome space and time.[64] Motor buses opened
up (new) possibilities and cars mobilized desires to undertake
excursions, to free oneself from the daily grind and go on a trip.
Every airplane combined together a variety of hopes to over-

come earthly bottlenecks and confinements. But aspirations for national strength and military superiority may also have become particularly audible and visual in the roar of the airplane's motor.

In the many older industrial sectors and factories, the situation was quite different. Many of the products did not mobilize a similar degree of "pride in the products," nor was it possible to organize production and labor processes "all of a piece." Old and new machines and buildings were and frequently remained closely juxtaposed. But even here there was an increased, new investment of capital. After the years of the depression, there was a considerably increased need for machines to be repaired, replaced and renewed.

However, the decisive factor was that the rubric under which the labor requirements were defined had not fundamentally changed. Regardless of the branch of industry, preference continued to be given to a "suitably exact" (passgenau) way of working (G. Schlesinger). The considerable increase in sales achieved by producers of machine tools, after the mid-1930s should not obscure the fact that the standards applied to the production of each item remained the same. Indeed these standards blocked a transition to a thoroughgoing mass production. This was true even in the technically most modern forms of production, such as airplane construction, a pillar of the armaments industry, which developed at a furious rate after 1933. It is not surprising that, with the slogan "Junkers Work – Quality Work," the Junkers Aircraft Company in Dessau made a direct reference to the standards of "manual capability and dexterity" needed to tend, to "run" and to look after their tool machines.[65]

Even in war production, at least in the manufacturing industries, the mode of performing on the job remained unchanged.[66] Every increase in the speed of running the machines, every effort to ease the input and output of semi-finished and final products, did not alter the standard of "proper work" among factory economists or factory engineers, or among masters, lead-hands and workers; "the sensibility located in their hands, the capacity for judgement and experience."[67] This reflected two things; first, the unevenness of the changes in the organization of work and production made it necessary to be able to build up a "cushion" in the event of breakdowns. Second, one's own value continued to be mediated through a conception of

91

"German quality work." Both of these aspects dictated extreme exactness in setting up the machine, in clamping the piece to be worked on, in testing the way the machine was running, in checking the alterations in the form of the part caused by cutting and forming techniques, such as cutting on a lathe or milling, drilling or polishing as well as hammering or pressing. This orientation was shaped by the security of experience, preserved in the eye's ability to measure and the fingers' ability to feel.

WORKER AND QUALITY WORK – SOCIAL STATUS AND SURVIVAL CHANCES

The National Socialist German Workers' Party – that is just about the same as over there (the former East Germany), the worker is the highest aristocracy that you could achieve. . . . It was possible for me as a worker's child to be troop leader (*Fahnleinführer*). And my underling, so you might say, was a graduate of the classical highschool (*Gymnasium*).[68]

The man who remembers things this way was born in 1925. His father, a trained fitter, then master with the navy, was for a long time unemployed, finally got a job in 1925 in bridge building and worked on temporary jobs in the Soviet Union. The son was an enthusiastic Hitler Youth and began an apprenticeship as a fitter in 1940. He lived in a heavily Catholic working-class district in the Ruhr. He was "a convinced Nazi" and "I would have denounced anyone." In the contemporary perception or in the memory of this (at that time, young) man, something had become possible under the Nazis that had "actually" been quite inconceivable. Someone from the "upper classes" had to obey a worker or a worker's son. The basis of the social hierarchy was no longer quite as fixed as one had previously been led to expect.

Others had experiences that signaled more an improvement of their survival chances than the overcoming of the barriers separating them from "those up there." Being a skilled worker, especially if your productivity was "above average," could "pay off" in a number of ways. For one thing, the chances were greater of doing well in a wage system based on increasing wage differentials. At the same time one could take personally

[Handwritten margin note: , Continuity after the seizure of power in 1933. (Lütke) · Continuity after the war. (Bartov)]

the official testimonials of respect c̲ quality workers. In concrete terms, spared constant supervision or advi factory, then one could develop or maintain one's *Eigen-Sinn*. And it from this a life-protecting, even life-saving benefit might emerge. As a worker born in 1923 reported, it was "to his advantage" that he was, respectively, a qualified skilled worker and a precision engineer "when I was in the army." Occasionally, the younger men got positions as mechanics, and stayed, in part, on the periphery of the main combat zones. For the somewhat older men it was sometimes possible to be designated "uk," that is unsuitable for military service, and thus to remain at home. According to a worker born in 1910:

> I was a diligent worker, never stayed away from work . . . was always punctual, and they needed people here, to do the work here, and we could do many things, we had to do everything here in the foundry. . . . We also had the foreigners [forced laborers] here, we had to train them as well and there were a lot of women among them.[69]

In war production, "German quality work" was often guaranteed by the prisoners who counted as "community aliens" or "sub-humans" in the eyes of the National Socialists and who were supposed to be "destroyed by labor."[70] But their products, just like those of the male and female "Aryan" Germans, had to achieve the "quality" which counted as a precondition for the "Final Victory" being striven for. In a speech which was part of the propagandistic mobilization for "total war" in the summer of 1943, the Armaments Minister Speer brought the collective projection shortly and sharply into focus: "Quality will [triumph] over the mass." The message was clear: "German work" would always be superior to the merely "quantitative" (output) "of the West"; it would triumph this time as well.

THE SYMBOLISM OF WORK AND THE LOGIC OF ACQUIESCENCE

[*In this final section, Lüdtke attempts to establish the lines of continuity connecting the "normality" of everyday life during the years before 1933 with popular experiences during the Third Reich.*] *Lüdtke supports Walter Benjamin's observations concerning the importance of the grand symbolic displays, such as the Nuremberg party rally, with which the Nazis attempted to forge a new, racial mass consciousness.* [*But Lüdtke argues that it was really the less dramatic, more "normal," well-established, everyday forms of symbolic practice associated with the world of manual work that gave the Nazis one of their most effective instruments for gaining the loyalties of many Germans. In its symbolic practices, which revolved around the central image of "the honor of labor," the Third Reich addressed working-class identities and gave expression to working-class needs that the trade unions and the labor parties of the Weimar era had all too often neglected. Nazism was thus able to occupy an important symbolic space largely ignored or abandoned by its enemies.*] [*And for some workers, Nazism provided more than simply symbolic satisfactions; Nazi insistence upon the "honor of labor" and the importance of "German quality work" could increase skilled workers' survival chances, although at the cost of making them de facto, if unwitting, accomplices of a murderous regime.*]

* * *

Heinz-Dieter Schäfer's thesis that the forms of mass acceptance of and participation in the Nazi regime after 1933 demonstrate a "split consciousness" has met with great approval. The world of experience, especially that of the "Final Solution of the Jewish Question," was perceived only "fragmentarily." Under the impression of actual terror and the (more widespread) threat of terror, an automatic mechanism of "making things disappear" was set in motion, which filtered out all unbearable perceptions. The offerings of order and "greatness," for individuals as for the simulated "community," were always permeated with mechanisms of anxiety, of "a hostile posture" toward the dictatorship which perpetually stimulated feelings of anxiety and helplessness that in turn produced "apathy, paralysis and an uncontrolled letting oneself drift along."[71]

By contrast, the argument presented here is that such observations by no means reflect the exceptional situation of a dictatorship. Rather, a site of contradictions, formed over the long term, where acquiescence and self-assertive (*eigen-sinnige*) distancing, agreement, but also the (very infrequent) setting of oneself in opposition were used in the daily practices of life and survival was now simultaneously stimulated and repeatedly pushed forward. The forms of acceptance were not restricted only to an "aestheticization of politics" staged "from above." This thesis of Walter Benjamin, formulated in 1935–6 in the very face of fascism, grasps only the one, spectacular side of symbolic practice.[72] Benjamin insistently drew attention to the "enormous festive processions," "monster meetings; mass sports events," and, above all, the war. According to Benjamin, these mass movements made it possible for the participants "to express themselves" but "certainly not to exercise their own rights." In two respects Benjamin fell victim here to the exaggeration of the isolation imposed upon the persecuted exile. On the one hand, he failed to see the continuation of previous ways of constructing meaning (*Deutungsweisen*). [At the same time, the variety of unspectacular everyday practices eluded him, in which in the work-place, in the neighborhood, in the family, but also in the "mass organizations," the participants themselves produced and experienced the fascination with and the utilization of the "new times."]

The National Socialist leaders and offices certainly did include the "great" gestures and scenes. Marches and mass performances were not just staged on 1 May 1933. Ley's attempt from the autumn of 1933, in countless "Houses of German Labor" to give permanent significance to his organization, the German Labor Front, can be understood as an attempt to "eternalize" the mass movement.[73] Here it stayed at the level of the gigantic; yet at the same time vague plans, starting in 1934, with the opening of the annual Reich Professional Contest (*Reichsberufswettkampf*), brought the appearance of leading Nazi "big-wigs" on to a large stage with considerable media effect.[74] And in 1937 the Reich Party conference of the NSDAP took place under the motto "The Party Day of Labor." The usual marches and speeches, the usual fanfare and flag dedication were supposed to embody "the triumph of labor"; so too was a "monumental well installation" which the city of Nuremberg provided as a gift at the opening of the party meeting. More precisely, the Lord Mayor presented "a model of this wonderful sculpture" (which was never actually built).[75] In an opening address, Hitler once again accentuated the factor of hard work; the construction of the new Germany could "only [be] the result of ceaseless industry." In this respect, his representative, Rudolf

Hess, went a step too far because he proclaimed, "that, through work, Germany [had already become] strong and free again." At the same time he gave a vivid example of the word-pictures with which the "everydayness" of industrial experiences should, so to speak, be summoned up and recalled "by everyone":

> Once dead workshops are filled with life, with eating and smoking. Wheels turn once again, forging presses move again, rollers roll again, train after train runs from one economic center to another, ship after ship comes and goes in once desolate harbors.

It was a cascade of trusted clichés and icons; clearly they were supposed to present (industrial) work to the participants in the mass marches, but also to the listeners and readers as an intoxicating, as a marvelous experience.

The mass rituals were, however, not everything by a long shot. The everyday connection of material achievements with sensual, tangible symbols became decisive, even when they remained limited to certain occasions. In every instance, experiences, anxieties and hopes could be seen to be addressed, which the labor movement of the Weimar Republic had scarcely even noticed. The recognition of the materiality of the work-place, with its hardships and unwholesomeness during work, made reference to key points of proletarian life and survival experiences. Brighter lighting or bigger windows, more spacious machine placement, the expansion of washing facilities or cloak-rooms, or, indeed, their provision for the first time, places to sit during breaks set apart from the machines – such symbolic announcements promised a new quality of recognition and practical welfare. And individual examples produced a striking reinforcement (of the message). Above all, who previously had publicly even conceded the importance of this side of everyday reality or even made an attempt at change? In this context of experience the symbolic references meant real improvements.

Among the hopes raised was also the hope for recognition. Outside the factory that meant, primarily, paid holidays (from Christmas 1937) as well as an actual right to a vacation. Inside the factory that could likewise have considerable, although also double-edged consequences – for example, in the case of worker's "self-supervision" in the motor and tractor factory Klockner-Humboldt-Deutz. The "factory leader", Dipl.-Ing. H.

Stein, selected 300 to 400 workers (probably "quality workers") and after 1937 and 1938 installed them among their colleagues as continuously present "self-supervisors." They got a lot of applause from the DAF and the Nazi Party. For the *Völkischer Beobachter*" this counted as undeniable proof of the "triumph of the German worker" who no longer needed the supervision of others. In any case, the factory won the "Golden Banner" of the DAF in 1940.[76]

The "honor of labor" alluded to "community" (*Gemeinschaft*), but at the same time turned to the individual. The picture language makes this concrete. Picture icons of muscular labor, toil and sweat reflected real-life experiences. They were intensively deployed in the Nazi picture press. However, photographs in illustrated newspapers, mainly in the factory newspapers of the 1930s, increasingly displayed bodies and faces that, despite all of the stylization of steeled corporality, not infrequently bore traces of the individual.[77] This, too, was not a complete novelty. The working-class press of the 1920s had, however, projected personal goals much more emphatically upon the symbols of the masses and the collective. By contrast, the individualizing work-symbols of the 1930s carried multiple meanings in a special way; they cited the picture of the worker, secure in his experience, who controlled the tool and the machine and thus referred to pride in work and the pride of the worker. But at the same time – and this was new – the half-length portraits and pictures of the worker's naked chest placed individual faces at their center-point. These pictures of individuals and of small groups seldom emphasized demonstratively heroicizing gestures. Much more often they carried a restrained documentary signature. To this extent it was perhaps possible for the first time to see openly addressed that "unhappy consciousness" about the worker's existence, that only a few workers put on display, but which certainly worried many more.

The life and survival of male and female industrial workers was fed from diverse sources. The calculation of interest connected itself with intense longings for the "good life." These longings not infrequently remained unspoken, but expressed themselves in moments of "self-assertion" (*Eigen-Sinn*) that involved the body – they were conserved and recalled in symbols. In self-assertive (*eigen-sinnige*) practice, the "many" were able anew to produce distance from the repeated daily expectations and compulsions. Moments of individual release, but also of individual fulfilment, were possible in and through *Eigen-Sinn*. Symbols certainly continued to have multiple meanings. They were able not only to incite *Eigen-Sinn*, but also to support agreement with the rulers; they could make a recognition which crossed class and political lines both visible and emotive. Above all, self-assertive (*eigen-sinnige*) demarcation and the sense of community delivered via symbols could easily expand itself. The capacity for submission as well as the pleasure of being involved were stimulated simultaneously. In case of doubt, one could make one's own worth visible in the form of a perfect product – just as easily in tank-treads as in locomotive wheels.

The field of force in which men and women workers and working-class wives found themselves in Nazi Germany was transformed. Silent as well as open violence increased perceptibly. But at the same time, a multitude of symbolic practices and presentations facilitated an altered self-perception. Equally decisive were concrete, sensual, as well as general-rhetorical, reinforcements of the "honor of labor." The diffuse rhetoric of the sense of "community" in the factories gave individual survival interests in the work-places – and in fact the self-assertiveness of the "quality worker" – increased legitimacy and opportunities. In this way, in an unprecedented fashion, hopes for a "good life" could be sensually experienced and felt to be justifiable. Naturally in the process a certain ambivalence was unavoidable; individual survival, especially the exploitation of the new chances, required continuous acquiescence and, not infrequently, active participation in the fascist mobilization of the economy for war. Survival and enjoyment of the "honor of labor" thus also meant becoming an accomplice to criminal policies.

NOTES

The full-length, German original of this article was published as " 'Ehre der Arbeit': Industriearbeiter und Macht der Symbole. Zur Reichweite symbolischer Orientierungen im Nationalsozialismus" in Klaus Tenfelde (ed.), *Arbeiter im 20. Jahrhundert* (Stuttgart: Klett-Cotta Verlag, 1991). The abridged version reproduced here is translated by David Crew, with the assistance of Alf Lüdtke.

1 For the planning and above all the arrangements and sequence of rituals celebrating the "Day of National Labor" on 1 May, see Eberhard Heuel, *Der umworbene Stand. Die ideologische Integration der Arbeiter im Nationalsozialismus 1933–1935* (Frankfurt/New York, 1989), pp. 42–187; for a transcript of the recording of Hitler's speech as well as a part of the radio programme for the chorus, see ibid, pp. 577–623. The declaration of 1 May 1919 as an official holiday celebrating labor remained a one-time gesture; the labor movement did not manage in the following years to make the proletarian day of struggle officially "acceptable" or to have it sanctioned by the state. On the occupation of the trade union houses and expropriation of their funds on 2 May 1933, see Heinrich August Winkler, *Der Weg in die Katastrophe. Arbeiter und Arbeiterbewegung in der Weimarer Republik 1930–1933* (Berlin/Bonn 1987), p. 867ff.; on an industrial center see Gerhard Hetzer, "Die Industriestadt Augsburg. Eine Sozialgeschichte der Arbeiteropposition" in Martin Broszat *et al.* (ed.), *Bayern in der NS-Zeit*, Vol. 3 (München/Wien, 1981), pp. 1–233, 93ff.

2 Ronald Smelser, *Robert Ley. Hitlers Mann an der "Arbeitsfront"* (Paderborn, 1989), p. 135ff.; see also Heuel, *Der umworbene Stand*, Chapters 4 and 5.

3 Heuel, *Der umworbene Stand*, p. 539ff., 505ff; on the following p. 531ff.

4 The numbers were very small. Between 1934 and 1942 proceedings were taken against 11,264 people (the numbers are missing for 1938); in 496 cases there was no verdict. After 1937 there was an unmistakable decline of actual prosecutions of "factory leaders" for neglecting their obligations, which had, in any case, been infrequent from the beginning; see Andreas Kranig, *Lockung und Zwang. Zur Arbeitsverfassung im Dritten Reich* (Stuttgart, 1983), p. 235ff.

5 R. Ley, "Ich gab die Menschen die Hand" in R. Ley, *Soldaten der Arbeit*, 2nd edn (München, 1939), pp. 69–79, p. 69f. (speech on 2 June 1937 in the Leuna Works); see also R. Ley, "Sechs aktuelle Fragen" in R. Ley, *Wir alle helfen dem Führer* (München, 1937), pp. 209–13, p. 209 as well as the picture caption "Nicht den Maschinen, den Menschen gilt das Interesse bei den Betriebsbesuchen Dr. Leys," ibid., between pp. 48 and 49; see also "W.K.," "Der deutsche Arbeiter zieht mit" in *Der Vierjahresplan*, Vol. 1, 1937, p. 24f.; Ley claimed to have had "innumerable conversations, man-to-man" during his factory visits "since the beginning of the new 4 year plan", in other words, since autumn 1936; ibid., p. 24.

6 R. Ley, *Die Deutsche Arbeitsfront, ihr Werden und ihre Aufgaben* (München, 1934), p. 11.

7 See Gerhard Paul, "Der Sturm auf die Republik und der Mythos vom 'Dritten Reich.' Die Nationalsozialisten" in Detlev Lehnert and Klaus Megerle (eds), *Politische Identität und nationale Gedenktage. Zur politischen Kultur in der Weimarer Republik* (Opladen, 1989), pp. 255–79.

8 The representational forms of "royalty" have recently become a theme of research; see David Cannadine and Simon Price (eds), *Rituals of Royalty. Power and Ceremonial in Traditional Societies* (Cambridge, 1987); the corresponding practices in Napoleonic France (and its satellites) but also under Napoleon III deserve closer consideration (for the appeal to a revolutionary icon see Maurice Agulhon, *Marianne au combat* (Paris, 1980); for the nomenclature and the – overwhelmingly – verbal symbolization of organized political groups in the Weimar Republic; Lehnert and Megerle (eds), *Politische Identität und nationale Gedenktage*; a discussion of rituals is also included but only for the SPD and the KPD; see the contributions by Manfred Gailus and Lehnert, ibid., pp. 61ff. and 89ff.; on visual and theatrical forms of representation see Dietmar Petzina (ed.), *Fahnen, Fäuste, Körper. Symbolik und Kultur der Arbeiterbewegung* (Essen, 1986) especially Gottfried Korff and Gerhard Hauk, ibid., pp. 27ff. and 69ff. For revolutionary-republican investiture ritual (i.e. the celebration of the ratification of the United States constitution 1788–9), see Jürgen Heideking, *Die Verfassung vor dem Richterstuhl. Vorgeschichte und Ratifizierung der amerikanischen Verfassung 1787–1791* (Berlin/New York, 1988), p. 709ff.

9 See, for example, Klaus Behnken (ed.), *Deutschland-Berichte der Sozialdemokratischen Partei Deutschlands (SOPADE) 1934–1940*, Vol. 4: 1937 (Frankfurt, 1980), p. 1290; Smelser, *Ley*, p. 300.

10 In general, see Peter Hüttenberger, "Nationalsozialistische Polykratie" in *Geschichte und Gesellschaft* (henceforth, *GG*) Vol. 2, 1976, pp. 417–42; on Ley, Smelser, *Ley, passim* and, in conclusion, p. 296 – with an important reference to the "new form of power" which the DAF was supposed to have exercised; this "diffuse power" depended upon "unceasingly collected pieces of individual information, upon service and upon wealth," ibid., p. 297.

11 The allusion to Max Weber's definition of power and domination should remind us of the connection between legitimation and the threat of force; certainly Weber either left open or simply did not acknowledge the question of the production and generation of "*belief* in legitimation" (my emphasis); see Max Weber, *Wirtschaft und Gesellschaft*, 5th edn (Tübingen, 1964), p. 38ff., as well as p. 157ff. but also p. 27.

12 In the NSBO and DAF press there are numerous factory reports in 1934 and 1935 which assume a similar posture; the otherwise nameless are given a voice or else step forward as "real" people in the (photographic) picture; see Heuel, *Der umworbene Stand*, p. 561ff.; for the effect of individual testimony see Michael Zimmermann, "Ausbruchshoffnung" in Lutz Niethammer (ed.) "*Die Jahre weiss man nicht, wo man die heute hinsetzen soll*" (Berlin/Bonn, 1983), pp. 97–132, especially p. 116.

13 For this interpretation of "symbols" see Victor Turner, *The Forest of Symbols. Aspects of Ndembu Ritual* (Ithaca/London, 1973), p. 27ff., especially p. 48ff.; see also V. Turner, "Symbols in African Rituals"

in Janet L. Dolgin *et al.* (eds), *Symbolic Anthropology* New York, 1977), pp. 183–94 as well as Raymond Firth, *Symbols. Public and Private* (London, 1973), p. 193ff.

14 On the unique characteristics of this individual self-distancing from *all* forms of expectation, which at the same time momentarily ignores cost-benefit calculations, see my article, "Cash, coffee-breaks, horseplay: *Eigensinn* and politics among factory workers in Germany circa 1900" in Michael Hanagan and Charles Stephenson (eds), *Class, Confrontation and the Labor Process* (New York, 1989), pp. 65–95, 78ff.

15 On this theme, in greater detail, see my attempt at a "thick description"; "Wo blieb die 'rote Glut'? Arbeitererfahrungen und deutscher Faschismus" in Alf Lüdtke (ed.), *Alltagsgeschichte, Zur Rekonstruktion historischer Erfahrungen und Lebensweisen* (Frankfurt/New York, 1989), pp. 224–82. This uncommonly "real" significance of symbols eludes Klaus Wisozky in his, in many respects, trenchant work; see K. Wisozky, *Der Ruhrbergbau im Dritten Reich. Studien zur Sozialpolitik im Ruhrbergbau und zum sozialen Verhalten der Bergleute 1933 bis 1939* (Düsseldorf, 1983), p. 99.

16 The example of the St Eligius festival, to honour the patron saint of, above all, metalworkers in a forge at the Renault company in the late 1920s, is also very stimulating on this theme; Noëlle Gérôme, "Das Sankt-Eligius-Fest in den Schmieden der Renault-Betriebe von Billancourt" in Friedhelm Boll (ed.), *Arbeiterkulturen zwischen Alltag und Politik* (Wien, 1986), pp. 143–54.

17 Heuel, *Der umworbene Stand*, p. 616; for the following, p. 618; for the text of the "eyewitness account," with the voices of the workers, which was transmitted at 10 o'clock, see ibid., p. 583ff.; Hitler spoke in the context of the main assembly after 8 p.m.

18 Adolf Hitler, "Rede auf dem Kongress der Deutschen Arbeitsfront in Berlin am 10. Mai 1933" in *Reden des Reichskanzler Adolf Hitler, des neuen Deutschlands Führer* (Berlin [1933]), pp. 50–6, here p. 55.

19 Curt Rosten, *Das ABC des Nationalsozialismus*, 6th, expanded, edn. (Berlin, 1933), p. 11; see Heuel, *Der umworbene Stand*, p. 311f.

20 Mason, "Bändigung der Arbeiterklasse in Deutschland. Eine Einleitung" in Carola Sachse, Tilla Siegel, Hasso Spode, and Wolfgang Spohn, *Angst, Belohnung, Zucht und Ordnung. Herrschaftsmechanismen im Nationalsozialismus* (Opladen, 1982), p. 37; Gerd Stein (ed.), *Lumpenproletarier-Bonze-Held der Arbeit. Kulturfiguren und Sozialcharaktere des 19. und 20. Jahrhunderts* (Frankfurt, 1985), p. 114ff. 149–209.

21 Heuel, *Der umworbene Stand*, pp. 386ff., 390ff.

22 Gisela Bock has shown the extent to which the racial-political guidelines of National Socialism were based upon the insistence on the differences between the genders (i.e. were based upon the "cult of the father" and upon "the cult of the male and the masculine"); see G. Bock, *Zwangssterilisation im Nationalsozialismus Studien zur Rassenpolitik und Frauenpolitik* (Opladen, 1986), p. 462. The homage to "the worker," in which Ernst Jünger put the crisis

mentality of counter-revolutionaries fixated upon the war into words in 1932 differed in both intention and argumentation from the tracts of leading National Socialists concerning "workers," despite several similarities. If factory work was to him and to his not inconsiderable circle of readers the example *par excellence* from the real world of the everyday nature of the global "friend-enemy" situation and of the necessity of "energy" and "order," then it made sense to perceive in "the worker" a wholly new world-historical "form." For Jünger that meant, "the only possible heir of Prussianism is the working class"(Jünger, *Der Arbeiter, Herrschaft und Gestalt* (1932) (Stuttgart, 1981), p. 69; for the following, p. 67. Naturally the "real existing" worker was for Jünger only the "manifestation" of a diffuse transformation toward a new world. Only in this future world could "work" be comprehended "as its inner necessity".

23 Mary Nolan, *Social Democracy and Society. Working-Class Radicalism in Düsseldorf, 1890–1920* (Cambridge, 1981), p. 138; Peter Friedemann, "Feste und Feiern im rheinisch-westfälischen Industriegebiet. 1890–1914" in Gerhard Hauck (ed.), *Sozialgeschichte der Freizeit*, 2nd edn (Wuppertal, 1982), pp. 165–85, p. 167.

24 Individual examples in Gottfried Korff, "Rote Fahnen und Tableaux Vivants. Zum Symbolverständnis der deutschen Arbeiterbewegung im 19. Jahrhundert" in Albrecht Lehmann (ed.), *Studien zur Arbeiterkultur* (Münster, 1984), pp. 103–40; see also Gerhard Hauk, "Armeekorps auf dem Weg zur Sonne." Einige Bemerkungen zur kulturellen Selbstdarstellung der Arbeiterbewegung" in Petzina (ed.), *Fahnen, Fäuste, Körper*, pp. 69–89.

25 See the collection of May Day placards and postcards in the Archiv der sozialen Demokratie, Bonn-Bad Godesberg; see also individual references, for example, to the Hamburg trade union house in 1906 and 1912–13 respectively in Roland Jaeger,"Von Merkur bis Bebel. Die Ikonographie der Industriekultur" in Volker Plagemann (ed.), *Industriekultur in Hamburg* (München, 1984), pp. 343–7, esp. 346f.

26 Karl Marx, *Das Kapital*, Vol. 1 [MEW 23] (Berlin/DDR, 1965), p. 192. This is paid too little attention in Detlef Stender's important reconstruction of the life histories of a worker in the fitting shop and another in the rolling mill of an aluminium factory, which is otherwise notable for its sensitivity to the many facets of and, at the same time, the interconnections between, experiences inside and outside the factory; see D. Stender, "Lebensgeschichten zweier Metallarbeiter" in Gert Zang (ed.), *Arbeiterleben in einer Randregion* (Konstanz, 1987), pp. 159–76, 160ff., 173ff.

27 See Carl Sonnenschein, one of the leading organizers of the "Volksverein für das katholische Deutschland" speaking in front of "Christian" metalworkers in 1911; *Der sittliche Wert der gewerkschaftlichen Arbeit*, 3rd edn (Duisburg [c. 1912]), p. 11f.

28 On this theme, with many instructive examples, Ulrich Engelhardt, *"Nur vereinigt sind wir stark" ... Die Anfänge der deutschen Gewerkschaftsbewegung 1862/63 bis 1869/70* (Stuttgart, 1977); see also the

collection of strike demands from the early 1870s in Lothar Mach-
tan, *Streiks und Aussperrungen im Deutschen Kaiserreich* (Berlin,
1984); for specific references to miners, see Klaus Tenfelde and
Helmut Trischler (eds), *Bis vor die Stufen des Throns. Bittschriften
und Beschwerden von Bergleuten im Zeitalter der Industrialisierung*
(München, 1986); also interesting for the 1880s; Hans-Josef Steinberg (ed.), *Mahnruf einer deutschen Mutter . . . sowie anderer Gedichte,
die Arbeiterinnen und Arbeiter an die Redaktion des illegal vertriebenen
"Sozialdemokrat" geschickt haben und die nicht abgedruckt wurden*
(Bremen, 1983).

29 See on this question Cora Stephen, *"Genossen, wir dürfen uns nicht
von der Geduld hinreissen lassen!" Aus der Urgeschichte der Sozialdemokratie* (Frankfurt, 1977), pp. 192ff., 212ff.

30 The discussion of real wage income is certainly still an open question; for a concise synthesis of the present state of the discussion,
see Gerhard Hohorst, *et al.*, *Sozialgeschichtliches Arbeitsbuch II:
Materialien zur Statistik des Kaiserreichs 1879–1914* (München, 1975),
pp. 97ff.; on the differences between strata within the working
class, and, where possible, for a discussion of stratum-specific
patterns of changing standards of consumption in individual
households at the beginning of the twentieth century, see Reinhard
Spree, "Klassen- und Schichtbildung im Spiegel des Konsumver-
haltens individueller Haushalte zu Beginn des 20. Jahrhunderts"
in Toni Pierenkemper (ed.), *Haushalt und Verbrauch in historischer
Perspektive. Zum Wandel des privaten Verbrauchs in Deutschland im
19. und 20. Jahrhundert* (St Katharinen, 1987), pp. 56–80, and also
Herman van Laer, "Die Haushaltsführung von maschinenbauarbei-
ter- und Textilarbeiterfamilien in der Zeit bis zum Ersten
Weltkrieg," ibid., pp. 152–84.

31 On the reflection of such experiences in attempts to carry on
through the "great crisis" after 1929, see my article "Hunger in
der Grossen Depression. Hungererfahrungen und Hungerpolitik
am Ende der Weimarer Republik," *Archiv für Sozialgeschichte*, Vol.
27, 1987, pp. 147–76.

32 Even among the organized, the numbers can be deceptive; not a
few of those who joined and paid contributions as relatively young
people, then left the organizations after one or two years. Only a
minority were engaged on a steady, enduring basis in the party or
trade union, or even in the numerous organizations which
attempted to accompany and to organize the various aspects of
working-class life. For the social democratic trade unions in the
Kaiserreich, this is shown by Klaus Schönhoven, *Expansion und
Konzentration. Studien zur Entwicklung der Freien Gewerkschaften im
Wilhelminischen Deutschland 1890 bis 1914* (Stuttgart, 1989), Part
III; on organizational "conjunctures," see Irmgard Steinisch, "Die
gewerkschaftliche Organisation der rheinisch-westfälischen Arbeiterschaft in der eisen- und stahlerzeugenden Industrie 1918 bis
1924" in Hans Mommsen (ed.) *Arbeiterbewegung und industrieller
Wandel* (Wuppertal, 1980), pp. 117–39 and also Elisabeth Domansky,

"Arbeitskampf und Arbeitsrecht in der Weimarer Republik" in Dieter Dowe (ed.), *Reprint: Gewerkschafts-Zeitung* Vol. 34, 1924, Introduction, pp. 31–80, 47ff., 58ff.

33 Adolf Levenstein, *Die Arbeiterfrage. Mit besonderer Berücksichtigung der sozialpsychologischen Seite des modernen Grossbetriebs und der psychophysischen Einwirkungen auf die Arbeiter* (München 1912); for the following, p. 51; for Levenstein in general, W. Bonss, "Kritische Theorie und empirische Sozialforschung" in Ernst Fromm, *Arbeiter und Angestellte am Vorabend des Dritten Reiches* (ed. W. Bonss) (Stuttgart, 1980), p. 19ff. Barrington Moore has quite rightly supported his thesis about the importance for Germany of demands for "fairness/justice" with references to Levenstein; see Barrington Moore, *Injustice. The Social Bases of Obedience and Revolt* (White Plains, N.Y., 1978) especially Chapter VI.

34 Very instructive on this question is Frank Trommler, "Die Nationalisierung der Arbeit" in Reinhold Grimm and Jost Hermand (eds), *Arbeit als Thema in der deutschen Literatur vom Mittelalter bis zur Gegenwart* (Königstein/Ts., 1979), pp. 102–25. For the Christian trade union movement, see also Sonnenschein, *Der sittlichen Wert*, p. 13ff.

35 K.-M. Bogdal, *Schaurige Bilder, Der Arbeiter im Blick des Bürgers* (Frankfurt, 1978), pp. 47ff., 117ff.

36 Trommler, "Nationalisierung," p. 112.

37 Johannes Reichert, *Aus Deutschlands Waffenschmiede*, 2nd edn (Berlin, 1918), p. 75; emphasis in the original.

38 Friedhelm Boll, *Frieden ohne Revolution? Friedensstrategien der deutschen Sozialdemokratie vom Erfurter Programm 1891 bis zur Revolution 1918* (Bonn, 1980), p. 104ff.

39 Jürgen Kocka, *Klassengesellschaft im Krieg. Deutsche Sozialgeschichte 1914–1918* (Göttingen, 1973), pp. 12ff, 43ff; Volker Ullrich, *Kriegsalltag. Hamburg im Ersten Weltkrieg* (Köln, 1982); Doris Kachulle (ed.), *Die Pohlands im Krieg* (Köln, 1982); Merith Niehuss, *Arbeiter in Krieg und Inflation* (Berlin/New York, 1985); Ute Daniel, *Arbeiterfrauen in der Kriegsgesellschaft* (Göttingen, 1989).

40 On the ADGB see my article " 'Deutsche Qualitätsarbeit', 'Spielereien' am Arbeitsplatz und 'Fliehen' aus der Fabrik" in Boll (ed.), *Arbeiterkulturen*, pp. 155–97, 182f.

41 See Michael Ruck, *Bollwerk gegen Hitler? Arbeiterschaft, Arbeiterbewegung und die Anfänge des Nationalsozialismus* (Köln, 1988), pp. 56–73.

42 See my article ' "Deutsche Qualitätsarbeit,' 'Spielereien' am Arbeitsplatz und 'Fliehen' aus der Fabrik" in F. Boll (ed.), *Arbeiterkulturen*, especially pp. 156ff, 174ff. For the "shopfloor" level, see Peter Schirmbeck (ed.), *"Morgen kommst Du nach Amerika." Erinnerungen an die Arbeit bei Opel 1917–1927* (Bonn, 1988), p. 58ff.: "On piece work" – it was here that the variety and the continuous nature of the interventions with which workers made the "production flow" possible could be recognized.

43 Vorstand des DMV (ed.), *Die Rationalisierung in der Metallindustrie* (Berlin [1932]), pp. 86f., 94f.

44 Unfortunately studies are lacking which would allow us to calculate distributions according, in particular, to region and industrial branch and which did not subsume the "strategic" groups of semi-skilled under the category of the unskilled. For the metal industry, see, however, the survey by the German Metalworkers' Union in 1931 (published as *Die Rationalisierung in der Metallindustrie*). Here, trade union representatives reported that skilled specialists had been "pushed out" of their jobs by semi- and unskilled workers in 10.5 per cent of the cases reported as rationalization from all of the individual branches; see ibid., p. 89. It is, however, impossible to reconstruct from the number of these "cases" either the number or the proportion of the people who were involved or affected in the metal industry in general (not to mention other branches of industry). Nevertheless, individual interviews show that new hirings of, above all, unskilled or semi-skilled workers provided opportunities to get work that was probably "qualified" as a "semi-skilled" lathe operator making component parts, a milling machine operator, a drilling machine operator or a tin shear worker, especially after 1934–5; see interviews with, respectively, five and thirteen retired workers, from the firms of Hanomag-Hannover and Henschel-Kassel in 1984 and 1985 (the transcript can be consulted in the Max-Planck-Institut für Geschichte). See also references from the United States automobile industry to the significance for the trade unions of new or "semi-skilled" specialists; see Babson, "Class, craft, and culture: tool and die makers and the organization of the UAW," *Michigan Historical Review*, Vol. 14, 1988, pp. 33–56. That workers were increasingly trained on the job ("Anlernen") is suggested by references from individual (large) enterprises; see on the Wernerwerk (Berlin, Siemens & Halske AG), Hachtmann, *Industriearbeit*, p. 87; see also the practice which can be observed in new wage agreements from 1937 onward of paying "non-specialist" workers as "trained specialists"; ibid., p. 59; see also F. Fendt, *Der ungelernte Industriearbeiter* (München/Leipzig, 1934), p. 18ff. (on the "new unskilled"), p. 27ff. (work tasks in specific industrial branches) p. 65ff. (wages), p. 75ff. (numbers). The references in Josef Mooser, *Arbeiterleben in Deutschland 1900–1970* (Frankfurt, 1984), p. 58ff., are very general.

45 On this topic generally, see Peter Hinrichs, *Um die Seele des Arbeiters. Arbeitspsychologie, Industrie- und Betriebssoziologie in Deutschland* (Köln, 1981).

46 Edgar Atzler, *Körper und Arbeit* (Leipzig, 1927).

47 Isolde Dietrich, "Massenproduktion und Massenkultur. Bürgerliche Arbeitswissenschaft als Kulturwissenschaft" in *Freizeit als Lebensraum: Arbeitende Menschen im Sozialismus – ihr Platz in der Freizeitkultur* vom Wissenschaftsbereich Kultur der Humboldt-Universität Berlin (Berlin/DDR, 1987), pp. 45–59.

48 Albert Vogler, 17 November 1929, facsimile of a letter to C. Arnold

(!recte: Arnhold), in *Arbeitsschulung* Vol. 1, 1929, p. 1. See also Heuel, *Der umworbene Stand*, p. 413ff.

49 Goetz Briefs, *Betriebsführung und Betriebsleben in der Industrie* (Stuttgart, 1934), pp. 23ff., 35, 51. Briefs, whose Institut für Betriebssoziologie was, moreover, installed at the Technische Hochschule Charlottenburg in 1928, complied explicitly and positively with the National Socialist design for the complete reorganization of industrial work relationships, ibid., pp. 131–42.

50 See Richard Lang and Willy Hellpach, *Gruppenfabrikation* (Berlin, 1922), especially p. 65ff. On Hellpach, who was elected president of the federal state of Baden 1924–5, and after 1933 came to the fore as a compliant supporter of the Nazis, who probably had an eye on keeping his position as an honorary professor and then as institute head, see H. Gundlach, "Willy Hellpach. Attributionen" in C. F. Graumann (ed.), *Psychologie im Nationalsozialismus* (Berlin, 1985), pp. 165–93.

51 Eugen Rosenstock certainly must have known about the experiment with group production; in any case, he was connected for a short time with Daimler and had run the company magazine there for a year in 1919. He proceeded from the assumption that for the workers, the motive for wage-labor was "Work and bread for everyone! . . . (not) the rational exploitation of human labour power." Attention had to be paid, in the first instance, to the "being" of the worker; only after this had been done could one begin "to speak . . . of increasing productivity and wages"; see Eugen Rosenstock, *Werkstattaussiedlung. Untersuchungen über den Lebensraum des Industriearbeiters* (Berlin, 1922), p. 89ff; for the following see also p. 79. This "existence" required, however, a "living relationship to the time and the place" of one's own "doing and working". His proposal admittedly tended towards a romantic utopianism; he wanted literally to give each of the individual workers their workplace; the "workshop settlement" was supposed to reconstruct the unity of living and working that would permit the [worker's] "being." Only then would work become "a piece of one's own life [and] life course."

52 On contemporary discussions and stereotypes, in the context of a European comparison, see Anson Rabinbach, "The European Science of Work. The Economy of the Body at the End of the Nineteenth Century" in Stephen L. Kaplan/Cynthia J. Koepp (editors), *Work in France. Representations, Meanings, Organization, and Practice* (Ithaca, London, 1986), pp. 475–513. On the design of contemporary investigations see Marie Bernays, "Untersuchungen über die Schwankungen der Arbeitsintensität während der Arbeitswoche und während des Arbeitstages. Ein Beitrag zur Psychophysik der Textilarbeit" in *Auslese und Auspassung der Arbeiterschaft in der Lederwaren-, Steinzeug-, und Textilindustrie* (Leipzig, 1912) [*Schriften des Vereins für Socialpolitik*, Bd. 135], pp. 183–389f., 382ff.

53 Hendrik de Man, *Der Kampf um die Arbeitsfreude* (Jena, 1927); for the following, p. 256f., p. 276.

54 Rex Hersey, *Seele und Gefühl des Arbeiters. Psychologie der Menschen-führung* (Leipzig, 1935); for the following pp. 74 and 78, respectively.

55 Cited in Hinrichs, *Um die Seele des Arbeiters*, p. 155.

56 On the positions taken by the ADGB trade unions in the "rationalization" debates see Gunnar Stolberg, *Die Rationalisierungsdebatte 1908–1933. Freie Gewerkschaften zwischen Mitwirkung und Gegenwehr* (Frankfurt/New York 1981).

57 *Arbeiter-Illustrierte Zeitung* (=AIZ), No. 6, 1928; for another case, see also Heinz Willmann, *Geschichte der Arbeiter-Illustrierten Zeitung 1921–1928* (Berlin 1974); the title picture No. 8, 1926 which also depicts a lathe operator.

58 For this reference to Theo Gaudig Essen I want to thank A. von Plato (Hagen) and R. Kania (Essen); see also my interview with Theo Gaudig in Essen on 4.9.1985.

59 Willi Bredel, *Maschinenfabrik N&K* [manuscript 1930] (Berlin/DDR, 3rd edn, Weimar, 1982), pp. 67ff., 74, 99ff.

60 De Man, *Arbeitsfreude*, p. 160.

61 De Man, *Arbeitsfreude*, pp. 158ff., 164. Cases on the theft of tools are particularly important and revealing; on this, see the memories of the *Gutehoffnungshütte* (GHH), which were recorded in 1939 and reflect the situation in the 1880s and 1890s; Historisches Archiv Haniel/GHH, Nr. 40016/9l

62 Schirmbeck (ed.). *"Morgen kommst Du nach Amerika,"* p. 83

63 See Hachtmann, *Industriearbeit im "Dritten Reich." Untersuchungen zu den Lohn- und Arbeitsbedingungen in Deutschland 1933–1945*, p. 75, and also Reinhard Berthold (ed.), *Produktivkräfte in Deutschland 1917/18 bis 1945* (Berlin/DDR, 1988), pp. 64–94. In both of these studies, few (large) factories are named, and in the contributions to the volume *Produktivkräfte* aggregate statements concerning technical developments or improvements dominate, concerning, for example, the parallel development of universal- and automatic special-purpose machines, or hardened metal tools and fast running equipment.

64 Inge Marssolek and René Ott, *Bremen im Dritten Reich. Anpassung–Widerstand–Verfolgung* (Bremen, 1986), p. 153f. (on Focke-Wulf and also Borgward, as well as on concentration camp labor); Dieter Pfliegensdörfer, " 'Ich war mit Herz und Seele dabei, und so, dass mir das gar nichts ausmachte.' Bremer Flugzeugbauer im National-sozialismus," *1999*, Vol. 3, 1988, pp. 44–103, p. 60ff., p. 64ff., see p. 49ff.

65 Hans Kern, "Innenwerbung für Wirtschaftlichkeit und Qualität. Zwei Werbeaktionen der Junkers Flugzeug- und Motorenwerke AG, Dessau" in *Zeitschrift für Organisation*, Vol. 12, 1938, pp. 275–85, p. 281ff., p. 285.

66 See Richard J. Overy, "Hitler's war and the German economy: A reinterpretation," *Economic History Review*, Vol. 32, 1985, pp. 272–91 291, p. 286.

67 Georg Schlesinger, *Psychotechnik und Betriebswissenschaft* (Leipzig, 1920), p. 15f, p. 51ff.
68 Life history of Gisbert Pohl in Alexander V. Plato, *"Der Verlierer geht nicht leer aus."* *Betriebsräte geben zu Protokoll* (Berlin/Bonn, 1984), p. 52; for the following, p. 54.
69 Reminiscence of Jan Wesel in Plato, *"Der Verlierer,"* p. 25. From 1943 the chances of being designated "uk" were significantly reduced.
70 For example, at Daimler-Benz, in airplane engine construction, in truck construction and in the production of tank parts; Hamburger Stiftung für Sozialgeschichte des 20. Jahrhunderts, *Das Daimler-Benz Buch. Ein Rüstungskonzern im "Tausendjährigen Reich"* (Nördlingen, 1987), Part II.
71 Heinz-Dieter Schäfer, *Das gespaltene Bewusstsein. Deutsche Kultur und deutsche Lebenswirklichkeit 1933–1945* (München, 1981), p. 146, p. 159.
72 Walter Benjamin, "Das Kunstwerk im Zeitalter seiner technischen Reproduzierbarkeit," *Gesammelte Schriften*, Vol. I, No. 2. (Frankfurt, 1974), pp. 471–509, p. 506.
73 On this theme, see Rainer Stommer, *Die inszenierte Volksgemeinschaft. Die "Thing-Bewegung" im Dritten Reich* (Marburg, 1985), p. 91, p. 93f.
74 Heuel, *Der umworbene Stand*, p. 409ff.; see also Artur Axmann, *Der Reichsberufswettkampf* (Berlin, 1938).
75 *Der Parteitag der Arbeit, vom 6. bis 13. September 1937. Offizieller Bericht über den Verlauf des Reichsparteitages mit sämtlichen Kongressreden* (München, 1938), p. 13ff., See also the cinematic representation of all "Party Days" after 1934, the effects of which can scarcely be overestimated; Martin Loiperdinger, *Der Parteitagsfilm. "Der Triumph des Willens" von Leni Riefenstahl. Rituale der Mobilmachung* (Opladen, 1987).
76 Martin Rüther. "Zur Sozialpolitik bei Klöckner-Humboldt-Deutz während des Nationalsozialismus: "Die Masse der Arbeiterschaft muss ausgespalten werden," in *Zeitschrift für Unternehmensgeschichte*, Vol. 33, 1988, pp. 81–117, p. 98ff. In November 1940, the "factory cell ombudsman" of the machine building shop 21 at Krupp used the reference to "self-calculation and self-checking" at Deutz to protest against the introduction of a stamping system at the beginning and the end of a particular piece-work job. He was nevertheless unsuccessful; see Historisches Archiv Krupp WA 41/6–10.
77 See Josef Winschuh, *Industrievolk an der Ruhr* (Oldenburg/Berlin, 1935); Peter Schirmbeck, *Adel der Arbeit. Der Arbeiter in der Kunst der NS-Zeit* (Marburg, 1984); see Krupp, *Zeitschrift der Kruppschen Betriebsgemeinschaft*, from issue 26 (1933/4); for example, issue 30 (1938/9), p. 161ff., p. 273; see also the text and picture book by Heinrich Hauser, *Opel, ein deutsches Tor zur Welt* (Frankfurt, 1937) and Hauser, *Im Kraftfeld von Rüsselsheim* (München, 1940); see also Thomas Lange, "Literatur des technokratischen Bewusstseins," *Lili. Zeitschrift für Literaturwissenschaft und Linguistik*, No. 40, 1989,

pp. 52–81, p. 61ff; see the photographic illustrations in Axmann, *Reichsberufswettkampf*, after pp. 168, 232, 321, 344; only word-pictures, which attempt to be all the more "poetic," can be found in Heinz Kindermann (ed.), *Ruf der Arbeit* (Berlin, 1942).

3

ANTINATALISM, MATERNITY AND PATERNITY IN NATIONAL SOCIALIST RACISM

Gisela Bock

Women's history is a relatively recent development in Germany but it has already begun to ask new questions about the the Third Reich. Did women play an active role in this, as in any other period of German history? If so, does this mean that German women must also share a certain measure of responsibility for Nazism's crimes? Or, as Gisela Bock asserts in the following article, were all women in the Third Reich the "victims" of a "sexist-racist" male regime which reduced women to the status of mere "objects."

In this essay, Bock examines those aspects of Nazi rule which she thinks most directly affected women – the cluster of measures that constituted a racist population policy. Although Nazism has sometimes been seen as a pronatalist regime, Bock argues that the essence of the population policies pursued by the Nazis were primarily antinatalist. The Nazis did not believe that all German women possessed the genetic capacity to produce desirable children and the regime focussed more of its attention on preventing the births of "inferior" or "worthless" children than on promoting population increase. The Nazis sought to purify the next generation of the Aryan race by forced sterilization and compulsory abortions. Of course, men, as well as women, whom the Nazis judged to be genetically inferior were also subjected to forced sterilization, yet Bock argues that women suffered more, both physically and emotionally, from the destruction of their ability to have children.

After the war began, Nazi antinatalism took on even more radical and destructive forms, aimed almost exclusively, Bock argues, at women. Nazi doctors conducted brutal experiments on Jewish and "Gypsy" women in concentration camps to find a cheap, quick way of

110

sterilizing hundreds of thousands of ethnically and eugenically "inferior" women. Bock also argues that sterilization policy was a forerunner of the Nazi "euthanasia actions" after 1939. In turn, the euthanasia program paved the way to the Holocaust itself, producing both the technology and the mentalities required for the systematic industrial annihilation of millions of Jews, the great majority of whom, Bock points out, were also women and children. Bock thus thinks that Nazism drew the gender lines quite brutally. The "racial struggle" that was the essence of Nazism, was waged by "men not just against men – such as in a traditional military war – but also against women as mothers" (p. 132).

* * *

Understanding the policy of the National Socialist regime towards women as mothers within a European perspective requires this issue to be placed in a context which allows the identification of similarities as well as differences between the National Socialist experience and that of other European countries. This can best be approached by examining three broad areas of research: first, those features of National Socialism which come close to, or are at least comparable with other countries' welfare reforms and which allow us to see Nazi Germany as a kind of welfare state (or as a society in the process of "modernization");[1] yet studies of the emergence of the European welfare states usually do not include women- and family-related National Socialist policies such as the introduction of child allowances in 1935/6. Second, there is the extreme opposite of social reform, i.e. National Socialist racism. Its various forms – particularly anti-Jewish and anti-Gypsy policy, race hygiene or eugenics – illustrate that in this respect National Socialism was unique, despite the fact that racism was an international phenomenon. It was unique most of all because, from its rise to power in 1933, it began to institutionalize racism at the level of the state, through innumerable laws and decrees which discriminated against those considered to be "racially inferior." National Socialism transformed racism into a state-sponsored race policy, and put into practice all its forms to a degree unheard of before and after. In this field too, women-related policies are rarely considered, even though women were half of all victims. Third, there is a growing body of research on women under

111

National Socialism and the regime's policy towards them. Its most salient common assumption is that National Socialism meant pronatalism and brought a cult of motherhood, that it used propaganda, incentives, and even force in order to have all women bear as many children as possible and to keep them out of employment for the sake of motherhood. Whereas research on National Socialist racism usually does not deal with women, research in women's history usually does not deal with National Socialist racism, and female victims of racism are mentioned marginally at best.

Yet, the number of such women – and the issue is, of course, not only one of numbers – is conspicuous. For the purpose of raising the population's "quality," of "race regeneration" or "racial uplift" (*Aufartung*), the National Socialist state pursued a policy of birth-prevention or antinatalism: through compulsory mass sterilization from 1933 on, through non-voluntary abortion from 1935 on, through marriage restrictions from 1935 on, through mass murder and genocide after 1939. Between 1933 and 1945, almost 200,000 women, 1 per cent of those of childbearing age, were sterilized on eugenic grounds. About 200,000 German Jewish women were exiled and almost 100,000 killed. Probably over 80,000 female inmates of psychiatric institutions and several million non-German Jewish women were killed in the massacres during the Second World War, and in addition an unknown number of non-Jewish non-German women. During the war, there were over 2 million non-German women who had to perform forced labour in Germany and on whom, particularly on those from Eastern Europe, hundreds of thousands of abortions and sterilizations were performed.

This chapter explores some of the features of National Socialist welfare policies, race policies and gender policies which focused on women as mothers and potential mothers. The first section deals with National Socialist racism in its form of antinatalism, of the prevention of "inferior offspring" for the purpose of "racial uplift." It shows that compulsory sterilization, though it was performed on both sexes, had in many respects different social and cultural meanings for women and men. The second section deals with National Socialist welfare reforms concerning procreation and the family. It shows that the view of National Socialist gender policies as essentially consisting of "pronatalism and a cult of motherhood" is largely a myth. Whereas Nazi antinatalism was revolutionary, unique and efficient, Nazi pro-natalism used largely traditional means; where it was novel, it resembled comparable family-centred welfare reforms in other European countries. The third section deals with some aspects of motherhood – or rather, of its opposite – in the massacres of the "race struggle" (*Rassenkampf*) during the second half of the regime.

In different ways, the three sections deal with a number of more general assumptions and results. First, just as National Socialist race policy was not gender-neutral, so National Socialist gender policy was not race-neutral. Second, the National Socialist welfare measures were comparable to those introduced in other countries around the same time, but they differed from them in important respects. They did not focus on mothers but on fathers, and most importantly, they were never universalized, because they had a definite limit in race policy which excluded the "inferior" from their benefits. Third, this limit, the inner dynamics of National Socialism and the comparison with other countries show that race policies were more crucial to National Socialism than were welfare policies, and that just as racism was at the centre of Nazi policies in general, it was also at the centre of Nazi policies toward women.

STERILIZATION POLICY OR ANTINATALISM FOR "RACE REGENERATION"

In June 1933, five months after Hitler came to power, his Minister of the Interior, Wilhelm Frick, gave a programmatic and frequently quoted speech on "population and race policy." It was intended to pave the way for the imminent sterilization law which had been prepared for by years of eugenic propaganda. Eugenic and compulsory sterilization had been advocated not only by National Socialists, but also – albeit for different reasons, though always in view of a perfect society – by many members of other political affiliations, including socialists and some radical feminists (not however by the Catholic Centre Party, because of the Pope's encyclical *Casti Connubi* of 1930 which spoke out against all artificial birth control, nor by moderate feminists such as Gertrud Bäumer, who in 1931 had taken a firm stand against eugenics, *Aufartung* and raising the population's "quantity and quality").[2]

Frick unrolled a "dismal picture." He pointed to the "cultural and ethnic decline," demonstrated by over a million people with "hereditary physical and mental diseases," "feeble-minded and inferior" people from whom "progeny is no longer desired," especially not where they show "above-average procreation." He went on to estimate that 20 per cent of the German population, i.e. another 11 million, were undesirable as mothers or fathers. He concluded that "in order to increase the number of hereditarily healthy progeny, we have first of all the duty to prevent the procreation of the hereditarily unfit." This project of state-run birth control became law on 14 July 1933, introducing compulsory sterilization. The official commentary stressed that "biologically inferior hereditary material" was to be "eradicated (*ausgemerzt*)," specifically among the "innumerable inferior and hereditarily tainted" people who "procreate without inhibition (*hemmunglos*)"; sterilization "should bring about a gradual cleansing of the people's body (*Volkskörper*)," and around 1.5 million people were to be sterilized, 400,000 in the short term. In fact, this was the number of those sterilized over the next decade, half men and half women, as well as an unknown but probably considerable number outside the law.[3]

All the sterilizations were compulsory; none came about by the free will of a sterilized person. Voluntary sterilization was forbidden by the same law (article 14), and frequently the police were employed, a possibility laid down in the law itself (article 12) and applied in 3–30 per cent of the cases, depending on regional variations. Almost all the sterilized were selected by doctors, psychiatrists, and other officials. Sterilization was decided by specially created courts, on which sat doctors, psychiatrists, anthropologists, experts in human genetics and jurists. Thus, birth control was not outlawed but introduced by law, for people considered to be of "inferior value" (*minderwertig*). Article 1 specified the kinds of "inferiority." They were described essentially in psychiatric terms, as intellectual and emotional "departures from the norm" which had been elaborated and declared as hereditary, since around 1900, by the science and policy of "race hygiene," "social hygiene," "procreation hygiene," "eugenics," "human genetics" or *Erb- und Rassenpflege*. Ninety-six per cent of the sterilizations were based on (in order of frequency) real or alleged feeble-mindedness, schizophrenia, epilepsy and manic-depressive derangement; the others on real or alleged blindness, deafness, "bodily malformation," St Vitus' dance and alcoholism. The sterilized were from all social classes and occupational groups, and their respective proportion corresponded to that in society at large. The quantitatively and strategically most important group were the "feeble-minded." They made up some two-thirds of all those sterilized, and almost two-thirds of them were women.[4]

The sterilization law did not provide for the sterilization exclusively of Jews, Gypsies, Blacks and other "alien" races but they were, of course, included; moreover, particularly Gypsies and Black people were sterilized both within and outside the 1933 law. None the less, the sterilization policy – and race hygiene as a whole – was a form of racism and an integral component of National Socialist racism. For racism means not only discrimination of "alien" races or peoples, but also the "regeneration" of one's own people, in so far as that was aimed at through discrimination of the "biologically inferior" among one's own people. For the theoreticians and practitioners of racism the "master race" was not already there, but had to be produced. In *Mein Kampf* Hitler had summarized current race theory in the mid-twenties: just as "one people is not equal to another," so "one person is not equal to another within one *Volksgemeinschaft* (ethnic community)," and therefore "the individuals within a *Volksgemeinschaft*" must be differently "evaluated," especially as regards the right to have children. He recommended the sterilization of "millions" of people. Later, a jurist in the Reich Ministry of the Interior summarized: "The German race question consists primarily in the Jewish question. In the second place, yet not less important, there is the Gypsy question.... But degenerative effects on the racial body may arise not only from outside, from members of alien races, but also from inside, through unrestricted procreation of inferior hereditary material." Like all racism, eugenics or sterilization racism used social and cultural criteria to define the "alien," "different," "sick," "inferior": namely emotional, physical, moral and intellectual criteria. The common denominator of all forms of National Socialist racism was the definition and treatment of human beings according to a differing "value" defined and ascribed by other human beings. The value criteria were declared to be "biology," as was the social and cultural field in which they were embodied: descent and procreation. The

115

common denominator not of all forms of Nazi racism but of its most dramatic forms was the attempt to "solve" social and cultural problems with means that were also called "biology": namely by intervening with body and life. Thus, in 1936 Himmler praised the sterilization law to the Hitler Youth: "Germans . . . have once again learned . . . to recognize bodies and to bring up this godgiven body and our godgiven blood and race according to its value or lack of value."[5]

The sterilization law was one of the first manifestations of National Socialist racism on a national and state level. Officials of the Reich Ministry of the Interior declared, referring to the sterilization law, that "the private is political" and that the decision on the dividing line between the private and the political is itself a political decision. In one respect, the sterilization law went even further than the anti-Jewish laws of 1933, since it ordered compulsory bodily intervention and was thereby the first of the Nazi measures that sought to solve social and cultural problems by "biological" means. The sterilization law, just as the anti-Jewish laws, made a political reality of the classical racist demand, proclaimed in Germany specifically by eugenicists: "unequal value, unequal rights" (*ungleicher Wert, ungleiche Rechte*).[6] For the "valuable" of both sexes sterilization was forbidden, and for the "inferior" of both sexes it was obligatory. For National Socialism, modern antinatalism took precedence over old-fashioned pronatalism, in terms of chronology as well as in terms of principle.

The sterilization law was officially proclaimed as embodying the "primacy of the state over the sphere of life, marriage and family"[7] and this primacy was particularly significant for women. All state interventions in the giving and maintaining of life, in begetting, bearing and rearing children, are important to women, and often more important than for men; their meaning for women may be different from that for men. In fact, sterilization racism, although it affected as many men as women, was none the less anything but gender-neutral. This is apparent above all from the three essential features of sterilization: bodily intervention, childlessness, and separation of sexuality and procreation. Other important gender differences included in the criteria for selecting those who were not to have children and the propaganda for sterilization.

For women, by contrast with men, the intervention meant a

major operation with full anaesthesia, abdominal incision and the concomitant risk. Shortly before the sterilization law was enacted, there was a debate as to whether such intervention on hundreds of thousands of women could be risked. But then the Propaganda Ministry announced that just as many women as men would have to be sterilized. The decision for mass compulsory sterilization of women meant violent intervention not only with the female body but also with female life. Probably about 5,000 people died as a result of sterilization, and whilst women made up only half of the sterilized, they were about 90 per cent of those who died of sterilization. A large number of them died because they resisted sterilization right up to the operating table and rejected what had happened even after operation. An unknown number of people, mainly women, committed suicide because of sterilization.[8] Hence, the first scientifically planned and bureaucratically executed massacre of the National Socialist state was the result of antinatalism, and women were its chief victims.

Childlessness has a different meaning for women and for men, just as having children does. Therefore, their reactions and forms of resistance to sterilization differed in many respects. Women as well as men protested against their stigmatization as "second-class human beings" – in thousands of letters to the sterilization courts that have been preserved – but women complained of the resulting childlessness far oftener than men, especially young women. Many tried to get pregnant before sterilization, and this resistance was important enough for the authorities to give the phenomenon a special name: (*Trotzschwangerschaften*) ("protest pregnancies"). For instance, one girl said that she had got pregnant in order "to show the state that I won't go along with this." The protest pregnancies were an important reason for extending the sterilization law, in 1935, into an abortion law: now abortions could also be performed for race hygiene reasons. In the case of such an abortion, sterilization also was compulsory.[9]

The separation of sexuality and procreation had a differing meaning for men and women. One doctor wrote about sterilized men in 1936: "Happy that nothing can happen to them any more, that neither condoms nor douches are necessary, they fulfil their marital duties without restraint." In relation to women it was another aspect of sexuality that was publicly discussed in the professional press. Tens of thousands of women who, as one of them asserted, did not "care at all about men" and had never had sexual intercourse were sterilized because, according to the opinion of the (exclusively male) jurists and doctors, the possibility of pregnancy through rape had to be taken into account. Therefore, the commentary to the law explicity laid it down that "a different assessment of the danger of procreation is necessary for men and for women," and in sterilization verdicts the following principle regularly appeared, and was prescribed by government decree in 1936: "In the case of the female hereditarily sick, the possibility of abuse against her will must be taken into account." Frequently compulsory sterilization was propagated as a means of preventing the "consequence" of a potential rape, namely pregnancy. The risk of "inferior" women being raped seemed to male contemporaries to be so high as to be a ground for the sterilization of women. In fact, sterilized women became objects of sexual abuse, both in the countryside, where sterilization quickly became generally known, and in cities, where sometimes soldiers or factory workers asked each other "on Mondays": "Did you not find a sterilized woman for the weekend?"[10]

The psychiatric diagnoses were largely gender-based. Those for women measured their "departure from the norm" against the norms for the female sex, and those for men against the norms for the male sex. To determine female "inferiority," heterosexual behaviour was regularly investigated, and negatively evaluated when the women frequently changed their sexual partner or when they had more than one illegitimate child. Men were less investigated on this issue, and the findings had no particular weight in the sterilization verdict. Women, not men, were tested as to their capacity and inclination for housework, for childrearing (also in the case of childless women) as well as to their capacity and inclination for employment. Men were assessed mostly for their work behaviour. The decisive criterion came to be *Lebensbewährung* ("conduct of life"), again prescribed by a government decree.[11]

These were, of course, not genetic but social and cultural criteria, because the sexes are social and cultural entities (like race or ethnicity). These sociocultural diagnoses were the reason why most of the women and more women than men, were sterilized for "feeble-mindedness." Thus, for instance, the sterilization verdict on Mrs Schmidt, mother of ten children, stated that while her "feeble-mindedness" had not actually been proved, she nevertheless "is to a quite unusual extent unclean and neglectful, and shockingly neglects her children and the household. Such uncleanness and neglect is however not conceivable with a more or less mentally normally disposed person." About 10 per cent of the sterilization trials ended with acquittal: in the case of women, when they could prove that they did their work, inside and outside the home, to the satisfaction of the doctors and lawyers of the sterilization court (who often came to inspect the household during the trial). This could not be shown by Luise Müller: she was condemned to sterilization because, according to the court decision, "her knowledge is confined to mechanically acquired information; she can indicate how to prepare various foodstuffs such as pudding, bread soup or rice soup, but only in the way usual at home."[12]

The sterilization policy was not carried on secretly – as was the later extermination policy – but almost entirely in public view. The population was virtually bombarded with antinatalist propaganda in the 1930s, and this propaganda was often directed specifically at the female sex. It contrasted starkly with the earlier feminist view on motherhood and the female sex. One of the official Nazi brochures, distributed in millions of copies in 1934, explained to women that their task was not prolific progagation but "regeneration." The female characteristic of maternalism (*Mütterlichkeit*) became the object of racist polemic and was treated as contemptible "sentimental humanitarianism" (*Gefühlsduselei*). Female gender difference, femininity and maternalism were to come to an end in National Socialist racism – even among "valuable" women. The Berlin doctor Agnes Bluhm, one of the early race hygienicists, wrote in 1934 in the journal of the dissolved Federation of German Women's Associations, *Die Frau*, about the "danger arising for women precisely from their *Mütterlichkeit*," since maternalism, "like any egoism, acts against the race." Like many male eugenicists, she polemicized against the "female instinct to care for all those in need of help." Of the fact that "woman, because of her physical and mental characteristics, is particularly close to all living beings, and has a particular inclination towards all living beings," it was said that there was "scarcely any worse sin against nature." In one women's magazine[13] the objection that

119

with sterilization "the National Socialist state was going against the laws of nature" was stated to be a false conclusion, because

> Until National Socialist rule, the German people neglected the laws of nature. . . . It not only disregarded the laws of heredity, of selection and of eradication (*Auslese und Ausmerze*), but directly opposed them, by not only keeping the unfit alive at the cost of the healthy, but even guaranteeing their procreation. . . . Every hereditarily sick German woman will, once she realizes this, take this operation upon herself in order to keep her whole race healthy. "But doesn't that mean she's sinning against life?" . . . What does life mean then? Just go to a lunatic asylum . . .

National Socialists by no means wanted children at any cost and they never propagated the slogan "Kinder, Küche, Kirche" which has been so often, but wrongly, ascribed to them. The biblical "Be fruitful and multiply" was often and explicitly rejected, as well as the assumption that "the State allegedly wants children at all costs." Indeed, this assumption was rejected in the propaganda and instructions from Goebbels' Ministry for Propaganda: "The goal is not: 'children at any cost,' but: 'racially worthy, physically and mentally unaffected childen of German families.' " An expert on large families stressed that "childbearing in itself is, from the race viewpoint, far from being a merit." Instead the point was "whether the biological basis," namely the hereditary value, was there "which alone makes many children into a value for the race."[14] In fact, not just a small minority of (sterilized) women were undesired as mothers, but somewhere between 10 and 30 per cent depending on the author of the estimate. On the other hand, those women who were considered desirable mothers were not a majority, but also a minority of about 10 to 30 per cent. The blood-and-soil ideologue Darré in a well-known publication divided women into four classes: those in the first should be encouraged to marry and have children; children of the second group, though not to be encouraged, were not objectionable; the third group should be allowed to marry, but where possible be sterilized beforehand; the fourth group should not marry and be sterilized at any cost. The head of the Party Race Policy Office considered it as "utopian" and "overoptimistic" to think that "almost all German women are worthy of procreation," and one of the most important sterilization promoters emphasized that even "those who are not hereditarily sick within the meaning of the sterilization law need by no means be worthy of procreation."[15] Never in history had there been a state which in theory, propaganda and practice pursued an antinatalist policy of such dimensions.

PRONATALISM, SOCIAL REFORM AND THE NATIONAL SOCIALIST WELFARE STATE

What is then the substance of the view which identifies National Socialist birth and gender policy as essentially pronatalist, as encouragement, incentive, or even compulsion to bear children, as a cult of motherhood and as an attack on women's employment for the sake of motherhood? How did National Socialism conceive of gender relations in this area, and what are the links between these issues and its race policy?

Again, current assumptions need to be revised. In Nazi Germany, as in other countries that were hit by the deep economic depression of the 1930s, the early polemics of Nazis and non-Nazis against women's employment remained largely ineffective. There were no Nazi laws against it, nor compulsory or mass firing of women from their jobs. Women's employment increased after 1933 (even though somewhat less than men's), and before as well as during the Nazi regime it was higher than in most western countries. The number of officially registered employed women rose from 11.5 million in 1933, when it made up 36 per cent of all employed persons and 48 per cent of all women between the ages of 15 and 60 years, to 12.8 million in early 1939 (within the German territory of 1937, but if most annexed territories are included, the number is 14.6 million), with the corresponding figures of 37 per cent and 50 per cent. In 1944, 14.9 million German women were employed (including Austria), making up 53 per cent of the German civilian labour force and well over half of all German women between 15 and 60 years.[16]

Along with the development from low employment to full employment to labour scarcity, largely because of the expansion of war industry, the number of female industrial workers increased by 28.5 per cent between 1933 (1.2 million) and 1936 (1.55 million), and by a further 19.2 per cent in the following two years. Not only did the number of employed single women rise, but even more that of married women and mothers. Between the Weimar period and the time before World War II, the number of married women in the labour force, and their proportion of all employed women, rose dramatically, and it almost doubled for married female workers in industry (21.4 per cent in 1925, 28.2 per cent in 1933 and 41.3 per cent in 1939; all married employed women: 31 per cent in 1925, 37 per cent in 1933, and 46 per cent in 1939). In 1939, more than 24 per cent of all employed women had children, and the married ones among them made up 51 per cent of all married employed women. As usual in the case of women, an unknown but considerable number must be taken into account as (more or less gainfully) employed outside official registration. During World War II, altogether about 2.5 million foreign women were brought to work, mostly by force, in German industry and agriculture to substitute – along with male foreign civilian workers and prisoners of war – for German men who were now at the battle lines. The lower their "racial value," the higher was the proportion of women among these workers and the heavier their work; among the Russian civilian workers, 51 per cent were women, and 58 per cent of all Russians working in the munitions industries were women.

The prohibition of free abortion through the old section 218 of the Penal Code was tightened up in 1933, but the additional stringency (sections 219 and 220) had little effect; what was instead effective was the introduction of legal eugenic and medical indications for abortion in 1935. The number of women on whom eugenic abortions were performed for the sake of the *Volkskörper*, often against their will and without their consent or knowledge and always combined with compulsory sterilization, was about 30,000. Voluntary abortions continued to take place, despite difficult conditions, at hundreds of thousands per year. By contrast with what is frequently asserted, the number of convictions for free and illegal abortion under section 218 did not rise during National Socialism, but fell by about one-sixth by comparison with the Weimar Republic (from 1923–32: 47,487 to 1933–42: 39,902).[17] The number of women who were forced to abort against their will or without their consent and who were compulsorily sterilized is over ten times as high as the number of the women convicted under section 218. During this period,

Gebärzwang (compulsory childbearing) did not go beyond what was usual before 1933, after 1945 or in other countries. National Socialist compulsion and terror was reserved for antinatalism, not for pronatalism. National Socialism did not nationalize the birth question, as often asserted, by compelling women into childbearing, but by preventing women from childbearing.

Instead, an increase in births was one of the goals of state welfare measures that were to assist those who wanted to have children, at a time when politicians still believed, or at least hoped, that economic support might influence men's and women's choice to have children. On the level of central government, they consisted mainly in three social reforms that were part of the much-publicized, largely tax-funded *Familienlastenausgleich* (relief of family burdens) which no longer conceived of family subsidies as poor relief but as independent state benefits. In 1933, marriage loans were introduced for husbands whose wife had been employed and gave up her job upon marriage (but from 1936 on, with full employment, she could keep it and was often pressed to do so). They were not paid in cash, but in the form of coupons to be used for the purchase of furniture and household equipment, and they were to be repaid at a modest interest and to be forgone by one-fourth per birth, i.e. up to the birth of four children (unless they were spaced with longer intervals, during which interest had to be paid). One of the main objectives of this loan was to lower the male marriage age and therefore men's need for prostitution. Second, in 1934 and 1939 the income tax was reformed to give heads of household increasing exemption amounts for spouse and children, and the income tax for the childless (couples as well as single men and women) was raised. Third, monthly state child allowances of 10 marks were introduced in 1936, payable from the fifth, three years later from the third child on. Initially, they were a form of poor relief, to be paid only to those below a certain income level; later on, the income limit was abolished. In international comparison,[18] such measures were not, or did not remain, unique: marriage loans were introduced in Italy, Sweden and Spain during the 1930s, and similar tax reforms and child allowances in most European countries between the late 1920s and the late 1940s. All national types of family allowances, including the German ones (but apparently with the exception of the French ones), shared one feature: they were not

123

to cover the costs of childbearing and raising, and particularly National Socialists warned that this should "not become a profitable business." But it deserves to be underlined that in most other countries child allowances were paid from the first or second child on.

None the less, National Socialist state subsidies differed from others in two major respects. One of them (although it resembled the model of the two other masculinist dictatorships, Italy and Spain) was their combination with sexism: they privileged fathers over mothers. The principle was laid down by a Nazi minister, Hans Frank, when he declared that "the concept of fatherhood has been handed down through age-old processes of natural law" and "the concept of father is unambiguous and must be placed at the centre of the financial measures." Here it was fatherhood, not motherhood, that was glorified as "nature": a nature, however, that did not exclude economic rewards – as in the case of women's nature – but included them. In Germany, this view may have been reinforced by current racial visions of "nordic patriarchalism" (*vaterrechtlicher Geist der nordischen Rasse*). It was the prospective husband who was entitled to the marriage loan. Family allowances went not to mothers, but to fathers – different from Britain, Sweden, Norway and in part also from France. German single mothers received child allowances only if the father of their children was known to the authorities. The tax rebates for the head of household brought by far the most substantial benefits, particularly for husbands in the upper income brackets. The husband's tax exemption for children was less significant than that for his wife: it was he who was being paid by the state for her housework (Goebbels had momentarily polemicized against the high rate of the husband's wife rebate).[19]

The "relief of family burdens" was meant to balance out, not the differing burdens of fathers and mothers, but the differing burdens of bachelors and fathers, so that – in the words of the State Secretary to the Ministry of Finance, praised by the head of the Party Race Policy Office – "a man will no longer be materially or morally worse off in competition with the so-called clever bachelor, merely because he has done his duty to his nation." The "duty" of begetting was considered more valuable than that of bearing and rearing children, women's contribution to procreation inferior to men's. This was not an old-fashioned cult of motherhood, but a modern cult of father-hood. Fatherhood deserved economic rewards from the state, motherhood was seen as incompatible with them. Accordingly, the male leader of the party's welfare organization (*Nationalsozialistische Volkswohlfahrt*, NSV) and its section "Mother and Child" condemned the "reward motive" (*Lohnmotiv*) of "selfish love" and stressed that

> there is no more beautiful image of selfless service than that of a mother with her children. She continues to care and to give, to show her child love upon love, never thinking whether she is going to get anything in return. . . . In the very moment she began to calculate returns, she would cease to be a good mother.[20]

The cult of motherhood was to some extent propaganda and ritual, the cult of fatherhood was propaganda and tough state policy. Of course it was not the family subsidies as such that were anti-woman, but the fact that they were refused to mothers and houseworkers.

None the less, it was the NSV section "Mother and Child" that supported mothers with many children, pregnant women and unmarried mothers, helping them to find employment, establishing kindergartens and offering vacations from home – not, however, as a right, but as poor relief, not as a new civic recognition by the state as in the case of fathers (and as to some degree in the case of the state-run Italian ONMI), but as a traditional handout.[21] Nazi women's organizations also sup-ported "valuable" mothers, but since they had no funds to offer, they offered courses on baby care. Whereas the NSV's support focused on the poor among the "valuable" and the women's organizations on women of all classes, and whereas single mothers with more than one child risked being taken to a steril-ization court, in 1936 Himmler created the *Lebensborn* organiza-tion in order to assist those mothers who bore children by men who were thought to belong to the racial elite, mostly SS-men. The *Lebensborn* was not an institution for forced breeding nor an SS bordello. It established well-furnished maternity hos-pitals (six in Germany, later nine in Norway, one in Belgium and one in France), mostly in the countryside. In Germany, about 7,000–8,000 women gave birth in such homes over the nine years of the *Lebensborn*'s existence (plus, 6,000 in Norway during the war), and about 55 per cent of them were single mothers. Before being admitted to the maternity homes, they were carefully selected, often by Himmler himself, according to the ethnic and eugenic credentials of the father of their child and of their own. But from 1939 on, the *Lebensborn* homes in Germany were used for those "valuable" children of the conquered territories in the East whose parents had been killed or who had been kidnapped in the course of Himmler's "search for nordic blood."[22]

For most women, there were only the cheap honours of Mother's Day and – for those with four children or more – the mother cross; the former was introduced in the 1920s (as in many other countries), the latter in 1939, years after the father-centred reforms, upon the French model of 1920 (in 1944 to be imitated in the Soviet Union). Even though the Nazi state enacted no law in favour of mothers as such, ten years after its beginnings, in 1942, it considerably improved the 1927 law for the protection of those pregnant women and young mothers who were employed – with the exception of Jewish, Polish and Russian women – in order to encourage them to combine employment and motherhood, particularly in war-work, but also in a long-term perspective. Maternity leave of six weeks before and six weeks after parturition remained as established in 1927 and was combined with a maternity benefit amounting to the full wage; agricultural and domestic workers were finally included, and the job continued to be protected against dismissal during pregnancy and four months after. The major innovation of the law was its provision for childcare services. However, maternity benefits were reserved to employed mothers only. Mothers were awarded state recognition and benefits only if they worked in addition outside their home. When in 1942 Robert Ley, the leader of the German Labour Front (the Nazi surrogate union) proposed to extend maternity benefits to non-employed women too, particularly the hard-working working-class mothers, Hitler rejected the proposal on the grounds that the state budget was needed for the "difficult tasks" of the next years:[23] the costs of military and non-military massacres.

The effect of pronatalist propaganda and of those welfare measures which included pronatalist goals was limited. The figures for the birth-rate (in 1933 they were among the lowest in Europe, along with Britain and Austria) increased by about one-third until 1936 (from a net reproduction rate of 0.7 to one of 0.9); then they remained almost stagnant, reaching no more than the level of the late 1920s, which had long been deplored as an expression of "birth-strike" and "race suicide," and they dropped again during World War II. Most of the increase was due to couples who had not been able to have the children they wanted because of depression and epidemics in the early 1930s and who made up for it when employment and income increased. The proportion of married women with four or more children (*viz.* the number proposed by Nazi demographers as "valuable" women's "duty") among all married women declined from 25 per cent in 1933 to 21 per cent in 1939. Those who married and had children from 1933 on limited their number to one, two or three children and thus followed the trend which had characterized Germany, as well as other industrialized countries, before the Nazi regime. The family benefits contributed not to an increase in births (even less the mother cross) but, at least before the war, to a growing belief in the capacity of the Nazi regime to overcome the depression. Whereas Nazi politicians had hoped that state welfare for children would increase their number, most men and women perceived it simply as a social reform that compensated for their low income and helped them survive with the children they wanted. Some women, including some Nazi women, protested openly against the reinforcement of male dominance through father-centred benefits, but such voices were silent after 1934.[24]

The behaviour of three particular groups illustrates both the specificity and the limits of the Nazi type of pronatalism as well as some motives for having children which usually remain hidden behind demographic figures. The leading Party functionaries, i.e. those "valuable" Germans who were the real objectives of pronatalism and who were closest to National Socialism, demonstrated that they believed in the pronatalist goals, if at all, only for others, but not for themselves. Nazi demographers deplored that of those functionaries who had married between 1933 and 1937, 18 per cent were still childless in 1939, 42 per cent had one child and 29 per cent had two children. Among the all-male SS members, 61 per cent were unmarried in 1942, and the married ones had 1.1 children on average; the same was true for medical doctors, who were the professional group with the highest membership figures in the party and the SS.

Obviously, there was an inverse relationship between adherence to National Socialism among the elite and the number of their children.[25] On the other side, one statistical group had a clearly above-average number of children: those whose claim for marriage loans and child allowances was rejected because of their "disorderly' conduct and their classification as "large asocial families." In respect of such people, Nazi demographers also deplored that up to half of the families with above-average numbers of children were to be considered undesirable.[26] The third group are those who produced two minor, but conspicuous, baby booms during World War II, when the average figures were declining, which were often noted and explained by contemporaries. In 1939, employed women, particularly of the working class, were forbidden to quit their job because they were urgently needed for the war economy – unless they were pregnant. Pregnant women and young mothers were also exempted from the labour conscription introduced in 1943. On both occasions, many women preferred to have children instead of working for the war, and this was one major reason why between 1939 and 1941, the number of employed women decreased by 500,000. All three groups illustrate – in different ways and to different degrees – that in Nazi Germany, the refusal to procreate and the use of contraceptives and abortion was not, as had been argued for other countries, an indication of political opposition.[27]

The second group is a pointer to the second outstanding feature of National Socialist state family benefits: their combination with racism. Race policy distinguished them from those in all other countries. None of the Nazi benefits was meant to be universally applied (not even to men and despite the abolition of the upper income limit), since those classified as *minderwertig* were excluded: parents or children who were considered eugenically or ethnically "unfit" – Jews (to whom even family-related tax rebates were denied), Gypsies, the physically, emotionally and mentally handicapped (particularly, but not only, the sterilized), "asocials," political opponents, labourers from eastern Europe. For instance, whereas in other countries and in Germany before 1933, a handicapped child was a reason for extending child benefits beyond the usual age limit, in Nazi Germany it was a reason for excluding it, and its parents,

128

entirely.[28] With respect to the "inferior," National Socialism pursued a policy not of family welfare, but of family destruction.

Government subsidies for marriage and procreation were not in themselves part of sexism and racism. They were a component of the emerging modern welfare states which for the first time in history subsidised the family, the sphere of male reproduction and female housework. But National Socialism combined them with sexism and with racism by privileging men over women and "valuable German" men over "racially inferior" men. The combination of the *Familienlastenausgleich* with racism was specific and unique to National Socialism; its combination with sexism was specific to it, as well as to other European dictatorships, and it distinguished them from the European democracies. Hence National Socialist birth and family policy consisted not of "pronatalism and a cult of motherhood," but of antinatalism and a cult of fatherhood and masculinity. Not a deterministic, but a historical continuity leads from there to the escalation of racism in the 1940s.

FROM ANTINATALISM TO GENOCIDE

During World War II, it was not maternity but its very opposite that came to play a significant role in the race policy of those years, including its murderous forms. The antinatalist "primacy of the state in the sphere of life" was now extended to a number of women who were far from being a minority and, more importantly, it implied the primacy of the state in the sphere of death.

When war was declared in 1939, legal sterilization was curtailed, mainly in order to liberate work-forces for war and massacre. But antinatalism took on other forms, directed almost exclusively against women. Early in the war, Polish women were sent back east upon pregnancy, and it seems that many deliberately took advantage of this method to be relieved from forced labour: their gesture was, again, babies rather than warwork. But from 1941 on, Russian and Polish women had to stay despite pregnancy, were encouraged and often forced to undergo an abortion, sometimes also sterilization, and often their children were taken away from them, in a complex interplay between Himmler's race experts, labour offices, employers and the medical profession. Particularly Russian women were purposefully put to work at "men's jobs" in the munitions industry so as to bring about miscarriages: a policy of war-work against babies. The plans for the conquered Eastern territories (particularly the *Generalplan Ost*) included a large number of carefully elaborated, voluntary and non-voluntary methods of decreasing the number of children born, which aimed almost exclusively at mothers and potential mothers.[29]

Around the same time, sterilization experiments were pursued in some of the concentration camps, under Himmler's command, particularly in Auschwitz and Ravensbrück, on Jews and Gypsies. Originally they were meant for sterilizing the Jewish "half-breeds" (*Judenmischlinge*) who were exempted from extermination. After the failure of experiments with chemicals and X-rays on women as well as men, the experiments focused on women only, through injections in the uterus. They were performed by Clauberg, who since 1934 had gained experience in sterilizing women and was searching for a "bloodless" method, i.e. without operations, complications, resistance and death. His method had advanced so far by 1943 that he considered he was able, with a team of ten men, to sterilize up to a thousand women per day. By now, the new procedure was aimed not only at female Jewish "half-breeds," but also at mass sterilizations of other women, hopefully – in Clauberg's words – "during the usual gynaecological investigation familiar to every doctor."[30] Jewish and Gypsy women in the camps became the model for the fate that in future was to be earmarked for hundreds of thousands of ethnically and eugenically "inferior" women.

National Socialist sterilization policy before 1939, called "prevention of unworthy life," was also a "forerunner"[31] of the "annihilation of unworthy life" ("euthanasia" or "action T4"). It started in 1939, and up to 1945 around 200,000 ill, old and handicapped people, mostly inmates of psychiatric clinics, women as well as men, were killed after having been selected as "incurable" or unable to work. Moreover, all Jewish inmates were killed, even without such selection, and therefore T4 was also the first phase of the systematic massacre of the Jews. Special killing gas was used for the first time in T4. It was for various reasons that National Socialist antinatalism led to this policy of massacre. It grew out of a mentality which saw sterilization not as a private and free choice, but as a "humane" alternative to killing for the sake of the *Volkskörper*, as an "elimination without massacre,"[32] as a political substitute for "nature" which "naturally" (i.e. without modern charity and medicine) would have prevented "unfit" people from surviving. Second, it was in sterilization policy that medical and psychiatric experts had already become used to dealing with bodily intervention and death, mostly that of women. Third, the very first victims of the massacre were 5,000 handicapped children up to the age of three years, i.e. precisely those whose mothers (and fathers) could not be identified before birth, since 1937, by means of the abortion and sterilization policy. Finally, many of those who had been active in, or had advocated, the policy of compulsory sterilization, were also active in the massacre of the ill – mostly doctors and other medical personnel – and many of them also played an important role in the genocide of the Jews.

In late 1941, the T4 gas chambers and their male personnel were transferred from Germany to the newly constructed death camps in the occupied eastern territories where they served for the systematic and industrial killing of millions of Jews and Gypsies, women as well as men. This transfer was not only one of technology, but also one of mentality and strategy, and it had significant gender dimensions which have by far not yet been sufficiently explored. Hundreds of thousands of Jews had already been killed before gas was used, mostly through mass shooting. The SS-men involved seem to have had considerable "psychological difficulties," particularly with shooting women and children, as was underlined, for instance, by the commandant of the Auschwitz camp; even Himmler and Eichmann became sick while watching executions which included women and children, and they asked for new methods to be developed. Gas technology was introduced, from late 1941, not only as a means to accelerate mass killing, but also because a " 'suitable' method," a "humane" alternative to overt bloodshed, was required which would relieve the SS-men of their largely gender-specific scruples.[33] The first mobile gas vans were applied mainly, sometimes exclusively, for the killing of women and children; "men, women and children" is the frequent description of the gas van victims. In the early phase of the massacre of the Jewish ghetto population, the majority of the victims were women.[34] When the stable gas chambers in Auschwitz were functioning, from late 1941, it was mostly

131

Jewish women, and particularly those with children who were selected for death right upon arrival – "every Jewish child meant automatically death to its mother" – whereas most able-bodied Jewish men were sent to forced labour. Almost two-thirds of the German Jews deported to and killed in the death camps were women, and 56 per cent among those Gypsies who were sent into the Auschwitz gas chambers;[35] the precise number of women among the other millions of dead will forever remain unknown. A recent study of the Nazi doctors in the death camps found that these men, who turned from healers into killers, were able to function largely because of male bonding, heavy drinking and their adaptation to an "overall Nazi male ideal."[36]

The leading massacre experts were by no means blind to such gender dimensions of genocide, and in 1943 Himmler exhorted his SS-men in a speech which summed up earlier reflections:

We came to the question: what about the women and children? I have decided to find a clear solution here too. In fact I did not regard myself as justified in exterminating the men – let us say killing them or have them killed – while letting avengers in the shape of children grow up.

Hence, Jewish women were killed as women, as childbearers and mothers of the next generation of their people. But Himmler went even further, placing the female victims at the centre of his own definition of genocide:

When I was forced somewhere in some village to act against partisans and against Jewish commissars, . . . then as a principle I gave the order to kill the women and children of those partisans and commissars too . . . Believe you me, that order was not so easy to give or so simple to carry out as it was logically thought out and can be stated in this hall. But we must constantly recognise that we are engaged in a primitive, primordial, natural race struggle.

Here, in the successful attempt to overcome male scruples towards a war of men against women, the National Socialist *Rassenkampf* in its most extreme form was defined as a deadly struggle of men not just against men – such as in a traditional military war – but also, and particularly, against women as mothers. The significance of this largely women-centred definition of "race struggle" has been recognized by some historians as one element of the singularity of the National Socialist genocide of the Jewish people.[37]

Female activists in Nazi race policies were a minority among the perpetrators and a minority among women generally, though a remarkably tough and efficient one. The more active among them were usually unmarried and without children. They were from all social classes except for the highest ones, and their participation in racist policies was mostly, as in the case of many men, a function of their job or profession. Whereas the sterilization policy was entirely directed by men, some of the female social workers and medical doctors helped select the candidates. Nurses in the six T4 killing centres assisted the male doctors in selecting and killing. Some women academics cooperated with their male superiors in Gypsy studies and laid the groundwork for the selection and extermination of Gypsies; for this purpose they used their easier access, as women, to Gypsies and Gypsy culture. Female camp guards who supervised women in the concentration camps came mostly from a lower or working-class background and had volunteered for the job in expectation of some upward mobility. Among all women activists, they were closest to the centre of the killing operations and responsible for their functioning; it is misleading to believe that "they did not affect the workings of the Nazi state."[38] National Socialist racism was not only institutionalized as a state policy, but also professionalized.

Historians, including some feminist ones, have argued that German women's share of guilt and responsibility for Nazi evil was to have adjusted to Nazism by believing in motherhood and by being nothing else but mothers and wives, a view that has been common, particularly among the left, for a long time.[39] But those women who participated in it did not believe in maternalism as a feature of the female sex, were rarely mothers and did not act as mothers; instead they adjusted themselves to male-dominated political, professional and job strategies, to professionalized race policy. More importantly, neither was the image of women as mothers at the core of the Nazi view of the female sex as a whole, nor was that view, to the degree that it played some role, specific to National Socialism. Instead, from the beginnings of National Socialism modern eugenics (race hygiene) had taken precedence over traditional procreative

133

ethics; within modern eugenics its "negative" (antinatalist) strand had taken precedence over its "positive" (pronatalist) strand, and within its "positive" strand modern welfare policy had taken precedence over the earlier fantasies of "genius-breeding." What was left of the latter was the more realistic and successful attempt at curtailing the procreation of allegedly "feeble-minded" people and of "inferior" peoples and, finally, to prevent the latter from living. This race policy, in all its complexity, was at the core of National Socialism, was its novelty and specificity; it shaped National Socialism's multiple views of women. Most of all, it broke with the maternalist image of the female sex. Under National Socialism, the values of maternity and maternalism, like human values in general, had reached an historical and international nadir.

When German women and men were liberated from this murderous regime, they were also liberated from state antinatalism. But paradoxically enough, the Allied Control Commission, the American Military Tribunal and later German jurisdiction maintained that on the one hand, the Nazi sterilization policy was neither a crime to be brought before a court nor part of the regime's racism (because sterilization laws existed also in the United States), and on the other hand, that child allowances (not, however, tax rebates) were part of the regime's racism and therefore payment had to be stopped. Thus in the late 1940s, when some European states, e.g. Britain and Norway, introduced child allowances as the first major reform of their fully developing welfare states, Germany was almost the only European country without child allowances.[40]

Both the East and West German constitutions included a clause on the equal rights of men and women, following the example of the Weimar constitution (which National Socialism had not bothered to abolish). In East Germany, which followed the model of the Soviet Union, equal rights were now interpreted as women's duty to perform extra-domestic work; domestic labour was downgraded (somewhat following Lenin's notorious scornful views on women's domestic work) and propaganda pressed housewives to take on a job and thereby help establish socialism and give precedence to the "We" instead of the "I," to the collectivity instead to selfishness.[41] This policy was reinforced by low wages and, in 1950, by maternity provisions for employed women (maternity leave with full wage replacement); necessitous mothers and widows received welfare grants only if they were incapable of performing extra-domestic work, often "asocial" unmarried mothers had their children taken away, and whereas all mothers received a single grant at the birth of the third and further children, a universal monthly child allowance was paid only from the fourth child on. In reaction to an extreme fertility decline and with the development of a "welfare socialism" in the 1970s, it was resolved that "the services of bearing and rearing children in the family are to be recognized and valued,"[42] by special female labour law (a forty-hour week for mothers who tended two or more children), temporary support for single mothers who wished to quit their job, and a paid "baby year" for mothers at the birth of second and further children.

Nor was mother-work as such valued by the early West German state, which also guaranteed equal rights in its constitution. Confinement benefit for employed women was improved; when child allowances (*Kindergeld*) were reintroduced in 1954, they functioned upon the older French model of employers' equalization funds and were paid to employed fathers of third and subsequent children. Only in 1964 the federal government took over the responsibility, universalizing and gradually raising the allowance as well as the number of eligible children; even though the law provided for payment either to the father or to the mother, it was usually the father who requested it. Until 1975, the major tool continued to be (breadwinner-focused) tax deductions for wife and children.[43] In 1979, the Social Democratic government introduced a (modestly) paid maternity leave of half a year (beyond confinement benefits), and in 1987, the Christian Democratic/Liberal government replaced it by a universal "childraising allowance" of up to 600 marks per month for a period of one and a half years. It differs from Lily Braun's similar ideal, suggested over eighty years before,[44] in two important features: it does not fully cover needs, and it is payable either to the mother or to the father, depending on who chooses child care instead of employment. Even though few feminists of the new women's movement have struggled for this reform, it would hardly have come about without the coincidence between the rise of the modern welfare state and the growth of women's movements in the twentieth century. It remains to be seen whether the difficult process of unifying Germany in a free welfare state will also recognize and respect the political and social rights of mothers and women generally.

NOTES

Reprinted from Gisela Bock and Pat Thane (eds), *Maternity and Gender Policies. Women and the Rise of European Welfare States, 1880s–1950s* (London/New York: Routledge, 1990), pp. 253–69.

1 G. A. Ritter, *Der Sozialstaat. Entstehung und Entwicklung im internationalen Vergleich* (Munich: Oldenbourg, 1989), esp. pp. 130–8; P. Flora and A. J. Heidenheimer (eds), *The Development of Welfare States in Europe and America* (New Brunswick: Transaction, 1981), esp. p. 83; H. Kaelble, *Auf dem Weg zu einer europäischen Gesellschaft. Eine Sozialgeschichte Westeuropas 1880–1980* (Munich: Beck, 1987).

2 W. Frick, *Bevölkerungs- und Rassenpolitik* (Langensalza: Beyer, 1933); A. T. Allen, "German radical feminism and eugenics, 1900–1918," *German Studies Review*, 1989, Vol. 11, pp. 31–56, esp. pp. 45–6; G. Bäumer, *Die Frau im neuen Lebensraum* (Berlin: Herbig, 1931), esp. pp. 207–10, 229–30; G. Bock, *Zwangssterilisation im Nationalsozialismus: Studien zur Rassenpolitik und Frauenpolitik* (Opladen: Westdeutscher Verlag, 1986), ch. 1.

3 W. Frick, *Bevölkerungs- und Rassenpolitik*; A. Gütt, E. Rüdin and F. Ruttke, *Gesetz zur Verhütung erbkranken Nachwuchses vom 14. Juli 1933* (Munich: Lehmann, 1934) (hereafter GRR), p. 60; G. Bock, *Zwangssterilisation*, ch. IV.3.

4 G. Bock, *Zwangssterilisation*, esp. pp. 182ff., 281, 302ff., 400, 421ff.

5 Quotes from A. Hitler, *Mein Kampf*, Vol. II (Munich: Eher, 1928), pp. 80–1; W. Feldscher, *Rassen- und Erbpflege im deutschen Recht* (Berlin: Deutscher Rechtsverlag, 1943), pp. 26, 118; B. F. Smith and A. F. Peterson (eds), *Heinrich Himmler: Geheimreden 1933–1945* (Frankfurt: Propyläen, 1974), pp. 54–5. For the Nazi concept of the "production" of the "master race" see H. Arendt, *The Origins of Totalitarianism* (New York: Harcourt Brace Jovanovich, 1968), ch. 12 with note 54. For the sterilization of Gypsies, Blacks and Jews see G. Bock, *Zwangssterilisation*, pp. 353–63.

6 GRR, p. 176; H. Burkhardt, *Der rassenhygienische Gedanke und seine Grundlagen* (Munich: Reinhardt, 1930), p. 93.

7 GRR, p. 5.

8 L. G. Tirala (Ministry of Propaganda), "Die wirtschaftlichen Folgen des Sterilisierungsgesetzes," *Volk und Rasse*, 1933, vol. 8, pp. 162–4; G. Bock, *Zwangssterilisation*, pp. 372–80.

9 G. Bock, *Zwangssterilisation*, pp. 280, 384 (quotes), 97–9, 386.

10 Quotes and documents in ibid., pp. 431, 396, 212, 398–9, 393.

11 Of 22 April and 22 August 1936; ibid., pp. 401–31, 322–5.

12 *Juristische Wochenschrift*, 1935, vol. 64, p. 2143; *Staatsarchiv Freiburg*, Gesundheitsamt Lörrach, no. 534.

13 E. von Barsewitsch, *Die Aufgaben der Frau für die Aufartung* (Berlin: Reichdruckerei, 1933), p. 14; she referred (like many others of the time and like earlier radical feminists such as Helene Stöcker) to Nietzsche's saying "Thou shalt not propagate, but elevate, the race" (see K. Anthony, *Feminism in Germany and Scandinavia* (New York: Holt, 1915), p. 94). A. Bluhm "Das Gesetz zur Verhütung erbkranken Nachwuchses," *Die Frau*, 1934, Vol. 41, pp. 529–38; J. Haarer, "Die rassenpolitischen Aufgaben des Deutschen Frauenwerks," *Neues Volk*, 1938, Vol. 6, no. 4, pp. 17–19; the following quote: M. Hess, "Das Gesetz zur Verhütung erbkranken Nachwuchses," *N.S.-Frauenwarte*, 1935, Vol. 4, no. 2, pp. 33–6. Among the women (and men) who actively opposed sterilization propaganda and activity, the Catholics were the most prominent and they referred to the papal encyclical *Casti Connubi* of 1930 which condemned eugenic sterilization.

14 "Richtlinien für eine bevölkerungspolitische Propaganda und Volksaufklärung," *Bundesarchiv Koblenz* (BAK), NS 18/712; *Partei-Archiv*, Nov. 1937, p. 19; W. Knorr, "Kinderreichenauslese durch das Rassenpolitische Amt der NSDAP in Sachsen," *Volk und Rasse*, 1936, Vol. 11, p. 270. Cf. G. Bock, *Zwangssterilisation*, pp. 122–3, 129–31.

15 R. W. Darré, *Neuadel aus Blut und Boden* (Munich: Lehmann, 1930), pp. 169–71; W. Gross, "Denkschrift zur Frage des unehelichen Kindes als Problem der deutschen Bevölkerungspolitik" (1944), BAK, R 22/485; H. Linden, minutes of a meeting on population policy 1935, *Auswärtiges Amt, Politisches Archiv*, Inland I Partei 84/4.

16 D. Winkler, *Frauenarbeit im "Dritten Reich,"* (Hamburg: Hoffman & Campe, 1977), esp. chs 2 and 5, pp. 198, 201; S. Bajohr, *Die Hälfte der Fabrik* (Marburg: Arbeiterpolitik, 1979), ch. 4, esp. p. 252; A. Willms, "Grundzüge der Entwicklung der Frauenarbeit von 1880 bis 1980," in W. Müller *et al., Strukturwandel der Frauenarbeit 1880–1980* (Frankfurt a.M.: Campus Verlag, 1983), p. 35. For the following figures see also R. Hachtmann, "Industriearbeiterinnen in der deutschen Kriegswirtschaft, 1936–1944/45" in *Geschichte und Gesellschaft. Zeitschrift für historische Sozialwissenschaft*, 19. Jg., 1993/ Heft 3, Juli/September, pp. 332–66.; C. Kirkpatrick, *Woman in Nazi Germany* (London: Jarrolds, 1939), ch. 7; U. Herbert, *Fremdarbeiter* (Bonn: Dietz, 1985).

17 Figures from *Statistisches Jahrbuch für das deutsche Reich*, 1926–1942, vols 45–59; G. Bock, *Zwangssterilisation*, pp. 160–3, 388. There were few convictions for sections 219 and 220. For a comparable situation in fascist Italy, see Detragiache, quoted in Saraceno's contribution to [the original] volume, G. Bock and P. Thane (eds), *Maternity and Gender Policies. Women and the Rise of European Welfare States, 1880s–1950s* (London/New York: Routledge, 1990), note 1.

18 The best overview is still D. V. Glass, *Population Policies and Movements in Europe* (first edn 1940; repr. London: Frank Cass, 1967). For

Nazi pronatalism and its impact see G. Bock, *Zwangssterilisation*, pp. 141–77.

19 Quotes from H. Frank, speech of 18 November 1937 (BAK, R 61/130); H. F. K. Günther, *Rassenkunde des deutschen Volkes* (Munich: Lehmann, 1923), pp. 345f., 274ff.; Goebbels' criticism (1941): BAK, R2/31097.

20 F. Reinhard, quoted in W. Gross, "Unsere Arbeit gilt der deutschen Familie," *Nationalsozialistische Monatshefte*, 1939, Vol. 9, pp. 103–4; Hilgenfeldt reporting to Bormann about a conversation with Himmler, 16 September 1942 (BAK, NS 18/2427).

21 J. Stephenson, *The Nazi Organisation of Women* (London: Croom Helm, 1981), esp. p. 164; see Saraceno's article in Bock and Thane (eds) *Maternity and Gender Policies*.

22 G. Lilienthal, *Der "Lebensborn e.V."* (Stuttgart: Gustav Fischer, 1985), esp. pp. 53, 66–7, 100, 113, 182–3, 242–4. Despite the *Lebensborn* children's privileges, they were not spared being killed if they were "incurably ill."

23 Documents in G. Bock, *Zwangssterilisation*, pp. 174–5.

24 C. Heinrichs, "Besoldung der Mutterschaftsleistung," *Die Frau*, 1934, Vol. 41, pp. 343–8; I. Reichenau (ed.), *Deutsche Frauen an Adolf Hitler* (Leipzig: Klein, sd, 1933), pp. 7, 15, 37. For the demographic figures see G. Bock, *Zwangssterilisation*, pp. 143–6, 151–7, 168 and 173.

25 K. Astel and E. Weber, *Die Kinderzahl der 29.000 politischen Leiter des Gaues Thüringen der NSDAP* (Berlin: Metzner, 1943), pp. 87, 114ff., 157, 161; Koller, "Haben Ärzte im Durchschnitt wirklich nur 1,1 Kinder?," *Deutsches Ärzteblatt*, 1942, Vol. 72, p. 343.

26 F. Burgdörfer, *Geburtenschwund* (Heidelberg: Vowinckel, 1942), pp. 157, 184; W. Knorr, "Praktische Rassenpolitik," *Volk und Rasse*, 1938, Vol. 13, pp. 69–73.

27 See Nash (note 41) as well as Saraceno (note 27) in Bock and Thane (eds), *Maternity and Gender Policies*. For the two baby booms see G. Bock, *Zwangssterilisation*, pp. 168–9.

28 D. V. Glass, *Population Policies*, pp. 106, 253, 293.

29 H. Heiber (ed.), "Der Generalplan Ost," *Vierteljahreshefte für Zeitgeschichte*, 1958, Vol. 6, pp. 317–18; G. Bock, *Zwangssterilisation*, pp. 442–51.

30 J. Sehn, "Carl Claubergs verbrecherische Unfruchtbarmachungs-Versuche an Häftlings-Frauen in den Nazi-Konzentrationslagern," *Hefte von Auschwitz*, Vol. 2, Oswiecim, 1959, pp. 3–32; R. Hilberg, *The Destruction of the European Jews* (New York: Holmes & Meir, 1985), Vol. III, pp. 940–6, 1081.

31 R. J. Lifton, *The Nazi Doctors. Medical Killing and the Psychology of Genocide* (New York: Basic Books, 1986), p. 22.

32 H.-W. Schmuhl, *Rassenhygiene, Nationalsozialismus, Euthanasie* (Göttingen: Vandenhoeck & Ruprecht, 1987), p. 40. For the 1942 decree, mentioned below, see G. Bock, *Zwangssterilisation*, pp. 358–9.

33 R. J. Lifton, *The Nazi Doctors*, p. 159, also pp. 15, 147; M. Broszat

(ed.), *Kommandant in Auschwitz* (Munich: DTV, 1963), p. 127; R. Hilberg, *Destruction*, Vol. I, pp. 332–4.

34 R. Hilberg, *Destruction*, Vol. II, pp. 690–1; Vol. III, p. 871; J. Ringelheim, "Deportations, deaths and survival: Nazi ghetto policies against women and men in occupied Poland," in T. Wobbe (ed.), *Nach Osten: Verdeckte Spuren nationalsozialistischer Verbrechen* (Frankfurt a.M.: Neue Kritik, 1991); J. Ringelheim, "Women and the Holocaust," *Signs*, 1985, Vol. 10, pp. 741–61; E. Kogon *et al.* (eds), *Nationalsozialistische Massentötungen durch Giftgas* (Frankfurt a.M.: Fischer, 1986), e.g., pp. 88, 91, 93–7, 105–8, 122, 131, 134, 158, 210–15.

35 L. Adelsberger, *Auschwitz* (Berlin: Lettner, 1953), pp. 126–8 (quote); M. Richarz, *Jüdisches Leben in Deutschland* (Stuttgart: Deutsche Verlags-Anstalt, 1982), Vol. 3, p. 61; J. Ficowski, "Die Vernichtung," in T. Zülch (ed.), *In Auschwitz vergast, bis heute verfolgt: Zur Situation der Roma (Zigeuner) in Deutschland und Europa* (Reinbek: Rowohlt, 1979), pp. 135–6.

36 R. J. Lifton, *The Nazi Doctors*, p. 462; see also pp. 193–6, 199, 231, 312–13, 317, 443.

37 By E. Jäckel, "Die elende Praxis der Untersteller," in *"Historikerstreit". Die Dokumentation der Kontroverse um die Einzigartigkeit der nationalsozialistischen Judenvernichtung* (Munich: Piper, 1987), p. 118. E. Nolte objected on the grounds that this massacre of women (and boys and old men) was self-evident; therefore it seemed to him superfluous to mention it specifically (ibid., pp. 229–30). Himmler's speeches: F. Smith and A. F. Peterson (eds), *Heinrich Himmler*, pp. 169, 201.

38 C. Koonz, *Mothers in the Fatherland* (New York: St Martin's Press, 1987), p. 405. For women's professional and job strategies in the context of race policy see R. Gilsenbach, "Wie Lolitschai zur Doktorwürde kam," in W. Ayass *et al.*, *Feinderklärung und Prävention*, Berlin, Rotbuch, 1988, pp. 101–34; H. Friedlander, in E. Katz and J. Ringelheim (eds), *Proceedings of the Conference "Women Surviving the Holocaust"* (New York: Institute for Research in History, 1983), pp. 115–16; G. Bock, *Zwangssterilisation* p. 208.

39 C. Koonz, *Mothers*, esp. chs 1 and 11. Some leftist writers assume that "among the persecuted and incarcerated, by far the majority were men" (R. Kühnl, "Der deutsche Faschismus in der neueren Forschung," *Neue politische Literatur*, 1983, Vol. 28, p. 71). For an influential criticism of this view see A. Tröger, "Die Dolchstoss legende der Linken: 'Frauen haben Hitler an die Macht gebracht'," in Berliner Dozentinnengruppe (ed.), *Frauen und Wissenschaft* (Berlin: Courage, 1977), pp. 324–55.

40 See V. Hentschel, *Geschichte der deutschen Sozialpolitik 1880–1980* (Frankfurt a.M.: Suhrkamp, 1983), pp. 139, 202; G. Bock, *Zwangssterilisation*, pp. 115–16, 244–6.

41 "Das 'Wir' steht vor dem 'Ich'," *Frau von heute*, 1959, Vol. 39, p. 2, quoted in G. Obertreis, *Familienpolitik in der DDR 1945–1980*

(Opladen: Westdeutscher Verlag, 1985), p. 146; also pp. 51–73, 119, 136–8, 155, 292–3.

42 E. Honecker, "Neue Massnahmen zur Verwicklichung des sozialpolitischen Programms des VIII. Parteitages" (1972), quoted in G. Obertreis, *Familienpolitik*, p. 292; also pp. 315–18.

43 U. Gerhard *et al.* (eds), *Auf Kosten der Frauen. Frauenrechte im Sozialstaat* (Weinheim and Basel: Beltz, 1988), pp. 83, 91–2, 195; P. Flora (ed.), *Growth to Limits. The Western European Welfare States Since World War II* (Berlin: De Gruyter, 1986–7), Vol. II, pp. 278–81.

44 Irene Stoehr, "Housework and motherhood: debates and policies in the women's movement in Imperial Germany and the Weimar Republic" in Bock and Thane (eds), *Maternity and Gender Policies*, pp. 213–32.

4

VICTIMS OR PERPETRATORS?

Controversies about the role of women in the Nazi state

Adelheid von Saldern

Gisela Bock portrays women as the victims of National Socialism, innocent of its crimes because it can scarcely be believed that they would have participated in the regime which oppressed them. But in her book, Mothers in the Fatherland, *Claudia Koonz contends that many women were "accomplices" to Nazism because the "emotional work" they performed for men in the "private sphere" of the family contributed to the stability of the Nazi system. In the following article, Adelheid von Saldern suggests, however, that few women can be regarded as simply "victims" or "perpetrators." The majority of German women experienced complex, ambiguous relationships with the Nazi regime which made it possible to be both "victim" and "perpetrator" at the same time. Indeed, von Saldern urges that we abandon the search for "pure types." She insists upon the significance of differences among women as well as between men and women in the Third Reich. Even as "victims," women experienced quite different fates; an Aryan woman, denied an abortion because she was deemed "genetically valuable" was certainly not the same kind of "victim" of Nazi racism as a Jewish or Gypsy woman who was forcibly sterilized, even murdered, because she was a "racial enemy."*

Von Saldern also rejects the argument that women could not have been directly involved in the functioning of the Nazi dictatorship because they were confined largely to the "private sphere" of the home and the family. Under Nazism, this "private sphere" was radically invaded by the perverted "public sphere" of Nazi ideology and arbitrary rule. The family was not a safe and sane haven, a "female sphere" insulated from the violence and brutality of the Nazi political system. But the fact that, until quite late in the war, private life appeared to remain relatively intact encouraged many women to tolerate, even

141

to support, the Nazi regime. Von Saldern points out that Nazism also constructed a specifically female sector of the "public sphere" which, though exercising no great influence upon the regime as a whole, none the less gave many women new opportunities to be active outside their homes and families. A variety of motivations caused some women to become actively involved, while others participated in a more passive fashion or simply abstained.

Von Saldern sees no easy way to determine the degrees of guilt and responsibility for Nazism that should be shouldered by different categories of women. But, as a first step, she suggests that clear distinctions be drawn between the effects of the structural conditions and relationships produced by Nazism and the choices that were or could be made by the individual women who had to operate within these structures. Even Nazism could not completely eliminate all freedom of choice; women still retained a certain ability to act as "responsible subjects." Only by discovering how they exercised that capacity can we arrive at a sound assessment of their "guilt" or "innocence." Above all, von Saldern emphasizes, it is important to avoid simplistic generalizations about women's "nature" which make it difficult to recognize the complex and contradictory variety of women's experiences or to understand what real women thought, felt and did during the Third Reich.

* * *

For a long time women were more or less excluded as subjects of historical research on the Third Reich, but the situation has begun to change during the past few years.[1] Historians have not, however, been able to agree in their evaluations of the role of women in the Nazi period; are women to be seen more as victims or as accomplices?[2] This controversial question has been posed and answered in quite conflicting ways with regard not only to Nazi Germany but for contemporary society as well.[3] The discussion of the role of women in the Third Reich has been stirred up by Claudia Koonz's book, *Mothers in the Fatherland*, published in 1987, which argues that the "emotional work" done by women for men contributed to the stability of the Nazi system. Her arguments have certainly not gone unchallenged and in what follows I want to sketch the main outlines of the current debate.[4]

WOMEN AS VICTIMS

In the existing literature, women have often been portrayed as the victims of National Socialism;[5] the Nazi system oppressed women, reduced them to mere objects who were therefore not able actively to defend themselves from National Socialism. It is certainly true that there were many women who were undeniably victims of the Nazi regime, above all Jewish women, but also Gypsy women, women in the resistance, and so on. There is also no doubt that, in general, women were the victims of structural discrimination in politics, society and the economy.[6] For example, the few women who occupied responsible positions in state and society before 1933 were forced out of their offices and professions.[7] Women's chances of being admitted to university and thus to the future functional elite of the Third Reich mostly declined (at least until the outbreak of the war).[8] Many young women had to work in badly paid agricultural jobs or as housemaids.[9] The list of discriminatory measures against women could be enlarged considerably and in so far as the term "victim" refers to these kinds of structural sexual discrimination it is quite applicable.

This, however, is not the core of the controversy among women's historians which becomes more evident when we take a look at Gisela Bock's discussion of sterilization. Bock argues that compulsory sterilization affected women more than men – especially in qualitative terms. Because women's identities were more closely connected to their sexual fertility, Bock thinks that forced sterilization did greater existential damage to women than to men. Bock sees an aggressive anti-feminism in Nazi sterilization practices which she thinks must be placed in the larger context of the Holocaust. Both Jews and women were to be regarded as "inferior." According to Bock, sterilization was a component of racial policy, which was supposed to purify the "racial body" by "removing the racially inferior"; here, Bock refers, in particular, to the estimated 4,500 women who died as a result of forced sterilization.

One of the merits of Bock's book is that it demonstrates the breadth of the application of eugenic ideas, all stemming from a common basic assumption, namely that it was both "necessary" and "possible" to cleanse a people of alleged "racial inferiors," either by preventing their reproduction or by isolating and killing them. Problems arise, however, from Bock's attempts to generalize and to extend her conclusions to all women. The Nazis did indeed think that women were, in general, inferior to men, but Bock fails to recognize that women's "inferiority" was a relative matter which did not imply evaluation in the sense of a racial policy. Aryan women might allegedly be "inferior" to Aryan men but both were members of a supposedly "superior race." By jumbling together very different meanings of "inferiority," Gisela Bock arrives at a conceptual equation of anti-feminism and anti-Semitism that is not convincing.[10]

Nevertheless, the evaluation of someone as "inferior" was based on different criteria for men and for women. Under certain conditions, promiscuous women were much more vulnerable than men to being labeled "inferior" – above all, if they came from a so-called "anti-social milieu." But, this sort of classification was, in any case, connected more with conservative-bourgeois values than with racist-fascist ideas. Bock supports her thesis that Nazi sterilization affected women more deeply than men by arguing that it damaged or destroyed women's social identity, which was based primarily on motherhood and fertility. Bock presumes that all women found their identity in child-bearing and motherhood, an argument which applied to some of the women who were sterilized but certainly not to all of them. As Atina Grossmann puts it, Bock comes "curiously close to implying that non-mothers are not really women."[11] Bock overstates her characterization of sterilization as a general policy of antinatalism. She argues that 1.6 million births were prevented by sterilization.[12] But this birth-deficit was, however, supposed to be compensated by increasing the number of children born to "valuable" parents, by tolerating illegitimate births (from "valuable" women) and by a strictly enforced prohibition of abortion. Thus the Nazi regime can equally well be seen as a pronatalist racial welfare state. Bock's interpretation of Nazi policy leads to the conclusion that all women were potential victims with the result that it is all too easy to argue that the number of women who shared direct responsibility for the Third Reich was negligible and that their involvement with the Nazi dictatorship was only a secondary phenomenon, purely a process of accommodation.[13]

Another key element in the present controversy is the question of whether women who were (co-)perpetrators can also be seen as victims. It is well known that the norms and values which had regulated the system of justice up until the Nazi era were replaced by their opposites, which, however, had become legitimate. The fascist system made it possible for people to commit certain crimes without facing punishment; indeed, these people were rewarded, even promoted. Only if the Nazi regime had gone so far as to force people to commit criminal acts could they be seen, in any meaningful sense, as victims of the dictatorship rather than as (co-)perpetrators. But in very few cases can this type of overt coercion be documented; even male and female concentration camp guards were usually allowed to change their jobs if they wanted to.[14] So when, for example, Helga Schubert describes women who made denunciations to the Gestapo (*Denunziantin*) as "victims of the dictatorship,"[15] we should ask whether this is not an inappropriate confusion of the perpetrators with the real victims, even if this was not Schubert's original intention. Dagmar Reese argues, however, that the precondition for becoming a perpetrator is "a person's freedom of choice" and "the ability to act as a responsible subject." In her case study of a woman worker at Siemens, who transferred to a job at the Ravensbrück concentration camp, Reese argues that this woman's social milieu, her gender-specific upbringing and education, as well as the political system, did not allow her to act as a responsible subject.[16] But what might be true in this one case becomes problematic when generalized because then we risk not finding any subjects who were (co-)responsible for their deeds.

THE PUBLIC SPHERE AND THE PRIVATE SPHERE

Claudia Koonz's book created a sensation among German women's historians by challenging the claim, advanced by many feminist scholars, that German women were largely innocent of responsibility for the crimes of Nazism because their activities were confined to the relatively "unpolitical" sphere of family life. Koonz argued that women who continued to maintain "normal" family life during the Third Reich made an invaluable contribution to the reproduction of the Nazi system, even if they themselves had no ideological motivations. In this next section of her article, Adelheid von Saldern reviews these conflicting conceptualizations of the relationship between the private domestic sphere and the public realm of state activity. She concludes that the arguments of both Koonz and her critics should be amended or expanded as follows:

1) *Adapting a framework of analysis suggested in the 1930s by Ernst Fraenkel, von Saldern argues that the apparent division between the private and the public spheres actually dissolved under the Third Reich. It is misleading to argue that women inhabited a relatively innocent, private sphere.*

2) *None the less, von Saldern thinks that the great majority of German women granted at least a passive acquiescence to the Nazi regime because it allowed them to conduct a relatively tranquil family life (so long as they were not numbered among the regime's many political and racial enemies) until the deaths of husbands, fathers and brothers on the Eastern Front and the massively destructive Allied bombing raids destroyed all illusions of normality.*

3) *Von Saldern also suggests that values and identities constructed by women in the private sphere (the ideal of "motherhood," for instance) may have led them to approve of, and sometimes even to become personally involved in, Nazi racial programs (for example, as social workers who conceived of their task as a kind of "social motherhood." After 1933, however, social work increasingly involved genetic/racial selections, resulting in the sterilization or murder of the biologically "unfit").*

4) *Finally, von Saldern points out that women were not simply confined to the home and the family but were brought in large numbers into Nazi organizations for women (such as the League of German Girls). This "special female public sphere" politicized private life, but it also transformed previously private concerns into public issues and gave many women new fields of activity outside the home.*

* * *

Much of the discussion of women in Nazi Germany revolves around the relationship between the public sphere and the private sphere.[17] Historians usually proceed from the assumption that the private, reproductive sphere was determined more by women and the public sphere more by men. The interrelationship between the public sphere and the private sphere has become a central issue in historical debates; were these two spheres intertwined or basically separate from each other? Was the private sphere infiltrated by the public? In the following comments, I will discuss the main interpretations that appear in recent literature and, at the same time, present some of my own thoughts on these issues.

Changes in the private sphere and the interconnections between public and private

Koonz claims that in the private sphere, women played a role that requires us to speak of guilt or at least of "complicity," rather than of innocence. But by focussing upon women's guilt, Koonz has laid herself open to attack.[18] As Gisela Bock puts it, "As long as the 'guilt' of women is seen as bearing and raising children, in the work done for the family and in the 'traditional' role of women, who were said to be at the center of National Socialist racial policy, there is hardly a chance of achieving a new view."[19] In particular, the following statement by Koonz has received much attention and criticism: "Far from remaining untouched by Nazi evil, women operated at its very center."[20] More specifically and concretely, Koonz argues that "When the SS man returned home, he entered a doll's house of *ersatz* goodness in which he could escape from his own evil actions."[21] But as Koonz does not differentiate sharply between the structural entanglement of the two spheres and the more subjective question of individual guilt and responsibility, her text lays itself open to misunderstanding.

Ernst Fraenkel's insights can be helpful in approaching the structural side of the problem. Fraenkel differentiated between the "prerogative state" (*Massnahmenstaat*), by which he meant the sphere dominated by Nazi illegality and injustice, and the "normative state" (*Normenstaat*), or the sphere under Nazism where the norms of pre-Nazi bourgeois society still survived. According to Fraenkel these two spheres were by no means insulated from one another; rather they were arranged in a hierarchy which always allowed the "prerogative state" to infiltrate the "normative state;" yet the *Massnahmenstaat* "only" partially utilized its hegemony.[22]

If we were to apply such an analysis to the situation of women – which Fraenkel did not do in his book[23] – we would have to conclude that women lived and acted in the *Massnahmenstaat* less than in the *Normenstaat*, which included the private sphere, the sphere of reproduction, family and housework, but which was infiltrated by the *Massnahmenstaat*. Indeed, Dagmar Reese and Carola Sachse argue that during the Third Reich, the private sphere was so radically invaded by the *Massnahmenstaat* that it makes little sense to speak of a "female space"; what remained was only an empty shell, which no longer enclosed differentiated concepts."[24] Fraenkel's approach may be more useful because he worked not with a picture of an empty shell, but rather two overlapping spheres, in which one dominated the other in an incalculable manner. Neither sphere was independent of the other; in the private sphere (*Normenstaat*), women (and men) were repeatedly confronted with regulations imposed by the public sphere, the *Massnahmenstaat*, when, for example, Jewish shops were boycotted, when the "block warden" (*Blockwart*) system was constructed in the neighborhoods,[25] when a neighbor was taken away or when the family was pressured to let their child join the Hitler Youth. Thus women could experience the *Massnahmenstaat* even when they were not directly connected with it as either victim or as perpetrator; a non-political, private sphere simply did not exist. As the deputy principal, *Studiendirektorin* Hedwig Forster, a committed Nazi, put it, the housewife should even boil fish in a National Socialist way.[26]

Separate spheres and an innocent private sphere? Arguments and counter-arguments

If analyzing the structural interconnections between the public and the private sphere is not thought to be a legitimate exercise, then arguments will have to be based solely on the examination of individual or group behavior. However, the existing literature displays certain methodological inconsistencies; some women's historians retain a structural approach instead of examining individual and group behavior. But rather than emphasizing the connections between the public and private spheres, these women's historians insist upon their separation, a division drawn along more or less gendered lines. They argue that women acted primarily in a "sane," non-political, private arena, an assumption which sometimes leads to a positive evaluation of women's activities in the Third Reich. Women are shown to have been able to cope with difficult situations, especially during the war, when women adapted to the steadily worsening conditions of everyday life so as to ensure the survival of their families. This literature stresses women's strength and ability to endure their own suffering.[27] Women's work in the Third Reich is presented as having been primarily oriented to "practical value" (*Gebrauchswert*) and involved with the natural resources of society, which are thought to have humanizing functions:[28] for example, Kuhn and Rothe stress women's "use-oriented" dealings with the "natural resources" of the society "in their social necessity and their humanizing functions."[29]

Windaus-Walser rejects such generalizations: "Was it not the race hygienists and eugenists of both sexes who claimed that their specific 'use-value orientation' in their dealings with the 'natural resource' of human beings was necessary for the society and had a humanizing function?"[30] Reese and Sachse disagree: "Modern race-hygiene was shaped by men as a science, as was its relationship to state and society . . . National Socialist racial policy was, doubtless, a male policy on the levels of scientific conceptualization, political decisions and administrative implementation."[31]

But can we really be so sure? Should we not also ask whether many women did not also support these "scientific" conceptualizations, these political decisions and administrative implementations? Did women really "only" endure such a policy because they were relatively powerless and were they "only" passively involved in the practical realization of racial eugenics?[32]

Just as there could be no completely innocent private sphere, so, too, the existence of any general cultural resistance, based upon "feminity," against the Nazi regime must be questioned. In the Third Reich, the original ideal of a life bound to natural resources suffered massive deformations – as did many other ideals – especially as a result of its connections with eugenic concepts. Female social workers provide one example of this process. They had initially wanted to transform the natural resource of "motherliness" into a humanitarian profession. But under the Nazis they often ended up preparing the way for the "selection" and elimination of so-called "inferior life," a process which was also justified on purportedly "humanitarian" grounds, such as "decreasing suffering" or "preventing damage to society."[33]

Different spheres, different values: two sides of the same coin

Ute Daniel describes a drifting apart of the norms and values which dominated in each sphere. While the private sphere was characterized by values such as personal intimacy and mutual responsibility, the public sphere, which included the political, was dominated by instrumental rationalization (*Zweckrationalität*), or, in other words, an "in order to" mode of thinking. For example: "In order to gain world power status, war had to be waged; in order to maintain the 'German race', Jews and others had to be exterminated."[34] In such a system of "instrumental rationalization," people were used as means to an end; the end itself was usually of a supra-individual nature. Moreover, in this system of instrumental rationalization, most Germans were given the impression that the negative side of the Third Reich "only" affected "aliens" and "outsiders" such as "non-Aryans", the opponents of the regime, homosexuals and, during the war, foreign workers and forced laborers. For most Germans, both men and women, private life continued to be "livable," even when, for the "others," it was not.[35] One of the compensations, the semblance of a relatively intact private sphere – at least until the loss of fathers and sons at the front and the long nights of bombing at home – and the relatively strong integration of women within this private sphere might explain women's toleration of the Nazi system.

At first glance, it appeared that nothing had changed in the private sphere in comparison with the preceding decades. But, in fact, a great deal had changed. The Nazi state which many women tolerated was a barbaric system, a system made possible by the passive acquiescence of the overwhelming majority of the German people. The continued existence of a seemingly intact private sphere made it easier for the Nazi system to wield power. But in uncovering this structural and functional interconnection between the private sphere and the public sphere, between a seemingly "pure and safe private world" (*heile Welt*) *and* "barbarism," it is not necessary to assume individual guilt. People's behavior did not have to change: although behavior in the private sphere may have remained "the same," its impact changed as an automatic consequence of the transformation of the public-political sphere.

The special female public sphere

In addition to the private sphere, women in the Third Reich were also given their own public sphere, although with very limited influence. Here a relatively autonomous field of activity within the general framework of National Socialist values and norms became possible for women, even though they were under the leadership of men at the very top. In 1936, for example, 11 million of the 35 million women in Germany were members of the *NS-Frauenschaft*.[36] By and large, these women, and especially those who were leaders, accepted the role allotted to them by the Nazi system. Many were more or less positively inclined to National Socialism. Although there was some grumbling and criticism in certain areas, this did not usually amount to serious (political) opposition. Of course, not all historians agree with this view, preferring, instead, to argue that women were "peculiarly resistant to National Socialism."[37]

In a rather different assessment, Claudia Koonz argues that "The state support of the female public 'sphere' offered women a counterbalance to the authority of husbands and fathers, of priests and pastors."[38] Similarly, Schmidt-Waldherr maintains that in the Nazi state it was women themselves who "were allowed" to transpose the Nazi concept of "mothers of the home" (*Hausmütter*) into the concept of "mothers of the folk" (*Volksmütter*) which was combined with a female public sphere although it remained relatively distinct from other fields of public activity.[39] And through their responses to the problems of everyday life, which were generally seen as women's tasks in the private sphere now transformed into public issues, the Nazis tried to fuse the private with the public spheres and to define women's roles in both. Such an intermingling meant that the private sphere became politicized. Carrying Schmidt-Waldherr's arguments further, we might say that women did not see this infiltration of politics into the private sphere as illegitimate or as a form of subordination. It may rather have been regarded as a welcome termination of a senseless division between the two spheres which enhanced women's social status and constructed an apparently productive synthesis between the "public" and the "private."

WOMEN AS PERPETRATORS

The terms "innocence" and "guilt," "victim" and "(co-) perpetrator" refer primarily to individual subjects, not to [social or political] structures. Ute Daniel and others have rightly pointed out that terms such as "victim" and "perpetrator" distract attention from more important questions, rather than focussing upon them. Such terms can at best be employed only as very rough descriptions of women as individuals responsible for their own actions.

Voting

"Hitler came into power through women": this has been a widely accepted stereotype.[40] Although the claim that women voted in disproportionate numbers for Hitler has been refuted or, at least, greatly relativized by historians,[41] it cannot be denied that women did vote for conservative parties, above all for the German National People's Party (DNVP) and the Catholic Centre Party (Zentrum). In a period of deepening crisis in state and society, the conservative political parties promised to protect the family and thus to maintain what many women regarded as the only quasi intact female sphere. Women's decision to vote conservative has to be seen as an act of "social logic." Moreover, church and religion appealed to many women. The strong, if contradictory, affinity of conservatism for National Socialism, particularly in the early 1930s, and the possible implications of such an affinity for women's history have, however, usually not been considered seriously. Neither has the fact that one third of female voters voted for the NSDAP in the last democratic election before Hitler's take-over.[42] How was it possible that in 1932 one-third of women voted for a party which, from our present point of view, was as anti-female as the NSDAP? Much of the existing literature talks in terms of deception and manipulation.[43] More sophisticated arguments suggest that a certain "social logic" was at work here and that many of the same reasons that moved women to vote conservative also caused them to support the Nazis. For example, Nazi propaganda for enhancement of the status of housewives and mothers met with some success among women to whom the Great Depression had denied alternative prospects. Claudia Koonz suggests that many women, especially those from the lower but also the middle classes rejected the type of emancipation symbolized by the "New Woman" of the 1920s, because it was at odds with their mentality, their view of society and their idea of the proper "gender-order." Helen Boak concludes that the Nazi movement "was not antiwoman, but against the emancipation of woman which it was thought took her away from her age-old role of wife and mother."[44] Koonz argues convincingly that Nazi women and even many conservative women approved of the possibility of expanding the "female sphere" in the Nazi system.[45] Despite its male-bonding culture, Nazism must also have appealed to women and to female "social logic." Windaus-Walser takes Nazi propaganda elevating the status of (Aryan) women as mothers seriously and she tries to decode the ways in which it might have addressed the interests and identities of many women, especially those who were mothers. She suggests that the "enhancement of female merits in the production of 'worthy' lives, as it was expressed in the National Socialist cult surrounding the Aryan mother" probably played an important role.[46] Windaus-Walser's argument could hardly be more at odds with Bock's interpretation of Nazism as fascist antinatalism. But Windaus-Walser does of course assume that women acted exclusively or primarily as "women" and "mothers," a position questioned by Dorothea Schmidt and Helen Boak.

Both Schmidt and Boak ask whether it was necessarily only gender-specific points of view which led women to vote for the NSDAP or the conservative parties.[47] Making use of both Weimar and present-day voting analyses, Schmidt suggests that it is not so much a party's specific position on women, but rather its general *Weltanschauung* that determines women's voting behavior. Boak claims that "Women chose to vote NSDAP for the same reasons men voted for the party – out of self-interest, out of a belief that the party best represented their own idea of what German society should be, even if they may have disagreed with the party's stand on individual issues."[48] Boak thinks that the party's attitude to women's role in society "did not play a decisive part in voters' choice and that what the Nazis had to say on this subject was to a large extent a reflection of the views held by the DVP, DNVP, Center party and BVP."[49]

Female anti-semitism

In her book, *Die friedfertige Frau*,[50] published in 1983, Margarete Mitscherlich contends that, as a rule, women who were anti-Semites or racists had taken over a male point of view. This argument has been widely accepted by women's historians. Projection of hate for the fathers (*Vaterhass*), the shifting of incestuous wishes on to Jews (*Rassenschändung*), rivalry, aggression, and so on, these unconscious psychological motives for the development of anti-Semitism were "relevant above all for the male psyche."[51] As a result of super-ego deformation, the ego-ideal of male anti-Semites was narcissistic. Because women generally had a weakly developed super-ego, female anti-Semitism could only be evaluated as a secondary phenomenon. Female anti-Semitism arose when the suppressed woman wanted to identify herself with the (anti-Semitic) male suppressor and adapted to his prejudices: "The tendency to adapt is in turn connected with her great fear of losing love."[52]

But Windaus-Walser has, with good reason, challenged this gender-specific interpretation of social psychological processes; weakly developed super-egos, a sufficient "pre-condition" for anti-Semitism, can be found among both men and women. Conflicts stemming from the Oedipus Complex can be found in women too; although the mother becomes the object of hate and rivalry, this mother hate can be transferred to men. Super-ego deformations, projections, idealizations and rejection mechanisms also appear in women. In short, Windaus-Walser cannot subscribe to any notion of the "blessing of female birth" and insists instead upon investigating women's contribution to the Nazi system: "What if National Socialism corresponded to the unconscious needs and inner psychological mechanisms of these women as well as to their conscious ideas? What if the hate felt by female anti-Semites did not differ from that of their male counterparts? What if women had not simply adapted to ('male') National Socialism but had made their own contribution to it?"[53] Women might, in fact, have delegated their murderous intentions to men: "Men then would have acted not only in their own name, but also in the name of women."[54] There was no specific female or male libido (or aggression), and, according to Windaus-Walser, there was only one anti-Semitism, which could of course be expressed in different ways.[55] Windaus-

154

Walser does not want to relativize the "deeds of the (male) actors," but rather to explore the broadly associated field, to which the attitudes and behavior of women also belonged, which made these deeds possible.

The issue of "female guilt"

Finally, we need to ask whether women as individuals shared the guilt of the Nazi regime, whether we can speak of a "specifically female guilt," a guilt, as Gisela Bock puts it, which should be looked for "in specifically female activities" in the traditionally separate private sphere.[56] Bock herself refuses to accept the notion of a "specifically female guilt" because she thinks that Nazi racial policy must not be confused with either the norms or with the reality of the "traditionally female sphere" and because the "real contribution of women to the Nazi crimes occurred in non-traditional functions external to the home."[57] But, once again, this argument neglects the structural interconnection of the private sphere and the public sphere. And while women certainly had less influence than men, they were by no means powerless, even though the particular scope for action and influence depended upon class and ethnic differences. Thus we cannot be satisfied with a description of women as merely the victims and the objects of Nazi policy who were simply forced to adapt to reality. The private sphere was by no means a safe and sane refuge; some women denounced their husbands.[58] Many mothers educated their children in the Nazi spirit; in other words, we must think in terms not only of the "power of the father" but of the mother as well.[59] The evaluation of female behavior is particularly complicated when it comes to women who supported their "Nazi-men" morally and psychologically.[60] The Nazis had a predilection for a pleasurable and cosy family life which became more important the more these men committed crimes in their work but did not want to lose the "decency" which they supposedly demonstrated at home in their role as good husbands and fathers. The influences that shaped intersexual relations were often complex and multi-layered. Because attitudes and gestures were frequently more important than "high-sounding phrases," there are few documentary sources which would allow us to explore this dimension of support for National Socialism; even oral history is often deficient when it comes to the subtle nuances of the intimate, private sphere.

There is no clear-cut answer to the problem of conducting empirical historical research on women's guilt. One reasonable approach involves constructing a socio-cultural reappraisal of individual or group biographical backgrounds and thereby reconstructing as exactly as possible the components which were self-determined *and* those which were determined by exterior forces, as well as the mixture of both.[61] Bock's attempt to make women as wives and mothers free of guilt is not very productive. Mothers' and wives' experiences were defined not only by the private but also by the public sphere. And the attitudes of women and also of juveniles in the female public sphere can often only be explained by looking at experiences formed in the private sphere.

It might be useful to look more closely at the women who were committed to the Nazi movement and its female public sphere. Activist women wanted to enlarge their own domain – children, kitchen, church, hospital and culture – and thus to influence society as women. For example, Renate Finkh, born in 1926, joined the Hitler Youth (*Hitlerjugend*) and assumed a leading position as *Jungmädelführerin* in 1940. Ambitious and proud of belonging to the elite of the so-called German "national community" (*Volksgemeinschaft*), she tried to influence the private sphere of other daughters and mothers so as to convince them of the Nazi ideology.[62] In her life, then, there was a mutual interaction between the female public sphere and the private sphere.

In her article on girls who were leaders of the League of German Girls (*Bund deutscher Mädel*), Dagmar Reese talks about "entanglement and responsibility" (*Verstrickung und Verantwortung*) but doubts that these particular teenagers can be seen as "mature individuals."[63] Yet Reese also defines her task as

> showing that active involvement in the League of German Girls made, or could have made, sense in the life situation of female juveniles – at the same time, however, emphasizing that this involvement had and still has a political dimension: women remain responsible for their behaviour.[64]

Reese presents four types of women: (a) the politically oriented leader; (b) the young woman prepared to adapt who primarily focussed upon protecting her social status; (c) the rebellious type who wanted to escape from home; (d) the social climber. With the possible exception of the first category, each of these different types of young women joined the BdM for reasons that derived more or less from their position in the private sphere. Again we are led to the issue of the entanglement of private and public spheres.

Reese is of course correct when she differentiates between the extent of the responsibility of each type. She holds the politically oriented leaders (type (a)) fully responsible for their acts. Reese analyses the behavior of the other types and especially of those in group (b) who were prepared to adapt, in terms of the relationship between the individual and a modern, sectionally organized system in which individuals are only "cogs in a wheel" (a relationship to which Hannah Arendt had earlier drawn attention). The system could be maintained because individuals limited their perceptions and made obedience their maxim.[65] Agreeing with Hannah Arendt, Reese states "that, in the case of adults, obedience means support, with the result that a system which appears to be passively tolerated" is in fact "actively maintained."[66] Men were, in general, more involved in political thought and action than were women. But we must also consider how narrowly the term "political" was defined at the time. Should "politics" perhaps not also include the societal norms and values of the Nazi regime [which both women and men helped to reproduce], such as the ideal of a "pure *Volk*" or the specifically Nazi development of "modernization?"[67]

Finally, there are strong arguments in favour of abandoning the search for "pure types" (i.e. for those who were "only" victims or "only" perpetrators) so as to focus more attention upon what can be called "mixed types." In the everyday realities produced by German fascism, ordinary men and women became complex and contradictory combinations of both victims *and* perpetrators, although this mixture of roles probably displayed gender-specific features because women were confined to minor political offices and to the less overtly Nazified everyday life of the private sphere. This meant that women were commonly co-observers, co-listeners and co-possessors of "guilty" knowledge, rather than co-perpetrators; their "complicity" consisted of passivity and toleration in the face of an action, but not the action itself. The investigation of such mixtures of opposites, of such "sites of contradiction" in their gender-specific forms can be productive not only because it reveals the complex subjectivity of women but also the complexity of all individual reactions, whether male or female, to Nazi attitudes and decisions.

"NEGATIVE PROPERTY?"

Female historians have the same right as male historians to different understandings of history and society and to different epistemologies. Female historians cannot and should not expect to achieve a homogeneous interpretation of the role of women in the Third Reich. The differences that separate historical assessments have, in part, arisen from differing viewpoints on the question of whether the disadvantages and subordinations to which women have been historically subjected can only be properly understood by those who identify "as much as possible" with the female gender. Some female historians certainly appear to think this type of identification is absolutely necessary. Consequently, women's history has been written with the aim of constructing a homogeneous gender history, free of contradictions, with which contemporary women can uncritically identify. The negative aspects have been left out, even though the price has sometimes – as in the case of the Third Reich – been high, amounting, indeed, to a denial that women acted as responsible subjects. Women's deeds have usually been evaluated "only" with regard to their inherent "social logic." Although this approach has provided an extremely worthwhile enrichment of the modern historiography of women, it should not allow us to ignore the impact of women's attitudes and actions upon the Nazi system as a whole.

Exactly why the "history of women in German fascism" should be integrated into a strategy of gender identification, as, for example, Kuhn and Rothe have done, remains a puzzle.[68] Nazi propaganda spoke of "the" women in general, but the real lives and experiences of women under Nazism varied greatly. Should we not rather identify with particular individual females or groups of women – for instance, with the many female political opponents of Nazism and the women resistance fighters, with Jewish women and the other real female victims of the Third Reich – while at the same time not ignoring "the others" who were structurally involved in the Nazi system or who, as individuals, were more or less "guilty?"[69]

Only a critical, as well as empathetic, approach to the history of women can produce the capacity for understanding which promotes the emancipation of women. And (female) historians should also discuss a question which Jean Amery asks about Germans in general and which Lerke Gravenhorst now addresses to women – namely, whether the history of women in the Third Reich must be appropriated as a kind of "negative property."[70] Whether the Nazi regime is presented primarily as a dictatorship exercised by men or by both men and women – with, of course, due recognition of the fact that power and responsibility were by no means equally shared – cannot be a small concern. Future research must discover how and to what extent the Nazi regime managed to integrate women. It must also explain why, as Hanna Lauterbach puts it, "most women [felt] that they themselves and all they valued were not suppressed by the regime and its ideology."[71] Was it all "just" a great historical misunderstanding? Did women mistakenly see fascism as a special type of "emancipation?"[72] Or had the decisive steps already been taken in the Weimar Republic as a result of widespread authoritarianism which, as Komann points out, prevented women from seeing the realistic chances offered them for emancipation and using them for the transformation of their wishes into social and economic autonomy?[73] Heilbrunn argues that religions which "train women to accept an inferior status, to exist only for the support and nurturance of men and children, are simultaneously training them for an authoritarian world."[74] Did religion play this role in the Weimar Republic and in the Third Reich and what role does religion play today?

The highly controversial interpretations of women's roles in the Third Reich which I have discussed in this article can be seen as the "female" side of the *"Historikerstreit."** This *"Historikerinnenstreit"* [conflict among historians of women] has focussed, in particular, upon the question of whether one half of the population (women) can be absolved of any real responsibility for the crimes of the (male) Nazi regime. Many women historians (but hardly any men) have participated in this *"Historikerinnenstreit."* On the other hand, it is quite remarkable that few women have contributed to the *"Historikerstreit."*[75] It will be important in the future to overcome these kinds of gendered divisions with regard to the most central issues of German historiography.

*The *Historikerstreit* or "historians' conflict" was a heated controversy in the late 1980s in which the German historian, Ernst Nolte, and the social theorist, Jürgen Habermas, played leading roles. Nolte claimed that the Holocaust was by no means a unique event in twentieth-century history and that genocide and totalitarian terror had not been invented by Hitler but by Stalin. Led by Habermas, Nolte's critics charged that his attempts to "relativize" the Holocaust, by comparing it to other genocides, amounted to nothing less than the "trivialization" of Nazi atrocities. The *Historikerstreit* did not produce a single piece of new evidence about the Holocaust or the Nazi regime. But it did show that certain historians were prepared to argue, as also were many leading conservative politicians, that the Nazi era should no longer be allowed to cast its shadow over the rest of Germany's modern history and over the identities of contemporary Germans.

NOTES

1 An earlier version of this article was published in *SOWI/Sozialwissenschaftliche Informationen*, Vol. 20, No. 2, 1991, pp. 97–104. I am very grateful to Gisela Johnson and David Crew for their assistance with this translation. I would also like to thank the participants in the discussion of an earlier version of this paper which was presented to a seminar in the German Department, University of California at Berkeley in March 1993.

2 Critical surveys of the historiography of women in the Third Reich are presented by Haubrich and Gravenhorst and – with somewhat different conclusions – by Reese and Sachse: Karin Haubrich and Lerke Gravenhorst, "Wie stellen wir heute moralische Wirklichkeiten von Frauen im Nationalsozialismus her?" in Lerke Gravenhorst and Carmen Tatschmurat (eds), *Töchter-Fragen. NS-Frauen-Geschichte* (Freiburg, i. Br., 1990) and Dagmar Reese and Carola Sachse, "Frauenforschung und Nationalsozialismus. Eine Bilanz" also in *Töchter-Fragen*, pp. 73–107; Gudrun Brockhaus also presents a critical discussion of the literature in which the thesis of "women as victims" dominates; see Gudrun Brockhaus, "Opfer, Täterin, Mitbeteiligte. Zur Diskussion um die Rolle der Frauen im Nationalsozialismus" in *Töchter-Fragen*, pp. 107–27.

3 See Christina Thurmer-Rohr, *Vagabundinnen. Feministische Essays* 3rd edn (Berlin, 1987); Beate Schaeffer-Hegel (ed.), *Frauen und Macht. Der alltägliche Beitrag der Frauen zur Politik des Patriarchats*, 2nd edn (Pfaffenweiler, 1988).

4 Gisela Bock, "Die Frauen und der Nationalsozialismus: Bemerkungen zu einem Buch von Claudia Koonz," *Geschichte und Gesellschaft*, Vol. 15, No. 4, 1989, pp. 563–79. I intend in this article not to review Koonz's book, but rather to present her main arguments, which I have sometimes exaggerated and sharpened so as to be able to

work out more precisely the differences, both methodological and interpretive, between Koonz and Bock.

5 See, for example, Annette Kuhn and Valentine Rothe (eds), *Frauen im deutschen Faschismus* (Düsseldorf, 1982); Gerda Szepansky, *"Blitz-mädel"*, *"Heldenmutter"*, *"Kriegerwitwe"* (Frankfurt, 1986).

6 See, for example, Ute Frevert, *Frauen-Geschichte. Zwischen Bürgerlicher Verbesserung und Neuer Weiblichkeit* (Frankfurt, 1986), p. 209; Georg Tidl, *Die Frau im Nationalsozialismus* (Wien/München/Zurich, 1984), pp. 35–41.

7 See, for example, Rita Thalman, *Frausein im Dritten Reich* (München/Wien, 1984), pp. 94–104.

8 Ibid., p. 104.

9 This change was produced by the introduction of the "Hauswirtschaftliches Jahr" (Housekeeping Year) and by the "Arbeitsdienst für Mädchen" (Labor Service for Girls).

10 Claudia Koonz draws a similar conclusion; see Claudia Koonz, "Erwiderung auf Gisela Bocks Rezension von 'Mothers of the Fatherland'," *Geschichte und Gesellschaft*, Vol. 18, No. 3, 1992, p. 396; see also Lerke Gravenhorst, "Nehmen wir Nationalsozialismus und Auschwitz ausreichend als unser negatives Eigentum in Anspruch? Zu Problemen im feministisch-sozialwissenschaftlichen Diskurs in der Bundesrepublik Deutschland" in *Töchter-Fragen*, p. 29.

11 Atina Grossmann, "Feminist debates about women and National Socialism," *Gender and History*, Vol. 3, No. 3, 1991, p. 355.

12 Gisela Bock, *Zwangssterilisation im Nationalsozialismus* (Opladen, 1986), p. 462.

13 Ibid., p. 139. See also Helga Schubert's argument that denouncers were victims; Helga Schubert, *Judasfrauen: Zehn Fallgeschichten weiblicher Denunziation im "Dritten Reich"*, 3rd edn (Frankfurt, 1990).

14 This information was given to me by Claus Füllberg-Stolberg (History Department, University of Hanover) who is directing a research project on women in Nazi concentration camps.

15 Schubert, *Judasfrauen*, p. 9; Schubert's intention (which can, however, be questioned) is to present denunciation as a "typically female" form of participation in the crimes of the Third Reich.

16 Dagmar Reese, "Homo homini lupus-Frauen als Täterinnen?" in *Internationale Wissenschaftliche Korrespondenz für die Geschichte der deutschen Arbeiterbewegung (IWK)*, Vol. 27, No. 1, 1991, p. 34.

17 Of course, the concept of the two spheres is an analytical construction which reflects the complexities of reality only in very approximate terms. In this discussion, I have omitted consideration of the professional realm, the sphere of production and other parts of the public sphere, because this does not touch upon this controversy. Although Jürgen Habermas has also worked on the private and public spheres, his focus differs from that of the *Historikerinnenstreit*; see Jürgen Habermas, *Strukturwandel der Öffentlichkeit* (Neuwied/Berlin, 1962).

18 This criticism is made not only by Bock ("Historikerinnenstreit,"

Geschichte und Gesellschaft) but also by Reese and Sachse ("Frauenforschung" in *Töchter-Fragen*, p. 101).

19 Bock, "Historikerinnenstreit", *Geschichte und Gesellschaft*, p. 404.

20 Claudia Koonz, *Mothers in the Fatherland. Women, the Family and Nazi Politics* (New York, 1987), p. 6.

21 Ibid., p. 420.

22 Ernst Fraenkel, *Der Doppelstaat* (Frankfurt, 1974), 1st edn (New York, 1940); the terms "prerogative state" and "normative state" are used in the 1941 English translation of Fraenkel's book by E. A. Shils, Edith Lowenstein and Klaus Knorr; see *The Dual State. A Contribution to the Theory of Dictatorship* (New York/London/Toronto, 1941), Introduction, pp. xiii–xiv: "By the Prerogative State we mean that governmental system which exercises unlimited arbitrariness and violence unchecked by any legal guarantees, and by the Normative State an administrative body endowed with elaborate powers for safeguarding the legal order as expressed in statutes, decisions of the courts, and activities of the administrative agencies."

23 Fraenkel was concerned "only" with legal issues.

24 Reese and Sachse, "Frauenforschung" in *Töchter-Fragen*, p. 102.

25 A "block warden" (*Blockwart*) was a person who had to observe and report on the behavior of the inhabitants of several houses.

26 Also cited in Adelheid von Saldern, "Die Situation der Frau im Dritten Reich", in Historisches Museum am Hohen Ufer (ed.), *1933 und danach. Hannover* (Hannover, 1983), p. 52.

27 Szepanksy, *Blitzmädel*, p. 9.

28 Kuhn and Rothe, *Frauen*, p. 18.

29 Ibid., p. 15.

30 Karin Windaus-Walser, "Gnade der weiblichen Geburt? Zum Umgang der Frauenforschung mit Nationalsozialismus und Antisemitismus," *Feministische Studien*, Vol. 6, No. 1, 1988, p. 105.

31 Ibid., p. 94.

32 Bock does not systematically analyze the role of women in the practical implementation of this policy but some of her references give the impression that women were reluctant to participate; Bock, *Zwangssterilisation*, pp. 208, 298, 302, 344, 392.

33 Examples in Angela Ebbinghaus (ed.), *Opfer und Täterinnen. Frauenbiographien des Nationalsozialismus* (Nördlingen, 1987); see also p. 7.

34 Ute Daniel, "Über die alltäglichen Grenzen der Verantwortung: Industriearbeit 1933–1945" in *SOWI/Sozialwissenschaftliche Informationen*, Vol. 20, No. 2, 1991, p. 85.

35 Ibid., p. 87.

36 Koonz, *Mothers in the Fatherland*, p. 457.

37 See, for instance, Jill Stephenson, *The Nazi Organisation of Women* (London, 1981), p. 170.

38 Koonz, "Erwiderung," *Geschichte und Gesellschaft*, p. 395.

39 Hiltraud Schmidt-Waldherr, "Konflikte um die 'Neue Frau' zwischen liberal-bürgerlichen Frauen und den Nationalsozialisten" in *Töchter-Fragen*, p. 181.

40 Annemarie Tröger and Jürgen Falter have commented critically upon this stereotype; see Annemarie Tröger, "Die Dolchstosslegende der Linken. 'Frauen haben Hitler an die Macht gebracht'" in Gruppe Berliner Dozentinnen (eds), *Frauen und Wissenschaft. Beiträge zur Berliner Sommeruniversität für Frauen*, July 1976 (Berlin, 1977), p. 326 and Jürgen W. Falter, *Hitlers Wähler* (München, 1991), p. 136.

41 Tröger, "Dolchstosslegende," *Frauen und Wissenschaft*, p. 327; see also Falter, *Hitlers Wähler*, pp. 136–46.

42 A precise analysis cannot be constructed, because gender was often not taken into consideration when the election data was originally collected; see Falter, *Hitlers Wähler*, p. 139.

43 The current trend in historical studies is to attempt to replace the "manipulation thesis" with other explanations, directed more at the analysis of social interests, milieux, mentalities and "social logics"; see also Frevert, *Frauen-Geschichte*, p. 207.

44 Helen L. Boak, " 'Our last hope': Women's votes for Hitler – A reappraisal," *German Studies Review*, Vol. 12, No. 2, 1989, p. 303. Boak refers to Thomas Childers, *The Nazi Voter. The Social Foundations of Fascism in Germany, 1919–1933* (London, 1983), p. 267.

45 Koonz, *Mothers in the Fatherland*, p. 55.

46 Windaus-Walser, "Gnade," *Feministische Studien*, p. 112.

47 Dorothea Schmidt, "Die peinlichen Verwandtschaften-Frauenforschung zum Nationalsozialismus" in Heide Gerstenberger and Dorothea Schmidt (eds), *Normalität oder Normalisierung* (Münster, 1987), p. 58.

48 Boak, " 'Our last hope'," *German Studies Review*, p. 303.

49 Ibid., p. 302.

50 Translated into English as *The Peaceable Sex: On Aggression in Women and Men* (New York, 1987).

51 Margarete Mitscherlich, *Die friedfertige Frau* (Frankfurt, 1985), p. 152.

52 Ibid., pp. 160, 156.

53 Windaus-Walser, "Gnade," *Feministische Studien*, p. 111.

54 Ibid.

55 These differences result from a "typical" female "mechanism of delegation" or "indirect participation," as well as from the relatively strict division which obviously exists between female wishes or phantasies, on the one hand, and female deeds, on the other.

56 Bock, "Historikerinnenstreit," *Geschichte und Gesellschaft*, p. 400.

57 Ibid., p. 401.

58 See the article by Klaus-Michael Mallmann and Gerhard Paul in this volume and also Klaus-Michael Mallman and Gerhard Paul, *Herrschaft und Alltag. Ein Industrierevier im Dritten Reich* (Bonn, 1991), p. 233.

59 See Windaus-Walser, "Gnade," *Feministische Studien*, p. 11.

60 See Claudia Koonz, "Mothers in the Fatherland: Women in Nazi Germany" in Renate Bridenthal and Claudia Koonz (eds), *Becoming Visible. Women in European History* (Boston, 1977), p. 470.

61 See, for example, Inge Marssolek's book about Helene Schwärzel's denunciation of Carl Goerdeler: *Die Denunziantin: Helene Schwärzel, 1944-47* (Bremen, 1993).

62 See Charles Schüddekopf (ed.), *Der alltägliche Faschismus. Frauen im Dritten Reich* (Berlin/Bonn, 1981), p. 68; further examples can be found in Renate Wiggershaus, *Frauen unterm Nationalsozialismus* (Wuppertal, 1984).

63 Dagmar Reese, "Verstrickung und Verantwortung. Weibliche Jugendliche in der Führung des Bundes Deutscher Mädel," *SOWI/Sozialwissenschaftliche Informationen*, Vol. 20, No. 2, 1991, p. 90.

64 Ibid., p. 91.

65 Ibid., p. 95.

66 Hannah Arendt, *Nach Auschwitz. Essays & Kommentare* (Berlin, 1989). Reese concludes from her interviews that it is usually only the "social climber" and "the rebellious type" who are prepared, after 1945, to reflect seriously upon their participation in the Nazi system; those who were willing "just" to adapt, tend to make light of the Nazi system because they were supposedly neither emotionally involved with the system nor existentially integrated into it; Reese, "Homo homini lupus" in *Internationale Wissenschaftliche Korrespondenz*, p. 96.

67 Ute Frevert takes the issue of "modernization" into consideration and – as a result – the possible positive impacts upon women's attitudes toward the Nazi regime: "Many reforms were absolutely attractive ..." Frevert mentions youth policy, the divorce law reform and the female NS organizations; Frevert, *Frauen-Geschichte*, p. 242. The question of "modernization" should be examined more closely in future research, although the term "modernization" must be disconnected from the "concept of enlightenment." Unless the Janus-face of modernization, i.e. the potential in "modernization" for barbarism, is made a central theme, the Third Reich could appear in an unwarranted positive light.

68 Kuhn and Rothe, *Frauen.*

69 In this article, there is, unfortunately, not room to discuss the rich history of politically motivated women who were part of the opposition to Nazism.

70 Jean Amery, *Jenseits von Schuld und Sühne* (München, 1980; 1966), p. 124; Gravenhorst, "Negatives Eigentum" in *Töchter-Fragen*, pp. 21, 25.

71 Hanna Lauterbach, "'Aber dann hätten wir ja nur noch Verbrecherinnen ...' Kommentar zur Diskussion über den Anteil von Frauen am 'Handlungskollektiv Deutschland'" in *Töchter-Fragen*, p. 143.

72 See Gudrun Brockhaus, "Opfer" in *Töchter-Fragen*, p. 123.

73 Margot Komann, "'Wie ich Nationalsozialistin wurde.' Eine kritisch-feministische Lektüre der Theodore Abel-Akten" in *Töchter-Fragen* p. 165.

74 Carolyn C. Heilbrun, "Women, Jews, and Nazism," *The Yale Review*, Vol. 77, No. 1, 1987, p. 78. The relevance of this statement for

the Catholic Church must be amended in one important respect; Catholicism was (and is) a form of authoritarianism that is not state-oriented. In many cases, this led to a special type of cultural resistance to the Nazi regime.

75 See Mary Nolan, "The *Historikerstreit* and social history," *New German Critique*, Vol. 44, Spring/Summer 1988, pp. 51–80; Adelheid von Saldern, "Hillgrubers 'Zweierlei Untergang' – der Untergang historischer Erfahrungsanalyse?" in *Normalität oder Normalisierung*, pp. 160–70; Adelheid von Saldern and Irmgard Wilharm, "NS-Geschichtsbild und historisch-politische Kultur am Wendepunkt" in Hannoversche Hochschulgemeinschaft (ed.), *Uni Hannover. Zeitschrift der Universität Hannover*, Vol. 14, No. 1, 1987, pp. 36–48.

5

OMNISCIENT, OMNIPOTENT, OMNIPRESENT?

Gestapo, society and resistance

Klaus-Michael Mallmann and Gerhard Paul

Ever since 1933, the Gestapo has been the ultimate symbol of that typically twentieth-century nightmare, the totalitarian police state. In the following article, Mallmann and Paul show, however, that the popular image of the Gestapo is a "myth" originally propagated by the Gestapo leaders themselves. After the war, historians perpetuated this myth of the "omniscient, omnipotent, omnipresent" Gestapo by taking the Gestapo leaders' statements of aims and ambitions as accurate reflections of everyday Gestapo practices. The "myth" of the Gestapo also gave the mass of ordinary Germans a convenient alibi; their failure to engage in serious resistance to the Nazi dictatorship could simply be seen as the inevitable consequence of the Gestapo's awesome power.

Mallmann and Paul dissolve these widely circulated images of Gestapo omnipotence and popular impotence by showing just how ill-equipped most Gestapo district offices were to perform the role of totalitarian "Big Brother." Local Gestapo offices simply did not have the manpower necessary to put into practice the increasingly grandiose directives issued by the Berlin central office. Indeed, the Gestapo would have been virtually "blind," had it not been able to draw upon the information produced by a "flood" of denunciations made by ordinary Germans against their relatives, friends and neighbors. The authors uncover a terrifying social landscape (not unlike the description of the former East Germany that is beginning to emerge from its voluminous secret police (Stasi) files) in which ordinary people eagerly helped to police one another. Most denunciations were generated not by political or ideological conviction but by anger, greed, hate and prejudice. Ordinary Germans used the Gestapo to settle scores with neighbors or relatives, to rid themselves of inconvenient spouses or to acquire Jewish property. The fact that this "plebiscitary" dimension of Nazi terror was by no means rational or predictable made the reality of the Gestapo even more frightening than the myth.

* * *

The story of the Gestapo is not least the story of its perception in the "distorted mirror" of omnipotence, omniscience and ubiquity. The aura of a perfectly operating secret police was preeminently an image created by means of propaganda, which was meant to intimidate but also to conceal its own structural deficits. Although this picture was in many respects a chimera – as we intend to show – it none the less gave reality its direction, indeed created its own unique reality, thereby furnishing the Gestapo with the aura of the most extreme criminological efficiency, which constituted a not insignificant part of its effectiveness, even though it was fictional. In 1941, at the German Police Convention, (Reinhard) Heydrich praised the fact that "The secret police, the criminal police and the security forces are shrouded in the whispered secrets of the political crime novel."[1]

The conceptions of the resistance fighters and of those in exile were also not left untouched by this carefully staged representation of the secret police, tracking down the regime's enemies with instinctual sureness. Right from the beginning this image especially impressed the left because the absence of mass resistance, their own growing social isolation, along with the decimation of their ranks – all this forced them to accept an explanation, which would not shake the basic foundations of their own worldview. The image of the Gestapo fabricated by the regime was just what was needed. The alleged perfection of the secret police's surveillance methods and the supposed efficiency of the Gestapo's omnipotent apparatus offered a "back door" through which the resistance could escape any confrontation with the reality of the shattered labor movement or the reasons that the possibility of an insurrection were fading. Because their own projections, patterns of interpretation and modes of thinking interfered with their perceptions, distinctly paranoid forms of perception were increasingly produced, which had very little in common with the reality of the state police, which indeed said more about the authors of these reports than about the actual subject being described.

For example: Franz Vogt, a former Social Democratic Party deputy in the Prussian *Landtag* and head of the Amsterdam working group of the German "Free" trade union mineworkers, maintained in 1936 that "One must assume that, in each factory, there is at least one informer for every twelve or fifteen workers."[2] In the years that followed, the "voyeurism" of the secret state police assumed even more abstruse forms in the consciousness of the illegal opposition: "The Gestapo has extended its spy network so much that it can now do without voluntary informers," claimed the Social Democratic "Germany Reports" of 1938. In Berlin, it was supposed to be "well known, that the Gestapo has a section of several thousand officials, designated by the technical term, 'Iron Reserve'. These are people who live quite inconspicuously in tenement buildings and whose functions are only known to the responsible (Nazi party) block leader."[3] The same tendency to see brown ghosts everywhere can also be found among the communists. In 1936 the KPD-section leadership in Forbach, who was responsible for the Saar region, reported that "individual miners have been permanently observed by spies on the way to and from their work as well as on the job."[4] Because the communist press in exile regarded National Socialism not as a mass movement but only as the executive committee of monopoly capitalism, it massively overestimated the numbers of agents implanted by the Gestapo, and drastically underestimated the extent of proletarian collaboration with the regime. The claim, that "the Gestapo [infiltrates] spies into the factories, in order to eavesdrop on the workers' conversations" was the product of tunnel vision;[5] the fact that there were large numbers of voluntary informers was ignored or dismissed as the act of traitors who had been bribed. The left was not pretending to be blind; it was.

After 1945 the myth of the all-powerful Gestapo, which totally left out of the picture the causes of the state police's successes, and which grotesquely exaggerated the unity of the regime, underwent a change in function. Eugen Kogon's book, *The SS-State*, which first appeared in 1946 and went through numerous subsequent editions, reluctantly provided the arguments for this view although it was more of an *ad hoc* eyewitness report than a fully developed scientific analysis.[6] In both the east and the west, the propagandistic attitudes of those formerly in power advanced to the status of a creed, capable of being supported by a majority and of creating consensus, which served as an instrument of collective political apology. The idea that a Gestapo agent had, so to speak, stood guard at every street corner, provided, once again, a suitable "escape hatch" – this time for the "man in the street" and his opportunistic acquiescence in the Nazi past. In his "classical" local study of the Nazi "seizure of power" in Northeim, William Sheridan Allen concluded that "The general feeling was that the Gestapo was everywhere" – even though in this small town in southern Lower Saxony, in addition to the regular police, there had only been one occasional informer for the security police, but not one single permanent Gestapo agent.[7] This model of the SS- or Gestapo-State as an unscrupulous clique dominating the German people, although a historical misrepresentation, provided absolution and so became a founding myth of both German states which managed to establish that Germans had been absolutely overpowered by their "criminal rulers," that they had been completely helpless against the "Nazi Socialist tyranny of violence," and thus also managed to conjure away the Gestapo and the SS as some kind of social enclave not really part of German society.[8]

Research on the Nazis and on the resistance also reproduced this separation and swallowed whole the myth of omnipotence and efficiency. Instead of penetrating the propagandistic obfuscation and analyzing the actual procedures of the "Prerogative State" (*Massnahmenstaat*), its regional topography, the way it was embedded in society, and above all the realities of its everyday practice, this literature has simply absorbed Heydrich's viewpoint, created by a bluff meant to "educate" the German people. The history of the Gestapo has become a one-dimensional success story of the omnipotent supermen in black. For Edward Crankshaw the Gestapo was a "highly professional corps."[9] Gerhard Schulz saw it as a perfectly functioning instrument of surveillance: "scarcely a politically significant initiative against the National Socialist regime went undetected."[10] And Friedrich Zipfel speculated that "it [would be] safe to assume that the network of spies was very tight and that the Gestapo was served excellently by its informers."[11] Especially Jacques Delarue's *History of the Gestapo* – still regarded as a standard work – was taken in by the great claims made by the Nazi police strategists: "Never before, in no other land and at no other time, had an organisation attained such a comprehensive penetration (of society), possessed such power and, reached such a degree of 'completeness' in its ability to arouse terror and horror, as well as in its actual effectiveness." As the informers of the Gestapo "spotted or overheard every German's slightest movement," the omniscience of the Gestapo was for Delarue as unquestionable as its omnipotence, both of which he quite simply derived from the Gestapo's formal functions. According to his circular argumentation at the level of an introductory seminar course: "in order to carry out its functions, the Gestapo had to be omnipotent."[12] The tradition of such thrillers extends, unbroken, right into the present. Jochen von Lang's book *Die Gestapo*, which appeared in 1990, conjures up the metaphysical dimensions of this omnnipotence as does Adolf Diamant's treatise on the Gestapo offices in Frankfurt and Leipzig.[13] Like their predecessors, both authors mistake intention for reality, confuse the program with the actual practice; they become completely intoxicated with the monstrosity of the Gestapo, but they do not give a single thought to the investigation of the actual ways in which it worked. Common to all of these studies is the fact that their evaluations are based not upon empirical study but largely upon a system of speculative supposition. The intentions of the Nazi police strategists concerning a comprehensive system of police control over German society has thereby achieved a certain retrospective historiographical reality.

However, the impression that in all these years there has only been stagnation would be false, though none of the important works even began to feel their way beyond the accepted dogma. For example, Hans Buchheim's "classical study" provided a vivid description of the fusion of the SS and the police, but he outlined only the framework within which the Gestapo operated, not, however its actual activity.[14] The same basic objection applies to all the other central studies of this topic; so, for instance, Heinz Hohne's *Orden unter dem Totenkopf* (*The Order of the Death's Head*), which was one of the first studies to correct the idea of a monolithic dictatorship and to focus attention upon the permanent polycratic conflicts and the system of structural self-hindrance,[15] the work of Shlomo Aronson, Christoph Graf and George C. Browder on the beginnings of the Gestapo[16] as well as the study of Gestapo head-quarters in the Prinz-Albrecht-Strasse by Johannes Tuchel and Reinhold Schattenfroh.[17] In spite of their excellent historiographical quality, these studies continued to be trapped in a traditional institutional history, did not push forward to an analysis of the Gestapo's repertoire of actions and ignored the interactions between the political police and society.[18] "One was much more interested in the designs and plans than in the actual ways in which this system operated," as the Canadian historian, Robert Gellately, quite rightly observes; "the prevalence of this perspective prevented historians from posing questions about the everyday practices of the police beyond the concentration-camps and the prisons; the entire social context remained unnoticed."[19] In addition, the distortion was increased by the perspective of a history written exclusively "from the top down." The focus of research was fixed on the Gestapo central office and the *Reich* main security office; but this bird's eye view from the Berlin center of operations, which was by no means the same as the realities of state policing at the local level, indirectly – and probably unintentionally – constructed the mystifying impression of omnipotence.

There is still no really detailed, empirical analysis of the ways in which the "Prerogative State" (*Massnahmenstaat*) actually functioned and, in particular, of the Gestapo as the central instance of organized, abnormal violence research which should also be a constitutive element of the study of resistance. Above all, the local Gestapo-offices – their structure, equipment and activities, their problems, mishaps and successes – have, until now, scarcely received systematic attention.[20] Even in the series of volumes, *Bayern in der NS-Zeit (Bavaria in the Nazi Period)*, published by the Institute for Contemporary History, which set new standards for all the research that followed, there was an inexplicable absence of even one monographic study of this issue, even though the now deceased director of the institute, Martin Broszat had demanded quite explicitly that the interaction between resistance and Nazi domination should be made a central topic of research.[21] On the contrary; despite this pathbreaking agenda, the idea that the Gestapo was everywhere crept into the "Bavaria project" as well. So, for example, without any closer examination or supporting evidence, Hartmut Mehringer wrote in his study of the KPD in Bavaria about "the increasing efficiency of the police apparatus of surveillance and persecution" whose "spy network [he claims to have been] ... almost perfect in the big cities after the autumn of 1933" and which had at its disposal "a whole army of internal informants" at the BMW company in Munich.[22] The omnipotent "big brother" had tacitly become a premise, not a theme of research.

This example is perfectly symptomatic of the current state of research; normally the examination of concrete Gestapo practices has been subsumed within research on resistance and has emerged – if at all – as a by-product of the numerous studies of oppositional behavior in individual cities and regions where it warrants, at the most, a thin section of one chapter.[23] As a rule, the *leitmotif* of omnipotence, omnipresence and omniscience, developed in Kogon's *SS-State* and perfected by Delarue, was simply filled with regional and local data. Even when a local secret police office, like the one in Gladbeck, turned out to have only four or six officers, it was still assumed that there the opponents of the regime had been placed "under permanent observation."[24] In most analyses, persistent observation and accurately directed terror became a kind of password or "missing link" which provided an effortless explanation for the fact that resistance had been crushed, frustrated or was, simply, absent. By mythologizing Gestapo terror, historians created a universal formula, a kind of modeling clay, that could be used to cover over every empirical crack in the picture, a universal solution, which without too much expenditure of thought seemed always to be appropriate. With this "self-activating" analysis a hermetically sealed circuit of interpretation emerged, based on circular arguments, whose premises could no longer be verified, whose results were already long since firmly established in advance. Endless studies give the impression that it is simply the names of the people and the places that are different.

However, some local and regional studies did initiate a new way of looking at the reality of the Gestapo. Whenever the bird's eye view from the Berlin central office was not uncritically reproduced, when attention was focussed upon domination and resistance in an area small enough to be observed in detail, where the local structures of social milieux and the concrete activities of the agencies of persecution became transparent, then the myth of the ubiquitous, efficient Gestapo began to crumble, provided that historians did not try, from the very start, to force the empirical findings into the procrustean bed of the Gestapo's omnipotent significance. Above all, Detlev Peukert's study of the communist resistance in the Rhine and Ruhr areas drew attention to inconsistencies in the historiographic picture of the Gestapo,[25] as did Inge Marssolek and René Ott in their monograph on Bremen.[26] But while these were more or less accidental by-products of local or regional investigations of resistance, which were not based upon a systematic approach to the Gestapo or upon a theoretically informed formulation of the questions, Reinhard Mann's study of Düsseldorf was able, for the first time, to demonstrate statistically the outstanding importance of denunciations within the state police's repertoire of practices.[27] Robert Gellately's work on the Gestapo district office in Würzburg – which appeared in 1990 – reinforced this perspective and, for the first time, brought German society centrally into the analysis of this Nazi institution of domination, although he concentrated his empirical investigation upon the persecution of the Jews and the surveillance of Polish workers.[28] Burkhard Jellonek's Münster dissertation on the repression of homosexuals, which appeared in the same year, limited itself neither to the normative aspect nor to the national level, but rather scrutinized in great detail the local offices in Neustadt, Würzburg and Düsseldorf.[29] Our own study of the district Gestapo office in Saarbrücken, published in 1991, which attempted to reconstruct police methods of proceeding against the various targets of persecution, should also be mentioned.[30] Although these studies certainly by no means redress all the deficits of existing research, they none the less permit – as a kind of interim reappraisal – several observations on the general structure, the methods of functioning and the effectiveness of state police activity at the local level, which cast new light upon the internal mechanisms of the "Prerogative State" (*Massnahmenstaat*) which, because of their relatively broad empirical basis, can lay some claim to a certain paradigmatic significance. If the Gestapo is not deprecated, as a propagandistically inflated subject, but rather observed in its normality and everyday routine, then it becomes especially clear that its own strength could scarcely have made it capable of playing the role of the ubiquitous "Big Brother." What stands out the most obviously is denunciation, almost overlooked until now, but frightening in its extent; it kept the machinery of terror going, and constituted a central component of the internal "constitution" of the Third Reich.[31]

It has become clear in all of these studies that the National

Socialist "Prerogative State" (*Massnahmenstaat*) was certainly no thoroughly rationalized mechanism of repression, in which one gear meshed precisely with the other, keeping the entire population under close surveillance. In quantitative terms alone, the Gestapo at the local level was hardly an imposing detective organization, but much rather an under-staffed, under-bureaucratized agency, limping along behind the permanent inflation of its tasks and of its own imaginings of the enemy. In January 1934, for example, the district office in Stettin, like the one in Frankfurt/Main had just forty-one officers, Koslin only twenty-nine. In 1935 the Gestapo in Braunschweig had only twenty-six employees, Hanover, forty-two, Bremen, forty-four, Bielefeld, eighteen; the district offices in Dortmund und Recklinghausen, responsible for the Eastern Ruhr and the Münster regions had a total of seventy-six and sixty-one employees, respectively, including those at their sub-stations.[32] In Düsseldorf, the district office, responsible for the Lower Rhine, the *Bergische Land* and the Western Ruhr region with a combined population of 4 million people, could call on the services of 281 agents in March 1937, including all of those at the sub-stations. Würzburg – responsible for all of Lower Franconia – had only twenty-eight officials.[33]

By comparison, Saarbrücken, with 113 employees at the end of 1935, and even 171 in July 1938, enjoyed a relatively luxurious provision of personnel; a similar density cannot be found in any other industrial region.[34] But despite these exceptionally high numbers, the impression should not be given that here was a criminological expedition force whose surveillance tasks were easy from the point of view of manpower. By far the largest number of these people were engaged, not as field operatives, but as office workers. In addition, something like seventy employees were allocated to the sub-stations and the border police. Finally, if one takes into consideration the numerous responsibilities of a regional Gestapo office as well as their explosive growth,[35] then this impressive level of staffing becomes a relative matter. Just like everywhere else outside of the metropolises of Berlin, Hamburg or Munich, endless departments were the responsibility of only one expert; not infrequently this person actually had to take care of several departments.[36] It would be nonsense to talk here of comprehensive surveillance or of omnipotence; as a rule, this was more or less a symbolic presence.

After the beginning of the war, the number of staff declined rapidly. In the autumn of 1941 the district office in Saarbrücken had only ninety-six employees including twenty-five administrative officials and office clerks.[37] The personnel in Neustadt and Würzburg were reduced and these district offices were downgraded to sub-stations of, respectively, the Saarbrücken and Nuremberg-Fürth offices.[38] From this point onward, there was no break in the complaints about manpower shortages and overwork. Despite the fact that the numbers of foreign workers and war prisoners continued to increase which meant, from the Gestapo's perspective, that an ever greater security risk had emerged, the district offices came more and more to resemble a "transit camp." There was a permanent coming and going which certainly did not permit continuity in the activity of individual departments as ever greater numbers of employees were seconded to the *Einsatzgruppen* or allocated to the commanders of the SD in the occupied territories.[39] "And so the once truly mighty Gestapo had become a Potemkin village" the *Kriminalrat* Franz Biereth, head of Section IV of the Saarbrücken district office wrote after the war. "Behind the façade which was still maintained there stood essentially a miserable, wretched skeleton."[40]

In quantitative terms, the Gestapo hardly represented a nursery of National Socialist fanaticism. An analysis of the composition of the personnel of the district offices in Würzburg and Saarbrücken confirms the opinion expressed by Dr Werner Best to the Nuremberg military tribunal that especially the political police was staffed with "officials of the previous police agencies" and that the proportion of SS "at first remained very small."[41] The purging of police ranks was confined to the top level; continuity in personnel remained dominant, as did the secondary virtues of duty and obedience which were deeply engrained in the dependent career civil service.[42] The core of the Gestapo was formed from the Political Department of the Weimar police – operating mostly under the designation IA – that contributed, in particular, its expertise in combatting the communists.[43] To increase personnel or to create new district branches – as in Trier or Saarbrücken – the Gestapo turned, above all, to security or criminal police officers, who saw a transfer as an advancement of their careers, which, however, meant that in the field of combatting political opponents, the majority of the officers were self-taught.[44]

Only two of the Gestapo officers in Würzburg, the head of the department and his successor, had joined the Nazi Party before Hitler's accession to power; in 1933, four more followed, the remainder joined only in 1937 and 1939, respectively.[45] So far, at least, as staffing was concerned, the regional office in Saarbrücken was certainly not the domain of the SS or of the party; only about 10 per cent of those employed here belonged to the SS in 1935, while 50 per cent were party members. The number of those who did not belong to any Nazi organization was, at 40 per cent, amazingly high; even the director of Department II – a complete career official – joined the NSDAP only in 1942.[46] This picture of a by no means fanaticized police unit becomes even more heterogeneous when one considers that numerous Gestapo officials in Saarbrücken had been members of republican parties before 1933 and even remained practising Christians.[47] It would be mistaken, in the face of such diversity, to view the Gestapo simply as the agent of Nazi ideology in the years before the war; in 1939, only 3,000 of its roughly 20,000 employees held an SS-rank.[48] More decisive than recruitment from within the Nazi sub-culture were the lines of continuity with the German police upon which the Gestapo could support itself; the fixation upon the authoritarian, nation state, the traditional canon of secondary virtues, the deification of law and order, the mentality of the "unpolitical" civil servant.[49]

With the war came important qualitative changes in the staff structure of district offices. In Saarbrücken, young criminal police assistants took the places of employees who had been conscripted. A new type of Gestapo official began to rise in the ranks, less technically competent than the criminological experts they replaced, and at the same time far more ideological. Complaints about their insufficient professional training and aptitude remained the order of the day until the end of the war. And the structural changes in qualifications, along with an increasing mobility of staff led to a considerable reduction in the Gestapo's striking power. While the categories of the persecuted steadily expanded (and this increase in the Gestapo's functions had, by itself, greatly overloaded its capabilities), the number of trained criminologists, schooled in interrogation techniques, became an ever smaller minority. This decline in intelligent police practice promoted the replacement of inherited police methods with confessions extorted with the use of force. It was at this point in its history that the reality of the Gestapo began to conform to its popular image as a brutal gang of thugs.[50]

But it does not really make sense to speak, as Kogon seems to insinuate, of a "social downgrading" of the top Gestapo leadership.[51] The top levels of the district offices in Westphalia and in the Saarland were hardly the playgrounds of social failures, but rather rungs in the career ladders of young academics, trained in law, often with doctoral degrees. These were "technocrats of power" for whom National Socialism signified not the utopia of the "people's community" but the claims to leadership of a new, non-doctrinaire elite.[52] So, for example, although Josef Gerum, head of the Würzburg office, was a Nazi "veteran fighter," he was hardly a "pampered child" of the movement. Born in 1888 – and thus almost a generation older than his colleagues – he was a member of the Bavarian police from 1917, joined the NSDAP in 1920 and, like Hitler, was confined to the Landsberg prison after the November 1923 *Putsch* attempt. None the less, the *Gauleiter* of the Main-Franconia region went so far as to demand that Gerum be replaced because, "I am convinced that while Gerum might perhaps fit the needs of the Russian Tscheka he is absolutely unsuited to the operations of our political police."[53]

Our picture of the Nazi "Prerogative State" (*Massnahmenstaat*), which is so colored by the organized death-factories, is almost completely contradicted by the examination of everyday life in the Gestapo local offices. Here traces of efficiency and flexibility are hard to find. Rather the bureaucratic tutelage exercised from Gestapo headquarters and fueled by a veritable mania for regulations and instructions reduced the local offices to the instruments of a paper war with a much more bureaucratic style than the concept of the *Massnahmenstaat* would lead us to believe. By far the largest number of employees were responsible for the routine functioning of the office, with filing documents, sorting card files and registering regulations; in vain, they struggled to achieve the orderly administration of a steadily swelling flood of cases, while at the same time tormenting themselves with restrictions and obstacles they themselves had produced. The required card file system could present only the pretense of perfection; in reality, it produced such a flood of information that many vital facts simply got lost. The evaluation of interrogations and the deposition of documents had long since failed to correspond to the much-vaunted Teutonic sense of order; for example, it took more than three years until the central office gave permission to the Saarbrücken station to procure a single modern wire-tapping system. The correspondence dealing with this matter fills an entire bundle of documents.[54] Bickering over the demarcation of authority, paper war and the sheer bureaucratic waste of energy generated permanent frictions that reduced efficiency and appears often to have produced an effect exactly the opposite of what was intended; the result often hindered rather than enhanced the construction of an efficient *Massnahmenstaat*.[55]

Quantitative as well as qualitative deficiencies in staff, high mobility of personnel as well as over-bureaucratization had many different effects upon the Gestapo's choice of actions. It was rarely the case that local offices were able to ferret out their own suspects; instead they acted primarily as collection points for outside sources of information upon which the Gestapo then decided whether or not to act. It was a "mail-drop" for all sorts of reports "from below," but hardly a detective apparatus. Its officials were desk-bound perpetrators, not well-versed criminologists working in the streets. They administered terror, but the initiative came primarily "from below." In his sample of case files of the Düsseldorf district office, Reinhard Mann came to the conclusion that only 15 per cent of all the proceedings were based upon observations made directly by the Gestapo or its own informers (*V-Leute*).[56] The Saarbrücken district office also seems to have engaged in very little real, direct surveillance, perhaps only in the last phase of a few cases.[57]

The Gestapo's actions against homosexuals provides a good example of the fact that it was primarily a reactive institution and its investigations required an outside impetus. In the Pfalz and Lower Franconia, where there was no real homosexual subculture which might have offered a starting-point for Gestapo raids, the district offices in Neustadt and Würzburg had to rely completely upon "Police Commissar Accident"; that is upon charges made by ordinary citizens or other public agencies. Otherwise they could only hope that confessions made by individuals under interrogation could produce a "snowballing effect." On the other hand, in the larger conurbation of the Düsseldorf government district, the Gestapo found a homosexual sub-culture with its own bars, red-light districts and toilets that continued to flourish throughout the Nazi era. For careerist young officers who wanted to acquire good marks and thereby recommend themselves for promotion it was relatively easy, by staging raids on well-known meeting places, to produce a successful record in this sector, which, after the *"Röhm-Putsch,"* Himmler announced was to be seen as the barometer of Gestapo and Kripo performance. But this did not destroy the nerve centers of the gay "scene" or really suppress same-gender sexuality; because of staffing deficiencies alone, one had to be satisfied with sporadic actions.[58]

Although the extent of co-operation with the regime varied considerably according to the time period, the region and the type of criminalized behavior, denunciations represented probably the most important resource of state police knowledge, both quantitatively and qualitatively. In the Würzburg station's district about 57 per cent of all cases of "race pollution" (*Rassenschande*) and friendly relationships with Jews went back to reports made by the population; only a single case can be traced back to the Gestapo's own observations.[59] Especially in cases where the disagreements of everyday life had been verbalized, denunciation was the Gestapo's most important source of information. In 87.5 per cent of all cases of "malicious slander against the regime" (*Heimtückefälle*) the Saarbrücken district office first became active after reports were made by publicans or their customers, colleagues at work, passers-by in the street or family members; only 8 per cent can be traced back to surveillance carried out by official institutions like the post office, the railway or the local police. And 69.5 per cent of all cases which were put into the category of "treason" or "high treason" by the public prosecutor in Saarbrücken were based upon denunciations.[60]

Neither working-class neighborhoods nor the shop floor were the preserves of an "unbroken" class culture. In Lower Franconia and the Saarland, at least, the (self-) mobilization of the population for the denunciation of deviant opinions was predominantly a lower-class phenomenon – "people with a degree of social power they never had before"[61] – and more a problem of the anonymous larger cities than of the smaller rural communities where people knew one another. And even within the private space of the family, the Gestapo found its helpers, above all women (several husbands were sent to concentration camps by their wives' denunciations and some of them even lost their lives). Political fanaticism was an important, but certainly not the only, cause; as a rule, it was more often conflicting worldviews, desires for emancipation and the lust for revenge that played a role. Just as denunciation in the factory or the pub was a predominantly male affair, so, in turn in the realm of the family, denunciation was, with few exceptions, a female domain.[62] The pattern of interpreting the Nazi system of domination as public male terror[63] falls short decisively, not least in this respect. It might certainly be supposed that informers, both male and female, were not completely aware of all the possible consequences of their actions, but cases can certainly be cited in which physical extermination was not only accepted as a possible consequence of a denunciation, but actually even deliberately intended; for example, the working-class woman in Saarbrücken who accused her husband, a former communist, of listening to the "enemy radio," just in order to make room for her lover. She told her son, "Your dad will go away and you will get a much better one."[64]

The phenomenon of mass denunciation, whose extent did not remain hidden even from attentive foreign correspondents,[65] was not something that the regime compelled by means of a law or a relevant directive; it was solely a matter of free will. Indeed the official reactions to these rampant denunciations were rather ambivalent; high dignitaries such as Frick, Gürtner and Thierack warned against denunciations which were all too often pure fabrications and, as a rule, motivated by self-interest. The district office in Saarbrücken complained about "anonymous letter writers" and the "constant expansion of an appalling system of denunciation."[66] Even Heydrich himself ordered that people who made "unjustified, exaggerated charges . . . with malicious intent" should be sent to a concentration camp.[67] But on the other hand, the unscrupulous nature of these denunciations, which continued to grow until 1941, corresponded with the inflation of the definition of "crime" and with the steady politicization of social behavior caused by ever-increasing threats of punishment.[68] And, in the end, they compensated for the Gestapo's considerable investigative deficiencies, although, at the same time – in a certain dialectical inversion – they also caused a great deal of the overloading of the Gestapo capabilities and frequently harnessed district offices to the pursuit of personal interests. To this extent, denunciations were both dysfunctional yet indispensable.

Against conspiratorial groups of the Communist or Social Democratic Parties, however, denunciation proved to be an almost useless weapon. The only recipe for success in this area was the use of paid informers and their number was limited. The mystifying assumption that the Gestapo possessed a wide range of agents and spies conforms in no way to reality.[69] The six-person information department of the district office in Nuremberg-Fürth – responsible for the entire area of Northern Bavaria – had at its disposal in 1943–4 somewhat more than eighty to 100 informers, who reported on the anti-regime attitudes, efforts and incidents that came to their attention. The Saarbrücken counterpart of this agency could call upon only fifty spies in 1939.[70] There were among them only a handful of top agents. But there were numerous occasional informers providing low-grade intelligence, "busy-bodies," "braggarts," "boasters" and "confidence men," as well as several "small-time crooks," who delivered falsified materials or simply invented stories about sabotage and resistance movements in the hope of a quick reward.[71] At least five of the informers working for the Saarbrücken district office were arrested for "intelligence fraud"; and for this reason, Albert Conrad, the most important agent in the organization tracking the Communist Party at the border, lost his life in Buchenwald.

As a rule, not true renegades but broken figures put themselves at the Gestapo's disposal.[72] We can identify three paths for the recruitment of informers; first, there were ultra-leftist communists who offered themselves up voluntarily. They had believed that a German October Revolution was just around the corner; but the Nazi takeover completely disoriented them. Now they tried to vindicate themselves for their political past, and at the same time capitalize on their knowledge, by making a complete about-turn. The second group consisted of people with personal problems which were compounded by disillusionment about the possibilities for resistance.[73] But a standard variant was the person forced, while in a Gestapo prison, to declare his/her readiness to co-operate.[74] These people were frequently promised their freedom and they were sometimes given financial assurances and the promise of a job in an enterprise deemed important for state security.[75]

The Gestapo district office in Saarbrücken managed to break into the illegal organizations of the Communist and Social Democratic Parties with the help of only half-a-dozen members of the first two groups. They made it possible to arrest individual couriers and middle-men, but never entire underground groups. By the spring of 1937, the Gestapo's paid informers had all been exposed. Thereafter, the district office lost contact with the illegal Communist Party and mostly groped around in the dark in this important field. From this point onward, the agents infiltrated by the Gestapo were unable to make further inroads into either the communist border organization, which functioned until the outbreak of the war, or the network of remaining small groups, which managed, even during the war, to engage in secret activities. The third group remained relatively ineffective because these people were looked upon with suspicion and mistrust from the very beginning. Even the Gestapo had to admit that

> People find it strange that these former party followers have no problem getting work in companies that are protected for reasons of state security, even though some of them were far more politically active than people who have already been denied jobs in these same enterprises.[76]

Hartmut Mehringer argues that a Gestapo informer, who managed in 1935–6 to establish contact with the top of the illegal KPD in Southern Bavaria, "represents a typical product of exactly this milieu and its development under the pressure of Nazi persecution." But this conclusion seems quite exaggerated.[77]

The intelligence weaknesses of the district office in Saarbrücken were by no means unusual, and were certainly not the famous exception which proves the rule. Already in 1937, the Gestapo had to concede that the Communist Party had improved its counter-intelligence work to such an extent that "people sent abroad disguised as exiles have no real prospect in the foreseeable future of being utilized for responsible (resistance) work."[78] In 1939 the complaint was made "that a series of Gestapo district offices across the *Reich* have not yet made contact . . . with communists who have been engaged in intensive work for some time now."[79] In 1941 the Prinz-Albrecht Strasse discovered that several district offices were not well informed about either popular opinion or the activities of "state enemies," "which can only be explained by a complete failure of the intelligence services"; in 1942 this conclusion was reconfirmed and it was even said that "there was simply no adequate intelligence service."[80] This problem – so it appears – hounded the Gestapo for the whole of the war. The "Reports on Important State Police Events" certainly offered occasional praise for arrests which were the result of "good preparatory work by the intelligence services"; nevertheless, individual arrests based upon denunciations continued to dominate. The appeal still had to be made for "an intensification of intelligence activities and sharp executive action against all the phases – repeatedly discussed here – of communist-marxist efforts."[81] Even Bormann's instruction of 1944 "to nominate the necessary number of trusted party members with experience in the relevant areas for voluntary work in the Security Police,"[82] in other words, to replace the spy-network that was in many places full of holes or even completely missing with so-called "golden pheasants" from the party, was unable to be of much help. These informants could not work undercover precisely because they were known in their neighborhoods to be Nazis; consequently, their surveillance was limited to observation "from outside."

Whereas denunciations or the reports of informers usually only made single arrests possible, interrogations, and above all the practice of "questioning under torture" (verschärften Vernehmung) was an investigative instrument unique to the Gestapo. The statements extorted here made sure that mass arrests could often develop from the capture of a single individual, especially in the persecution of the left-wing parties. Here a lot remains in the shadows. Excesses, including torture, should not lead to the projection of a general "picture of the Gestapo as (only) a collection of brutal SS-thugs bent upon crippling their victims."[83] Still, the number of confessions is astounding. The erosion of the left-proletarian milieu and the crisis of meaning within the resistance that raged between the German-Soviet Pact and the turning-point of Stalingrad – seems to have been especially important in allowing the Gestapo to make inroads into the ranks of the resistance.[84]

The intelligence provided by every sort of state and local authority – the population registration, labor and health offices, the railway and the Post Office, the criminal police and the local constabulary – was also quite indispensable. This co-operation generally worked without any friction. But in the Saarland there developed what the head of the district office described in 1942 as a permanent "guerilla war" as the Gestapo tried to shift on to the local police the responsibility for its own deficits in the areas of investigation, surveillance and making arrests.[85] In many cases, requests for help met with blatant obstructionism or informal sabotage, because those working at police head-quarters did not want to let themselves be downgraded to the role of messenger boys for the Gestapo. On the other hand, individual police officers demonstrated an almost fanatical devotion to working with the Gestapo. Although the extent of the actual official assistance varied greatly, and local social considerations also interfered, the regular police did help to give real substance to the Gestapo's aura of omniscience and omnipotence. And in many villages no unit of the secret state police ever put in an appearance; just as [before 1933] the rural police shaped the face of authority thus bestowing the façade of continuity and legality upon the Nazi "state of emergency."[86] On the other hand, the "Security Service" of the *Reichsführer SS*, shoved off at an early stage into the field of surveying popular opinion, played a largely marginal role in state police investigations; its importance has been greatly overestimated by historians.[87]

These observations can be summarized, tersely, as follows; paid informers exposed conspiratorial groups and voluntary denunciations ran dissent to ground. Or in other words, the oppositional impulses and activities of workers were, as a rule, eliminated from within their own ranks; fears of the Gestapo were largely home-made. These plebiscitary strains of terror question the cliché of a society held together by brutal force exercised from above and demonstrate that, as both unpaid denouncers and paid informers, elements of the working class, were indispensable wheels in the machinery of persecution who helped in quite concrete ways to shape the *Massnahmenstaat*. Without the army of voluntary informants from the general population and the state administration, the Gestapo would have been virtually blind. And without the official co-operation of the criminal police, the constabulary and the gendarmes, it would not have been able to carry out the tasks it had been assigned. "Although there were remarkably few Gestapo people on the ground," according to Gellately, "there were many professional and amateur helpers on whom they could rely."[88] Although the Gestapo was certainly the final authority, in most cases, it was not the driving force. It interrogated, selected, made decisions, deported or delivered cautions; but it was scarcely able to engage in investigations by itself. The widespread collaboration with the regime, the acceptance of terror by society, cancelled this deficit and provided the Gestapo with many ears, in the immediate vicinity of the regime's political opponents. The concept of "mass crime" therefore has a double meaning; these were crimes that affected masses of Germans, but a large part of the German population also participated in these crimes.

At the same time, the structural intelligence deficiencies of the Gestapo and its dependence upon denunciations, informers and spies whose statements were often unusable in a proper court of law, encouraged the police increasingly to take the administration of "justice" into their own hands; by decreeing the use of "protective custody" or by shoving people into a concentration camp, the Gestapo could avoid handing over cases to the public prosecutor's office. Faced with the permanent expansion of its functions, the progressive criminalization of new groups of the population and the steady increase in the sheer numbers of people arrested, the Gestapo engaged less and less in the detailed, time-consuming process of furnishing proof of a crime, which was, in any case, frequently unsuccessful. The astonishingly high degree of amateurism combined with excessive demands corresponded quite logically with an increasingly liberal use of arrest orders which saved the Gestapo the trouble of laboriously collecting real evidence; people were now sent to concentration camps on the mere suspicion of "anti-state activity." The Gestapo's use of judicial criminal prosecution increasingly became the statistical exception, favored, as a rule, only in "air-tight" cases.[89]

Inside the secret state police, people were well aware of these weaknesses. In the autumn of 1934, the Gestapo reported a "permanently continuous growth of the communist movement in almost every part of the *Reich*," and complained "that with the far too small forces of the political police, a really intensive and, above all, successful combatting of communism was simply not possible" because "only after weeks, or even months of extensive investigation, is it possible to collect enough evidence to initiate criminal proceedings in a court of law." It would therefore be absolutely "inadequate . . . to combat the KPD using only the procedures of the criminal law"; a more "comprehensive struggle" would require "intensified use of protective custody."[90] The Gestapo district office in Saarbrücken made it crystal clear to a potential informer that it "did not attach much value to denunciations that lacked concrete evidence."[91] Heydrich drew the logical conclusion and freed his subordinates from the burden of finding evidence by allowing "people who had been active communists before 1933 and were now suspected of illegal activity" to be taken into protective custody and transferred to a concentration camp.[92]

From this point onward, the repression of communists – and increasingly of Social Democrats – was based primarily upon a system of insinuation and suspicion, a model that assumed the permanent nature of political convictions, which then appeared to be repeatedly verified by the charges of neighbors and colleagues, Nazi block wardens and the police.[93] This was a collective enterprise of projection that said less about the organized resistance than about the fantasies and imagined enemies of the persecutors. A report about the long-time chairman of the Social Democratic Party branch in Frankenholz in the Saar reads as follows:

> Johann Kessler always showed himself to be a vicious communist who defended the status quo to the very last. Even today Kessler is politically unreliable and should be handled with care. Bürgermeister J. in Hocherberg hopes that Kessler will be "taken somewhere" as soon as possible.[94]

Gestapo officers assumed the role of bureaucratic lords over life and death; they decided which individual cases, from among the multitude threatening to suffocate them, they would deal with and in what way. They might simply drop a case but they could also classify people who had come to their attention according to the danger they represented to the state based on the record of their past life. In this system of insinuation, the concrete facts of any case were pushed more and more into the background; in most cases, real proof of anti-state activity could not be found. Everything depended upon the "feel" of the case; the suspect's reputation and former convictions aroused suspicion and this suspicion, in turn, justified the "justice" that the police themselves administered. Sometimes, there were "illegals," who – if they had previously belonged to the Communist or Social Democratic Parties – were simply transported to a concentration camp, without being recognized as members of the resistance. This procedure of projecting guilt by implication terrorized and destroyed, but it was also structurally blind and did not take systematic aim at the resistance, which came only accidentally into its sights and was often not even properly identified.[95]

The inadequacies of the Gestapo thus created no real buffer against terror, but rather an opaque, ultimately incalculable domain with no laws, in which, whether or not someone got caught up in the machinery of destruction depended, quite accidentally, upon the person working on the case and his state of mind. It was, therefore, not least the structural weaknesses of this system of terror which contributed to its progressive radicalization. The permanent overloading of this system created fears of threats which found an outlet in preventive measures, thus constructing a vicious circle; from the concern to eliminate ever new sources of danger there emerged additional tasks, further overloading and a commensurate growth of paranoia.[96] On the other hand, the Gestapo displayed a much lower level of systematic procedure and criminological intelligence than the previous literature suggests and the possibilities for surveillance were by no means so "totalitarian" that resistance was, from the outset, condemned to catastrophe. The internal fragmentation of the *Massnahmenstaat* and the structural deficiencies of its agencies permitted a variety of free spaces and niches into which people could withdraw. The number of paid informers, the only effective weapon against conspiratorial groups, was limited and could not be increased at will; the Gestapo had no magic wand. The cumulative radicalization with its over-extension of police resources and over-exertion of the Gestapo's own strength even produced the paradox that once the war began, the resistance's chances to be active increased objectively.

Closely inspecting the ways in which the state police

approached and disposed of cases and shifting the perspective away from the history of institutions and toward a history of the effects of the *Massnahmenstaat* casts a completely new light upon the possibilities for conspirational resistance, but above all, upon the significance of popular complicity with the regime, upon the popular instrumentalization of terror and upon the disputed issue of whether the "brown" violence had arisen from within the German population or had simply swept over it. A social history of terror as an integral component of German social history during the Nazi period, that tries to close the gaps between our detailed knowledge of the Gestapo's duties and its real activities and resources, must proceed from the assumption that denunciations were the key link in the interactions between the police and the population, that they were among the most important factors which kept the system of terror going. "That conclusion," Robert Gellately quite rightly observes, "suggests rethinking the notion of the Gestapo as an 'instrument of domination'; if it was an instrument it was one which was constructed within German society and whose functioning was structurally dependent on the continuing cooperation of German citizens."[97] This viewpoint, in turn, in which Germany no longer appears as "the first occupied territory"[98] and the Gestapo is no longer seen as a foreign institution imposed upon the population, but rather as one rooted in German society, requires a real change in the paradigm which has guided research until recently; instead of the image of a state capable of (almost) perfect surveillance of the whole population we need now to see a society that produced mass denunciations.

In the preceding discussion, we hope to have clearly differentiated our analysis from previous opinions on this topic by working out new aspects of the functioning of the Nazi *Massnahmenstaat*. The utility of this attempt at a new interpretation would seem to be less questionable than its empirical scope and its ability to adjust to contradictory results. The significance of the intelligence groundwork produced by the IA departments under the Weimar police commissioners, remains unclear, even though this question demands attention because of the considerable continuity in personnel and also because of the dominance of anti-communist activities in the last phase of the Republic as in the first years of the Nazi era.[99] Moreover, there were undoubtedly top agents like, for example, "V–10" at the Münster district office to whom doors were opened everywhere, who allegedly worked for years as a courier for the illegal SPD without being discovered.[100] There were certainly also regional Gestapo offices – in Hamburg, for example – which even as late as August 1944 had the considerable number of 265 employees at its disposal.[101] However, the Nazi regime was quite definitely not in the position to engage in comprehensive surveillance or perfect repression. Although the Nazi regime's aspirations were totalitarian, the reality was not. We must therefore agree with Hans Mommsen who concludes that "The decisive cause of the German catastrophe was not the Nazis' superior manipulative capabilities or their techniques of rule, but rather the lack of resistance in German society to the destruction of politics. The Third Reich can, in this respect, be historicized without thereby questioning the special importance of National Socialism."[102]

NOTES

1 *Völkischer Beobachter*, 17 February 1941.
2 Franz Vogt, "Die Lage der deutschen Bergarbeiter," reprinted in Detlev J. K. Peukert and Frank Bajohr, *Spuren des Widerstands. Die Bergarbeiterbewegung im Dritten Reich und im Exil* (München, 1987), pp. 133–53, quotation, p. 140.
3 *Deutschland-Berichte*, No. 8, August 1938, pp. 864, 866.
4 Report of 27 October 1936, Institut für Geschichte der Arbeiterbewegung Berlin (= IfGA), I 2/3/318.
5 *Deutsche Informationen*, 3 October 1936; see Allan Merson, *Communist Resistance in Nazi Germany* (London, 1985), p. 50f.
6 Eugen Kogon, *Der SS-Staat. Das System der deutschen Konzentrationslager* (Frankfurt a.M., 1946).
7 William Sheridan Allen, *The Nazi Seizure of Power. The Experience of a Single German Town, 1930–1935* (Chicago, 1965), p. 178.
8 See Alf Lüdtke, "Funktionseliten: Täter, Mit-Täter, Opfer? Zu den Bedingungen des deutschen Faschismus" in Alf Lüdtke (ed.), *Herrschaft als soziale Praxis. Historische und sozialanthropologische Studien* (Göttingen, 1991), pp. 559–90.
9 Edward Crankshaw, *Die Gestapo* (Berlin, 1959), p. 18.
10 Gerhard Schulz, *Die Anfänge des totalitären Massnahmenstaates* (Köln–Opladen, 1974), p. 211.
11 Friedrich Zipfel, *Gestapo und Sicherheitsdienst* (Berlin, 1960), p. 18.
12 Jacques Delarue, *Geschichte der Gestapo* (Düsseldorf, 1964), pp. 9, 89, 91.
13 Jochen von Lang, *Die Gestapo. Instrument des Terrors* (Hamburg, 1990); Adolf Diamant, *Gestapo Frankfurt am Main. Zur Geschichte einer verbrecherischen Organisation in den Jahren 1933–1945* (Frankfurt

a.M. 1988); Adolf Diamant, *Gestapo Leipzig. Zur Geschichte einer verbrecherischen Organisation in den Jahren 1933-1945* (Frankfurt a.M., 1990).

14 Hans Buchheim, "Die SS – das Herrschaftsinstrument" in *Anatomie des SS-Staates*, Vol. 1, 4th edn (München, 1984), pp. 13–212; see also Gunter Plum, "Staatspolizei und innere Verwaltung 1934–1936," *Vierteljahreshefte für Zeitgeschichte* (= *VZG*), Vol. 13, 1965, pp. 191–224.

15 Heinz Höhne, *Der Orden unter dem Totenkopf. Die Geschichte der SS* (Gütersloh, 1967).

16 Shlomo Aronson, *The Beginnings of the Gestapo System. The Bavarian Model in 1933* (Jerusalem, 1969); Shlomo Aronson, *Reinhard Heydrich und die Frühgeschichte von Gestapo und SS* (Stuttgart, 1971); Christoph Graf, *Politische Polizei zwischen Demokratie und Diktatur. Die Entwicklung der preussischen Politischen Polizei* (Berlin, 1983); George C. Browder, *Foundations of the Nazi Police State. The Formation of Sipo and SD* (Lexington, 1989).

17 Johannes Tuchel and Reinold Schattenfroh, *Zentrale des Terrors. Prinz-Albrecht-Strasse 8: Hauptquartier der Gestapo* (Berlin, 1987); see also Friedrich Zipfel, "Gestapo und SD in Berlin" in *Jahrbuch für die Geschichte Mittel- und Ostdeutschlands*, Vol. 9/10, 1961, pp. 263–92; Reinhard Rurup (ed.), *Topographie des Terrors. Gestapo, SS und Reichssicherheitshauptamt auf dem "Prinz-Albrecht-Gelände". Eine Dokumentation* (Berlin, 1987).

18 With regard to the problems involved in writing a social history of police see Alf Lüdtke, "Zur historischen Analyse der Polizei in Deutschland. 'Rechtsstaat' und gewaltsame Herrschaft" in Philippe Robert and Clive Emsley (eds), *Geschichte und Soziologie des Verbrechens* (Pfaffenweiler, 1991), pp. 107–20; Alf Lüdtke, " 'Sicherheit' und 'Wohlfahrt'. Aspekte der Polizeigeschichte" in Alf Lüdtke (ed.), *"Sicherheit" und "Wohlfahrt". Polizei, Gesellschaft und Herrschaft im 19. und 20. Jahrhundert* (Frankfurt a.M., 1992), pp. 7–33.

19 Robert Gellately, "Gestapo und Terror. Perspektiven auf die Sozialgeschichte des nationalsozialistischen Herrschaftssystems" in Lüdtke (ed.), *"Sicherheit" und "Wohlfahrt,"* pp. 372f.

20 On the institutional dimension of the Gestapo see Bernd Hey, "Zur Geschichte der westfälischen Staatspolizeistellen und der Gestapo" in *Westfälische Forschungen*, Vol. 37, 1987, pp. 58–90; Bernd Hey, "Die westfälischen Staatspolizeistellen und ihre Lageberichte 1933–1936" in Anselm Faust (ed.), *Verfolgung und Widerstand im Rheinland und in Westfalen 1933–1945* (Köln, 1992), pp. 30–9; Jörg Kammler, "Nationalsozialistische Machtergreifung und Gestapo – am Beispiel der Staatspolizeistelle für den Regierungsbezirk Kassel" in Eike Hennig (ed.), *Hessen unterm Hakenkreuz. Studien zur Durchsetzung der NSDAP in Hessen* (Frankfurt a.M., 1983), pp. 506-35, restricts his analysis to the beginnings of the Third Reich, and does not investigate the Gestapo's actual mode of operation. Although the district office in Kassel had only ten employees in June 1933 and only twenty-four in the summer of 1935, Kammler

still supposes their omnipotence (p. 506); some interesting details can be found in the following editions of Gestapo files; for Aachen, Bernhard Vollmer (ed.), *Volksopposition im Polizeistaat. Gestapo-und Regierungsberichte 1934–1936* (Stuttgart, 1957); Robert Thévoz and Hans Branig/Cécile Lowenthal-Hensel (ed.), *Pommern 1934/35 im Spiegel von Gestapo-Lageberichten und Sachakten*, 2 vols (Köln/Berlin, 1974); Jörg Schadt (ed.), *Verfolgung und Widerstand unter dem Nationalsozialismus in Baden. Die Lageberichte der Gestapo und des Generalstaatsanwalts Karlsruhe 1933–1940* (Stuttgart/Berlin/Köln/Mainz, 1976); Thomas Klein (ed.), *Die Lageberichte der Geheimen Staatspolizei über die Provinz Hessen-Nassau 1936–1939*, 2 vols (Köln/Wien, 1986); Klaus Mlynek (ed.), *Gestapo Hannover meldet . . . Polizei und Regierungsberichte für das mittlere und südliche Niedersachsens zwischen 1933 und 1937* (Hildesheim, 1986); Margot Pikarski/Elke Warning, *Gestapo-Berichte über den antifaschistischen Widerstandskampf der KPD 1933–1945*, 3 vols (Berlin Ost, 1989–90); Peter Brommer, "Zur Tätigkeit der Gestapo Trier in den Jahren 1944/45" in *Jahrbuch für westdeutsche Landesgeschichte*, Vol. 18, 1992.

21 Martin Broszat, "Zur Sozialgeschichte des deutschen Widerstands," *VZG*, Vol. 34, 1986, p. 295.

22 Hartmut Mehringer, "Die KPD in Bayern 1919–1945. Vorgeschichte, Verfolgung und Widerstand" in Martin Broszat and Hartmut Mehringer (ed.) *Bayern in der NS-Zeit*, Vol. 5 (München/Wien, 1983), pp. 103, 130, 142.

23 See Hans-Josef Steinberg, *Widerstand und Verfolgung in Essen 1933–1945* (Hannover, 1969), pp. 59–64; Kurt Klotzbach, *Gegen den Nationalsozialismus. Widerstand und Verfolgung in Dortmund 1930–1945. Eine historisch-politische Studie* (Hannover, 1969), pp. 239–41.

24 Frank Bajohr, *Verdrängte Jahre. Gladbeck unter'm Hakenkreuz* (Essen, 1983), p. 160; in a similar tone, see also Reinhard Bein, *Widerstand im Nationalsozialismus. Braunschweig 1930 bis 1945* (Braunschweig, 1985), p. 38f.

25 Detlev Peukert, *Die KPD im Widerstand. Verfolgung und Untergrundarbeit an Rhein und Ruhr 1933 bis 1945* (Wuppertal, 1980), pp. 116–30, 278–87, 372–81.

26 Inge Marssolek and René Ott, *Bremen im Dritten Reich, Anpassung–Widerstand–Verfolgung* (Bremen, 1986), pp. 176–83.

27 Reinhard Mann, *Protest und Kontrolle im Dritten Reich. Nationalsozialistische Herrschaft im Alltag einer rheinischen Grossstadt* (Frankfurt a.M./New York, 1987), pp. 147–76, 287–305.

28 Robert Gellately, *The Gestapo and German Society. Enforcing Racial Policy, 1933–1945* (Oxford, 1990); see also Gellately, "The Gestapo and German Society. Political Denunciation in the Gestapo Case Files," *Journal of Modern History*, Vol. 6, 1988, pp. 654–94.

29 Burkhard Jellonek, *Homosexuelle unter dem Hakenkreuz. Die Verfolgung von Homosexuellen im Dritten Reich* (Paderborn, 1990), pp. 176–326.

30 Klaus-Michael Mallmann and Gerhard Paul, *Herrschaft und Alltag.*

Ein Industrierevier im Dritten Reich (Bonn, 1991), pp. 175–268, 284–97, 318–26.

31 Until recently, there have been only the following discussions of this problem; Martin Broszat, "Politische Denunziation in der NS-Zeit. Aus Forschungserfahrungen im Staatsarchiv München" in *Archivalische Zeitschrift*, Vol. 73, 1977, pp. 221–38; Peter Hüttenberger, "Heimtückefälle vor dem Sondergericht München, 1933–1939" in Martin Broszat, Elke Fröhlich and Anton Grossmann, *Bayern in der NS-Zeit*, Vol. 4 (München/Wien, 1981), pp. 509–18; Helga Schubert, *Judasfrauen. Zehn Fallgeschichten weiblicher Denunziation im Dritten Reich* (Frankfurt a.M., 1990).

32 Thévoz/Branig/Lowenthal-Hensel, *Pommern 1934/35 im Spiegel von Gestapo-Lageberichten und Sachakten*, Vol. 1, p. 24; Diamant, *Gestapo Frankfurt am Main*, p. 20; Bein, *Widerstand im Nationalsozialismus*, p. 38; Mlynek, *Gestapo Hannover meldet . . .* p. 15; Marssolek/Ott, *Bremen im Dritten Reich*, p. 179; Hey, "Zur Geschichte der westfälischen Staatspolizeistellen und der Gestapo," p. 66.

33 Bundesarchiv Koblenz (= BAK), R 58/610, "Personalstatistik der Staatspolizei," 31 March 1937.

34 See Mallmann and Paul, *Herrschaft und Alltag*, pp. 198–203.

35 See Mann, *Protest und Kontrolle im Dritten Reich*, pp. 148–55.

36 See also Gellately, *The Gestapo and German Society*, p. 46.

37 BAK, R 58/856; Landesarchiv Saarbrücken (= LAS), Stapo-Stelle 7, 11, 19, 20, 24.

38 BAK, R 58/241, Decree of the "Chef der Sicherheitspolizei" and SD, 30 May 1941; the dates for the staff of the Stapo-Leitstelle Düsseldorf in the last phase of the war are missing; see Mann, *Protest und Kontrolle im Dritten Reich*, p. 155.

39 On the changes in the staff during 1943–4, see LAS, Stapo-Stelle 29; for Hamburg see also Gertrud Meyer, *Nacht über Hamburg. Berichte und Dokumente* (Frankfurt a.M., 1971), p. 74.

40 *Die Neue Saar*, 11 May 1951.

41 *Der Prozess gegen die Hauptkriegsverbrecher vor dem Internationalen Militärgerichtshof Nürnberg 14. November 1945–1. Oktober 1946* (= IMG), Vol. 20 (Nürnberg, 1948), pp. 142, 160.

42 On the Political Police in Prussia during the Weimar Republic see Graf, *Politische Polizei zwischen Demokratie und Diktatur*, pp. 5–107.

43 See Gellately, *The Gestapo and German Society*, pp. 50–7; on the continuity of personnel in Bremen, see Inge Marssolek and René Ott, *Bremen im Dritten Reich*, p. 176: in Hamburg, see Helmut Fangmann, Udo Reifner, Norbert Steinborn, *"Parteisoldaten". Die Hamburger Polizei im "Dritten Reich"* (Hamburg, 1987), pp. 51–62, in Munich, see Aronson, *Reinhard Heydrich und die Frühgeschichte von Gestapo und SD*, pp. 127–76; on the activities of the Political Police see the local examples given by Bernd Klemm (ed.), " . . . *durch polizeiliches Einschreiten wurde dem Unfug ein Ende gemacht". Geheime Berichte der politischen Polizei Hessen über Linke und Rechte in Offenbach 1923–1930* (Frankfurt a.M./New York, 1982).

44 On the composition of the personnel in the Trier and Saarbrücken

district offices see Mallmann and Paul, *Herrschaft und Alltag*, pp. 181f., 203f.

45 See Gellately, *The Gestapo and German Society*, pp. 58f., 76.

46 Berlin Document Center, NSDAP-Mitgliederkartei, file Eugen Schwitzgebel; Zentrale Stelle der Landesjustizverwaltungen Ludwigsburg, Verschiedenes 10.

47 For more details see Mallmann and Paul, *Herrschaft und Alltag*, pp. 205f.; for similar information see also Hey, "Zur Geschichte der westfälischen Staatspolizeistellen und der Gestapo," p. 67.

48 Robert Lewis Koehl, *The Black Corps. The Structure and Power Struggles of the Nazi SS* (Madison, 1983), p. 159.

49 On the myth of the Schupo as a republican corps see Peter Lessmann, *Die preussische Schutzpolizei in der Weimarer Republik. Streifendienst und Strassenkampf* (Düsseldorf, 1989); see also Hsi-Huey Liang, *Die Berliner Polizei in der Weimarer Republik* (Berlin/New York, 1977).

50 See Mallmann and Paul, *Herrschaft und Alltag*, p. 207f.

51 Kogon, *Der SS-Staat*, p. 370.

52 See Hey, "Zur Geschichte der westfälischen Staatspolizeistellen und der Gestapo," p. 64f., 88f.; Mallmann and Paul, *Herrschaft und Alltag*, pp. 208f.; for similarities with the leadership of the district office in Karlsruhe, see Schadt, *Verfolgung und Widerstand unter dem Nationalsozialismus in Baden*, pp. 34f.; see also Karl Paetel, "Die SS. Ein Beitrag zur Soziologie des Nationalsozialismus," *VZG*, 1954, pp. 1–33; Gunnar C. Boehnert, "An Analysis of the Age and Education of the SS-Fuehrerkorps, 1925–1939," *Historical Social Research*, Vol. 12, 1979, pp. 4–17; Friedrich Zipfel, "Gestapo and the SD: A Sociographic Profile of the Organizers of Terror" in Stein U. Larsen, Bernt Hagtvet, Jan P. Myklebust (eds), *Who were the Fascists. Social Roots of European Fascism* (Bergen/Oslo/Tromso, 1980), pp. 301–11.

53 This quotation is taken from Jellonek, *Homosexuelle unter dem Hakenkreuz*, p. 267; see also Gellately, *The Gestapo and German Society*, pp. 59, 67.

54 LAS, Stapo-Stelle 32.

55 See Mallmann and Paul, *Herrschaft und Alltag*, pp. 210–14; see also Jellonek, *Homosexuelle unter dem Hakenkreuz*, p. 331.

56 Mann, *Protest und Kontrolle im Dritten Reich*, p. 292.

57 See Mallmann and Paul, *Herrschaft und Alltag*, pp. 223f., 238–41.

58 See Jellonek, *Homosexuelle unter dem Hakenkreuz*, pp. 188–200, 232–42, 277–302.

59 Gellately, *The Gestapo and German Society*, p. 162.

60 See Mallmann and Paul, *Herrschaft und Alltag*, pp. 241–5; LAS, Generalstaatsanwalt 218.

61 Gellately, *The Gestapo and German Society*, p. 153.

62 On the motives and the structures of denunciations see ibid., pp. 130–58; Mallmann and Paul, *Herrschaft und Alltag*, pp. 229–34; for examples of denunciations see also Klaus-Michael Mallmann and Gerhard Paul, *Das zersplitterte Nein. Saarländer gegen Hitler* (Bonn, 1989), pp. 22f., 47f., 96f., 108f., 112f., 286f.; Klaus-Michael

Mallman und Horst Steffens, *Lohn der Mühen. Geschichte der Bergarbeiter an der Saar* (München, 1989), pp. 231f.; Lawrence D. Stokes, *Kleinstadt und Nationalsozialismus. Ausgewählte Dokumente zur Geschichte von Eutin 1918–1945* (Neumünster, 1984), pp. 905–8.

63 For example, Claudia Koonz, *Mothers in the Fatherland. Women, the Family and Nazi Politics* (New York, 1987); for a more critical position on this issue see Gisela Bock, "Die Frauen und der Nationalsozialismus," *Geschichte und Gesellschaft*, Vol. 15, 1989, pp. 563–79; Dagmar Reese, "Homo homini lupus-Frauen als Täterinnen," *International Wissenschaftliche Korrespondenz zur Geschichte der deutschen Arbeiterbewegung*, Vol. 27, 1991, pp. 25–34; Adelheid von Saldern, "Opfer oder (Mit-)Täterinnen? Kontroversen über die Rolle der Frau im NA-Staat," *Sozialwissenschaftliche Informationen*, Vol. 20, 1991, pp. 97–103.

64 LAS, Landesentschädigungsamt, MDI 6264.

65 See, for example, William L. Shirer, *Berliner Tagebuch. Aufzeichnungen 1939–1941* (Leipzig/Weimar, 1991).

66 Geheimes Staatsarchiv Preussischer Kulturbesitz Berlin-Dahlem (= GStAB), Rep. 90 P, No. 9, H. 10, Report of Stapo-Stelle Saarbrücken for November 1935. Similar comments were made by the leader of the Stapo-Stelle Karlsruhe in an interview in 1934; reprinted in Schadt, *Verfolgung und Widerstand unter dem Nationalsozialismus in Baden*, pp. 303–6.

67 BAK, R 58/243, Decree Chef der Sicherheitspolizei, 3 September 1939; for other references see Gellately, *The Gestapo and German Society*, pp. 138–43, 148–51.

68 On the cycles of denunciation, see Mann, *Protest und Kontrolle im Dritten Reich*, p. 294; on the developing criminalization, see Mallmann and Paul, *Herrschaft und Alltag*, pp. 252–64.

69 For example, Zipfel, *Gestapo und Sicherheitsdienst*, p. 13; Bein, *Widerstand im Nationalsozialismus*, p. 39; Diament, *Gestapo Frankfurt am Main*, p. 23; Walter Otto Weyrauch, *Gestapo V-Leute. Tatsachen und Theorie der Geheimdienste. Untersuchungen zur Geheimen Staatspolizei während der nationalsozialistischen Herrschaft* (reprinted Frankfurt a.M., 1988 and 1992). For criticisms of Weyrauch see Robert Gellately, "Situating the 'SS-State' in a social-historical context: recent histories of the SS, the police, and the courts in the Third Reich," *The Journal of Modern History*, Vol. 64, 1992, p. 349.

70 Elke Fröhlich, "Die Herausförderung des Einzelnen. Geschichten über Widerstand und Verfolgung" in Martin Broszat, Elke Fröhlich, (ed.), *Bayern in der NS-Zeit*, Vol. 6 (München/Wien, 1983), p. 212; for impressive references about the actions of Gestapo agents and informants, see ibid., pp. 182–90, 209–27; on the agents of the Stapo-Leitstelle Hamburg, see Meyer, *Nacht über Hamburg*, pp. 81f., 91f.; on the Stapo-Saarbrücken, see Mallmann and Paul, *Herrschaft und Alltag*, pp. 215–23; see also Gellately, *The Gestapo and German Society*, pp. 61–4.

71 For Hamburg, see Meyer, *Nacht über Hamburg*, p. 169 and for

Bielefeld, see Hey, "Zur Geschichte der westfälischen Staatspolizeistellen und der Gestapo," p. 68.

72 For Augsburg, see Gerhard Hetzer, "Die Industriestadt Augsburg. Eine Sozialgeschichte der Arbeiteropposition" in Martin Broszat, Elke Fröhlich, Anton Grossmann (ed.), *Bayern in der NS-Zeit*, Vol. 3 (München/Wien, 1981), p. 171.

73 Typical of this attitude is the complaint of the former leader of the KPD in the Saar region, Paul Lorenz, who was later an agent of the Gestapo; see IfGA, I 2/3/107, Lorenz to ZK of the KPD, 5 October 1934.

74 For a typical example, see LAS, Oberster Säuberungsrat V OSR 153/50.

75 Typical, for example, is LAS, Landesentschädigungsamt MDI 6206 and Stapo-Stelle 40.

76 BAK, R 58/265, Rundbrief Gestapo of 15 December 1938.

77 Mehringer, "Die KPD in Bayern," p. 157; criticisms of this position in Peukert, *Die KPD im Widerstand*, p. 124f.

78 BAK, R 58/498, Rundbrief Gestapo of 31 June 1937.

79 Bundesarchivabteilung Potsdam (= BAP), St. 3/62; Report of Gestapo for the first quarter of 1939.

80 BAP, St. 3/68, Report of Reichssicherheitshauptamt (IV A 1) of 15 January 1941; BAP, St. 3/70, Report of Reichssicherheitshauptamt of 31 January 1942.

81 BAK, R 58/213, Meldungen wichtiger staatspolizeilicher Ereignisse of June and November 1944.

82 BAP, Filmsammlung, Film 3902, Reichsverfügungsblatt NSDAP of 31 May 1944.

83 Jellonek, *Homosexuelle unter dem Hakenkreuz*, p. 240.

84 See Mallmann and Paul, *Herrschaft und Alltag*, pp. 234–8. Mann found that 13 per cent of all cases of the Stapo-Leitstelle Düsseldorf were the result of confessions produced by Gestapo interrogations; see, *Protest und Kontrolle im Dritten Reich*, p. 292.

85 LAS, Polizeipräsident 185, Stapo-Stelle Saarbrücken to Polizeipräsident Saarbrücken, 13 August 1942.

86 For details on co-operation between the Gestapo and traditional institutions see Mallmann and Paul, *Herrschaft und Alltag*, pp. 233–6, 278–91; see also the statement of the deputy-leader of the Stapo-Stelle Düsseldorf in *IMG*, Vol. 20 (Nürnberg, 1948), p. 176.

87 See Mallmann and Paul, *Herrschaft und Alltag*, pp. 269–78; Gellately, *The Gestapo and German Society*, pp. 137 and 65f.; on the SD see, especially, George C. Browder, "The SD; the Significance of Organization and Image" in George Mosse (ed.), *Police Forces in History* (London/Beverly Hills, 1975), pp. 205–29; see also G. C. Browder, "Die Anfänge des SD. Dokumente aus der Organisationsgeschichte des Sicherheitsdienstes des Reichsführers SS," *VZG*, Vol. 27, 1979, pp. 299–324; G. C. Browder, "The Numerical Strength of the Sicherheitsdienst des RFSS," *Historical Social Review*, Vol. 28, 1983, pp. 30–41; also important is the edition of files by Heinz Boberach (ed.), *Berichte des SD und der Gestapo über Kirchen und Kirchenvolk*

in Deutschland 1934–1944 (Mainz, 1971); see also Boberach (ed.), *Meldungen aus dem Reich. Die geheimen Lageberichte des Sicherheitsdienstes der SS 1938–1945*, 17 vols (Herrsching, 1984); for the local example of Bielefeld see Bernd Hey, "Bielefeld und seine Bevölkerung in den Berichten des Sicherheitsdienstes (SD) 1939–1942" in *70. Jahresbericht des Historischen Vereins für die Grafschaft Ravensberg* (Bielefeld, 1976), pp. 227–73; Peter Brommer, *Die Partei hört mit. Lageberichte und andere Meldungen des Sicherheitsdienstes der SS aus dem Grossraum Koblenz 1937–1941* (Koblenz, 1988).

88 Gellately, *The Gestapo and German Society*, p. 72.
89 See Mallmann and Paul, *Herrschaft und Alltag*, pp. 246–9.
90 BAP, St. 3/9/I, Bericht über den Stand der kommunistischen Bewegung in Deutschland, October 1934.
91 IfGA, I 2/3/107, Report of KPD-Abschnittsleitung Forbach/France of 20 September 1935.
92 BAK, R 58/264, Decree of Gestapo, 29 July 1935.
93 On the co-operation between the Gestapo and the National Socialist formations see Mallmann and Paul, *Herrschaft und Alltag*, pp. 226–99; Dieter Rebentisch, "Die 'politische Beurteilung' als Herrschaftsinstrument der NSDAP" in Detlev Peukert and Jürgen Reulecke (eds), *Die Reihen fast geschlossen. Beiträge zur Geschichte des Alltags unterm Nationalsozialismus* (Wuppertal, 1981), pp. 107–25.
94 LAS, Staatsanwaltschaft 331, Mayor of Höcherberg to Stapo-Stelle Saarbrücken of 9 November 1939.
95 See Mallmann and Paul, *Herrschaft und Alltag*, pp. 206f., 249–51; LAS, Justizvollzugsanstalt, Gefangenenpersonalakten 1935–1944.
96 On the cumulative radicalization, see Mallmann and Paul, *Herrschaft und Alltag*, pp. 264–8.
97 Gellately, *The Gestapo and German Society*, p. 136.
98 Zipfel, "Gestapo und SD in Berlin," p. 263.
99 See, for example, on the KPD in the Rhine province, 1932; Landeshauptarchiv Koblenz, 403/16779–16781, 16783.
100 See the reports in BAP, P. St. 3/6 and also Hauptstaatsarchiv Düsseldorf, RW 34/33/
101 Meyer, *Nacht über Hamburg*, pp. 293–300.
102 Hans Mommsen, "Nationalsozialismus als vorgetäuschte Modernisierung" in Walter A. Pehle (ed.), *Der historische Ort des Nationalsozialismus. Annäherungen* (Frankfurt a.M., 1990), p. 46.

6

THE "HITLER MYTH"
Image and reality in the Third Reich
Ian Kershaw

The Nazi Volksgemeinschaft *promised not so much an impossible
return to the pre-industrial past, as a society free of the contradictions
and "irritations" of everyday life in the industrial age. But beneath
the ideological representations of the smoothly functioning, monolithic*
Volksgemeinschaft, *the real contradictions of modern industrial
society remained. Frustration and disappointment with the realities of
everyday life under National Socialism led ordinary Germans to
grumble and complain, but seldom to engage in behavior that can be
appropriately termed "resistance." Why? Organized terror played a
central role. But the most important mechanism of social integration
in Nazi Germany was Hitler's charismatic leadership. The "Hitler
myth" secured the loyalty to the regime of even those who opposed the
Nazi movement itself. Millions of ordinary Germans believed that
the Führer would certainly right all wrongs in Nazi Germany
(especially those committed by his lieutenants, the so-called "little
Führers"), if only these abuses could be brought to Hitler's personal
attention. Hitler's foreign policy and military successes also convinced
ordinary Germans (at least until Stalingrad) that the Führer was a
brilliant, indeed infallible, statesman and general who was leading
Germany to world power. The "Hitler myth" was not just a cunning
triumph of Goebbels' propaganda machine; mass belief in the charismatic leader was the inevitable corollary of the disappointments of
quotidian existence in the Third Reich. In the "Hitler myth," ordinary
Germans found compensation for the tensions, anxieties and frus-
trations of everyday life under National Socialism. By the time the
Allied bombing raids and German defeats in Russia had begun to
deflate this myth, the Führer was already the prisoner of his own
propaganda image. Convinced of his own infallibility, Hitler plunged
Germany into absolute defeat and collapse.*

In this brief excerpt, Ian Kershaw summarizes the main components of the "Hitler myth," its significance for the Nazi regime, and the reasons why even the total devastation of Germany did not completely dispel all vestiges of the "Hitler myth" in the years after 1945.

* * *

We have explored the main components of the popular image of Hitler and their blending into a leadership "myth" of remarkable potency and resilience. The gulf between the fictive figure, manufactured by propaganda on the foundations of pre-existing "heroic" leadership ideals, and the genuine Hitler is striking. Difficult though it is to evaluate, the evidence of the receptivity to the portrayal of Hitler's image which we have examined has pointed to seven significant bases of the "Hitler myth." In each case the contrast between image and reality is stark, the "mythical" content unmistakable.

Firstly, Hitler was regarded as a personification of the nation and the unity of the "national community," aloof from the selfish sectional interests and material concerns which marked the normality of "everyday life" and created the damaging divisions in society and politics – the selfless exponent of the national interest, whose incorruption and unselfish motives were detachable from the scandalous greed and hypocrisy of the Party functionaries. Secondly, he was accepted as the single-handed architect and creator of Germany's "economic miracle" of the 1930s, eliminating the scourge of mass unemployment which continued to plague other European nations, revitalizing the economy, providing improved living standards, and offering a new basis of lasting prosperity. Thirdly, as shown most clearly in the popular reactions to the massacre of the SA leadership in 1934, Hitler was seen as the representative of "popular justice," the voice of the "healthy sentiment of the people," the upholder of public morality, the embodiment of strong, if necessarily ruthless, action against the "enemies of the people" to enforce "law and order." Fourthly, as the example of the "Church Struggle" showed, Hitler was widely viewed – even by prominent Church leaders with a reputation for hostility to Nazism – as personally sincere, and in matters affecting established traditions and institutions as a "moderate" opposed to the radical and extreme elements in the Nazi Movement, but largely kept in the dark

198

about what was actually going on. Fifthly, in the arena of foreign affairs, Hitler was commonly regarded as an upholder and a fanatical defender of Germany's just rights, a rebuilder of the nation's strength, a statesman of genius, and for the most part, it seems, not as a racial imperialist warmonger working towards a "war of annihilation" and limitless German conquest. Sixthly, in the first half of the war Hitler appeared to be the incomparable military leader who, nevertheless, as a former Front soldier and one distinguished for bravery knew and understood the "psychology" of the ordinary soldier. Even after the war turned sour he continued to be seen by many as the epitome of Germany's unwavering will to certain victory. Finally, there was Hitler's image as the bulwark against the nation's perceived powerful ideological enemies – Marxism/Bolshevism and, above all, the Jews. This image presumably registered most strongly among those sections of the population whose exposure to ideological "schooling" was greatest – particularly, therefore, among committed members of the Party and its affiliates. Fear of Bolshevism and the prevalent anti-Marxism in the German middle classes, made even more acute through the shrill tones of Nazi propaganda, unquestionably formed a wide negative base of Hitler's popularity. But, strikingly, Hitler's personal preoccupation with "the struggle against the Jews" does not appear to have figured as a leading component of his image for the bulk of the population.

That the crass inversion of reality caricatured in these aspects of the popular image of Hitler was in large measure a product of the deliberate distortions of Nazi propaganda has been made abundantly clear in the preceding chapters. Even though at best only partial success was attained in "imposing" this image on the still unbroken socialist/communist and catholic subcultures, where there were strong ideological counters to acceptance of the "Hitler myth," and on sections of the upper classes whose status-conscious elitism provided a continuing barrier to the appeal of populist leadership images, there can be no doubt that the penetration of the propagated "Hitler myth" was deep, especially, but by no means only, among the German middle classes. After 1933, Nazi propaganda, largely uncontested now that opponents within Germany had been silenced, could almost deify Hitler. Goebbels, as we saw, ranked his creation of the public Hitler image as his greatest propaganda triumph.

Yet, cynical though its "manufacture" was, the excesses of the Führer cult after 1933, and the extent of its penetration, are inconceivable without the realization that, in the crisis conditions of the early 1930s, it had touched upon and articulated (even if in extreme and distorted fashion) long-standing and pervasive elements of the bourgeois political culture in Germany.

Of these, the most crucial arose from the disparities between the superficial attainment of national unity and the internal divisions of the German nation-state since its creation in 1871, and the gulf between the immense world-power aspirations and the modesty of Germany's actual achievements in international relations. From Bismarck's time onwards, "national unity" in the new nation-state not only received exaggerated emphasis, but was focused on the rejection of internal "enemies of the Reich" (Catholics, socialists, ethnic minorities) and, increasingly under Wilhelm II, was linked to varying notions of German expansionism. The internal divisions grew more rather than less apparent, however, enhanced by the populist politics from the 1890s onwards, and the imperialist ambitions, though more and more strident, were gravely disappointed. The ideological basis was there for the fundamental divides which the war, defeat, and revolution openly exposed, and which provided the Weimar Republic from its inception with an extremely weak base of legitimation, especially among the bourgeoisie and elites. The extensified fragmentation of Weimar politics and eventual decline into little more than interest politics[1] in the face of mounting internal crisis, entirely delegitimized the State system itself, wholly discredited pluralist politics, and paved the way for a full acceptance – already by 1932 of around 13 million Germans – of a new basis of unity represented in an entirely novel political form personalized in Hitler's "charismatic" leadership.

In such conditions as prevailed in the last phase of the Weimar Republic, of the total discrediting of a State system based upon pluralist politics, the "functional" leadership of the bureaucrat and the Party politician as the representatives of the impersonal "rational-legal" form of political domination, imposing laws and carrying out functions for which they are not personally responsible and with which they are not identifiable, lost credibility. Salvation could only be sought with a leader who possessed *personal* power and was prepared to take *personal* responsibility, sweeping away the causes of the misery and the faceless politicians and bureaucrats who prevail over it, and seeming to impose his own personal power upon the force of history itself.[2] In reality, of course, the fascist variant of "charismatic leadership" – there are obvious parallels in the Mussolini cult – was not only superimposed on existing bureaucratic power, but created new, extensive apparatuses of bureaucratic administration, and led not to diminished but to massively increased bureaucratic interference in all spheres of daily life. In this paradox, we see the essence of the heightened detestation of the new breed of Party "functionaries," the agents – along with the traditionally disliked State civil servants – of this bureaucratized control, and the popularity of the Führer, whose personal power was idealized and elevated to a plane where it seemed to be executed outside the realms of "everyday life."

An extract from a speech to the Reichstag in April 1939 illustrates well the personalized claims Hitler made for "his" great "achievements" and how far these rested on "national" rather than specifically Nazi ideals and aspirations. These "achievements" provided the basis on which Hitler, more than any politician before him, had been able to integrate not only the German middle classes, but the vast majority of the population who, on particular aspects of policy, could often reveal heated antagonism to the specific manifestations of Nazi rule affecting their daily lives. In his speech, on 28 April 1939, Hitler provided the following catalogue of achievements which, in the view of most ordinary Germans, could only be taken as a breathtaking list of personal successes:

> I have overcome the chaos in Germany, restored order, massively raised production in all areas of our national economy. . . . I have succeeded in completely bringing back into useful production the seven million unemployed who were so dear to all our own hearts, in keeping the German peasant on his soil despite all difficulties and in rescuing it for him, in attaining the renewed flourishing of German trade, and in tremendously promoting transportation. I have not only politically united the German people, but also militarily rearmed them, and I have further attempted

to tear up page for page that Treaty, which contained in its 448 articles the most base violations ever accorded to nations and human beings. I have given back to the Reich the provinces stolen from us in 1919. I have led back into the homeland the millions of deeply unhappy Germans who had been torn away from us. I have recreated the thousand-year historic unity of the German living-space, and I have attempted to do all this without spilling blood and without inflicting on my people or on others the suffering of war. I have managed this from my own strength, as one who twenty-one years ago was an unknown worker and soldier of my people.[3]

For the great mass of Hitler's audience, the political and economic recovery of Germany, which he was trumpeting as his own personal achievement, was a goal in itself. For Hitler and the Nazi leadership, it provided only the base for racial-imperialist conquest and a war of annihilation. It remains for us to ask how the popular Hitler image we have examined contributed towards the growing strength of the regime and towards making possible this war, which, from what we have seen, most Germans – though prepared to fight if necessary – had been only too anxious to avoid.

The "Hitler myth" can be seen as providing the central motor for integration, mobilization, and legitimation within the Nazi system of rule. Its functional significance has to be examined in the context of its importance for the "non-organized" masses, whose image of Hitler has been the central concern of this work, for the Party faithful, and for the Nazi and non-Nazi elites.

No one was more aware of the functional significance of his popularity in binding the masses to him, and hence to the regime, than Hitler himself. He pointed out that the strength of the regime could not depend on "the laws [!] of the Gestapo alone," and that "the broad mass [of the population] needs an idol."[4] On another occasion, he commented that the ruler who was dependent only upon executive power without finding "the way to the people" was destined to failure.[5] His well-documented fear of loss of personal popularity and the corresponding growth in instability of the regime[6] is further testimony of his awareness of the centrality of the integratory force of his role as Führer. This integration was largely affective, for the most part forging psychological or emotional rather than material bonds. But its reality can scarcely be doubted. And at moments of internal crisis – such as in June 1934 – the regime was stabilized and its leadership given extended room for manoeuvrability through the surge in Hitler's popularity and the strengthening of bonds of identity between people and Führer. In his portrayed public image, Hitler was able to offer a positive pole in the Third Reich, transcending sectional interests and grievances through the overriding ideal of national unity, made possible through his necessary aloofness from the "conflict sphere" of daily politics, separating him from the more unpopular aspects of Nazism.

Hitler recognized that enthusiasm and willingness for self-sacrifice could not be conserved, and were bound to fade when confronted with "the grey daily routine and the convenience of life."[7] He saw, therefore, that the masses could be bound to him only through constant psychological mobilization, demanding ever recurring successes. Until the middle of the war, the successes came, and spectacularly so, especially in the arena of foreign policy and military affairs, bringing many Germans who were far from Nazis into close identification with Hitler, revamping sagging morale, forcing open acclaim, prompting active participation – if shallow and largely ritualized – in support of "his" achievements, disarming potential opponents, making objections to Nazi policy difficult to formulate. This was, for example, undoubtedly the effect of the plebiscites staged in 1933, 1934, 1936, and 1938, in which the massive acclamation, though the product of intense propaganda and coercion and obviously in no sense a true reflection of the state of opinion, nevertheless reflected genuine widespread approval and admiration for Hitler's accomplishments and persuaded waverers to fall in line.[8]

The plebiscitary acclamation which could always be mobilized by Hitler provided him with an unassailable base of popularity, and as such offered the regime legitimation both within Germany and in the eyes of foreign powers, allowing the scope for further mobilization and a gathering momentum of Nazi policy. The massive popularity of Hitler, recognized even by enemies of the regime, formed therefore a decisive element in the structure of Nazi rule in Germany. It goes far towards helping to account not only for the high and growing degree of relative autonomy from non-Nazi elites enjoyed by Hitler and the Nazi leadership, but also – as the counterweight to terror, repression, and intimidation – for the weakness of resistance to the regime. The "Hitler myth" and terror were in this sense two indispensable sides of the same coin, ensuring political control and mobilization behind the regime. It is no coincidence, therefore, that terroristic repression escalated wildly in the final phase of the waning regime as the binding force of Hitler's popularity weakened and collapsed.

For the mass of "non-organized" Germans, the "Hitler myth" functioned through the stimulation of popular acclaim – recurrent but always temporary – for *faits accomplis*, for coups which had been brought about, successes already attained, rather than for a clear set of policies in train. One main role of the Party was to ensure that the appropriate degree of acclamation was produced. But for the activists in the Party and its affiliates, the integratory and mobilizing functions of the "Hitler myth" were not confined to support for current attainments, but rested on the incorporation in Hitler of the "idea" of Nazism itself, determining future utopias to be won as well as past glories achieved. The centrifugal forces of the Nazi Movement were held together in great measure by the ideals embodied in the image of the Führer; social disappointments and disillusionment could be transcended and overcome by participation in the Führer's great "struggle" and ultimate satisfaction in the brave new world to come. For the activist and "committed" core of the Movement, especially for the younger element, the perceived Führer image stood symbolically for ideological precepts – preparing for a show-down with Bolshevism, acquisition of *Lebensraum*, "removal of Jews" – which were "directions for action"[9] long before they were realizable objectives. Without such ideological precepts bound up in the "representative figure" of the Führer, the dynamism built into the permanent mobilization of the Party and its affiliates is largely unthinkable. Not detailed plans of a Party programme, but his role as the embodiment of a cosmic struggle against irreconcilable internal and external enemies of immense power and magnitude ultimately bound the Party faithful to Hitler.

And where the coming mortal conflict with Bolshevism sharpened among Nazi activists the preparedness and taste for uncompromising and brutal struggle, the idea of *Lebensraum* and limitless German expansionism provided a future panacea for all national ills and current personal dissatisfactions, the "removal of Jews" offered a current, exising target to be attained, even if the road to the goal was unclear. Based as it was on principles of race, with the figure of the Jew as the focal point of all hatred, and with the Führer as its ideological and organizational fulcrum, the Nazi Movement needed no regular orders or directions from Hitler to step up the pace of anti-Jewish actions and discrimination, pushing the government and the State bureaucracy into action, and always therefore increasing the radicalizing momentum of racial policy.

In such ways, the Führer image functioned, in integrating the potentially disintegrative forces within the Nazi Movement on a different plane among the Party "faithful" than among the broad mass of "non-organized" Germans, in mobilizing the boundless energy and misplaced idealism of the fanatics and activists through orientation towards long-term "cosmic" and "utopian" goals, and through offering legitimation for action undertaken against ideological and racial "enemies of the State."

The significance of the "Hitler myth" has to be seen, finally, on a third level which preceding chapters have not sought to explore systematically; that of its function for the elites – both the non-Nazi "national-conservative" elites and the power-groups within the Movement itself.

For non-Nazi, "national-conservative" power-elites in the economy and in the army, Hitler's "charisma" had in itself never been a decisive factor, even though by the early 1930s it seems clear that substantial sectors of especially the "intellectual elite" had succumbed in varying degrees to the Führer cult.[10] For the traditional elites, it was not charisma but pragmatic power considerations which aligned them with Hitler. The erosion of their political and social "basis of legitimation," stretching deep into the pre-war era, had reached a critical level during the Weimar Republic.[11] Hitler was able to offer them a new mass base for the apparent consolidation of their leadership positions within the framework of an authoritarian system, together with the prospect of Germany attaining a position of hegemony within Europe and even world power status. For his part, Hitler needed their support to gain and consolidate power. This was the well-known basis of the *entente* between the dominant forces of the traditional "power-elite" and the Nazi leadership in January 1933.[12]

However little "charisma" had come into these considerations in 1933, there seems no doubt that the "Hitler myth" – or significant elements of it – played an important role in shaping the behaviour of the conservative elites in the following years in at least two ways. Firstly, misplaced conceptions within the elites of Hitler as a man whom they could trust and "work with," in contrast to the Party radicals, integrated the disparate sectors of the elites and mobilized their support behind the Nazi leadership in the critical early years at the same time that Hitler's popularity provided the mass base of legitimation for the presumed reassertion of their own spheres of domination. Important figures from within the "national-conservative" elites who later played prominent roles in resistance to Nazism – such as Ernst von Weizsäcker in the bureaucracy, Carl Goerdeler in the economy, and Henning von Tresckow in the military – were all prepared to distance Hitler in the early years from their mounting criticism of the radicals in the Movement.[13] Their path into fundamental opposition was, partly for this reason, a hesitant one, and their objections to the regime for long less than fundamental.[14]

Secondly, their underrating of the "caesaristic" elements of Hitler's mass charismatic base meant that, far from providing a new foundation for the power of the traditional elites, as they had hoped, the plebiscitary acclamation for the Führer enabled Hitler's own power to detach itself from its likely shackles and develop a high degree of relative autonomy, at the same time reducing former dominant groups like the army to "power-elites" proper to merely "functional élites,"[15] unable to check Hitler himself and the "wild men" of the Nazi Movement, even when wishing to do so. In cementing the basis of the Führer's pivotal position, the "Hitler myth" had been instrumental in establishing a situation in which the traditional elites could become outflanked by the specifically Nazi elites. Unlike the position in classic "Bonapartist" theory, therefore, the Dictator and his entourage could not be edged aside by the traditional "ruling class" once the economy had been stabilized. The dynamic driving-force of the "Hitler myth" allowed, in fact, no stabilization or "normalization," but rather conditioned circumstances in which the traditional "ruling class" became ever more subsumed in and dependent upon the "behemoth"[16] of the Nazi State which it was no longer able to control in its mad rush to destruction.

From the early 1920s onwards, Hitler had built up his power base in the Party above all on the strength of the bonds of personal loyalty with his "paladins," the second-rank Nazi leaders and *Gauleiter*. Hitler's personal magnetism, his unique demagogic talents, his strength of will, apparent self-confidence and certainty of action, and his indispensability to the Movement (which had fractured without his leadership following the ill-fated Putsch of 1923), all provided the foundations of charismatic authority of extraordinary strength within his own entourage, resting upon bonds of personal loyalty. For his part, Hitler always felt most at home in the company of his closest group of "fellow fighters" from the "time of struggle." He realized that their loyalty was the firmest basis of his own personal power, that he needed them as they needed him. His hatred for those who crossed him having once shared the bond of mutual loyalty was unbounded, but equally he never forgot old services performed, and, apart from the "Night of the Long Knives" in June 1934, he did not resort to purges within the Party.[17]

The institutionalization of Hitler's charismatic leadership, first of all within the Party during the 1920s and then within the State after 1933, served a crucial function in sealing the bonds between Hitler and the subordinate Party leadership. The integrative function was the decisive one here. The fragmentation of the Nazi "elite" groupings had shown itself plainly in 1924, and the inner-Party factionalism and opposition in the early 1930s had been countered only through the strength of Hitler's personal position. After 1933, too, the ferocious personal enmities and political conflicts within the Nazi elite, which otherwise would have torn the system apart, were resolved only in Hitler's own charismatic authority – in his indisputable position as the base of Nazism's popular legitimacy and the embodiment of Nazism's "idea."

These Party leaders were of course closer to the real Hitler than were the mass of ordinary Germans or even the mass of Party activists. What is striking, therefore, and of importance for the drive and dynamism of the regime, is that the undiluted "Hitler myth" – the fully-fledged cult of the "superman" Leader in all its glorification – embraced the Nazi elite almost in its entirety, and was not simply regarded cynically as a functional propaganda manufacture. If the glorifying speeches and writings of subleaders during the Third Reich itself[18] are no proof of this, the behaviour of Nazi leaders arraigned at Nuremberg and post-war memoirs (for all their obvious apologetics) demonstrate it conclusively.[19]

Even after the war and the revelations of Nuremberg, Alfred Rosenberg called Hitler the "driving force and untiring motor of the great achievements of the National Socialist State."[20] For Hans Frank, the Führer had been "a sort of superman" in whom he had believed "without reservation" and whom he regarded as being right "in all decisive matters."[21] Albert Speer, the ambitious, calculating, and rational power technician who had climbed to the top of the ladder, and who distanced himself most clearly from Hitler at Nuremberg and in his memoirs, admitted that he had seen in the Führer something approaching "a hero of an ancient saga" and, after the victory in France, as "one of the greatest figures in German history."[22] And the former head of the Hitler Youth, Baldur von Schirach, who retained even at Nuremberg a naive attachment to Hitler, indicated in his memoirs the effect on Hitler himself of the constant toadying and sycophancy which surrounded him, shielding him from rational criticism or genuine debate, and bolstering his increasing detachment from reality. Von Schirach pointed out that "this unlimited, almost religious veneration, to which I contributed as did Goebbels, Göring, Heß, Ley, and countless others, strengthened in Hitler himself the belief that he was in league with Providence."[23]

As these memoirs (in which the element of self-defence based upon complete submission to the Führer does not contradict the apologists' genuine belief in his power and the extreme personal devotion to him) clearly suggest, Hitler's own person gradually became inseparable from the "Führer myth." Hitler had to live out more and more the constructed image of omnipotence and omniscience. And the more he succumbed to the allure of his own Führer cult and came to believe in his own myth, the more his judgement became impaired by faith in his own infallibility,[24] losing his grip on what could and could not be achieved solely through the strength of his "will." Hitler's capacity for self-deception had been profound ever since the mid-1920s, if not earlier, and was vital in order to carry conviction among his immediate entourage about the greatness of his cause and the righteousness of his path towards attaining it. But as his success within the Movement, within the German State, and on the international stage grew until it knew no bounds, so the self-deception of the "conviction" ideologist magnified to the extent that it ultimately consumed all traces of the calculating and opportunist politician, leaving in its place only a voracious appetite for destruction – and ultimately self-destruction. In this sense, the "Hitler myth" was a fundamental component of the underlying instability of the Nazi regime and its untrammelled dynamic of destruction.

It would have been expecting too much to imagine that the once-mighty "Hitler myth" might disappear overnight in 1945, disintegrating along with the mortal remains of the Führer himself and being scattered with the ashes of the Third Reich. Not only had its hold been too strong for that among considerable sections of the population, but the conditions of the immediate post-war era were miserable enough for many to compare them unfavourably with the peacetime era under Nazism.

An early post-war opinion survey undertaken by the United States occupying forces in October 1945 among a representative sample of the population of Darmstadt suggested differences in attitudes towards Nazism among those under nineteen years of age and older Germans. As many as 42 per cent of the youth, compared with 22 per cent of the adults, thought the reconstruction of Germany could best be carried out by "a strong new Führer." According to the report, ". . . a considerable difference appeared in the attitude towards Hitler, the majority of the youth offering an opinion being ready to excuse Hitler as a good man with bad advisers, while the majority of the older people condemned Hitler as an evil individual."[25] The Nuremberg Trials lifted the scales from the eyes of many Germans, and later OMGUS surveys reported that only one in eight (12 per cent) of those questioned in the American Zone recalled trusting Hitler as Leader up to the end of the war, while 35 per cent claimed never to have trusted him and a further 16 per cent to have kept faith in him only until the outbreak of war.[26]

Nevertheless, around one in two Germans in both the American and the British Zones – and a percentage on the increase – thought that National Socialism had basically been a good idea, badly carried out, and were far more favourably disposed to it than to communism.[27] Good social conditions, good living conditions, full employment, unified State and government, and order and security were the attributes, in that order, picked out as the best thing about National Socialism.[28] As late as 1950, 10 per cent of a nation-wide opinion survey sample in West Germany regarded Hitler as the statesman who had achieved most for Germany – second only to Bismarck.[29] In summer 1952, around a quarter of the population had a "good opinion" of Hitler.[30] A tenth of those questioned thought that Hitler was the greatest statesman of the century, whose true greatness would only be recognized at a later date, and a further 22 per cent thought that, while he had made "some mistakes" he had nevertheless been an excellent head of State.[31] Around a third of those questioned still opposed the attack on Hitler's life on 20 July 1944.[32] In 1953, some 14 per cent still voiced their willingness to vote again for a man such as Hitler.[33]

A sample of youth in north Germany interviewed in the late 1950s still revealed significant traces of the "Hitler myth": he had done much good in abolishing unemployment, punishing sexual criminals, constructing the motorways, introducing cheap radio sets, establishing the Labour Service, and reinstating Germany in the esteem of the world. He had been an idealist with many good ideas at first, only later making errors, turning out to be basically evil, and becoming insane and a mass murderer.[34]

The decisive drop in the level of Hitler's posthumous popularity came during the era of the "economic miracle" under Adenauer and Erhard. By the mid-1960s, only 4 per cent were reporting that they might be willing once again to vote for someone like Hitler.[35] By this date, only about 2 or 3 per cent thought Hitler has achieved more than any other leader for Germany. (Adenauer had, by now, far outstripped Bismarck as the favourite in these stakes.)[36] Even so, the number of those who believe that Hitler would have been one of the greatest German statesmen of all time had it not been for the war remained relatively high, though this figure too had fallen sharply (from 48 per cent in 1955 to 32 per cent by 1967).[37]

210

By the mid-1960s, admiration for Hitler was almost entirely confined to the residual extreme radical Right, the neo-Nazis. During the first years of the Federal Republic, from 1949 to 1953, when the Right was staging something of a recovery, attempts had been made to distinguish between "insane Hitlerism" and the positive aspects of National Socialism.[38] But as this phase of radical Right optimism died away from 1953, it was replaced in the hard-core by professed adherence to the Nazi past and outright glorification of Hitler.[39] The basic tenor of the publications of the extreme Right has scarcely altered since that date. The short-lived revitalization of the neo-Nazi Right which saw the temporary rise to prominence of the NPD [National Democratic Party] between 1966 and 1968 brought a very minor revival of positive views about Hitler and Nazism. In 1968, 6 per cent of the West German population (compared with 4 per cent in 1965 and 1967) reported their willingness to vote again for a man such as Hitler.[40] The "Hitler Wave" of publications during the 1970s appears to have contributed to renewed and open glorification of Hitler on the extreme Right.[41] Hitler is still today regarded there in "heroic" terms as a "great statesman" and "significant personality," whose foreign policy achieved German power and autonomy, while his failure and the loss of the war are put down to sabotage from within, and the war itself attributed not to Hitler but to the meddling of the western powers in a German-Polish conflict.[42] Systematic sampling of West German voters carred out in 1979–80 indicated that 13 per cent of all voters in the Federal Republic had a consolidated extreme rightist "world view"; 14 per cent responded positively to the statement that "we should again have a Leader who would rule Germany with a strong hand for the good of all,"[43]

Though these figures shock, they need to be put into perspective. Since 1945, West Germany has become a "normal" liberal democracy, with close affinities to the political systems of other western countries. These countries, too, have their unreconstructed fascists and Nazis, their residual lunatic right-wing fringe, and their broader bands of sympathizers with various aspects of rightist thinking. And apart from the peculiarities of the relationship with the German Democratic Republic, the structural problems of the West German State are in the main those common to most (and less acute than in many) advanced capitalist industrial societies of the present: problems of social equality and distribution of wealth, and of maintaining in an era of world-wide recession the economic growth so central to the legitimacy of post-war liberal democracies; problems of the exploitation (and often ruination) of limited natural resources in the interests of the economy; problems of national defence in a nuclear age; and the corresponding problems of containing and absorbing often justified social and political protest without destroying civil liberties and undermining the very essence of the liberal democratic state.

The socio-economic problems in West Germany as elsewhere have given rise to an inevitable resurgence of hostility towards ethnic and other minorities, and have put some pressure on the political system itself (reflected in the emergence of the part ecological, part anti-nuclear, part general social protest "Green Party"). But the specific features and structural characteristics of the German socio-political culture in the short-lived and ill-fated nation-state, which conditioned the manufacture and appeal of the extraordinary "Hitler myth," were largely swept away in the whirlpool of change arising from total defeat, and were completely banished in the process of long-term change deriving from post-war reconstruction. Unlike the 1920s and 1930s, the current socio-economic problems, acute though they are, have not seen a marked upswing in the political fortunes of the extreme Right. Crucially, they have not produced, nor do they appear likely to do so, a damaging crisis of legitimacy for the State.

Only such a crisis, of almost inconceivably devastating proportions – such as might follow a major war – could so undermine and destroy the existing pluralist political structures that a new form of fascist-style charismatic leadership might appear to sizeable proportions of the population to be a viable and attractive solution. Without wanting to appear too sanguine, and without trivializing the persistent phenomenon of right-wing extremism and the need to maintain vigilance against it, the full realization of the responsibility which Hitler bears for the untold agonies suffered by millions has so discredited everything he stood for in the eyes of sane persons everywhere that, except in circumstances beyond the scope of our realistic imagination, it is difficult to see that there could be a resurrection or a new variant of the once-mighty "Hitler myth," with its power to capture the imagination of millions.

Old myths are, however, replaced by new as the combination of modern technology and advanced marketing techniques produce ever more elaborate and sophisticated examples of political image-building around minor personality cults, even in western democracies, aimed at obfuscating reality among the ignorant and gullible. The price for abdicating democratic responsibilities and placing uncritical trust in the "firm leadership" of seemingly well-intentioned political authority was paid dearly by Germans between 1933 and 1945. Even if a collapse into new forms of fascism is inherently unlikely in any western democracy, the massive extension of the power of the modern State over its citizens is in itself more than sufficient cause to develop the highest level possible of educated cynicism and critical awareness as the only protection against the marketed images of present-day and future claimants to political "leadership."

NOTES

Reprinted from Ian Kershaw, *The "Hitler Myth." Image and Reality in the Third Reich* (Oxford/New York: Oxford University Press, 1987), pp. 253–69.

1 See T. Childers, "Interest and Ideology: Anti-System Politics in the Era of Stabilization 1924–1928" in G. Feldman (ed.), *Die Nachwirkungen der Inflation auf die deutsche Geschichte* (Munich, 1985), pp. 1–20.

2 See A. Gorz, *Farewell to the Working Class* (London, 1982), pp. 58–9, 62–3.

3 M. Domarus (ed.), *Hitler, Reden und Proklamationen 1932–1945* (Weisbaden, 1973), p. 1178; S. Haffner, *Anmerkungen zu Hitler* (Munich, 1978), p. 44.

4 H. Picker, *Hitlers Tischgespräche im Führerhauptquartier 1941 bis 1942* (Stuttgart, 1963), p. 248; H. von Kotze and H. Krausnick, *"Es spricht der Führer", 7 exemplarische Hitler-Reden* (Gutersloh, 1966), p. 46.

5 von Kotze and Krausnick, *"Es spricht der Führer,"* p. 46.

6 See A. Speer, *Erinnerungen* (Frankfurt am Main/Berlin, 1969), p. 229; and also T. W. Mason, "The Legacy of 1918 for National Socialism" in A. Nicholls and E. Matthias (eds), *German Democracy and the Triumph of Hitler* (London, 1971), pp. 215–39.

7 *Lagebesprechungen im Führerhauptquartier*, ed. H. Heiber (Berlin, 1962), p. 287.

8 See A. Schweitzer, *The Age of Charisma* (Chicago, 1984), pp. 86–7.

9 M. Broszat, "Soziale Motivation und Führer-Bindung des Nationalsozialismus," *Vierteljahreshefte für Zeitgeschichte*, Vol. XVIII, 1970,

p. 405. The following reflections owe much to this stimulating article.

10 See W. Struve, *Elites against Democracy. Leadership Ideals in Bourgeois Political Thought in Germany, 1890–1933* (Princeton, 1973), p. 433; F. Weinstein, *The Dynamics of Nazism. Leadership, Ideology and the Holocaust* (New York, 1980), pp. 66–7; H. Mommsen, "Zur Verschränkung traditioneller und faschistischer Führungsgruppen in Deutschland beim Übergang von der Bewegungs- zur Systemphase" in W. Schieder (ed.), *Faschismus als soziale Bewegung* (Hamburg, 1976), p. 165; and H. Mommsen, "Der Mythos des nationalen Aufbruchs und die Haltung der deutschen Intellektuellen und funktionalen Eliten" in *1933 in Gesellschaft und Wissenschaft*, ed. Pressestelle der Universität Hamburg (Hamburg, 1983), p. 134.

11 K.-J. Müller, "Nationalkonservative Eliten zwischen Kooperation und Widerstand" in J. Schmädeke and P. Steinbach (eds), *Der Widerstand gegen den Nationalsozialismus* (Munich, 1985), pp. 25–6; R. Baum, *The Holocaust and the German Elite* (London, 1981), pp. 52–3, 178ff., 183ff.

12 See K.-J. Müller, "Nationalkonservative Eliten zwischen Kooperation und Widerstand" in Schmädeke and Steinbach (eds), *Der Widerstand*, pp. 25–6.

13 Ibid., pp. 28–30.

14 The ways in which conservative opposition groups, even when actively conspiring to destroy the regime, could accommodate – without, of course, identifying with them – central parts of Nazi ideology in their "world view" has recently been shown with regard to the "Jewish Question." See C. Dipper, "The German resistance and the Jews," *Yad Vashem Studies*, Vol. XVI, 1984, pp. 51–93.

15 See K.-J. Müller, *Armee, Politik und Gesellschaft in Deutschland 1933–1945* (Paderborn, 1979), pp. 39–47.

16 See F. Neumann, Behemoth, *The Structure and Practice of National Socialism* (London, 1942).

17 See M. Kater, "Hitler in a Social Context," *Central European History*, Vol. XIV, 1981, pp. 257–60; Schweitzer, *The Age of Charisma*, p. 66f.

18 See Schweitzer, *The Age of Charisma*, p. 82.

19 See, e.g., G. M. Gilbert, *Nuremberg Diary* (London, 1948), pp. 186–96; and D. Jahr, "Die Einstellung der engeren NS-Elite zur Persönlichkeit und politischen Strategie Adolf Hitlers," Ruhr-Universität Bochum Magisterarbeit, 1984.

20 A. Rosenberg, *Letzte Aufzeichnungen, Ideale und Idole der nationalsozialistischen Revolution* (Göttingen, 1955), p. 328.

21 H. Frank, *Im Angesicht des Galgens* (Munich, 1953), pp. 139, 322.

22 Speer, *Erinnerungen*, pp. 177, 184.

23 B. von Schirach, *Ich glaubte an Hitler* (Hamburg, 1967), p. 160.

24 According to Otto Dietrich, Hitler began around 1935–6 "to hate objections to his views and doubts in his infallibility," wanting "to speak but not to listen" – O. Dietrich, *Zwölf Jahre mit Hitler* (Cologne/Munich, n.d. [1955]), pp. 44–5. And Fritz Wiedemann

claimed it had been impossible to contradict a leader "who immediately became aggressive if the facts did not fit into his conception" – F. Wiedemann, *Der Mann, der Feldherr werden wollte* (Velbert/Kettwig, 1964), p. 90, and see also pp. 73–4, 89.

25 IfZ, OMGUS-Akten, 5/234–2/2. 13 Oct. 1945.

26 A. J. and R. L. Merritt (eds), *Public Opinion in Occupied Germany. The OMGUS Survey, 1945–1949* (Urbana, 1970), pp. 30–1.

27 Ibid., pp. 32–3; A. J. and R. L. Merritt (eds), *Public Opinion in Semisovereign Germany. The HICOG Surveys, 1949–1955* (Urbana, 1980), p. 7; IfZ OMGUS-Akten, 5/233–3/2, reports from 11 June 1948; 5 Jan. 1949; 11 Feb. 1949 from the British Zone Public Opinion Research Office, Bielefeld.

28 IfZ, OMGUS-Akten 5/233–3/2. 11 Feb. 1949.

29 *Jahrbuch der öffentlichen Meinung, 1947–1955*, ed. E. Noelle and E. P. Neumann (Allensbach, 1956), p. 132. K. D. Bracher, *The German Dictatorship* (Harmondsworth, 1973), p. 589, states that as many as 32 per cent of West Germans in 1953 thought that Hitler had been possibly the greatest statesman of this century, but this seems to be a misreading of the figure in the opinion polls given for Bismarck, not Hitler.

30 *Jahrbuch der öffentlichen Meinung 1947–1955*, p. 135.

31 Ibid., p. 136.

32 Ibid., p. 138.

33 Merritt and Merritt, *Public Opinion in Occupied Germany*, p. 62, n. 17.

34 W. Jaide, "Not interested in politics?" in W. Stahl (ed.), *The Politics of Postwar Germany* (New York, 1963), pp. 368–9.

35 Merritt and Merritt, *Public Opinion in Occupied Germany*, p. 62, n. 17.

36 *Jahrbuch der öffentlichen Meinung 1965–1967*, ed. E. Noelle and E. P. Neumann (Allensbach, 1974), p. 201.

37 Ibid., p. 144.

38 H.-H. Knuetter, "Ideologies of Extreme Rightists in Postwar Germany," in Stahl (ed.), *The Politics of Postwar Germany*, p. 224.

39 Ibid., pp. 244–6.

40 Merritt and Merritt, *Public Opinion in Occupied Germany*, p. 62. Presumably for mainly tactical reasons, only a third of the NPD adherents questioned admitted their readiness to vote again for a man such as Hitler.

41 For the commercial "marketing" of Hitler during the 1970s, see C. H. Meyer, "Die Veredelung Hitlers. Das Dritte Reich als Markenartikel" in W. Benz (ed.), *Rechtsextremismus in der Bundesrepublik* (Frankfurt am Main, 1984), pp. 45–67.

42 *5 Millionen Deutsche: "Wir sollten wieder einen Führer haben . . ." Die SINUS-Studie über rechtsextremistische Einstellungen bei den Deutschen* (Reinbek bei Hamburg, 1981), pp. 54–5.

43 Ibid., pp. 78–9.

Part II

THE "RACIAL COMMUNITY" AND ITS ENEMIES

7

LABOR AS SPOILS OF CONQUEST, 1933–1945

Ulrich Herbert

In the three years since the unification of Germany, the "foreigner problem" (Ausländerfrage) has become a major political issue. But it is seldom publicly acknowledged that foreign labor has been an important element of the modern German workforce, in both quantitative and qualitative terms, for at least the last hundred years. Real or imagined memories of earlier experiences with foreign workers have deeply influenced, indeed distorted, popular perceptions of the "problem" of foreign labor from the early twentieth century to the present.

By the end of the Second World War, there were some 7.5 million foreign workers in Germany, most of whom had been forced into working for the German war effort. The racism of the Nazi regime allowed forced labor to be exploited with no particular concern for the health or the lives of the coerced workers. In the book from which the following chapter is taken, Ulrich Herbert shows that forced and slave labor in Nazi Germany had its roots in a long tradition of discrimination against foreign workers in which even German workers participated to some degree.* Wilhelmine Germany (1890–1918) employed workers from all over Europe, but Poles were the most significant contingent and appeared to constitute the most important political and cultural threat. Polish workers were admitted only as temporary or "seasonal laborers" and had to submit to special legal regulations which deprived them of most of the rights allowed to "native" Germans. During the First World War, Russian and Polish civilian workers, who before 1914 had been required periodically to leave Germany, were now forced to stay in the country and their

---

*See Ulrich Herbert, *A History of Foreign Labor in Germany, 1880–1980. Seasonal Workers/Forced Laborers/Guest Workers* (Ann Arbor: University of Michigan Press, 1990).

movements and work habits were subjected to harsh controls. Thousands of Belgians were also more or less forcibly deported to work in Germany industry. But this transition to forced labor was disguised by the pre-war traditions of discrimination and control directed, in particular, against the Poles. To many Germans, forced labor practices in the First World War seemed no more than the "toughening and tightening of regulations due to war, and therefore justified."† *These (false) memories of forced labor during the First World War in turn helped to desensitize many Germans to the Nazis' barbaric exploitation of forced labor during the Second World War.*

By the time the Nazis came to power in 1933, foreign labor was of only marginal importance to the German economy; the mass unemployment created by the Great Depression had drastically slashed the numbers of foreigners who could find work in Germany. Until 1939, the numbers of foreign workers in Germany remained low, a sign of the Nazis' racial prejudices and their commitment to economic autarky. But after the war began, the Nazis faced a growing labor shortage. Unwilling to mobilize German women for industrial war production, the Nazi regime had no alternative but to turn increasingly to the forced labor of foreigners. Yet the influx of millions of Russian POWs, Poles and other, supposedly "inferior," nationalities into wartime Germany, threatened to become a racial nightmare. To ensure that politically and racially "dangerous" contacts between Aryan Germans and foreign workers would be kept to a minimum, the Nazis set up a draconian system of racial apartheid.

The conditions under which forced labor was performed during the Second World War were extremely brutal, often amounting to "annihilation by work," malnourishment and mistreatment. Herbert argues, however, that the treatment of forced labor should not be confused with the fate of the European Jews. Indeed, the author shows that the decision in favor of a massive deployment of foreign workers and POWs in the Reich, especially the Russeneinsatz in the autumn of 1941, eliminated any lingering "economic" considerations that might have been raised as objections to the implementation of the "Final Solution"; Jews could now be murdered en masse *precisely because they were not needed to perform slave-labor for the Reich.‡*

Most Germans did not even question the presence of millions of

†Ibid., p. 116.
‡See, most recently, Ulrich Herbert, "Labour and Extermination: Economic Interest and the Primacy of *Weltanschauung* in National Socialism," *Past and Present*, No. 138, February 1993, pp. 144–95.

forced and slave-laborers in Nazi Germany, or their own position of racial privilege over these foreigners. After 1945, few Germans appear to have felt any real guilt about the exploitation of foreign labor during the Second World War; in their minds, the "deployment of foreign labor" (Fremdarbeitereinsatz) had no real connection with other Nazi atrocities.

* * *

FOREIGN WORKERS AND THE GERMAN WAR ECONOMY

"Russeneinsatz": the deployment of Russians

After lightning-fast victories over Poland and France, the German leadership was confident of an equally speedy victory when Hitler decided to embark in the summer of 1940 on "Operation Barbarossa" and attack the Soviet Union. Their overconfidence in a sure victory was also the reason why no thought was given to the deployment of Soviet labor, civilian and POW, and no preparations were undertaken for such an eventuality. Rather, plans were developed for resettling many millions of Soviet citizens to the northern regions of the Soviet Union. In May 1941 in Milan, a group of experts summed up such plans as follows: "Many tens of millions have become superfluous in this entire area and will die or have to emigrate to Siberia."[1]

Plans of the military leadership for dealing with the anticipated hordes of Soviet POWs were also prepared in line with this basic perspective. Although a minimum of two to three million prisoners was expected, no housing, food provisions, or transports were organized for such massive numbers of POWs. Christian Streit, who has studied the fate of Soviet POWs, has commented in this regard:

> There was no doubt, on the basis of the plans of the Economic Staff Oldenburg in the Wehrmacht Supreme Command, that a large proportion of the prisoners as well as the civilian population would starve to death as a result. At this juncture, there was no interest in preserving the lives of these prisoners for purposes of labor exploitation in the German economy.[2]

221

The deployment of Soviet prisoners for labor purposes in the Reich was even expressly forbidden; employment of prisoners was permitted only for the "immediate needs" of the troops.[3]

The consequences of these decisions were enormous. A few short weeks after the beginning of the war against the Soviet Union, Soviet prisoners began to die in massive numbers as a result of starvation and disease: some 60 per cent of the 3,350,000 Soviet prisoners taken by the Germans before the end of 1941 died, 1.4 million of them before September. Of the 5.7 million Soviet POWs captured by the Germans during the course of the war, an estimated 3.3 million died in German custody.[4]

Already in August 1941, but at the latest by mid-September, it was evident that expectations entertained by the German top echelon of being able to bring the war against the Soviet Union to a swift victorious conclusion by the end of 1941 had been ill founded. When the German advance on Moscow ground to a halt, it gradually became clear that preparations would have to be made for a longer, drawn-out war of attrition rather than another *Blitzkrieg*. This necessitated a rethinking of the entire concept of the war economy. In particular, all hopes had been dashed for a speedy return by German soldiers on the eastern front to their jobs back home, and the manpower shortage once again took on threatening proportions, now to a greater and more serious extent than had been the case in 1939 and 1940. Half a million vacancies were reported in agriculture, 50,000 in mining, 300,000 in the metal industry, and 140,000 in construction, so that the German war economy was now unable to function without a further massive injection of foreign labor.

The mining industry in the Ruhr led the way in utilizing Soviet labor in the Reich, an option that was still strictly rejected by the party leadership and the SS. After a lengthy dispute, in which the content of the altercations and the positions of the disputants were similar to those that had characterized the debates over the deployment of Polish workers, Hitler and Göring gave the basic go-ahead in October and November 1941 for deploying Soviet prisoners of war and civilian workers. The regulations issued by Göring on 7 November 1941, left no doubt about the future character of the *Russeneinsatz*:

The place of German skilled workmen is in the armaments industry. Shoveling dirt and quarrying stones are not their job – that's what the Russian is for. No contact with the German population, in particular no "solidarity." As a matter of principle, the German worker is always the boss of any Russians. Food provision is a matter for the Four-Year Plan. The Russians can arrange their own food (cats, horses, etc.). Clothing, housing, maintenance a bit better than what they had back home, where some lived in caves. Supervision: members of the Wehrmacht during work, as well as German workers acting as auxiliary police. Range of punishment: from limitations on food rations to execution by court-martial, generally no additional stages are recognized.[5]

Taken in their entirety, Göring's guidelines are the extreme expression of the compromise reached in the autumn of 1941: Russian workers were to be deployed but under conditions of maximum exploitation, the worst imaginable treatment and food, and the threat of the death penalty, even in the case of minor transgressions.

After the fundamental decisions had been made in favor of deploying Soviet labor, the responsible authorities in the Reich proceeded on the assumption that the German labor problem had been basically solved in view of the vast reservoir of prisoners in the East. In actual fact, however, it became clear that the greater proportion of the prisoners in the Wehrmacht camps in the East had already died; moreover, of those still alive, there were only a small number who were still fit to endure the rigors of transport and subsequent deployment. In February 1942, the high-ranking ministerial official Mansfeld commented in retrospect:

The current difficulties besetting labor deployment would not have arisen had a decision been made in proper time for a *large-scale deployment of Russian prisoners of war.* There were 3.9 million Russians available; of these, now only 1.1 million are left. It will be extremely difficult to increase the number of Russian POWs currently deployed (400,000).[6]

Consequently, the German labor administration now had to resort to the recruitment of Soviet civilian workers instead of the administratively more simple procedure of deployment of prisoners of war. This entailed substantial problems – not only in terms of organizational effort but also ideologically.

As a result, measures were adopted in the spring of 1942 to render the deployment of foreign workers more effective, now in particular the recruitment of Soviet civilian workers. Another objective of these measures was analogous to the decrees on Poles of March 1940: to ensure that the treatment of Soviet laborers would be in keeping with the racial principles of the Nazi regime.

The entire sphere of labor deployment was centralized by the creation of the post of Plenipotentiary for Labor Deployment (*Generalbevollmächtigter für den Arbeitseinsatz* – GBA), to which the Gauleiter of Thuringia, Fritz Sauckel, was appointed. This served in particular to coordinate the recruitment campaigns of the occupied countries and the utilization and treatment of foreign workers. Sauckel's principal task was to bring as many foreigners as possible to Germany in the shortest amount of time. In addition, he was entrusted with the job of singing the praises and selling the successes of National Socialist foreign-laborer policy by means of rather crude and emotional propaganda. In contrast, his actual influence on basic decisions regarding such policy was of less importance.

On 2 February 1942, the RSHA issued the so-called Decrees on Eastern Workers (*Ostarbeitererlasse*). "Eastern worker" (*Ostarbeiter*) was now the official term for Soviet civilian workers, and these new regulations were similar in their basic contours to those that had been issued for Polish workers, though they went further in respect to several important points.

If one summarizes these decrees, together with the supplementary regulations, the following picture emerges: quartering was in closed residence camps, fenced in and segregated by sex; families of Eastern workers were housed together. Return to the East was ordered for those unfit for work, juveniles under 15 years of age, and pregnant women. There was a prohibition on freedom of movement and leaving of the camp, except for work, and supervision during leisure time by the German Labor Front (DAF). Excursions were to be organized as a possible reward, with the requisite German escort. Work was to be organized as much as feasible in closed groups. Any feeling of solidarity between Russian and Germans was to be prevented. Supervision and guarding duties were to be handled by plant guards, professional security personnel, and German workers acting as auxiliary plant police. The camps were to be managed by camp directors appointed by the political security officer of the plant. Guarding of female Russian workers would be done by males as well. There was to be a strict requirement for wearing a badge marked OST. Russian agents and senior inmates would be utilized. Mail privileges were to be allowed twice a month. There was a prohibition on any pastoral assistance, and ruthless suppression, even by the use of weapons, of any disobedience. A special system of punishment was to be instituted: penalties such as cleanup duty, assignment to penal labor gangs, withdrawal of hot meals for up to three days, arrest for periods up to three days; camp directors were allowed to inflict corporal punishment (flogging). All other punishments were to be the sole prerogative of the Gestapo. Inmates who attempted to escape were to be sent to "labor re-education camps" and to concentration camps. The death penalty was to be introduced for capital offenses, political offenses, and sexual intercourse with Germans.[7]

In addition to the fears regarding racial purity and the ethnic dangers to national-cultural policies associated with any massive employment of Russians in the Reich, political objections and misgivings of the security authorities were also a factor operative here: namely their apprehension that Bolshevik workers from the East might influence their German fellow workers politically, thus engendering bonds and expressions of solidarity between German and Soviet workers. In accordance with these fears, it was made unmistakably clear and emphatic in the Decrees on Eastern Workers and the numerous plant regulations on their implementation that German workers, as a matter of principle, had to conduct themselves at all times as workers in a senior and superior capacity vis-à-vis the Russians. Contacts between Germans and Russians, moreover, were to be restricted to only the most essential job-related instructions. The limitation on deployment in labor gangs was also designed to serve this aim.

In their entirety, these *Ostarbeitererlasse* can be viewed as the virtually complete and concrete practical implementation within foreign-labor deployment of the racist principle predicating a division into *Herrenmenschen*, i.e. members of the "master race," and *Untermenschen*, i.e. members of a "subhuman" species of mankind. Heydrich had also proclaimed this in unmistakable fashion in December 1941:

> Though the economic perspectives that must be taken into account have been clearly recognized as having immediate pertinence, any attempt to postpone the issues of race and integrity of national culture [*Volkstum*] until the postwar period should be resolutely opposed. How long the war may last is uncertain, and the danger is mounting with every passing hour. Unfortunately, the deployment of foreigners was initiated without any supervision and guidance in respect to recruitment, deployment, treatment, etc., so that it is becoming more and more difficult now to take steps to intervene and guide the process. However, the deployment of Russians, at present in the planning stages, offers us this opportunity. That is an opportunity that must – and will – be taken advantage of, due to the special dangers these peoples pose.[8]

We have dealt previously in the main with offices of the war economy – the Office for the Four-Year Plan, the Ministry of Agriculture, the Economic and Armaments Office in the Supreme Command (OKW), and the labor administration authorities – when examining the driving forces behind the mass deployment of foreign labor. Yet what role did the private economy have in these efforts?

This question has been much discussed in the secondary literature, and Marxist scholars in particular have singled out industry as the "driving force" behind the massive deployment of foreign labor.[9] Yet it has been shown that the proportion of Polish POWs and civilian workers deployed in the industrial sector during the initial years of the war was quite negligible, and French prisoners of war were largely concentrated in agriculture. Moreover, the first attempts to deploy Poles in mining, for example, were viewed by mine management as having been of little practical success. What was decisive for industry was that the skilled manpower that was mainly required there needed an initial fairly lengthy period of on-the-job training before such workers could be profitably utilized. However, since expectations at first were running high that the field campaigns would be relatively short and swift, industry harbored hopes that its German work force, inducted for military service, would

226

soon be back on the job. For this reason, the demand for foreign workers, especially by the large enterprises, was comparatively limited during the *Blitzkrieg* phase of the war – aside from a few branches such as construction.

This was also true of the period in 1941 before and several months after the invasion of the Soviet Union. There were a small number of requests submitted to the authorities – for example, from industry in the Ruhr – for Soviet workers as early as July 1941, but such requests initially remained isolated instances. The greater majority of the industrial firms were still biding their time in the hope of reemploying discharged German soldiers that coming winter after a quick victory over the Soviet Union. Yet when it became clear by the autumn that a quick end to the conflict was not in sight – and in the wake of the fundamental decision by Hitler and Göring giving the green light for the deployment of Soviet labor – industry also prepared to put large numbers of Russian civilians and prisoners of war to work.

This decision was made for the western sector of the Reich by the Northwest District Group of the Economic Group Iron on 19 November 1941. It was stated there: "People will have to accommodate to the notion of deploying Russian labor." In view of the military situation, it had become evident

that, seen over the long haul, the only wise and safe move economically was to acquire Russian laborers. . . . Consequently, since we will not be able to avoid deployment of Russians, what must now be done is to examine whether the Northwest Group should not attempt by unified action to postpone for as long as possible the date of this exchange.[10]

However, since such a move was regarded as futile, the group voted at that session to accept the deployment of Soviet labor in industry in the Ruhr.

This does not offer proof of the "openly criminal conception of forced labor conscription [*Verschleppung*] among the leading German monopolies, their initiative and leading role in mass conscription and relocation during all phases of the war."[11] It is not possible to confirm that thesis empirically. Rather, what is evident is that the representatives of big industry abandoned their plans for the imminent postwar period only with great reluctance, since it was their conviction that the war had already been won. Only very reluctantly did they begin, by basic acceptance of a policy of deployment of Russians, to orient their thinking in terms of a long war of attrition. Their original goal had been the predominance of German industry in Europe, its macroregional hegemony – not any massive enterprise of training and deployment of Soviet workers in German firms.

The recruitment campaigns were initiated beginning in the winter of 1941 in those parts of the Soviet Union occupied by the Wehrmacht. However, the practice of induction and deportation implemented by the German authorities involved, drawn from the labor administration, the Wehrmacht, and the SS, had little in common with recruitment in the general and accepted sense of the concept. Based on experience in Poland, the German authorities issued regulations stipulating how manpower contingents imposed on the various districts were to be recruited, using a system of compulsory draft and conscription based on age group. There were a small number of volunteers in some regions during the early weeks, but the German authorities proceeded on the assumption right from the start that "voluntary recruitment . . . would not prove successful."[12]

A report from a German mail censorship office dated November 1942 gives an indication of what these recruitment campaigns looked like in actual stark practice:

> Men and women, including teenagers aged 15 and above, [are being] picked up on the street, at open-air markets and village celebrations and then speeded away. The inhabitants, for that reason, are frightened, stay hidden inside, and avoid going out into public. According to the letters perused, the application of flogging as a punishment has been supplemented since about the beginning of October by the burning down of farmsteads or entire villages as a reprisal for failure to heed the orders given to the local townships for making manpower available. Implementation of this latter measure has been reported from a whole series of localities.[13]

Using such methods, the German authorities succeeded in a short span of time in bringing enormous numbers of workers from the Soviet Union to Germany. From April to December 1942 alone, a total of some 1.3 million civilian laborers were transported into the Reich for deployment, amounting to an average of 40,000 per week, 50 per cent male, 50 per cent female. The average age of the deportees was about 20, but many of them were considerably younger, including 15- and 16-year-olds recruited for labor in the Reich. In addition, approximately 450,000 Soviet prisoners of war were sent as labor conscripts to the Reich in 1942, so that by the end of the year there were already more than 1.7 million civilian and POW workers from the Soviet Union on the job in German enterprises. The greater proportion of these were utilized in industry, which was reeling under the burden of constantly boosted production demands following the reorientation to the prospect of a protracted war of attrition in the winter of 1941–2.[14]

The German authorities also intensified their hiring and recruitment measures in the western occupied countries and in Poland, increasingly utilizing coercive measures of compulsion, such as the introduction of compulsory service in France as well. The upshot was that the numbers of conscripted civilian workers from the West rose – along with an intensification of the resistance movements in the respective countries. The German secret service reported in the summer of 1942 regarding the situation in France that

> further segments of the indifferent mass of the population had [gone over] to the oppositional camp as a result of the law on compulsory labor service. . . . In many circles today, one encounters an atmosphere of bitter rejection of everything German. . . . Even if that is not manifested in open rejection, there is an obvious and unmistakable danger that a substantial proportion of the population has become more receptive toward hostile agitation than was previously the case.[15]

The spread of partisan groups in the Soviet Union can also be attributed to a substantial degree to the deportation policy pursued by the occupying German troops.[16]

Change in political direction

If one examines the policy and practice of foreign-labor deployment during 1942 in context, it is evident that the regime invested considerable efforts in bringing more and more mass transports of laborers to Germany, especially from the Soviet Union, and that the organization and administration of foreign-labor deployment had been rendered more effective. On the other hand, however, the central primacy of racial theory still overrode any economic considerations. The working and living conditions of the eastern workers and the Soviet POWs were extremely poor while those of the Polish workers were little different. Laborers from western countries were somewhat better off, yet their situation was far worse than that of the domestic German work force. Thus, a racist hierarchy was visibly manifest everywhere in concrete practice, becoming ever more established and entrenched: Germans, workers from the West, workers from the East – in descending order. The extensive exploitation of workers from Eastern Europe was the product of the notion that it was quite easy to deport many more millions of them into the Reich: they constituted a virtually inexhaustible and readily available labor pool. Consequently, their productivity levels remained comparatively low, and their actual effectiveness for the National Socialist war economy was far less than their massive numbers on the job might suggest.

However, a change developed after the crushing German defeat at Stalingrad in early 1943 and the apparent turning point in the war that this defeat signaled. For the first time, it became clear to both the leadership and the greater mass of the German population that the principal question was not when the war would be won – but rather how a total defeat could be avoided. The increased demands for replacement of losses raised by the armies on the eastern front had led once again to a serious manpower shortage in Germany beginning in the late autumn of 1942 due to the induction of workers employed in armaments production as well. By the first half of 1943, the German war economy was lacking some 1.5 million workers. These gaps could not be filled by utilizing the previous methods of a step-up in recruitment for foreign labor. It is true that the regime shifted to a policy of inducting more German women for work in industry as a stopgap measure; however, the actual figures (see Table 1) indicate that this had only limited practical effectiveness.

Table 1 Female employment in Germany during World War II (in millions)

May	Total	German Women Employed in Industry	% of All Those Employed
1939	14.6	2.75	25.1
1940	14.4	2.66	26.5
1941	14.1	2.70	26.0
1942	14.4	2.60	26.0
1943	14.8	2.74	25.7
1944	14.8	2.70	25.0

Rather, it had become absolutely necessary to pursue another tack: the productivity levels of the foreign workers in Germany, in particular those from the Soviet Union, had to be drastically increased (Table 2). Here lay the greatest untapped potential. Yet this presupposed a corresponding improvement in food provisions, better treatment, as well as a political revaluation of the *Ostarbeiter* to a certain degree.

That was also the direction taken by a political and propagandistic initiative launched by various Reich agencies under the direction of the Propaganda Minister Goebbels. Proceeding on the assumption that Germany, as Europe's protective wall, was waging a war against Bolshevism but not against the Russian people, he coined the slogan "European Workers against Bolshevism" to suggest the existence of common interests shared by the workers employed in Germany from the countries under Wehrmacht occupation and the workers from the Soviet Union.

Table 2 Productivity levels of foreign workers and POWs in the Rhineland and Westphalia, mid-1943, in comparison with the average productivity of German workers in the same job (in percentage)[17]

Eastern workers	80–100
Female eastern workers compared to all German workers	50–75
Female eastern workers compared to German female workers	90–100
Poles	60–80
French	80–100
Belgian	80–100
Dutch	60–80
Italian, Yugoslav, Croatian	70–80
POWs in mining	50
POWs in metal industry	70

It should be noted that distinctly political considerations were regarded here as more important than racial factors, constituting a shift in the war aims previously propagated by the leadership. This was accompanied by a campaign to improve the living and working conditions of the eastern workers, the purpose of which was to spark a rapid rise in worker productivity levels.

While Goebbels's European initiative had little impact on the actual foreign policy of the regime, a number of changes were introduced subsequently in the policy toward foreign workers, especially in respect to Soviet labor. Thus, food rations were beefed up, extensive training measures introduced, and concessions made in regard to easing restrictions on leaving the camp and employment options within the factories.[18] At the same time, however, all discriminatory regulations of the security authorities remained in effect, and the system of punishment was made even more severe. In any event, these changes provided the factories with a possibility to utilize their Soviet workers more effectively; indeed, from the middle of 1943 on, almost all plants and factories were able to report rising productivity levels.

At the same time, recruitment of civilian workers was expanded throughout Europe by ever more brutal methods. The regime leadership actually succeeded in bringing approximately 2.5 million more foreign civilian workers and POWs into the Reich between early 1943 and the end of the war – despite the avalanche of military defeats. Approximately 600,000 of them were Italians. In the aftermath of Mussolini's downfall in July 1943, the German authorities had interned Italian soldiers who refused to continue to fight for the Germans in work camps inside the Reich, deploying them there as laborers. These Italian military internees – popularly known as "Imis" or "Badoglios" (after the name of the new Italian head of state) – found themselves, together with workers from the Soviet Union, perched on the lowest rung of the racist hierarchy; they were exposed to a particular degree of wrath and fury of the Germans over the supposed Italian "betrayal" of the cause.[19] With their addition, there were now some seven million foreigners laboring for the Germans inside the Reich. The overwhelming majority of these persons had been conscripted for labor against their will and were working under conditions that steadily deteriorated in the face of the imminent defeat now looming ever more clearly on the horizon, the increasing brutality of the German authorities (as well as of many German foremen and fellow workers on the job), and the devastation of German cities bombarded by Allied air raids.

Every second worker in agriculture in August 1944 was a foreign conscript; in mining, construction, and the metals industry, the corresponding figure was roughly every third worker. In the summer of 1944, approximately one-third of the total foreign labor force in the Reich was deployed in agriculture, one-third in heavy industry, and the remainder in other sectors of industry. The predominance of agriculture, which had characterized the deployment of foreign workers until early 1942, had disappeared. Two-thirds of all Polish and French POWs were employed in agriculture while those workers that had been added since 1941 were largely deployed in the industrial sector.

Of the 5.7 million registered foreign civilian workers in Germany in August 1944, 1,924,912 were women, amounting to precisely one-third. However, these female workers came largely (87 per cent) from the East; among males, the corresponding figure was 62 per cent. The lower the individual group of foreigners in the political and racist hierarchy of the Nazis, the higher the percentage of females, ranging from 3 per cent female among the Hungarians (who were allied with the Germans) to some 51 per cent of the workers from the Soviet Union.

Thus, this brief survey of the statistics on foreign workers in Germany in the final year of the war indicates the following: fully one-fourth of all those employed in the German economy were foreigners; in agriculture and armaments-related industries, they made up approximately one-third of the work force. The deployment of millions of foreign workers and prisoners of war during World War II made it possible for Nazi Germany to continue the war effort long after its own labor resources had been depleted. Without these foreign workers, the war would have been lost for Germany by the summer of 1943 at the latest. At the same time, however, the deployment of foreign laborers allowed the regime to maintain a high level of provisions for the German population right down to the last phase of the war. In this way, it managed both to retain the loyalty of the population and to avoid having to induct large numbers of German women for work in industry. . . .

233

WAR ECONOMY AND IDEOLOGY: THE PRACTICE OF FORCED LABOR

Extensive exploitation

As a result of the guidelines issued by Göring in November 1941, the *Ostarbeitererlasse*, and corresponding regulations laid down by various labor and food provision agencies, the working and living conditions of the Soviet civilian workers and POWs were in such a shocking state that reports began to come in from all over the Reich a short time after the arrival of the first transports from the East: the situation in respect to food provisions for eastern workers and Russian prisoners of war was catastrophic; their housing arrangements were inadequate; and the wages paid to a civilian worker were so low after the deduction of a supplementary tax (the so-called surtax on eastern workers [*Ostarbeiterabgabe*]) that the work offered no incentive for encouraging higher productivity. Numerous factories and firms complained to the responsible civilian and military authorities that effective performance on the job could no longer be expected of Soviet workers, given the poor nourishment they were receiving. The firm of Krupp in Essen reported in April 1942, for example:

> Among the civilian Russian workers – who, aside from a few exceptions, arrived here in excellent physical condition – the typical edemas due to lack of proper nourishment have likewise already begun to appear. In the view of our company physicians, their physical decline is due exclusively to the inadequate nourishment they are receiving. In this connection, we would like to emphasize that the rations we provide them are strictly in keeping with official regulations. More than 30 per cent of our Russian prisoners of war are already unfit for work due to inadequate diet, and 12 have already died in the camp.[20]

The regulation to utilize Soviet workers only in the framework of labor detachments also impeded an effective and useful deployment of their labor for the respective firms. There were now enough workers available, but the actual relief provided by the employment of Russians for the factories operating under heavy production pressure was substantially less than originally estimated. Their productivity was without exception below 70 per cent, and in many instances less than 50 per cent of that of comparable German workers – although the factories concurred in their reports that the productivity levels of such workers approximated those of Germans when they were provided with an improved diet.

The causes at the root of this development, seemingly so absurd from an economic point of view, were not simply the welter of decrees and regulations issued by the authorities. Rather, a key factor was attitudinal: an approach adopted by those responsible at the central and the local level in the government offices and the firms, according to which the Russian was considered worthless from a racial perspective, incapable of any higher-level and more skilled performance on the job. Moreover, it was reasoned, providing the Russian workers with food would serve only to place a burden on maintenance of the German population. "If one of them isn't worth a damn, another one can be found who is. The Bolsheviks are human beings without souls – if a hundred thousand die, a few hundred thousand will come in their stead," stated a representative of the German Labor Front in Essen to a Krupp factory manager who had complained that the Soviet workers assigned to him were close to death by starvation and consequently totally unable to work.[21] It is true that there were various initiatives for improving the situation of eastern workers and Soviet POWs – yet until the spring of 1943, nothing had been done aside from an easing of restrictive regulations regarding work in gangs.

Thus, the system of *Fremdarbeitereinsatz* in Germany at the end of 1942 was riddled with profound contradictions. A halt or even reduction in the deployment of foreigners, as had been demanded by the SS and certain sections of the party, was completely out of the question in light of the pressing needs of the war economy. The more the military situation of the Reich deteriorated, the more the regime was dependent on foreign labor. This necessitated an approach presupposing treatment of these workers in terms of their job productivity and greater integration into German life, on the job and off. However, such enhanced integration harbored a certain danger: racist caricatures propagated by German propaganda of the Russian *Unter-menschen* might dissolve and evaporate as a consequence of closer contact. If the productivity of the foreign workers, in particular from the Soviet Union, were to be increased, the National Socialist vision of a postwar Europe dominated by a German master race would be undermined and compromised – and the very meaning of a Nazi victory laid open to question.

Specifically in the metals industry, many firms that were interested in an effective deployment of the workers assigned to them – and that had even in some cases begun to train the Russian workers – subsequently developed their own guidelines for treatment and also issued supplementary rations to their workers.[22] The maintenance and augmenting of worker efficiency became an overriding central principle in deployment of foreign labor in the majority of firms. This plan was first successfully implemented in connection with workers from western countries and then increasingly with Soviet civilian workers as well. Beginning in 1943, these tendencies were also supported by the political leadership and were promoted by eased regulations regarding treatment as well as a campaign to increase the productivity of eastern workers by improved on-the-job training.

The attempt to optimize the exploitation of the labor, specifically in the case of eastern workers, was promising and attractive in the eyes of the firms because they did not need to show any consideration for the impediments of social policy and legislation, such as were present when employing German workers, especially women. Eastern male and female workers thus became highly sought after as laborers, because of their cost-attractiveness and effectiveness on the job.

Attitudes had therefore undergone a sea change. While industry in particular had resisted the deployment of Russians initially because of the numerous restrictions on their utilization, the meager rations they were allotted, their poor physical condition, and a widespread aversion to Soviet workers both among management and on the shop floor, management now demanded more and more contingents of additional *Ostarbeiter* once these restrictions had largely been remedied or removed. From a purely economic standpoint, the employment of foreigners, eastern workers included, had become quite worthwhile and profitable in Germany, and had even taken on the dimension of an intriguing feasible option for the postwar period. One of the directors of the Fieseler Works summed up this estimate in a speech given in June 1943 in the following words:

By means of the deployment of foreign workers, the German nation has, for the first time, adopted and exploited on a massive scale the activity of auxiliary peoples [*Hilfsvölker*]. The nation has learned from this and amassed new experience. It will be useful and wise even during the war, and after its conclusion at the latest, to gather together this wealth of experience in some competent office.[23]

Yet the example of mining illustrates that the primacy of productivity had not by any means become the dominant factor everywhere throughout German industry. The working and living conditions, especially of the Soviet workers, were unusually poor in this branch and remained so right up until the end of the war. By late December 1942, fully 28 per cent of all workers in the coal mines of the Ruhr region were foreigners, three-fourths of these *Ostarbeiter* and POWs. However, a few short weeks after their arrival, the physical condition of the civilian workers who had been allocated for work in the mines had deteriorated drastically to a critical point, in a manner similar to that of the POWs. Their physical condition initially had been quite good.

Before the summer of 1942, the approximately 25,000 Soviet workers in the mines of the Dortmund district had not as yet been effectively deployed. A Dortmund mining official reported as follows on this problem: "For example, there are frequent instances of Russian POWs who collapse after a short time in the pits. They are seized by lethargy down in the mines and must be brought again to the surface on a stretcher or by some other means."[24]

Even as late as the end of 1942, approximately every sixth Soviet miner was deemed unfit for work, and the average productivity of the others was 37 per cent of average levels customary among their German counterparts. Whoever was unfit for work among the Soviet prisoners of war was sent back after some time to the "main camp" (*Stalag*), where many of them subsequently died. A large number of mines even refused later on to send the prisoners they had been assigned back to the camp, "especially since only a very small proportion of them will ever return from there," as the Association of Mines Hibernia tersely noted.[25]

There were repeated complaints about maltreatment along with the poor diet they were given. A circular letter of the Mining Group Ruhr stated:

Complaints are repeatedly lodged with the Wehrmacht and the civilian authorities that treatment of the Russian prisoners of war is still deficient in a number of mines, that flogging and maltreatment have still not been eliminated, and that there is a complete lack of any humane treatment either down in the pits or on the surface. This serves to indicate that just and proper care for the prisoners of war allocated to these mines – or even a modicum of interest in them – is indeed nonexistent. How else can one explain the daily attrition due to death, the transport back to camp of totally emaciated candidates for the graveyard, individuals who have been toiling for months?[26]

Foremen and pit foremen were those principally guilty of such acts of maltreatment, yet there are a fair number of reports about excesses perpetrated by German miners directed against Russians.

Starting in 1943, management in various mines likewise undertook efforts to improve the output of Soviet workers, but these efforts met with little success. Deficient diet, poor health, high mortality rates – these remained characteristic features of the deployment of foreign laborers in the mining industry. "Thus, for example, 90 Sov. POWs had to be returned from one mine to their home camp in the past three months. A number of these POWs could no longer be saved," stated a communication sent by the command of Defense District VI to the Dortmund Mining Authority in May 1943.[27]

At the beginning of 1944, there were 181,764 Soviet prisoners employed throughout the entire mining sector, yet in the first half of that year a total of 32,236 departures were officially recorded. A breakdown of the figures for mining in Upper Silesia during this period indicates just what was meant by such "departures." Of the 10,963 Soviet prisoners of war registered there as departures, 7,914 had been "returned to prison camp because of illness;" 1,592 had been "transferred to hospital due to illness"; 639 had been reported as having "died while on work gangs"; and 818 were reported to have "fled."[28]

Descriptive accounts detailing the horrific living conditions of the foreign workers in mining, especially those from the Soviet Union, were familiar to both mine management and the authorities. Thus, there were reports by the commissions of the representatives of the protecting powers of the International Red Cross and German escort officers on their visits with POW work gangs in the mines. A report filed in September 1944 listed the principal abuses and defects as follows:

1) POWs are flogged.
2) POWs were forced to work standing in water without rubber boots.
3) POWs were lacking a second blanket, even at the end of October 1943.
4) Their quarters are frequently overcrowded, infested with vermin, and a quiet night's sleep is by no means certain.
5) POWs come with wet clothes from the pits and return to the pits with wet clothing, since there is no opportunity for drying of clothing in their quarters.
6) The examination to determine whether they are fit for work in the mines is very superficial. A civilian doctor, for example, examines up to 200 prisoners an hour as to their fitness for work.
7) Extremely high incidence of accidents. Shifts frequently go down into the shaft without a German skilled workman present among the POWs. Regulations on accident prevention are posted only in the German language.
8) Food is available in sufficient quantity but is frequently mediocre in quality.
9) Sick persons are often not brought to the doctor promptly.
10) Sick POWs still in need of care and treatment are released and sent back into the pits prematurely.[29]

The mines involved often reacted to such reports with a lack of understanding and critical judgment. The management of the Essen Steinkohle mine commented, for example:

> The zeal with which the German authorities show such solicitous concern for the well-being of the foreigners is indeed remarkable. In order to reach a proper attitude toward such efforts and instructions, one's own sober thoughts on such matters are always helpful regarding the question: to what extent have such offices previously

concerned themselves with a similar degree of seriousness about the well-being of our own German workers? And the foreign workers, comfortably quartered and well fed without exception – insofar as they are housed on company premises, or are employed there – are well off in every respect. These persons can well endure their fate at a moment when the German people is fighting for its very survival.[30]

The hierarchy of racism

Given such a vast number of foreign workers, it is quite impossible to arrive at any summary generalizing statement in respect to their living conditions. Rather, there were substantial differences in the concrete situation of the various groups of foreign workers and POWs; these differences were in accordance with a combination of specific criteria.

The criteria of race and ethnic affiliation are the most precisely identifiable of these yardsticks. The workers from western countries were in a worse position than native Germans but in a far better position than workers from the East when it came to food rations, the interior furnishings and physical state of living quarters, work hours and wages, skilled employment; this likewise held true in regard to regulations of security policy, such as the system of punishment, social intercourse with Germans, mistreatment, etc. A hierarchy arose on this basis, an insidious pecking order: French civilian workers ranked above all others from western countries (Belgium, Netherlands); after these came workers from southern European countries either allied with or dependent on Germany (Hungarians, Romanians, Slovenians, Greeks, Serbs, Croatians). Those workers were followed on a lower rung by laborers from Czechoslovakia (the so-called Protectorate Bohemia and Moravia), and beneath them were the Poles. At the bottom of the heap were workers from the Soviet Union – along, since the summer of 1943, with the Italian military internees. In addition, there were certain gradations discernible between Ukrainians and Russians on the one hand, and civilians and prisoners of war on the other. The concentration camp inmates who were deployed in increased numbers in the armaments industry during the last year of the war formed their own special category far beneath the bottom rung of this racist ladder, since their exploitation as forced laborers was not tempered by any sort of treatment oriented in terms of criteria of productivity on the job. In actual practice, nonetheless, differences between the situation of Soviet workers, for example, and the Jewish concentration camp inmates began to blur in many factories during the chaos characterizing the final phase of the war.

In concrete practice on the shop floor, these gradations, regimented by a bewildering plethora of decrees, were naturally not implementable in all details. Yet one is repeatedly warranted in concluding from the reports of local factory and government officials directly involved that this hierarchy corresponded quite closely to the structure of prejudice and bias marking the attitude of persons in positions of authority in the industrial firms and the camps – as well as within a broad segment of the population. One's belonging to a specific *Volkstum*, a specific national ethnic background, determined to a pronounced degree the actual fate of the individual laborer.

Supplementary to a classification based on nationality or *Volkstum*, there was also categorization based on sex. This had an impact and various repercussions particularly on female eastern workers. In order to ward off the "dangers to the blood" threatening the folk body politic from the deployment of workers of an alien ethnic substance as seen by the regime leadership, recruitment squads in the East were instructed to recruit male and female workers in equal numbers. Thus, approximately, one-third of the Polish workers were female, and a bit more than half of the Soviet civilian workers. In the factories, they were subject to the same requirements and demands as the men but were paid even lower wages. Moreover, they were relatively defenseless against sexual advances and harassment by German superiors and camp directors. The files of the Düsseldorf Gestapo offices, for example, are full of cases in which German camp directors had coerced sexual favors from female eastern workers, whose average age was about 20 – either by taking advantage of their official position or simply by force.

Another factor of central importance in determining the living conditions of the foreigners was the specific branch and firm in which they were employed, what camp they were housed in and, especially since the end of 1942, whether they were deployed in an urban area or in the countryside. The aforementioned example of mining indicated just how terrible were the conditions of the civilian workers and prisoners of war from Eastern Europe concentrated in this branch. In the metal industry, in contrast, the situation of workers in some instances was clearly better. It was a tremendous advantage to be able to work in agriculture, particularly when it came to provision of an adequate diet. This developed even to the point where the authorities would send emaciated, half-starved Soviet laborers to work for a period of time in agriculture in order to "fatten them up again" – that was the official term.[31] During the last two years of the war, many forced laborers attempted to escape by their own wits and wiles from mining and other branches, such as construction, and find a job and lodgings – generally illegally – with a farmer.

Yet the fact that there were often striking differences between conditions in the various individual camps and factories is a good indication that the official regulations, despite all the frenetic regimentation, still permitted a great deal of leeway and that the essential factor in this regard was the behavior of those who held positions of responsibility in the factories and camps. The man or woman lucky enough, for example, to have a supervisor or foreman who allowed extra rations to be given to Russian workers without a special permit had far better prospects of surviving his or her ordeal of *Arbeitseinsatz* in Germany without permanent physical damage than did another foreign worker. The latter stood defenseless and at the mercy of those persons with the authority to decide his fate in the factory and camp – exposed to their harassment, maltreatment, corruption, and inordinate thirst for power. Those survival prospects were also enhanced for any worker fortunate enough to have a camp director who did not choose to curtail the extremely brief rest breaks allowed the camp inmates by engaging in additional hassling and harassment – or who avoided any involvement in the exceptionally widespread, corrupt, underhanded dealings and trafficking in food rations allotted to the foreigners.

The behavior of the Germans who had some concrete connection with the labor utilization of some seven million foreign workers in the Reich – which surely amounted to many thousands of individuals – becomes more important as a factor

242

the more one focuses on the actual realities of foreign-worker deployment during World War II, moving beyond the plane of political ideology and administrative bureaucracy. The German population here was not a mass of passive onlookers – rather, that population was included as an active factor in the conceptions of National Socialist policy: how the foreign forced laborer actually fared on a day-to-day basis was dependent on the behavior of individual Germans in the workplace, the camps, or the public sphere.

After the Allies commenced heavy bombing raids on urban centers, an increasingly important factor for foreign workers was whether they were living in the countryside or in the metropolitan areas exposed to aerial bombardment. Eastern workers, Poles, and prisoners of war were not allowed to enter the public air-raid shelters, and many camps did not even have trenches to retreat to during an air raid.[32] For foreign workers in the large metropolitan centers, there now began a period of constant fear – in a number of towns, genuine panic broke out among the foreigners, who were not properly protected against the airborne assaults. The commander of the camp in Hemer noted: "A large proportion of attempts to escape are due to panic.... For example, 32 Soviet POWs fled from their work in a large labor battalion in the endangered district of Dortmund-East, and in interrogation after being captured, they repeatedly indicated the frequent air bombardments as a reason for trying to escape."[33] Since the camps for foreigners were generally located in the inner-city areas close to factories, they were especially exposed and vulnerable to the destructive fury of the airborne attacks. However, since the first priority for clearing-up operations and repairs went to plant premises and residential neighborhoods located in areas populated by Germans, and camps for foreigners were relegated to the bottom of the list for such postraid operations, if included at all, the living conditions of inhabitants in these camps deteriorated drastically in the aftermath of an attack and often remained seriously deficient for extended periods.

Thus, camp doctors reported on conditions in a camp for French prisoners of war in Essen in the wake of an air assault as follows:

The camp houses 640 French prisoners of war. It was

largely devastated by an airborne attack on April 27th of this year. At the present time, conditions in the camp are insufferable. There are still 315 POWs housed in the camp, yet 170 of these are no longer quartered in barracks but rather in an underpass of the railway line Essen–Mülheim along Grunert Strasse. This underpass is damp and not suited for permanent occupancy by human beings. . . . There are two wooden bunk beds available for sick workers. As a rule, medical treatment is administered out of doors in the open.

In September 1944, half a year after the original attack, another doctor reported on this same camp: "The POW camp on Nöggerath Strasse is in a ghastly, deplorable state. People are living in ash cans, doghouses, old ovens and self-constructed makeshift huts. Their food rations are barely adequate."[34]

Thus, along with nationality, sex, and the specific conditions prevailing in individual branches of industry, factories, and camps, an additional salient factor shaping the living conditions of the foreign laborers was the degree of exposure of their camp to bombardment: whether their camp had been largely devastated or was still relatively intact. The range of circumstances in which foreign workers found themselves living was indeed extremely broad and diverse.

Despite all need to differentiate in this regard, one can justifiably contend that the criterion of nationality or race was most strongly manifested in the differing living conditions of the foreign laborers. The regular reports submitted by mail censorship offices contain empirical data on these dimensions. For example, workers from Western Europe were given the same pay as Germans for the strenuous physical work they had to perform but frequently were assigned jobs below their level of qualification and experience. Their hours were also by and large similar to those demanded of German workers, and they complained just as much as their German counterparts about the frequent overtime and Sunday shifts. A common focus for complaints was the quality of food dished out by the kitchens and canteens in the factories and camps. Complaints about the size of the portions were less common as a criticism. One bitterly castigated restriction was the sheer impossibility for most western workers to be given a vacation in order to return home for a visit. The German authorities had made this more difficult and finally even forbidden home leave since some of those who had gone home on vacation had not returned.

In material terms as well, the situation in which workers from Western Europe found themselves was completely different from that of their German counterparts. But more pointed and drastic in their impact were the instances of humiliation and discrimination so frequently reported. Demeaning punishments (for example, floggings as a penalty for overextending one's allotted home leave) and various harassments made it abundantly clear to these laborers that they were not welcome guest workers in the Reich – but rather, at least in the majority of cases, were citizens of defeated enemy countries in a land governed by a terroristic dictatorship. A French worker wrote home in 1942: "I hope it'll soon be over with . . . because people here think like a bunch of wild men. . . . You literally bite off your own fingers since its prohibited to open your mouth and complain; you just have to keep it all to yourself.[35]

Nonetheless, the civilian workers from the West stood on the highest rung of the racist hierachy; the place accorded to Soviet civilian workers and prisoners of war, in contrast, was far down at the bottom of this political-ideological pecking order. Their living conditions were palpably worse even than those of the Poles and generally far poorer than those enjoyed by western workers. Excessively long hours; a poor diet, wages, housing, and clothing; deficient medical care; barbed wire; defamatory abuse; and maltreatment – these are what characterized their situation as forced laborers in the Reich. Even the report writers of the Nazi official agencies who investigated the living conditions of eastern workers and POWs in order to uncover possibilities and angles for stepping up their productivity levels were agreed on that point. Thus, a commission of the Economic Staff/ East wrote the following on its impressions during a tour through the Ruhr region in November 1943:

> In the districts we visited, the eastern worker is generally left to his fate, aside from in a small number of exemplary firms, since he is viewed solely as an easily replaceable means of production conscripted from the vast eastern region. The firm directors have, almost uniformly, no understanding of the heart of the issue pertaining to the

eastern worker and do not wish to become interested in this matter. As a consequence, even the most necessary and essential things, such as food and lodging, leave something to be desired, are inadequate, prepared with indifference, dirty – indeed, in some instances mediocre beyond any possible standard or criterion.... One comment was quite instructive: "The eastern worker is very tough. He works at his job until he collapses to the ground, and then all that is left for the doctor is to issue a death certificate." ... The mood among eastern workers was – aside from a small number of exceptions where it could be characterized as quite good – generally one of discontent, in some instances catastrophically bad. Thus, for example, it will be impossible to extinguish the image of wretchedness and misery [we saw] in the camp of the Bochum Association:... workers run down and in a poor state of health, rotten morale, the camp neglected and filthy, inadequate diet, floggings, families torn apart, attempts to escape even by women. Food as a premium, a prize – first productivity, then reward. The directorship of the camp has no understanding of the problems.[36]

In the summer of 1943, an official of the Foreign Office inspected several camps for eastern workers on his own initiative and reported the following:

Despite the officially allotted rations for eastern workers, it has been possible to establish beyond any doubt that the diet in the camps indeed consists of half a liter of turnip soup for breakfast, a liter of turnip soup at noontime in the factory and, for dinner in the evening, a liter of turnip soup. In addition, the eastern worker receives a daily ration of 300 grams of bread. This is supplemented by a weekly ration of 50 to 75 gr of margarine and 25 gr of meat or meat products, which are distributed or withheld according to the whim of the camp directors.... Large quantities of food are sold in a kind of black market. This food allocated for the eastern workers is purchased by other foreign workers and then sold to the eastern workers at exorbitant prices.... It should also be noted that most female workers have a greater fear of giving birth in the camp than of death itself. I myself witnessed female workers from the

East lying on the steel springs of beds without a mattress, and in this condition they were forced to give birth.... The greatest scourge of the camp is TB, which is also widespread among the workers under 21 years of age. It should be underscored that within the framework of the sanitary and health conditions the eastern workers find themselves in, German and Russian factory doctors are prohibited from prescribing any medicines for these workers. Those who are sick with TB are not even isolated from the others. The sick are compelled by flogging and beating to go about the performance of their work duties, because the authorities in the camps question the jurisdictional authority of the doctors treating such patients. I have no idea why the German authorities are "importing" a large number of children from the occupied territories to Germany. Yet it is well established that there are numerous children between the ages of 4 and 15 in the camps and that these children have neither parents nor any other relatives in Germany. It is apparent that such children are worthless when it comes to promoting German war aims. The state of their diet, health, and material deprivation certainly do not contribute to strengthening the "morale" of the eastern worker. He is beset by a general apathy in which he is bereft of hope when it comes to life. Thus, for example, women are beaten in the face with nail-studded boards. Men and women, as punishment for the most minor transgression, are locked in freezing concrete dungeons and left without food in the dead of winter, after having been forced to remove their outer clothing. For reasons of hygiene, eastern workers are hosed down with cold water during the winter out in the assembly grounds of the camp. As penalty for the mere theft of a few potatoes, hungry eastern workers are executed in extremely brutal fashion before the assembled inmates of the camp.[37]

Primacy of productivity or priority of ideology?

In spite of such conditions, which – as indicated by the relatively broad coverage in reports by German *Arbeitseinsatz* authorities –

were no exception, the National Socialists nonetheless succeeded during the final two years of the war in significantly raising the output and job productivity levels for Soviet workers as well. Various factors played a decisive role in this regard: first and foremost, the frequently encountered linkage between food and output level, and the widespread introduction of the piece-work system. Of central signficance was also the constant expansion of the systems of supervision and punishment of both the Gestapo and the factory police and raiding squads.

In addition, psychological factors must likewise be taken into consideration. Maintenance of one's sense of personal worth and identity by means of doing good work was of a certain importance precisely for those persons who had no other weapon except their performance on the job to use as a defense against their general oppression and the bitterness and spite with which they were ill treated and abused by their superiors. This was especially true in the case of women. It was specifically the female workers from the East, generally very young, who were highly sought after as workers in industrial firms from 1943 on: they performed well, were paid at a paltry rate, and, significantly, were located beyond the pale when it came to social policy: the protection measures embodied in German social legislation for woman workers were not applicable in their case. In contrast to their male counterparts, they were regarded as being especially tractable – the German authorities had no fears about rebelliousness or resistance where they were concerned. In their role as Soviet forced laborers and women, they were subject to a double oppression, since they were often exposed to and at the mercy of sexual advances and harassment by camp directors and other German superiors, as well as by Soviet male workers.

The regulation stipulating that at least 50 per cent of the workers brought to the Reich from Poland and the Soviet Union had to be women was intended by the German authorities to help prevent sexual contact between Germans and nationals from alien peoples. Yet the upshot of this policy was that the number of children born from Polish and Russian parents in Germany rose, and this was a scandalous situation, especially in the eyes of party circles.

Pregnant workers from Poland and the Soviet Union had initially been sent back home, but employment bureaus and the police soon began to harbor suspicions that such pregnancies had been intentional – induced as a way to be able to leave Germany. Consequently, possibilities for an abortion were expanded in the case of pregnant Poles and eastern workers, beginning in the spring of 1943. However, many lower-level authorities approved of a far more brutal approach when it came to such pregnant women. A report from the *Generalgouvernement* stated: "Among those returning from the Reich are a large number of pregnant women; these women were released from work and allowed to return home, since they are soon due to give birth. The frequency of such cases makes it reasonable to conclude that their condition is intentional." The suggestion was made to take these children from their mothers after birth: "Children endowed with good blood could be placed in homes, while the others would have to be administered special treatment [*Sonderbehandlung*]. It is my opinion that this would immediately dampen the desire to bear children among these Polish girls."[38] *Sonderbehandlung* was, of course, the euphemism of the National Socialist authorities for execution. Thus, what is recommended here in an incredibly cynical and brutal manner is nothing short of the murder of a portion of the children borne by these Polish workers, while taking the racially valuable infants away from their mothers and raising them in children's homes.

Subsequent to this, Himmler arranged with the Plenipotentiary for Labor Deployment at the end of 1942 not to ship any more foreign workers from the East back home in cases of pregnancy. Rather, children of "good racial stock" borne by these women were to be brought up as Germans in special homes; children of "inferior racial stock" were to be gathered together at assembly stations for children. Himmler expressly remarked that a "pompous term" of some sort ought to be coined as a name for such assembly stations.[39] The RSHA then issued a related degree on 27 June 1943: its content embodied a consistent practice and implementation of race-biological principles in these questions. The care centers for children of "inferior racial stock" borne by Polish and Russian workers were now called "nursing homes for the children of foreigners" (*Ausländerkinder-Pflegestätten*) and were to be staffed by foreign personnel.

There would be a different approach when it came to children of "good racial stock":

The necessity to prevent the loss of German blood to alien peoples has been intensified in the wake of the casualties suffered during this war. It is therefore important to preserve (when feasible) the children of foreign women – who have in their veins a certain amount of German or racially similar blood and can thus be regarded as valuable – for the German nation, and consequently to educate them as German children.

This was the reason given to justify a complicated procedure of "racial examination." If the result proved "positive," the infants were placed in special homes after being weaned and separated from their mothers. In the case of western workers, this was done only with the consent of the mother; in the case of eastern workers and Polish women, no such formal consent was needed. In addition, "mothers who were of especially valuable racial stock and who satisfied the requirements of the *Lebensborn* were to be admitted to SS homes for mothers, and their children were to be granted formal guardianship."[40]

In the subsequent period, numerous such Nursing Homes for the Children of Foreigners were set up, often on the initiative of the firms where these foreign mothers were employed. This was the case, for example, in the firm of Krupp in Essen. The children's home Buschmannshof was opened in Voerde near Dinslaken in 1943 because, as the Krupp camp superintendent later explained, the number of children of eastern workers had continued to soar and there was no longer sufficient space in the Krupp hospital in Essen.[41] This is why the children were being cared for in Voerde by a segment of the Russian mothers under the direction of a German woman. Of the 120 children in the home, at least 48 died as a result of a diphtheria epidemic between the autumn and winter of 1944. This epidemic was apparently caused by the poor diet the children had been subjected to. The camp with all inmates and guard personnel was evacuated to Thuringia at the end of the war without the mothers having been informed. The documentation on these instances does not permit a definite and more accurate determination of the fate of these children.

Yet a second related instance proves that they were treated as unnecessary mouths to feed: second- or even third-class human beings whose lives had little value in the eyes of the authorities.

In May 1944 in the village of Velpke n
likewise opened a similar children's I
of eastern workers deployed in the
children, if necessary, were forcibly re
The director of the home was an et
ported by four female eastern work
and Russian children housed there between May and December
1944; of these 96 died in that period due to epidemics, malnu-
trition, and general debility, although they had been admitted
to the home in good health and with warm clothing. A communication written by SS Lieutenant-General Hilgenfeldt to
Himmler makes it clear that such conditions were the rule rather
than the exception. Hilgenfeldt had visited one of the homes
for eastern children and wrote on 11 August 1943:

> The present treatment the children are receiving is, in my
> opinion, appalling. Here there is only a situation of
> "either/or." Either there is no desire to keep these children
> alive – and then they should not be allowed to slowly
> starve to death, siphoning off many liters of valuable milk
> in this way from the provisions of the general population.
> Or the intention is to raise the children in order to be able
> to make use of them later on as workers. If that is the
> case, then they must be properly fed so that they will be
> fully utilizable some day as laborers.[42]

Even in the final two years of the war, the continuity of a radical
implementation of race-biological principles in dealing with eastern workers and Poles is quite evident and manifest in the actions
taken by the party and the SS, in cooperation with factory
authorities, toward these children of "alien national stock"
(*fremdvölkisch*) and their mothers. The implementation of racial
principles in the selection of infants from "good racial stock" and
"poor racial stock" is a grim indication that the regime wished
only temporarily to yield to the pressures and constraints of the
economy and the shortage of manpower and that it had merely
postponed certain options regarding radical solutions based on
the dictates of racial doctrine. Yet when it came to infants who
were not utilizable for purposes of labor deployment, it was possible, already at that time, to proceed according to racist methods
envisioned for application to all Soviet and Polish workers after a
victorious conclusion to the war.

These then were the basic contours of National Socialist policy toward conscripted foreign workers in the final two years of the war: on the one hand, a shifting of the process of selection based on racial criteria to spheres not directly relevant for labor deployment, continuity in the special system of penalties and in the imposition of repression, with punishment and harassment meted out according to the way the war was going; on the other, initiatives to liberalize regulations governing treatment, particularly in order to equalize the status of workers from West and East under the banner of an "anti-Bolshevik defensive struggle to protect Europe."

Concentration camp prisoners and conscripted labor

If previous mention was made of the potential labor reservoir at the disposal of the German authorities in countries occupied by the Wehrmacht, the reference was solely to civilian foreign workers and POWs under the control and authority of the German labor administration or the department for prisoners of war within the Wehrmacht Supreme Command (OKW). However, the prisoners under the authority of the SS in the concentration and extermination camps, particularly the millions of European Jews, were not encompassed by the organization net of foreign labor deployment. Yet the fate of European Jewry and the decision made in November 1941 to conscript massive numbers of Soviet civilians and prisoners of war are intertwined in a macabre way.[43]

The decision to push ahead with a massive conscription and deployment of Russian civilian workers and prisoners of war in November 1941 also constituted one of the prerequisites opening up the way for a transition to mass liquidation of the Jews in the SS camps. By conscripting massive numbers of Soviet citizens, it became possible to deflect or in effect neutralize pressures and constraints flowing from the exigencies of the war economy for deployment of Jews as laborers. Rather, this even facilitated the removal of Jewish workers from industries crucial to the war effort; meanwhile, their mass extermination was initiated and soon accelerated to a murderous tempo.

At the same time, however, the perspective of possible *Arbeitseinsatz* for Jews continued to exist in an official sense, and it was given repeated manifest and visible embodiment in the

selections carried out on the ramps of the extermination camps
– be it only for purposes of deception and camouflage, be it "in
order to maintain the fiction that only those unfit for work were
being killed," as emphasized by Hans Mommsen. Thus, "the
politics of genocide [remained] within the murky twilight of
the presumed necessity of conscripted labor."[44]

In the summer of 1943, some 15 per cent of the total number
of 160,000 registered prisoners in concentration camps were
employed in camp repair operations under the supervision of
the Economic and Administrative Main Office (*Wirtschafts- und
Verwaltungshauptamt* – WVHA) of the SS, while 22 per cent were
classified as unfit for work. The remaining 63 per cent, some
100,000 inmates, were divided among the construction projects
of the SS, various SS economic enterprises as well as a
number of private firms.[45] The number of Jewish prisoners in
this group was quite small. Even in the spring of 1944, the
Ministry of Armaments proceeded on the assumption that there
were only 32,000 concentration camp inmates actually deployed
in the armaments industry.

At the same time, there was a total of 165 subsidiary camps
(*Nebenlager*) of the 20 main concentration camps; of the former,
130 were located within the borders of the Reich.[46] Exact deter-
minations are difficult since there are discrepancies between the
figures given by the SS and those given by the Speer Ministry.
What is clear, though, is the minor importance that the deployment of concentration camp inmates had for the armaments
industry until early 1944.

This did not change until the stream of conscripted foreign
civilian workers and POWs began to run dry. There had been
indications of this as early as the autumn of 1943, and Speer
turned to Himmler in February 1944 with a request "to assist
armaments production to a greater degree than previously by
deploying concentration camp inmates in functions that I regard
as especially urgent," since "the inflow of foreigners has been
on a considerable decline for some time now."[47]

This heralded the beginning of the last, dramatic subchapter
in the deployment of concentration camp inmates as laborers in
Germany. A large proportion of the concentration camp labor
gangs, directly utilized in private industry, were not set up until
during this particular period. This development was of major
importance for the aircraft industry and, in part closely linked

with this, the program to relocate the production plants for key armaments components to underground sites.

Already in August 1943, a decision had been made in the top leadership echelon of the regime to go ahead with production of the rocket A 4 (the so-called *V-Waffe*), using concentration camp inmates in subterranean production sites. The code name for the project was "Dora." Construction of the complex of underground caves in Kohnstein in the Harz Mountains was to be carried out by Office C of the WHVA under the direction of SS Lieutenant-General Dr Hans Kammler.[48]

This project, steamrolled ahead under enormous pressure of time, had horrendous consequences for the concentration camp prisoners deployed there. Kammler's slogan was: "Don't worry about the victims. The work must proceed ahead in the shortest time possible."[49] Specifically during the first phase of construction in the autumn and winter of 1943–4, the number of dead reached enormous proportions: of some 17,000 inmates transported to work in Dora up to March 1944, 2,882 had died. Here, too, the causes underlying the high rate of mortality were the ready expendability and easy replaceability of the inmates performing largely simple – but physically strenuous – tasks, working under heavy pressure of time, deficient diet, and extremely poor living conditions. These mortality rates began to decline only after the residential camp had been completed and production had commenced. Until that point however, the inmates were usually totally worn out and depleted a few short weeks after their arrival.

On the basis of these experiences – Speer had alluded to the "sensational success" achieved in Dora – Kammler was given the task in December 1943 of expanding the system of subterranean caves and shafts for armaments production, especially of aircraft. In this way, 425,000 square meters of subterranean or bunker-protected production surface was created. Entire factories or sections of factories were relocated there immediately after completion of these underground facilities.

Projects of such a magnitude were possible only using concentration camp inmates because only the SS had a labor reservoir of such proportions at that time at its disposal in the camps. Correspondingly, the number of concentration camp inmates rose during the final year of the war; Soviet and Polish prisoners now made up the majority. These contingents in turn consisted in part of foreign workers, who had been interned in concentration camps because of some transgression, and in part of workers who had been brought back by the retreating German armies from territories evacuated in the East – i.e. workers who had been forcibly deported.

At the end of 1944, the total number of concentration camp prisoners reached some 600,000. Of these, 480,000 were regarded as "fit for deployment as laborers." Based on estimates of the head of the WVHA, Pohl, some 140,000 were deployed in operations under the Kammler staff, approximately 130,000 more were employed in construction projects of the *Organisation Todt*, and 230,000 were in private industry.[50]

Yet the access of the SS to non-Jewish concentration camp inmates was not sufficient to supply the needed manpower. In April 1944, the transfer of armaments production and the construction of massive bunkers demanded a further 100,000 workers. Apparently proceeding on the basis of a suggestion from the *Organisation Todt*, Hitler determined on 6 and 7 April 1944, that he would "personally contact the Reichsführer of the SS and have him supply the approximately 100,000 necessary men from Hungary by provision of large contingents of Jews."[51] This was in strict contradiction with the principle that had been adhered to until then of keeping the Reich *judenfrei* – a policy that since the end of 1941 had served to frustrate all attempts by German firms to retain their skilled Jewish workers, especially in view of the fact that Soviet workers in virtually unlimited supply had been placed at the disposal of industry.

But now the main question was how best to facilitate the relocation of armaments production, threatened by aerial assault, to subterranean vaults. The standing principle of not deploying Jews for work in the Reich but rather of killing them either outright or after a short time, was momentarily set aside – this after the greater proportion of European Jewry had already been liquidated.

A short time after this, those officials responsible for the relocation of the aircraft industry to subterranean production chambers tried to obtain Jewish camp inmates as forced laborers and commented: "We have to get another 100,000 Hungarian Jews or something similar down here."[52] That was also approved, and the deployment was ordered of 200,000 Jews from Hungary for work on the "large projects of the *Organisation Todt* and other tasks essential to the war effort." However, they were to be deployed exclusively as concentration camp inmates of the SS, because "a so-called open deployment for work in enterprises within the Reich," which the minister of armaments had apparently recommended, was out of the question. That was "due to fundamental considerations . . . since it would contradict the policy of *Entjudung* of the Reich, which in the meantime has by and large been brought to completion."[53]

When the German Wehrmacht occupied Hungary on 19 March 1944, some 765,000 Jews had fallen into German hands. Deportations commenced on 15 April and by July an estimated 458,000 Hungarian Jews had already been sent to Auschwitz. Approximately 25 per cent of the Hungarian Jews were not murdered immediately: of the 458,000 deported to Auschwitz, some 350,000 were gassed and 108,000 shipped out to be deployed as forced laborers.[54]

These 108,000 survivors were divided into contingents of 500 each and sent to transit camps in Germany. Since in the meantime the flow of foreign workers had nearly dried up, more and more firms in the Reich were demanding that they be provided with concentration camp inmates – even if these were Jews. The latter were kept under very stringent conditions in regard to security, housing, and segregated deployment. The number of work detachments from the permanent home camps had risen rapidly since the spring of 1944. The list of German firms that had set up external subcamps and begun to utilize concentration camp inmates grew ever longer and included numerous well-known companies.[55] The working and living conditions of the inmates were quite diverse and depended on the type of job, the place of the individual inmate in the hierarchy of the SS, as well as the behavior of the firm management of the camp commanders, guards, and foremen on the job. The Jews in particular suffered under especially onerous and difficult conditions.

However, the situation was much worse in the concentration projects of the *Organisation Todt* and of the Kammler staff, because hellbent speed was of the essence for them. Conditions there for the inmates were correspondingly appalling: the poor food, atrocious accommodations in caves detrimental to health, the murderous, breakneck tempo of work, and the unceasing inflow of new prisoners being packed and crammed into the often already jammed camps – these factors interacted, compounding the misery. The upshot was the creation of hellish human inferno in the camps of the construction projects toward the end of 1944, with a rate of mortality that limited the life of the individual inmate to an average of several short months. The massive deployment of concentration camp inmates in the gigantic construction projects of the final phase of the war, designed to serve to protect the German armaments industry from destruction and assure continuity of production below ground, cost the lives of massive numbers of forced laborers on a scale that was truly outrageous. The value of a person did not exceed what his physical strength was able to provide for a short span of a few weeks. Work and destruction here became synonyms for hundreds of thousands of harried human beings in a program of *annihilation by labor*. Several general aspects should be emphasized on the basis of this brief sketch of developments.

1) The utilization of foreign civilian workers, prisoners of war, concentration camp inmates and Jews as forced laborers was not resorted to during the war based solely on considerations of the needs of the war economy – rather, it was likewise generally geared to political-ideological criteria, especially those of race. In the process, aspects bound up with the war economy emerged into the foreground during the course of the war (a) parallel to the deterioration of the war situation and, in particular, to the worsening manpower shortages, and (b) graduated in accordance with the ranking of the various individual national groups in the racist hierarchy of the National Socialists. The utilization of enemies of National Socialism – defined on the basis of whatever criteria – as forced laborers in the Reich constituted an ideological concession to the constraints of the war economy and was in each instance the product of compromise. The brighter the prospects for victory, the more radically were ideological objectives adhered to and implemented; the worse the war situation, the greater the concessions to economic points of view.

2) The decision in favour of a massive deployment of foreign workers and POWs in the Reich, especially the *Russeneinsatz* in the autumn of 1941, was one of the prerequisites facilitating implementation of the policy of the "Final Solution" against European Jewry without giving any longer-

term consideration to aspects of *Arbeitseinsatz*. The thesis that the policy toward the Jews had a central primary aim – namely, their exploitation as forced laborers – is untenable. Instead, it is more accurate to contend that the policy of the "Final Solution" was implemented beneath the camouflaging cover of forced labor deployment.

This development becomes clear in the phase of preparations for the "Final Solution": on the one hand, the unfitness for work of the Jews concentrated in the ghettos, a physical incapacity brought about in a calculated manner by those in political power, accelerated the decision to murder them. On the other hand, the deportations, carried out within the framework of the fiction of *Arbeitseinstaz* in the East, were announced although no corresponding preparations had yet been undertaken. The fact that only a relatively small proportion even of the Jews not immediately murdered in the concentration camps were ever actually utilized is attributable to contradictions and competition in respect to ultimate objectives between the various SS agencies, organizational incompetence, and inadequate preparations.

Those same negative factors underlay the entire program of deployment of concentration camp prisoners as forced laborers. That program was implemented and operative until the very end of the war, bedeviled by extraordinarily high mortality rates and relatively low efficiency in respect to the needs of the war economy. Primarily, however, it was a consequence of the primacy accorded the racist-motivated objective of annihilation over all economic aspects. On the one hand, this intention to annihilate was legitimated – or, more precisely camouflaged – by references made by those who were in positions of responsibility to problems of organization, personal animosities, competition over area and scope of authority, as well as references to problems of social policy and policy of food provision, etc. But all this tended more to camouflage that intention or served even as a self-justification for the perpetrators.

3) German industry and the Speer office, which was closely associated with it, dealt with the question of forced labor – principally, or even exclusively – from the standpoint of

the war economy and the question of effectivity. In each instance, they made use of that group of workers that was available in sufficient numbers and promised the best return on investment. Initially, this meant skilled workers from western Europe. When they were no longer available in adequate supply, it entailed resorting to Poles – and then to Russians, later to concentration camp prisoners, and finally, in the last year of the war, to Jews. That final development was in contrast to the failure of efforts by numerous German firms in the first half of the war to maintain their traditional Jewish work force. Their interest in retaining Jewish personnel had at that time been compensated and offset by enhanced possibilities for utilizing Soviet labor.

Unlike the practice in the enterprises of the SS, where punishment and an ideologically motivated annihilation of concentration camp inmates were largely predominant, private industry was interested in the fate of the inmates – in both a positive and negative sense – only to the extent that it was bound up with boosting production. This perspective encompassed both an approach that tried to go easy on and spare individual skilled workers as well as the annihilation of enormous masses of prisoners slaving away on the crash construction projects during the final months of the war, rushed through at an infernal tempo and predicated on the principal criteria of speed and the total expendability of the individual inmates working as forced laborers. The paradigm for such projects, as far as the treatment of inmates was concerned, had been the construction of the Buna Works of IG-Farben in Auschwitz.

If the destruction of ideological enemies was the ultimate goal for the SS – and temporary labor deployment, if necessary, a means to that end – then the principal aim for industry was increasing production at the lowest possible cost or the building of subterranean production sites as rapidly as possible. To achieve such objectives, the death of the forced laborers as a result of the work necessary to attain the goal, given certain prerequisites, was seen by industry as a means. Precisely because in the overwhelming majority of cases there was no personal interest on the part of management, for example, in treating prisoners badly or annihilating them for ideological reasons, the structural aspect of this process emerges more clearly into view. That aspect cannot be attributed to the individual moral fiber of a given factory owner. Rather, it indicates the degree to which the orientation to production, efficiency, and profit in the intensified situation of the war economy during the final two years of the war – and in the framework of the political objectives of the Nazi regime – accepted the death of laborers as part of the bargain, quite literally so. Indeed, that orientation virtually presupposed their death in the final phase of the war.

4) However, any attempt to reduce the policy of mass annihilation of the National Socialists solely or largely to underlying economic, rational interests fails to recognize that the mass destruction of opponents in an ideological sense itself constituted a rationally founded political aim in the eyes of the National Socialists, in particular the proponents in their ranks of a consistent and systematic racism. Racism was not some sort of mistaken belief serving to mask and cloak the true interests of the regime, which were in essence economic. Rather, racism was the very lodestar of the system, its unwavering fixed point.

Opposition and resistance

In view of the inhumane and brutal practices of the race agencies and racist authorities of the Nazi regime and the living conditions that eastern workers, in particular, were compelled to endure, it is reasonable to ask whether – and if so, to what extent – foreign workers succeeded in efforts to resist and defend themselves. Given the inordinate might of the National Socialist security authorities, opposition and resistance manifested itself during the early phase of the war largely in various forms of refusal to work: outright escape, loafing on the job, in part even in agreement with their German fellow workers to go slow. Such manifestations were generally individual and spontaneous reactions to unbearable working and living conditions.

However, to the extent the difference became ever greater between the express aim of the National Socialist authorities to achieve total regimentation and control of the life of the foreign workers on the one hand, and the exigencies and constraints arising from the concrete deployment of millions of foreign laborers on the other – a practice that necessarily was not amenable to full and total control – a kind of informal substructure developed among foreign workers and POWs in the camps. This involved a steadily expanding and ramifying sphere of black market and illegal activities, attempts to escape from work, informal solidarity, along with components of the use of force and suppression. In many respects, it was more a mirror image than counterimage of the Nazi system of suppression yet often enough provided many foreign workers with their only option for survival.

The individual elements of expressly manifested resistance, however, were not directly linked. Not until 1943 is it possible to interconnect more closely the various individual phenomena, involving an entire scale of behavioral patterns.

Most common and widespread were forms of individual provision of essentials: attempts to improve by one's own efforts the inadequate diet in the camps by means of barter and exchange; black marketeering; selling of small, self-made objects for daily use; or even by the theft of food. The point of departure for such activity was in many instances the corruption rampant among camp directors and other Germans who were involved with the system of food provision for the foreign laborers. That corruption was present everywhere and spread rapidly during the final phase of the war. The differing level of food provisions allotted to the various groups of foreign workers based on pecking order likewise contributed to the flowering of a black market in foodstuffs in the camps.

In March 1944, Reich authorities were given a report stating:

> The poor diet of the eastern workers is contributing significantly to the growth of a black market, since the French in particular, along with others from western countries, are engaging in a lively trade in bread with the eastern workers. The average price for a pound of bread sold on the black market to eastern workers is 10 Reichsmark.[56]

Among workers from the West, in contrast, the preferred item in such trafficking was documents – given the excessive concern of the Nazis for bureaucratic form and papers, this was one avenue that held out a fair prospect of obtaining, however underhandedly, the necessary documents for the return trip home. Taken as a whole, nonetheless, these were all manifestations of one salient development: the widening gap between the decrees of the Reich authorities and the actual realities of the deployment of conscripted laborers in the camps, firms, and factories. It was that gap that made it possible for foreign laborers to attempt to improve their own living conditions under the iron blanket of police regimentation and control.

This development was manifested most strongly and evidently in the burgeoning number of attempts by foreign workers to escape during the last two years of the war (Table 3).

The greater proportion of those who tried to flee were soon recaptured – also because the authorities reported every foreigner who failed to appear at his job or in the camp as having escaped, even if he or she had only disappeared for a short time or was wandering around homeless in the ruins of an inner-city area that had been devastated by a bombing raid. Nonetheless, many were successful either in returning to their homeland or – in the majority of cases – in changing their camp, factory, or city in this way.

These attempts to flee from the job were in the main the individual actions of numerous workers, each acting alone. Yet their concerted impact led to a substantial increase in the degree of disorganization of foreign-labor deployment. Together with the various types of loafing on the job, such escapes constituted the most important and effective forms of resistance against the Germans. They were in keeping with the political and social situation of foreign workers in the Reich and combined a relatively low level of risk for the individual with a

Table 3 Escapes by foreign workers, 1943[57]

February	20,353
March	27,179
April	27,172
June	30,000
July	38,000
August	45,000
December	46,000
Monthly average	ca. 33,000

comparatively high degree of effectiveness and immediate payoff.

Organized political resistance by the foreigners had no prospect of success as long as the power of the Gestapo and the loyalty of the German population as a whole to the regime remained so strong and seemingly unshakable, as was the case until the spring of 1943. Only after that – parallel to the development of German resistance against National Socialism – do we find the first signs of organized and explicitly political resistance among foreign workers, here in particular Soviet laborers.

The German defeats on the eastern front in the winter of 1942–3 were the signal for various groups of Soviet antifascists to begin to build up genuine, concrete resistance cells. The most important of these groups was the Fraternal Cooperation of Prisoners of War (*Brüderliche Zusammenarbeit der Kriegsgefangenen* –BSW), which was the largest and best-organized resistance movement among foreigners uncovered by the Gestapo during the war.[58] Starting from a small nucleus of captured Soviet officers trained in illegal methods of struggle, the BSW spread until May 1943, especially in southern Germany, and had contact persons in numerous camps for Soviet prisoners of war and civilian laborers. It had been set up from above to below, along the lines of the classic type of illegal party organization, was centrally led by a group of officers and political commissars and adamant in its adherence to the programmatic line of the organization, with its own statutes, membership dues and system of representatives. Politically, it was oriented to the aim of a mass uprising by foreign workers that would overthrow the Nazi regime from within.

In constrast, their concrete praxis consisted mainly of assistance in escapes and the exercising of pressure on German camp directors and firm managers to improve the living conditions of the POWs and the civilian workers. However, its centralist structure made it possible for the Nazi authorities, once they had managed to get on its track, to uncover the entire organization in a relatively short time and to smash it completely in the spring of 1943.

Ferreting out the clandestine network was much more difficult in the case of groups operating in decentralized fashion, especially when they were integrated into the formal substructure among the foreigners. Such groups can be increasingly identified from early 1944 on. In the spring of 1944, the SD of the SS reported:

> The advance of the Soviet armies, the events in Italy, and, last but not least, the terror attacks on German cities are leading eastern workers in the Reich to a strengthening of their identity and self-confidence. This increasingly pronounced shift in mood is awakening the hope among workers from the East that they will soon be able to return to their homes and is increasingly engendering among them thoughts of taking up an active struggle against the Germans.[59]

From this juncture on, the Gestapo noted the existence of organized resistance groups in virtually every larger city in the Reich, especially among Soviet workers; the number of such groups multiplied significantly as the summer approached. The focus of their activities lay principally in aid in preparing and carrying out escapes, provision of illegal papers, care of the sick, organizing of food provisions, neutralizing of informers, etc. Many of the programmatic statements uncovered by the Gestapo mentioned the need to organize weapons, but no such weapons were found in actual fact in the possession of these organizations and committees. This is an indication that the program calling for preparations for a revolt and uprising was rather a distant, longer-term objective; in the spring of 1944, the main task at hand was to strengthen the foundation of these organizations and attempt slowly to advance their speed.

However, there is a dearth of data on the majority of such organizations. The Gestapo reports after the discovery of groups and the arrest of their members only seldom contain information regarding the actual scope of the activities of these resistance fighters. Yet it is noteworthy that such associations of Soviet workers could be found throughout the entire length and breadth of the Reich. For the period from March to September 1944, there are reports on such groups of Soviet workers from thirty-eight cities, involving a total of at least 2,700 activists or arrested members.[60]

If the degree of effectiveness of these groups is not measured by their programmatic longer-term aim of a mass uprising but rather in terms of the existing conditions and possibilities, it becomes quite evident that there was a considerable increase

264

and expansion of antifascist resistance by Soviet workers during the last year of the war. That is especially true in those cases where such resistance developed from the matrix of the immediate living and working conditions of the foreign laborers. This entailed a limitation for organizations operating in a small area and, at least initially, doing without any supraregional interconnections and networking, but was a stronger insurance against premature discovery and destruction of the organization. Forging ties with German resistance groups, a development that the German security authorities were especially heedful and suspicious of, was among the intended aims of many groups; however, only in a small number of cases can it be shown that such ties existed.

Taken in their entirety, the scope and spread of resistance activities among foreign workers, especially Soviet, during the last year of the war indicate that it was here, in the ranks of these workers, that the greatest resistance potential of all against the National Socialist regime existed in Germany. Moreover, these groups posed a special threat in the eyes of the German security authorities for another salient reason: it must be assumed that they enjoyed a far greater degree of sympathy or support among the mass of foreign civilian workers and prisoners of war than did the largely isolated German resistance groups, communist or social-democratic in orientation, within the broader German population.

From forced laborer to displaced person

The final weeks of the war became a virtual inferno, especially for the foreigners living in the large urban areas. In the cities that had been most devastated, such as Cologne or the urban centers of the Ruhr, the numbers of foreign workers and POWs wandering around aimlessly without food or shelter and reported as escapees increased. In various parts of town, many hundreds of workers, largely Soviet, were living in the ruins of the destroyed houses and had to try to scrape by and survive until the end of the war, now on the near horizon. Some such workers formed gangs that attempted by theft and plundering to obtain foodstuffs and defend themselves by armed force against persecution by the security police. This went as far as genuine shoot-outs with the Gestapo, as reported in connection with events in Cologne.[61]

The number of incidents of theft and plunder also increased dramatically among the German population beginning in early 1945, yet such plundering was generally blamed on foreigners. The security police reacted to this by an excessive show of force; everywhere in the large metropolitan areas, foreign "plunderers" were arrested and – since the RSHA had delegated the lower Gestapo authorities the right to order executions independently where deemed necessary – often shot on the spot. When the front approached ever nearer and Gestapo officials began to abscond, there were often mass executions, in part unbelievable in their magnitude, carried out literally at the last minute.

Thus, for example, 67 foreigners, mainly eastern workers, were executed in Duisburg during the final days of the war, 35 in Essen, 23 in Bochum, more than 200 in Dortmund. Only a few days before American troops had reached the area, 208 eastern workers – 129 men, 77 women, and 2 small children – were executed in Suttrop in the Sauerland at the order of SS General Kammler. The explanation for this given by General Kammler was that although there had not as yet been any plundering or riots by workers from the East in this area, such excesses were definitely likely and preventive action had to be taken.[62]

This murderous frenzy of the National Socialist authorities during the final days of the war, when the collapse of the Reich appeared imminent and certain, cannot be explained solely by mustering a series of rational reasons. Precisely the last case mentioned indicates that it was not principally the deeds of the homeless eastern workers but rather their very existence that was felt to be an unacceptable provocation. After all, these foreigners, wandering about in the chaos of the final phase of the war, represented the quintessence of everything that National Socialism had been fighting against. "Plundering" eastern workers also constituted a fulfillment of all those racist anxieties that people had harbored against them since the very beginning of the program of foreign-labor deployment. Finally, what had always been feared was now happening: the Russian turned plundering and murdering bandit.

The acts of "plunder" by eastern workers were thus able to serve to deflect interest from the burgeoning criminality spreading among German *Volksgenossen* and to soothe one's potentially bad conscience about the treatment that had been meted out to foreigners in general and Soviet workers in particular in the preceding years. This "plundering" acted to balance the scales, so to speak, for the crimes and abuses committed against them and could thus be avenged mercilessly and unhesitatingly, heedless of any scruples.

However, for many foreign workers, the time of travail and suffering did not come to an end with the arrival of Allied troops. It is true that the Allies succeeded in a short time in making sure that the millions of foreigners in Germany at the end of the war – designated by the general label Displaced Persons (DPs) – would have proper provisions and food; that indeed was a considerable organizational feat in itself.[63]

But difficulties reared their head as soon as it came even to the question of repatriation of the DPs. Most of the laborers from western countries were brought back to their home areas in the first few days and weeks after the liberation or set out on their own, homeward bound. Already at Yalta, the Western Allies had agreed with Stalin that all Soviet citizens should be sent back immediately, be repatriated to the Soviet Union.

Nonetheless, a quite substantial number of Soviet prisoners of war and civilian workers were suspected by the Soviet authorities of having collaborated with the Germans – and this did not only involve members of the Wlassow Army, who had fought directly on the German side against the Soviet Union. Rather, there were indications that the suspicion of collaboration was more general and encompassed a large segment of the civilian forced laborers and Soviet prisoners of war. It is surmised that there were severe repressive measures implemented against them after their repatriation. Yet the historical literature still lacks a full study of the subsequent fate suffered by these Soviet DPs; aside from conjectures and a small number of eyewitness reports on shootings, there are very few solid and reliable data available.[64]

Except for a few tens of thousands, all DPs were gradually repatriated. A number of those who remained – many of them Poles – tried to emigrate to North America, but a substantial number also stayed on in West Germany classified as homeless foreigners. . . .

Racism in Nazi Germany was not restricted solely to the

relationship toward the Jews. Even less was it limited only to the diehard party-line proponents or the stratum of functionaries within the system. Rather, the National Socialist system of forced labor demonstrated that a model of National Socialist society, based on a hierarchy shaped by blantantly racist criteria, was indeed capable of functioning. It demonstrated that such a system of domination, organized according to values that smacked of atavism, was able to reduce and defuse the social tensions within the class structure of German society substantially, if not render them totally meaningless, by means of terror against members of "inferior" races or nationalities and visible preferential treatment for members of the German "master race." In their importance, such tensions of a social-class nature were relegated to a secondary position after differences based on nation and race. The reports about the mistreatment of foreigners in factories are only the intensified, extreme, and by no means typical expression of this development.

Most Germans evinced little interest in the fate of the foreigners. Their concern for their own survival under National Socialism left them little time or opportunity to view the misery of the foreign workers as anything special or out of the ordinary. The foreigners were simply there, part of the workaday scenery. They belonged as much to the everyday reality of the war as ration cards or air-raid bunkers. The discrimination of workers from Eastern Europe was tolerated as something just as matter-of-fact and given as were the daily work detachments of half-starved laborers marching through the streets of the towns to their jobs in factories. Their own privileged position *qua* Germans *vis-à-vis* these workers was also nothing exceptional, leastwise nothing that one would wish to expend any extra thought on. Yet this was precisely what constituted the essential ingredient underlying the functioning of the system of National Socialist forced labor for foreigners: the concrete practice of racism here became truly a daily habit, a dimension of everyday life.

However, there is in this matter-of-factness the basis for another form of continuity: a continuity characterized by an absence of awareness, a failure to register the actual continuity that exists. In memories of the National Socialist dictatorship, and in the public debate on its deeds, the foreign workers play no important role. In the recollections of older persons, they generally surface rather as a kind of marginal and obvious presence. In memory, they are not sorted and filed away as a specific topic or recollectional rubric in connection with the war, National Socialism, or crimes by the SS but rather are included under some diffuse category of private life that does not appear to have any direct connection with the actual war and with Nazism.[65] The fact that foreigners were deployed as workers in Germany during the war is not regarded as being something specific to Nazism.

The deployment of foreign workers and prisoners of war in Germany does not, in the West German public sphere, have the historical status of being anything special – a set of practices and programs that indeed made history. As far as the deployment of *Fremdarbeiter* during World War II is concerned, there is not now – nor has there ever been – any feeling of guilt in Germany, any widespread perception that there was some sort of injustice and crime perpetrated here. This then was an unresolved issue that persisted as a burden from the past, compromising the practice of the recruitment and hiring of foreign workers resumed some ten years later in the Federal Republic, an unredeemed mortgage of failed awareness.

NOTES

Reprinted from Ulrich Herbert, *A History of Foreign Labor in Germany, 1880–1980: Seasonal Workers/Forced Laborers/Guest Workers*, translated by William Templar (Ann Arbor: University of Michigan Press, 1990).

1 Wirtschaftspolitische Richtlinien für Wirtschaftsorganisation Ost, Gruppe Landswirtschaft, 23 May 1941, Nuremberg Doc. EC 126, IMT, 36, p. 135.
2 Christian Streit, *Keine Kameraden: Die Wehrmacht und die sowjetischen Kriegsgefangenen 1941–1945* (Stuttgart, 1978), p. 79.
3 Order, Sect. POWs, Wehrmacht Supreme Command (*Abteilung Kriegsgefangene des OKW*), 16 June 1941, BA/MA, RW 4/v. 57, fol. 95.
4 Streit, *Keine Kameraden*, p. 136.
5 Order by Hitler, 31 October 1941, as decree of the Wehrmachtsführungsstab, OKW, Nuremberg Doc. EC 194, Nürnberger Nachfolgeprozesse, fall VI, Anklagedokumentenbuch 67. The decree is signed by Keitel. Decree by Göring, 7 November 1941, Nuremberg Doc. PS 1193, IMT, 27, p. 56ff. and Nuremberg Doc. PS 1206, ibid., p. 65ff; likewise for the following.
6 Lecture by Mansfield, 19 February 1942, memo, Wirtschafts- und Rüstungsamt, Nuremberg Doc. PS 1201, GStAB 1 Js 464, Doc. II.11, emphasis in original.

7 Decree, Reichsführer of the SS and Chief of the German Police (RFSS), 20 February 1942, "Einsatz von Arbeitskräften aus dem Osten," an die Höheren Verwaltungsbehörden ("Deployment of Workers from the East," to Higher Administrative Authorities), in *Allgemeine Erlasssammlung des RSHA und RFSS (AES)*, BA RD 19/ 3, pt. 2a IIIf, pp. 37–41; "Allgemeine Bestimmungen über Anwerbung und Einsatz von Arbeitskräften aus dem Osten" ("General Regulations on Recruitment and Deployment of Laborers from the East"), RFSS, 20 February 1942, ibid., pp. 24–35; Decree, RFSS to all State Police Offices, 20 February 1942, ibid., pp. 15–23.

8 Heydrich, 3 December 1941, Konstituierende Sitzung des "Arbeitskreises für Sicherheitsfragen beim Ausländereinsatz" (initial formative meeting of the Working Group for Security Questions in Connection with the Deployment of Foreigners), Protocol BA R16/ 162, fol. 1. This *Ausländer-Arbeitskreis* developed in subsequent years into the central coordinating body for *Ausländereinsatz* in respect to all fundamental questions.

9 D. Eichholtz, *Geschichte der deutschen Kriegswirtschaft*, 2 vols (Berlin [GDR], 1971–85), Vol. 1, p. 85.

10 Protocol, meeting of 19 November 1941, BA R 13/I 373.

11 Eichholtz, *Kriegswirtschaft*, Vol. 1, p. 89.

12 Army High Command 2 to Heeresgruppe B, n.d. (Spring 1942), published in part in N. Müller, ed., *Deutsche Besatzungspolitik in der UdSSR, Dokumente* (Cologne, 1980), p. 293f.

13 Report, Auslandsbrief-Prüfstelle (Inspection Office for Foreign Mail), Berlin, on letters from occupied eastern territories evaluated in the period 11 September to 10 November 1942, Nuremberg Doc. 018 PS, IMT 25, p. 77f.

14 *Der Arbeitseinsatz im (Gross-) Deutschen Reich* (1942).

15 Report on general atmosphere, Militärverwaltungschef (Military Administrative Chief) in France, on recruitment during the period 10 October 1942 to 9 November 1942, BA R41/267, fol. 240.

16 F. Hoffmann, "Die Kriegsführung aus der Sicht der Sowjetunion," in *Der Angriff auf die Sowjetunion*, ed. H. Boog *et al.* (Stuttgart, 1983), Vol. 4, *Das Deutsche Reich und der Zweite Weltkrieg*, pp. 752–7.

17 M. Odenthal, *Die Entwicklung des Arbeitseinsatzes in Rheinland und Westfalen unter besonderer Berücksichtigung der Ausländer und Kriegsgefangenen 1938–1943* (Essen, 1944), p. 63.

18 Instructions, "Allgemeine Grundsätze für die Behandlung der im Reich tätigen ausländischen Arbeitskräfte" ("General Principles for Treating Foreign Workers Active in the Reich"), the product of lengthy negotiations by various authorities dealing with *Ausländereinsatz* regarding changes in regulations on treatment, especially of Soviet prisoners; circular of Reich Chancellery, 5 May 1943, Nuremberg Doc. 205 PS, IMT 25, p. 298ff.

19 Herbert, *Fremdarbeiter*, p. 259ff.; cf., for example, *Meldungen aus dem Reich*, 9 December 1943, 28 December 1943, 7 January 1944 in H. Boberach (ed.), *"Meldungen aus dem Reich"*.

20 Fred. Krupp AG Essen to *Rüstungskommando Essen*, 2 April 1942, BA/MA RW 19 WI/IF 5/176, fol. 79.
21 Communication, Kruppsche Lokomotiv- und Wagen-Fabrik to Krupp-Hauptverwaltung (Krupp Locomotive and Car Factory to Krupp Central Management), 25 February 1942, Nuremberg Doc. D 361, IMT 35, p. 78.
22 Report, Mitteldeutsche Motorenwerke, Leipzig, 12 March 1942, IfZ, MA 41; report, Linke-Hoffman-Werke Breslau, 18 February 1942, Nuremberg Doc. NI 5236; report, Chamber of Industry and Commerce Hesse to Reich Chamber of Economy, 26 August 1942, BA R 11/1241, fols. 96ff.
23 Lecture, 22 June 1943, in Kassel, cited in *Deutschland im Zweiten Weltkrieg*, ed. Wolfgang Schumann and Gerhart Hass, 6 vols (Cologne, 1974–85), Vol. 4, p. 489f.
24 Economic situation report, *Oberbergamt* (Chief Mining Authority) Dortmund, 31 August 1942, StAM, Bergamt Dortmund A 4/48.
25 Discussion of managing directors, Zechenverband Hibernia, 7 June 1944, BgBA Bochum 32/740.
26 Circular, Bezirksgruppe Steinkohle Bergbau Ruhr to members, no. 43, 29 January 1943, BA R 10 VIII/56, fols. 36ff.
27 Communication, 10 May 1943, StAM, Bergamt Lünen, A III, no. 76.
28 Wehrmacht Supreme Command to Pleiger, 4 September 1944, BA R 10 VIII/57, fols. 27ff.
29 Ibid., fol. 58.
30 Essen Steinkohle to Bezirksgruppe Ruhr, 7 April 1943, Nuremberg Doc. NI 3012 (F).
31 OKW/Kriegsgefangene (Wehrmacht Supreme Command/War Prisoners), 12 January 1942, BA R 11/1240, fol. 112. The Supreme Command (OKW) even had some difficulty justifying these measures in ideological terms. It excused the 18 December 1941 guidelines for better treatment of prisoners with the remark: "The new measures for the physical strengthening of Soviet prisoners are for the sake of expediency and do not affect the intellectual or political-philosophical attitudes and views of the Soviets as such." BA R11/1240, fol. 102.
32 For the entire period of the war in the city of Essen, there was a total of 77 deaths as a result of aerial bombardment for every 1,000 inhabitants in the German residential urban population; for foreigners, the comparable figure was 138 per 1,000; cf. Schadensmeldungen beim Essener Polizeipräsidenten (Damage Reports, Essen Chief of Police), 28 July 1942 to 29 November 1944, Case X, Dok. Ihn No. 996, G 16.
33 Report, Camp Commander, Stalag VI A, Hemer, 2 January 1945, BA R 10 VIII/56, fol. 63.
34 Stinnesbeck to Jäger, 12 June 1944, Nuremberg Doc. D 335, IMT 35: 75f.; Jäger to Kruppe, 2 September 1944, Nuremberg Doc. D 339, Case X, B 45.
35 Auslandsbrief-Prüfstelle (Inspection Office, Foreign Letters), Frankfurt/Main, 5 March 1943, BA R 41/268, fol. 46.

36 Wirtschaftsstab Ost-Chefgruppe Arbeit, Reich Ministry for Occupied Territories, report, n.d. [December 1943], pertaining to inspections, 24 November–5 December 1943, Nuremberg Doc. NI 3013 (F).

37 Notes, Legation Councillor Starke, Foreign Office, 16 August 1943, Nuremberg Doc. NG 2562.

38 Suggestion of an unknown authority in the "Warthegau," n.p., n.d. [1942], in *Położenie polskich robotników przymusowych w Rzeszy, 1939–1945*, ed. C. Luczak (Poznań, 1975), Vol. 9, *Documenta occupationis*, Doc. no. 137.

39 Vorlage des Ausländer-Referats (Draft document of Section on Foreigners), RSHA for Himmler, 23 December 1942, GStAB I Js4/64, Doc. B 77, fols. 4–7; decree of GBA (Plenipotentiary for Labor Deployment), 15 December 1942, BA NS 5 I/263; Telex by Himmler to RSHA, 31 December 1942, GStAB 1 Js 4/64, Doc. B 77, fol. 7.

40 Circular decree, Reichsführer SS, 27 June 1943, in AES 2 A IIIf, 137ff.

41 Herbert, *Fremdarbeiter*, p. 249f.

42 Hilgenfeldt to Himmler, 11 August 1943, Nuremberg Doc. NO 4665, Case XI, no. 336, fols. 85ff.

43 On this entire complex, which can be treated here only in brief, see my detailed comments in U. Herbert, "Arbeit und Vernichtung: Ökonomisches Interesse und Primat der 'Weltanschauung' im Nationalsozialismus" in *Ist der Nationalsozialismus Geschichte?* ed. D. Diner (Frankfurt, 1987), pp. 198–237; also F. Pingel, *Häftlinge unter SS-Herrschaft* (Hamburg, 1987).

44 H. Mommsen, "Die Realisierung des Utopischen: Die 'Endlösung der Judenfrage' im 'Dritten Reich,' " *Geschichte und Gesellschaft*, Vol. 9, 1983, pp. 381–420, here p. 415.

45 Himmler to Speer, June 1943, quoted in R. Hilberg, *Die Vernichtung der europäischen Juden: Die Gesamtgeschichte des Holocaust* (Berlin, 1982), p. 621.

46 Schieber to Speer, 7 May 1944, BA R 3/1631; Wirstchafts- und Verwaltungshauptamt (Economic and Administrative Main Office) (WVHA) to Himmler, 5 April 1944, Nuremberg Doc. NO 020.

47 Speer to Himmler, 23 February 1944, BA R3/1583.

48 "Führerbesprechung" by Speer with Hitler, 19 to 22 August 1943, quoted in W. A. Boelcke (ed.), *Deutschlands Rüstung im Zweiten Weltkrieg: Hitlers Konferenzen mit Alfred Speer 1942–1945* (Frankfurt, 1969), 291. Cf. also Manfred Bornemann and Martin Broszat, "Das KL Dora-Mittelbau," in *Studien zur Geschichte der Konzentrationslager*, ed. M. Broszat (Stuttgart, 1970), pp. 155–98, here p. 165; R. Fröbe, "Wie bei den alten Ägyptern: Die Verlegung des Daimler-Benz-Flugmotorenwerkes Genshagen nach Obrigheim am Neckar 1944–45," in *Das Daimler-Benz-Buch*, ed. K. H. Roth *et al.* (Nördlingen, 1987), pp. 392–470.

49 Cited in Bornemann and Broszat, "Das KL Dora-Mittelbau," p. 165.

50 Testimony by Pohl to Nuremberg Tribunal, 25 August 1947, *Trials of War Criminals*, Vol. 5 (Washington, 1950), p. 445.

51 Discussion of Dorsch (OT) with Hitler, 6–7 April 1944, BA R3/1509.

52 Sauer, 14 April 1944, Nuremberg Doc. NG 1563.

53 Himmler to WVHA and RSHA, 11 May 1944, Nuremberg Doc. NO 5689; RSHA to Foreign Office, 24 April 1944, Nuremberg Doc. NG 2059.

54 R. L. Braham, *The Politics of Genocide: The Holocaust in Hungary* (New York, 1981); Raul Hilberg, *The Destruction of the European Jews* (New York, 1961), p. 631.

55 The *Verzeichnis der Konzentrationslager und Aussenkommandos, Bundesgesetzblatt*, 1977, TI, 1787–1852, encompasses 1,634 concentration camps and external subcamps (*Aussenkommandos*) that existed for a brief or longer period during the war. The overwhelming majority of the external subcamps came into existence only starting with the end of 1943, and particularly the early summer of 1944. A realistic estimate of the total numbers of such *Arbeitskommandos* at the end of 1944 is approximately 1,000, with some 500,000 to 600,000 prisoners; cf. Affidavit Sommer, 4 October 1946, Nuremberg Doc. NI 1065.

56 Communication, Ausländer-Referent (Adviser on Foreigners) in RHSA Hässler, 16 March 1943, to Ausländer-Arbeitskreis (Working Commission on Foreigners), Protocol ZAVO, GStAB 1 Js4/64 Doc. C 30, 34ff.

57 List presented by RSHA to Himmler, autumn 1943, BA R 58/1030, fol. 221; meeting, Ausländer-Arbeitskreis, 17 June 1943, 30 September 1943, BA R 16/162.

58 J. A. Brodski, *Im Kampf gegen den Faschismus: Sowjetische Widerstandskämpfer im Hitlerdeutschland 1941–1945* (Berlin [GDR], 1975), pp. 226–368.

59 *Meldungen aus dem Reich*, 21 February 1944.

60 Herbert, *Fremdarbeiter*, 320ff.

61 Ibid., 327ff.

62 Cited in "Urteile des Landgerichts Hagen, 17 November 1959," in *Justiz und NS-Verbrechen*, 22 vols, ed. A. L. Rüther-Ehlermann and C. F. Rüther (Amsterdam, 1969ff.), Vol. 16, No. 486.

63 W. Jacobmeyer, *Vom Zwangsarbeiter zum Heimatlosen Ausländer: Die Displaced Persons in Westdeutschland 1945 bis 1951* (Göttingen, 1985).

64 There are virtually no reliable sources. However, the reports of exiled Russian authors should be read with a certain degree of caution, e.g., A. Petrowsky, *Unvergessener Verrat* (Munich, 1963), or N. Tolstoy, *Die Verratenen von Jalta* (Munich/Cologne, 1977). Informative, yet in many respects also of questionable serious historical value is N. Bethell, *Das Letzte Geheimnis: Die Auslieferung russischer Flüchtlinge an die Sowjets durch die Alliierten* (Frankfurt/Berlin, 1980).

65 U. Herbert, " 'Apartheid nebenan': Erinnerungen an die Fremdarbeiter im Ruhrgebiet," in *Die Jahre weiss man nicht, wo man die heute hinsetzen soll*, ed. L. Niethammer (Berlin/Bonn, 1983), pp. 233–66.

8

THE GENESIS OF THE "FINAL SOLUTION" FROM THE SPIRIT OF SCIENCE

Detlev J. K. Peukert

In the following article, Detlev Peukert argues that the growth of the modern welfare state in early twentieth-century Germany was inspired by, and, in turn, nourished a "Utopian" view of social policy. Drawing on the "knowledge" constructed by the newly emerging "human sciences" – pre-eminently, sociology, psychology and criminology – welfare professionals maintained that just as medical science had learned to cure diseases previously thought to be hopelessly fatal, so, too, modern social welare would be able to heal the body social. The Weimar Republic (1919–33) represented the high point of this enterprise when social policy became firmly anchored in the state. But it was also during the Weimar Republic that the "limits of the welfare state" were revealed for the first time. German society proved to be a very sickly patient, especially after 1929, when the Great Depression, mass unemployment and state welfare cutbacks created previously unimaginable material deprivation and social dislocation. But rather than accepting the fact that German history had frustrated their ambitions, welfare experts began to redefine their Utopia. If German society as a whole could not be cured of its social problems, then healthy individuals must be protected from the influence of the "incurables." The "scientization" of the social and the "medicalization" of social problems had, so Peukert argues, opened the door to a new and distinctly modern "pathology" which found its ultimate expression in the Nazi program of separation of the "healthy" German Volk *from its "degenerate" racial and biological enemies* (Ausgrenzung), *followed by their sterilization or extermination.*

Racism offered a way out of the normative crisis produced by the triumph of science and reason over religion. Although nineteenth-century medical science had been able to prolong life, it could not

274

overcome death; and, unlike religion, it offered no spiritual consolation for this failure. Peukert argues that racism solved these problems by shifting attention from the individual body to the Volkskörper (the "eternal," genetic "body" of the German race or Volk). Although each individual must eventually die, the "healthy" race could survive. But while racism promised immortality for each individual's "healthy" genes, it also made the "elimination" of the "unfit" carriers of "deficient genes" a duty owed by the current generation to its posterity. This prescription had murderous results during the Third Reich, when the Nazis sought to "purify" the race, not only by exterminating the Jews, but also by sterilizing or killing the mentally ill and the physically handicapped, "deviant" youths, prostitutes and vagrants or Gypsies and homosexuals.

* * *

"DER TOD IST EIN MEISTER AUS DEUTSCHLAND" ("DEATH IS A MASTER FROM GERMANY")

If the unappetizing episode of the *Historikerstreit** has one redeeming feature from a historical point of view, it is that after endless wrangles about "fascism" and "Hitlerism," "intentionalism" and "functionalism,"† attention has been concentrated on

*The *Historikerstreit* or "historians' conflict" was a heated controversy in the late 1980s in which the German historian, Ernst Nolte, and the social theorist, Jürgen Habermas, played leading roles. Nolte claimed that the Holocaust was by no means a unique event in twentieth-century history and that genocide and totalitarian terror had not been invented by Hitler but by Stalin. Led by Habermas, Nolte's critics charged that his attempts to "relativize" the Holocaust, by comparing it to other genocides, amounted to nothing less than the "trivialization" of Nazi atrocities. The *Historikerstreit* did not produce a single piece of new evidence about the Holocaust or the Nazi regime. But it did show that certain historians were prepared to argue, as also were many leading conservative politicians, that the Nazi era should no longer be allowed to cast its shadow over the rest of Germany's modern history and over the identities of contemporary Germans.

†"Intentionalists" have stressed the systematic, step-by-step implementation, under Hitler's direct and explicit orders, of a long-standing plan for the extermination of European Jewry. In contrast, "functionalists" stress the greater importance of historical contingencies and of the "cumulative radicalization" of the Nazi regime between 1933 and 1945; they tend to see the "Final Solution" as the product, not only of Hitler's will, but as the (changing) outcome of competition amongst various Nazi agencies and leaders. "Functionalists" argue that extermination was not the only "answer" proposed for the "Jewish problem," but that the war made other projects, such as the creation of a vast Jewish "reserve" on the island of Madagascar, unfeasible, while at the same time

the single event around which any history of the National Socialist era must be written; namely, Auschwitz.[1]

Unfortunately, however, it must be said that the story of the *Historikerstreit* has been one of constant departure from, and evasion of, this central theme. The debate has been about the "Gulag" rather than "Auschwitz." Admittedly, in this respect it has not merely obeyed a certain inevitable logic of self-censorship. Even among writers who have been seriously and painstakingly concerned to understand how the policy of a "Final Solution" could emerge and be put into practice, the debate has inevitably widened out into a historical reconstruction of contexts and pre-histories, despite the fact that categories of historical explanation break down in the face of the horror of the policy's implementation.[2]

The effect of years of research has been that historians have moved away from a picture of the origins of the "Final Solution" which, while simplistic, also had the merit of simplicity; a picture of Hitler and his closest accomplices stricken with racial mania, making deep-laid plans to translate their fantasies into reality and then implementing these plans with demonic thoroughness, while keeping the fact from public knowledge throughout.

Today we know how complex and contradictory were the processes that led to the gradual and growing radicalization of Nazi racial policies and extermination methods, with their outcome in the murder of millions of Jews, Gypsies, people with mental and physical handicaps, and the "unproductive" and "asocial," as well as the subjection of the so-called *Ostvölker*.[3] We also know how the Nazis' racial policies were inextricably bound both with their domestic and foreign policies, and with the pattern – at first sight so normal – of German society; in other words, with everyday life, which despite its banality, or even perhaps because of it, became literally deadly for millions of people.[4]

---

dissolving all remaining constraints on mass murder. While the "intentionalists" tend to see the Nazi regime as relatively coherent and unified in its structures and purposes, the "functionalists" argue that the Nazi "state" was, in fact, a relatively incoherent constellation of competing organizations and interests (Gestapo, SS, DAF, Four-Year Plan, etc.), over which Hitler rather loosely presided.

Speaking schematically, we can list a number of processes, deeply rooted in the everyday life of German society, which were contributory factors in causing these racial policies to be implemented in the form of practices of extermination:

1) The escalation of the terror unleashed in the occupation of Poland and the Soviet Union led to mass-produced murder (Commissar Order, *SD-Einsatzgruppen*, treatment of prisoners of war).

2) The forced employment of millions of foreign workers meant that the *völkisch* hierarchy of *Herrenmensch* and *Untermensch* became a structural feature of daily life. This context made feasible the scheme of "annihilation through work" both inside and outside the concentration camps.

3) An anthropological racism, with anti-Semitism as its centerpiece, became radicalized in the following stages; bans on emigration; deportations to the East; unsystematic mass killings and, finally, systematic mass killings.

4) Paralleling this, a eugenic or "social-hygienic" racism became radicalized; that is, the programme of negative eugenics, proceeding via the mass compulsory sterilization of the so-called "genetically unhealthy" to the systematic murder of the allegedly incurable mentally or physically ill. Here, the techniques of mass murder were tested out, ranging from selection and deportation to the gassing of the victims and the concealment of the facts from the public.

5) In steadily widening areas of social policy, health policy, education policy and demographic policy, a ruling paradigm and guide to action became established whereby people were divided into those possessing "value" and those lacking "value." "Value" was to be selected and promoted, and "non-value" was to be segregated and eradicated. Large-scale social planning of a highly modern mind was harnessed toward the establishment of a racist Utopia in which the social question would be "finally solved."

6) By no means least in importance, the characteristic Nazi tension between the "normative" state and "prerogative" state, the chaotic "system" of jurisdictions and the rivalries between wielders of power led to a growing reliance on ever more radical "solutions" to self-inflicted problems.

7) Finally, behind this twofold radicalizing dynamism of form

277

and content, there was the intrinsically unstable motive force of the National Socialist movement, forever taking flight into the future, and of the elite cartel led, in the movement's name, by Hitler. Since to have stood still would have meant a loss of identity, and since the positive purport of the "national community" (*Volksgemeinschaft*) remained exceedingly vague, the regime inevitably drifted into an increasingly radical negative concentration on the eradication of a worldful of enemies.

All of these factors, combining in varied ways with regard to time, place and subject-matter, played a part in causing the racist Nazi Utopia to come to fruition in the deadly machinery of the "Final Solution." In other words, all monocausal explanations of the origins of the "Final Solution" are inadequate. Nevertheless, we can and must ask whether this tangle of causes does not contain one central thread which might explain the origins of the decision, unparalleled in human history, to use high technology to annihilate certain abstractly defined categories of victims. Such a thread, according to the view to be argued in this paper, is not to be found in the traditional history of anti-Semitism and the persecution of the Jews, despite the fact that Jewish victims constituted by far the largest group on the charge-sheet of Nazi terror up to 1945. Rather, what was new about the "Final Solution" in world-historical terms was the fact that it resulted from a fatal racist dynamism present within the human and social sciences. This dynamism operated within the paradigm of the qualitative distinction between "value" and "non-value." Its complement in practical terms was the treatment of the *Volkskörper*, or "body" of the nation, by means of "selection" and "eradication." What emerged was an abstract process of selection based on this factitious racist definition of a holistic national entity, and a scheme for a high-technology "solution" based on cost-benefit analysis. The "Final Solution" was a systematic, high-technology procedure for "eradicating," or "culling," those without "value." It operated in terms of the dichotomies "healthy/unhealthy" with reference to the *Volkskörper* ("racial body"), "normal/deviant" with reference to the *Volksgemeinschaft* ("national community"), and *Volk/Volksfremd* ("racial community"/"community alien") with reference to the nation and the race.

Recent research has shown that separate strands in the tangle of causes leading to the Final Solution were present in the most varied domains. The potential for good and ill inherent in the human and social sciences, and in the professions associated with them, was the central common factor. From this perspective, of course, the crimes of the Nazis are not the only historical event of relevance – if, that is, we regard these crimes, not as a lethal outbreak of anachronistic barbarism, but as one among other possible outcomes of the crisis of modern civilization in general.

Recent studies of the development of psychiatry under National Socialism,[5] of the history of the compulsory sterilization program,[6] of genetics, eugenics and medicine,[7] of social policy and demographic policy,[8] of education,[9] of the treatment of the "asocial" and foreign workers,[10] of the persecution of the Gypsies,[11] of the persecution of the Jews in the context of everyday life,[12] and of racism as a form of cultural expression,[13] have thrown up so many interconnected findings[14] that it seems legitimate to make a first attempt at an inclusive schematic interpretation. I readily admit that my interpretation has arisen out of my own research in the area of the history of social welfare education[15] and that it must naturally be subject to scrutiny and revision in the light of findings in the other individual areas mentioned. Nevertheless, any theory of the genesis of Nazi racism must transcend these individual fields, since racism itself transcended them, both in its theory and its practice.

The common racist factor in the disciplines and professions of the human and social sciences is the differential assessment and treatment of people according to their "value," where the criteria of "value" are derived from a normative and affirmative model of the *"Volkskörper"* as a collective entity, and the biological substratum of "value" is attributed to the genetic endowment of the individual. This broad definition of racism deliberately includes the views of theories and scientists who would certainly not have regarded themselves as "racists" merely by virtue of the fact that their theories and methods were centered on the tripartite model of "value," the *Volkskörper* as collective entity and the hereditary character of the relevant attributes. To include them is to take account both of the point that the character of National Socialism in general and of its racism in particular were an amalgam of different inputs and tendencies, and of the historically vital fact that the process that evolved into the "Final Solution" was one of cumulative radicalization in which the most deadly option for action was selected at every stage. In other words, the broad current which became the Final Solution was fed by numerous smaller currents which, taken singly, had perhaps never been intended, nor desired, by their authors to lead to such a result.

In order to understand the specific role played by racist thinking in the history of the modern human sciences and the professions corresponding to them, we must go back to the turn of the century. This was the period that saw the rise of the theories, and, more importantly, the practices, involving a scientific approach to human beings which have since put their stamp, for good or ill, on modern life.

THE HUMAN SCIENCES AND THE UTOPIAN DREAM OF A "FINAL SOLUTION"

By about the turn of the century, a scientific approach to the study of human beings and to the tackling of social problems had become a broadly practicable project for the first time. A breakthrough in scientific medicine had occurred, achieving notable success in combating epidemic diseases. This gave rise to the expectation that all the major diseases would be effectively combated, or even eradicated, in the foreseeable future. Drawing an analogy with the combating of disease, psychology and educational theory held out the prospect of scientific diagnosis of the personality and methods of therapy that would eliminate ignorance and social maladjustment. As prevention and cure spread through urban mass society, a new paradigm of social hygiene, targeted at the social causes of illnesses and deviance, became established. Increasingly, medicine took into its sights both the body of the individual and the collective "body" of the nation. As the state took it upon itself, through social policy, to deal with risks to individual welfare such as illness, accident and senile decay, so welfare services became professionalized and a new academically trained class of social workers was created and underwent rapid expansion.

Within a few decades, then, there had arisen a network of scientific and academic theories and methods on the one hand,

and of social welfare institutions and practices on the other, designed to solve the "social question." The complexity of the issues involved meant that these new approaches were soon forced to reach out beyond the more restricted problem areas which had originally given rise to them, and they now set themselves up, in terms both of self-image and of their mode of practical and administrative intervention, as key agents in the shaping and regulation of modern everyday life.

Increasingly, the scientific and academic disciplines and the social welfare institutions and professions began to claim to be able to provide comprehensive solutions to all "social questions." To be sure, the frustrating fact had to be faced from the outset that means were finite and successes limited. Accordingly, much of the subsequent history of these disciplines and institutions swung between the dual poles of their claim to comprehensive validity and control, on the one hand, and the depressing fact of their limited efficacy, on the other. It would have been possible to curb the sense of frustration by taking stock and scaling down the claims. It was also possible, however – and this was the more likely eventuality, given the astonishing breakthroughs made by the human and social sciences around the turn of the century – that the frustrating and recalcitrant features of social and human reality would be seen as obstacles that had to be surmounted by yet more rapid advance.

In the course of this evolution, the human and social sciences and professions acquired considerable new prestige, and the range of issues they were held competent to address was greatly enlarged. The emergence of the new social-scientific discourse in the domains of both theory and practice also coincided historically with drastic changes in social and living conditions at the turn of the century. We must briefly outline these changes here.

The so-called "demographic transition" involved a major upheaval in key elements of the life-cycle.[16] Traditional death-rate patterns, with high infant and child mortality, the ever-present risk of death in adult life, and relatively early death in old age, gave way to the modern mortality pattern: low infant and child mortality, reduced risk of death in adult life, and very high old-age mortality in line with the increased mean level of life expectancy. Death, in other words, largely ceased to be an everyday phenomenon, and reappeared only at the far end of the life-span in a less understood form. This alteration in the fundamental experience of life and death forced people to seek new existential answers; psychologically, indeed, we have still not come to terms with the banishment of death from daily life. The failure gave rise to a whole host of mechanisms of defence and repression.

The same applies to the role of the body, its health and sickness. Scientific medicine, public hygiene and social insurance meant that concern with the body increased enormously. The new message was a "natural" – in this context, a rational and scientific – attitude to the body. The practical achievements of medicine, but more especially its faith in therapeutic progress, led to an idealization of youth and health;[17] the decline of the body through illness and aging was to be defied, or at least deferred, as long as possible. The tension between the bodily ideal and individual bodily decay was to be overcome not only by science but also in respect of those individuals affected. The obvious move was for the actual target of scientific effort to switch from the individual, whose case in the long run was always hopeless, to the "body" of the nation, the Volkskörper.

Bound up with these changes was the youth cult, itself fed from many sources. One of its wellsprings was undoubtedly the demographic transition, which first produced a quantitative expansion on a scale hitherto unknown, and then, with the shift toward the two-child family, instigated a process of qualitative transformation as parents became able to afford to devote more intensive care to their offspring. On top of this came the social and cultural thrust of innovation at the turn of the century, which made for a downgrading of the experience of the older generation and an identification of modernity with youthfulness.[18]

The youth cult reflected more than merely demographic changes. It signaled the decisive breakthrough of modern forms of life that occurred around the turn of the century and that entitle the period to be called (by analogy with cultural history) the beginning of the "classical modern" era. Industrialization, urbanization, mass society and the permeation of everyday life with technology are merely some of the markers of this sociocultural modernization process. They were also the key concepts invoked in a vigorous process of self-scrutiny and debate conducted in the name of cultural criticism, social reform and life-style reform. The debate was mirrored by the arrival of a new sense of vitality not only among the avant-garde, but in the everyday lives of the masses. This, in turn, entailed unprecedented efforts at reorientation. Traditional sources of meaning and ritualized structures in everyday life failed to provide answers to the new questions. The drive for innovation devalued the experience of the older generation, yet for a long time it was unclear what new kinds of outlook would replace it.

Undoubtedly, these complex processes of upheaval in life-patterns were viewed, for the most part, favorably at the turn of the century and were seen as indicators of the advancing realization of the enlightenment ideal of the greatest happiness of the greatest number. It seemed that the human sciences and social professions would abolish the limitations of the human condition, or at least continue to push back their frontiers.

Implicit within this faith in progress, however – which was very closely bound up with the new spirit of vitality in the new scientific and social professions – was a fundamental sense of insecurity, as critical contemporaries were quick to point out. Illness, aging and death might have been banished from modern day-to-day experience, but they lay in wait on the dark side of the modern sense of vitality, more threatening and less understood than before, ready to usher in the extinction of the individual.

Siegfried Kracauer, writing in 1929, diagnosed this phenomenon in his acute analysis of modern white-collar culture and its *neue Sachlichkeit* ("new objectivity") optimism during the brief span of the "golden twenties":

> It is, however, a mark of the *neue Sachlichkeit* altogether that it is a façade behind which nothing lies concealed. It has not been wrested from the depths; it is an aping of profundity. Like the rejection of old age, it springs from a dread of confrontation with death.[19]

Making death a taboo, idealizing the body, the cult of youth and the façade-like character of modern consumer culture all became collective repositories of meaning so quickly, primarily because of the fact that the long-term historical process of secularization had by now reached the masses and everyday life. The cohesive force of Christian constructions of meaning continued to diminish, as did the influence of religious rituals on major life-events and the social environment.

At the turn of the century, then, the gap created by the decline of religious influence on everyday life in industrial society was so great, and the conquest of the world by secularized, scientific rationality was so overwhelming, that the switch from religion to science as the source of a meaning-creating mythology for everyday life took place almost without resistance. The result, however, was that science took upon itself a burden of responsibility which it would soon find a heavy one. In order that we may better understand this process whereby a religious-based mythology of everyday life was converted into one legitimized by science, we should look for a moment at the question of the evolution of the world religions before the era of secularization.

Max Weber regarded theodicy as the central dynamic impulse behind the evolution of world religions. The vindication of an omnipotent and just God in a world so obviously dominated by suffering and injustice generated repeated shifts toward rationalization, stretching the conceptual frameworks of the different world religions to their logical limits. We can see the evolutionary dynamism within the human and social sciences as analagous to the pressure toward rationalization generated by theodicy; as a result of the process of secularization, the sciences were now promoted into the role of supplying the key concepts in the repository of everyday constructions of meanings. This science-based "logodicy" is equally the product of the borderline but universal experiences of suffering and death. It asks the question: how can the rationalist, secular ideal of the greatest happiness of the greatest number be vindicated, given that it is rebutted in the case of each individual by illness, suffering and death? The borderline, or extreme experience of death, cannot ultimately be explained away by means of scientific rationality alone, so long as death remains beyond science's reach. A "logodicy" of the human sciences accordingly drives the sciences into irrationality. It inevitably becomes fixated upon the Utopian dream of the gradual elimination of death, even while this dream is unfailingly frustrated in the life of each particular individual. The obvious escape from the dilemma is to split the target of scientific endeavor into the merely ephemeral body of the individual and the potentially immortal body of the *Volk* or race. Only the latter, specifically its undying material substratum in the form of the genetic code, can guarantee the undying victory of science itself.

Naturally, this abstract, ideal-type process can be discerned only in partial and mixed form in the actual thinking of individual scientists and theorists. It need not be an ever-present influence governing thought and action. It is, however, basic and permanent and has the corrosive force of existential doubt. It is also entirely subject to the business-cycle of history. In periods of social and scientific growth and advance, it finds expression in an almost boundless faith in progress; obstacles are minimized, the future seems assured, the message is "Not yet, but soon!" Indeed, the exact boundary between optimism and delusions of grandeur may not always be clearly apparent. Armed with the skepticism of hindsight, we are struck by the fantasies of omnipotence prevalent in the sciences and social professions at the turn of the century.[20] In times of crisis and the deceleration of progress, on the other hand, the grand designs are stalled as they repeatedly come up against insurmountable obstacles. The optimistic, utopian vision of the *Volkskörper* is stripped of its universality and is instead defined in negative, restrictive terms. The central concern now becomes that of identifying, segregating and disposing of those individuals who are "abnormal" or "sick."

The numerous varieties of racism, and particularly the institutionalized racism of the Nazis, added a ready-made armoury of weapons to the science-based search for an irrational solution to the "logodicy" of death. The paradigm here was the *Volkskörper qua* object of scientific aid and cure. The body of the individual might indeed be an obstacle to therapeutic success, but all that was needed was a decision; whether it could be cured, and hence, admitted to the ideal *Volkskörper*, or whether it should be eliminated – in which case the *Volkskörper* would again assume its ideal character after all.

Ideologically speaking, National Socialism offered a perfect validation of the primacy of the *Volkskörper*, with its doctrine of individual hereditary "value" and "non-value." Aesthetically speaking, it backed this up with its idealized body-images of steel-hard maleness, voluptuous femaleness and, generally, youthful health with its promise of immortality.[21] The split between the individual and national "body" also allowed the borderline experience of death to be explained away. In this sense, National Socialism reintroduced a language for negotiating the fact of death. In racist ideology, individual death and the ephemeral nature of individual existence are secondary in comparison with the eternal life of the *Volkskörper* and the perfectible genotype. Within the irrational logic that was National Socialism's hallmark, the nurture and improvement of the immortal *Volkskörper* in fact gave death a double "significance": in the form of heroic death and in the form of "eradication" (*Ausmerze*).

The eudemonistic sentiment that pervades Himmler's secret speeches justifying the "Final Solution" was, therefore, desperately serious. So, too, was the belief of numerous prominent scientists that the concentration camp experiments, "euthanasia" and "criminal biology," while harsh in their effects on the individual, were justified not only because they affected solely those without "value" but because they would secure the well-being of future healthy and normal members of the *Volkskörper*.

FROM MASS WELL-BEING TO MASS ANNIHILATION

It must be clearly emphasized that the ideal-type account given so far of the inner logic that led the human and social sciences to find their self-validation in racism depicts an extreme logical possibility; it does not imply that such an evolution was absolutely inevitable. On the contrary, it can be said that everyday mythologies, whether legitimized by religion or science, are only very rarely pushed to their logical limits. As a rule, it is an assortment of inconsistent and hence practicable half-measures, eclectically adapted to the inchoate structures of everyday life, that is used as a basis for action.

This was the case in the normal situation of work in the fields of science and social policy. A doctor, for example, might care selflessly for all of his patients and yet simultaneously cling to the Utopian vision of a *Volkskörper* of the future, freed of all hereditary defects. Like [Alfred] Grotjahn [1869–1931], he might be a [prominent, socialist] doctor concerned with public health and social hygiene, an impassioned champion of the welfare of those at the bottom of the social scale, and yet at the same time call for the sterilization of 30 per cent of the population on grounds of genetic defects. Naturally, too, doctors and social workers who derived moral certitude from religious or other beliefs were able to remain immune to racist ideas of "value" or at least to the barbarous consequences of such ideas. Historically speaking, this option remained open; such alternative ways of thinking and acting were possible. But there was also the racist option of the primacy of the *Volkskörper* over the individual, and of the "valuable" over the individual without "value."

The thesis of this essay is that the origins of the "Final Solution" can be established historically as follows: 1) We can show how the racist implications of the human and social sciences, in their function as constructors of meanings in everyday-life mythologies, might arise; 2) We can outline the possible alternatives that might result from these initial conditions and those options which, in the actual historical context, did in fact result; 3) We can reconstruct the concatenation of circumstances within which the racist option prevailed; 4) We can state the conditions in which the racist Utopia was radicalized into a program for action and implemented in the form of the lethal technology of the "Final Solution."

The current state of research does not yet enable us to translate this scheme into a total history of racism in the Nazi state, one that includes an account of its roots in the nineteenth century. We know enough, however, to be able to point to parallel, if very varied, sets of racist processes in the most disparate scientific disciplines and social professions. The history of one such area, which has been the subject of my own detailed research, may serve as representative of many others. This is the field of social welfare education.[22]

Social welfare education evolved, as a halfway house between educational policy and social welfare policy, to fill a loophole in the system of social control of young people that had arisen within the contradictions of modern industrial society. The loophole was to be filled by a higher cultural standard of youth service provision and a battery of youth welfare measures designed to rectify social deviance.

The most important phases of evolution were as follows:

1) The perception of the problem and a formulation of desired solutions to the problem, in accordance with the social reform aspirations and science-based progressivism of the 1880s and 1890s.

2) A phase of institutionalization, at first experimental and then very rapidly spreading to become the norm, still entirely governed by the optimistic goal of using state intervention to secure for "every" child the educational right to "physical, mental and social fitness" (1900–22).

3) A phase of routinization and crisis of confidence, particularly when room for manoeuvre becomes financially restricted in the 1920s. The old optimism now survives side by side with a new sense of frustration, and the first seeds of an alternative vision to that of comprehensive educational provision begin to take root. Proposals are already being put forward for a law of "detention" – or, euphemistically, "protection" – which will cover all those who fail to achieve the educational goal of "fitness," whether on objective or subjective grounds of "unfitness" or "ineducability." Legal schemes for compulsory detention of the "ineducable," however, break down both because of the unknown cost and because of internal self-contradictions in the attempted definitions of "ineducability." If the definition is kept narrow, then it does not catch all the social deviants intended, since they cannot be taken into custody as criminal or insane. But if the definition is made sufficiently wide to include them, then the overall number of those affected escalates so rapidly as to make a mockery of due legal process.

4) The search for new ideas by established educators, disturbed by the contradictions thrown up by work in the field, becomes intense in the crisis years 1928–33. The specific crisis within the field of youth welfare education, symptomatized by revolts and scandals in young people's homes, coincides with a self-critical debate among educational reformers on the "limits of educability" and "limits of education." In turn, within the context of the general crisis in the welfare state, these changes affect, and are affected by, the new program of welfare retrenchment. Among the various alternative proposals generated by this crisis debate, a new way of viewing the educational problem gradually gains ground as welfare provision is cut back. Social and educational provision has to run the gauntlet of cost-benefit trade-off. Services are allocated in accordance with their prospect of achieving immediate return, and the implicit

guiding criterion becomes the "value" or otherwise of those receiving the services or the educational provision. "Lesser value" is not necessarily defined in terms of hereditary tendencies, but it may be. By the final years of the Weimar Republic the new paradigm of selecting those of "value" and segregating those of "lesser value" has already begun to displace the previous paradigm of universality of provision and correction. This change of paradigm is reflected in the amendment to the Reich Youth Welfare Law of November 1922, when the "ineducable" are excluded from reform-school education. The racist doctrine of the genetic "value" of the individual gave the imprimatur of theory to practical policies that were already coming into effect.

5) When the Nazis came to power in 1933, the paradigm of selection and elimination, already dominant, is made absolute. What is new is not the paradigm *per se*, but the fact that its critics are forced into silence. In addition, through a voluntary pre-emptive act of obedience, racist terminology is elevated into the *lingua franca* of the human sciences and social welfare professions. And, as yet another change, one single branch of modern social thought, namely racism, receives supreme state backing and is given ever-greater scope to test its theories and methods and put them into practice.

6) After 1933, racism has an unprecedented operational license and is systematically implemented on a colossal scale, as in the compulsory sterilization of the so-called "genetically unhealthy." Yet, despite this and despite the constant establishment of new procedures of "special treatment" for the racially stigmatized in concentration camps, the racist paradigm of selection and eradication encounters the same crisis of confidence as that faced by the universal-provision paradigm ten years earlier. The "positive" racism underlying the system of youth welfare provision based on heredity rapidly comes up against limits which rebut its Utopian claims. Racist theorists accordingly start searching all the more stubbornly for ways of vindicating their views through the "negative" racism of segregation and eradication. While the image of an immortal, healthy *Volkskörper* remains vague, the catalogue of deviances that are to be eradicated becomes even more detailed and specific. This negative

radicalization of the racist Utopia becomes the vital guiding thread in the evolution of Nazi policy. "Eradication" more and more overtly becomes the favored option, although up to the outbreak of war no final choice has yet been made among the various ways of implementing it, which range from physical segregation and sterilization, via killing by neglect, to killing by design.[23]

7) With the outbreak of the war, and the issuance of the order calling for the systematic murder of those deemed "unworthy of life" (lebensunwertes Leben), the crucial step is taken from the racist Utopian dream to its realization in the "Final Solution." It is no accident that this move occurs at the focal point of one of the scientific professions. Indeed, the process whereby the racist definition of the victims of the "Final Solution" is now expanded makes plain that it is the eugenic, racial-hygiene variant of racism that has provided the key component parts of the machinery of mass murder; the notion of "non-value," removing ethical status from those affected; the anonymity of the process of categorization of the victims in terms of hereditary characteristics (largely specious in any case); long-standing preceding administrative practices involving institutions of segregation; and, finally, the scientific and technological input involved in the construction of the apparatus of murder itself. Anti-Semitism based on racial anthropology supplies the graphic and traditionally legitimized scapegoat image that helps to serve as the basis for the expansion of the categories of the victim. But the specifically modern character of the "Final Solution" derives from the swing to racial hygiene in the human and social sciences.

8) In the next phase, within the machinery of murder now running and incorporating ever-wider groups of people, the human sciences and social professions are engaged in a parallel process of theoretical and institutional generalization aimed at an all-embracing racist restructuring of social policy, educational policy, and health and welfare policy. The debates and drafts dealing with the "Law for the Treatment of Community Aliens" (Gemeinschaftsfremde),[24] the full implementation of which is abandoned in 1944 only because of the state of the war, unite the disorganized and conflicting separate disciplines and agencies of the Nazi state, typically,

in the negative project of identifying enemies.[25] The abortive projects of the 1920s to rescue progressivist welfare education by putting the "ineducable" into compulsory detention now resurface in the catch-all definition of *Gemeinschaftsfremde*, a category which potentially threatens everyone falling under it with police custody, if not imprisonment or death: "failures," "ne'er-do-wells," "parasites," "good-for-nothings," "trouble-makers" and those with "criminal tendencies."

Nazi racism, the professed goal of which had been to secure the immortality of the racially pure *Volkskörper*, in practice inevitably became converted into a crusade against life. It found its fulfilment in the ever-expanding mass production of murder of all those it defined as "unworthy of life." It found its final Utopian refuge from the borderline experience of death in the unbridled infliction of death upon others.

The fact that National Socialism followed this path does not mean that such a path was inescapable. On the contrary, several critical junctures and strategic shifts were required before the eudemonistic Utopian dream of the victory of science and social reform over mass poverty, ignorance, illness and death was transformed into the mass-destructive Utopia of racist purification of the *Volkskörper* through the "eradication" of lives of "lesser value." The strategic shifts included the following: 1) From the individual *qua* object of support to the social and national "body"; 2) From care for the needy to selection of those of "value" and eradication of those of "lesser value"; 3) From the ideal of the greatest happiness of the greatest number to a cost-benefit accounting of provision and likely return, based on the "value" of those eligible for support; 4) From self-indulgent delusions of technological and scientific grandeur to self-reproducing high-technology mechanisms of annihilation.

None of these shifts was inevitable, although all of them represented options implicit in the hybrid role of the human and social sciences in the modern world. It was owing to the particular character of historical change in Germany that the fatal sequence of choices was made, each in a specific historical situation, that led to the appalling logical extreme of the "Final Solution."

International comparisons can help to explain which aspects

of the crisis of the human sciences and of the mirage of a racist solution were specific to the German national tradition and which ones were bound up with the problems of modernization in general. Both crisis and solution, after all, were evident in other countries, albeit in different forms. Advance in the human sciences and in social policy was an international phenomenon, as was the growing associated tendency for the scientific and social professions to assert their claims in the social field. Racism was international, too, both in its more archaic guise as racial anthropology and in its more modern, eugenic, racial-hygiene version.

As far as specifically German national factors are concerned, we can cite the extraordinary acceleration in the process of modernization around the turn of the century and the corresponding explosive debate on cultural criticism, social reform and life-style reform. The level of institutionalization and bureaucratization within the social professions may well also have been particularly high. But distinctive national factors can really be discerned only in the crisis years of the late 1920s, when the general crisis of modernization in German society and the economy coincided with a deep-seated crisis of political legitimacy. And the vital factor leading to the radicalization of racism, and, eventually to the "Final Solution" was the character of the Nazi dictatorship. The German case was paradigmatic in as much as it revealed the lethal potential implicit in a general process of historical change; it was the product of national factors in as much as only the latter converted this potential into reality.

Let us pick out two critical episodes in the German case once again. First, the general crisis of modernization at the end of the 1920s promoted the change of paradigm to one of a policy of selection and eradication and then, with the Nazi seizure of power, gave racism a new institutional framework and a horrifying new source of energy. Second, the situation between the outbreak of the Second World War and the invasion of the Soviet Union, when the Nazis' racist Utopianism became progressively more radical in the negative "eradication" sense, gave rise to the appalling machinery of murder and the deaths of millions in the "Final Solution."

The process, it should be said, did not unfold without opposition. Resistance came from victims and their relatives; from a

292

not inconsiderable number of scientists and members of the social professions; from individuals who could not, and would not, suppress their detestation of racism and the results to which it was leading; and, indeed, though in varying degrees, from many non-fascist organizations, particularly the Catholic Church. Catholics, as religious absolutists, found it easier than Protestants, with their leaning toward non-transcendental rationality, to hold out against an ideology which sanctified the *Volkskörper* and deprived those of "lesser value" of their status as human beings. This fact can be explained if, as it has been argued here, we view the roots of modern racism as lying in the problem of legitimation in a secularized world. A secularized world no longer provided final answers; it had no way of pointing beyond itself. Once the façade of a non-transcendent everyday mythology had been shattered by crisis, the search was on for "final solutions."

The "death of God" in the nineteenth century gave science dominion over life. For each individual human being, however, the borderline experience of death rebuts this claim to dominion. Science therefore sought its salvation in the specious immortality of the racial *Volkskörper*, for the sake of which mere real – and hence imperfect – life could be sacrificed. Thus the instigators of the "Final Solution" finally achieved dominion over death.

AFTER AUSCHWITZ

The watchword for the human and social sciences in 1945, after the frenzy of the "Final Solution," was "Back to normal!" The distinctive character of daily life in the last years of the war and the first years of peace was certainly part of the reason for this. Millions had died in battle, at home or as refugees, and these deaths were experienced by the survivors with a directness and intensity that overshadowed memories of the "Final Solution," which, ostensibly, had taken place far from home. Post-war distress encouraged people to turn inward and deal with the more manageable dimensions of their own fate, leaving the fates of the millions who were unknown to them to pale into insignificance. It was in similar fashion that the scientific and social professions, which had shed their inhibitions under National Socialism, now rapidly reverted to the routines of everyday enquiry.

Thus, apart from the small group prosecuted in the Nuremberg doctors' trial, most scientists and professionals who had committed or been implicated in crimes found it possible to resume a post-Nazi normality directly where their pre-Nazi routine had broken off. Since there were few prosecutions even of those who had been guilty of offences in a juridicial sense, those who had been involved in planning, establishing, testing out, constructing and operating the machinery of the "Final Solution," yet were not technically liable to prosecution, could actually be pronounced "innocent."

At the same time, the destructive frenzy of the firing squads and gas chambers had furnished a *reductio ad absurdum* of the racist Utopia of a "neat and tidy" final solution to all the questions besetting modern society. Disillusionment set in even among those who had been tempted by the Utopian dream in the euphoric early years of the regime or during the period of German domination over the European continent.

Those, however – and most fell into this category – who attempted, by returning to "business as usual," simply to evade coming to terms with the Nazi past, were also obliged to try to revert to a pre-crisis mentality as far as their respective sciences and professions were concerned. The sense of crisis that had been sufficiently unsettling before the Nazi seizure of power to infect the human sciences with racism now had to be as firmly banished from consciousness as the Nazi years themselves.

Even among those scientists and academics, including some educational reformers, who had preserved their integrity and had been persecuted by the Nazis, coming to terms with the past took place in a selective fashion, either because there might be a sense of complicity or because of feelings of impotence. The result, with Nazi sympathizers and persecution victims in the scientific professions alike, was a blockage of any systematic analysis of the way in which their professions had been entangled in the history of racism in general and of National Socialism in particular.

There were only a few exceptions to this rule. One was the publication of documents by Mitscherlich,[26] which was initially criticized vehemently by members of the medical profession and then used as a pretext for closing off any settling of accounts with the past. In the early post-war years, there were also a good number of publications from a religious point of view which, not without reason, attacked National Socialism as part of a wider critique of secularism, but which never went beyond calling for a return to old Christian values and, hence, merely erected a moral and theological superstructure on top of a scientific base that was not itself called into question.[27] Altogether, it was far easier for Christian apologists in the 1950s to accede to the domination of science over everyday life by shutting out all problematic implications.

Just as the German economy in the 1950s resumed the path of growth abandoned in 1914, so the human sciences and social professions, by shedding their Nazi ideological baggage and the beliefs and atittudes acquired during the debate about "crisis" and "limits," returned to the unproblematic normality which they had abandoned in the quest for Utopian final solutions in the 1920s.

What of the present day? What can we do now? We shall not find a way forward unless we continue with the task, so far only partially tackled, of restoring awareness of what actually happened in the past. The fact that a younger generation is now represented in all the disciplines and professions of the human and social sciences is a help here, not only because this generation bears no personal responsibility for the past, but because after a quarter of a century of normality, *Wirtschaftswunder* ["economic miracle"] and faith in progress, a sense of running up against limits is reappearing once again. This sense of crisis makes it possible – indeed, makes it imperative – to raise questions about the historical crisis that preceded the upsurge of Nazi racism. A purely factual reconstruction of past events is possible only if, at the same time, we engage in a theoretical debate about options and opportunities within the disciplines and professions of the human and social sciences, past and present.

In any case, skeptical questions are increasingly being raised about the viability and substance of our everyday mythologies; about our images of youth and age, illness and health, life and death; about the moral categories we bring to bear in our dealings with others, notably those different from ourselves. Recent debates about foreign migrants and AIDS present a conflicting picture. On the one hand, we can see the continuing survival of a discourse on segregation, untouched by any historical self-consciousness. On the other hand, however, there is a considerable body of opinion pleading for the tolerance and responsibility that spring from an awareness of German history and of the genesis of the "Final Solution" from the spirit of science.

NOTES

The German original of this article was published as "Die Genesis der 'Endlösung' aus dem Geist der Wissenschaft" in Detlev J. K. Peukert, *Max Webers Diagnose der Moderne* (Göttingen: Vandenhoeck & Ruprecht, 1989), pp. 102–21.

1 *"Historikerstreit." Die Dokumentation der Kontroverse um die Einzigkeit der nationalsozialistische Judenvernichtung* (Munich, 1987).
2 Dan Diner (ed.), *Ist der Nationalsozialismus Geschichte? Zu Historisierung und Historikerstreit* (Frankfurt, 1987); Heide Gerstenberger and Dorothea Schmidt (eds), *Normalität oder Normalisierung? Geschichtswerkstätten und Faschismusanalyse* (Münster, 1987).
3 See the engaging discussion by Hans Mommsen, "Die Realisierung des Utopischen: Die 'Endlösung der Judenfrage' im 'Dritten Reich,' " *Geschichte und Gesellschaft*, Vol. 9, 1983, pp. 381–420.
4 *Alltagsgeschichte der NS-Zeit. Neue Perspektive oder Trivialisierung?* Kolloquien des Instituts für Zeitgeschichte (Munich, 1984); Detlev Peukert, *Volksgenossen und Gemeinschaftsfremde. Anpassung, Ausmerze und Aufbegehren unter dem Nationalsozialismus* (Cologne, 1982) [translated as *Inside Nazi Germany: Conformity, Opposition and Racism in Everyday Life* (London/New Haven, 1987)] and Detlev Peukert and Jürgen Reulecke (eds), *Die Reihen fast geschlossen. Beiträge zur Geschichte des Alltags unterm Nationalsozialismus* (Wuppertal, 1981).
5 Klaus Dörner, "Nationalsozialismus und Lebensvernichtung" in *Vierteljahreshefte für Zeitgeschichte*, Vol. 15, 1967, pp. 121–52; Ernst Klee, *"Euthanasie" im NS-Staat. Die "Vernichtung lebensunwerten Lebens"* (Frankfurt, 1983); Ernst Klee, *Dokumente zur "Euthanasie"* (Frankfurt, 1985); Ernst Klee, *Was sie taten, was sie wurden. Ärzte, Juristen und andere Beteiligte am Kranken- und Judenmord* (Frankfurt, 1985); Dirk Blasius, *Der verwaltete Wahnsinn. Eine Sozialgeschichte des Irrenhauses* (Frankfurt, 1980); Dirk Blasius, *Umgang mit Unheilbarem. Studien zur Sozialgeschichte der Psychiatrie* (Bonn, 1986); Hans-Walter Schmuhl, *Rassenhygiene, Nationalsozialismus, Euthanasie. Von der Verhütung zur Vernichtung "lebensunwerten Lebens," 1890–1945* (Göttingen, 1987); see also the survey of the literature by Clausjürgen Schierbaum, "Aussondern des 'Unwerten,' " *Neue Politische Literatur*, Vol. 32, 1987, pp. 220–32.
6 Gisela Bock, *Zwangssterilisation im Nationalsozialismus. Studien zur Rassenpolitik und Frauenpolitik* (Opladen, 1986), provides an excep-

tionally thorough source review and detailed historical account, and is also a penetrating theoretical study that lays the foundations for future research. My article here is greatly indebted to Bock's reconstruction of the internal logic and phases of evolution of racism.

7 Gerhard Baader and Ulrich Schultz (eds), *Medizin und Nationalsozialismus. Tabuisierte Vergangenheit-Ungebrochene Tradition?* (Berlin, 1980); Benno Müller-Hill, *Tödliche Wissenschaft. Die Aussonderung von Juden, Zigeunern und Geisteskranken 1933–1945* (Reinbek, 1984); Alfons Labisch and Florian Tennstedt, *Der Weg zum "Gesetz uber die Vereinheitlichung des Gesundheitwesens" vom 3. Juli 1934* (Düsseldorf, 1985).

8 Hans-Uwe Otto and Heinz Sünker (eds), *Soziale Arbeit und Faschismus. Volkspflege und Pädagogik im Nationalsozialismus* (Bielefeld, 1986); Heidrun Kaupen-Haas (ed.), *Der Griff nach der Bevölkerung. Aktualität und Kontinuität nazistischer Bevölkerungspolitik* (Nördlingen, 1986). The subtitle of this latter study gives an indication of the problems arising from the style of research it represents. Such work has the undoubted merit of recovering long-neglected aspects of racial, health and demographic policy as continuing historical processes and thus helping to explain the specific shape they adopted under National Socialism. The group of authors pursuing this line of research, however, centered around Karl Heinz Roth and Götz Aly, repeatedly creates obstacles to reaching a balanced assessment of its own achievements by fusing analysis with indictment and by confusing continuities with identical phenomena. The constant propagandistic tone of these writers casts doubts upon the reliability of the evidence they cite and rules out the possibility of any nuanced, scholarly discussion. Nevertheless, their findings must be taken into account by all serious historians and used as a spur to new research. See especially the series *Beiträge zur nationalsozialistischen Gesundheits- und Sozialpolitik* (Berlin, 1985ff.), five volumes of which are now available: *Aussonderung und Tod; Reform und Gewissen; Herrenmensch und Arbeitsvölker; Biedermann und Schreibtischtäter; Sozialpolitik und Judenvernichtung.*

9 Ulrich Hermann (ed.), *"Die Formung des Volksgenossen." Der "Erziehungsstaat" des Dritten Reiches* (Weinheim/Basel, 1985); Heinz-Elmar Tenorth, *Zur deutschen Bildungsgeschichte 1918–1945* (Cologne/Vienna, 1985).

10 Wolfgang Ayass, *"Es darf in Deutschland keine Landstreicher mehr geben." Die Verfolgung von Bettlern und Vagabunden im Faschismus* (Dissertation; Kassel, 1980); Ulrich Herbert, *Fremdarbeiter. Politik und Praxis des "Auslandereinsatzes" in der Kriegswirtschaft des Dritten Reiches* (Berlin/Bonn, 1985).

11 Michael Zimmermann, "Die nationalsozialistische Vernichtungspolitik gegen Sinti und Roma," *Aus Politik und Zeitgeschichte*, Vols 16/17, 1987, pp. 31–45.

12 Ian Kershaw, "Antisemitismus und Volksmeinung" in Martin Broszat and Elke Fröhlich (eds), *Bayern in der NS-Zeit*, Vol. II

(Munich/Vienna, 1979), pp. 281–348; see also the contributions by Mommsen, Allen, Wiesemann and Luchterhand in Peukert and Reulecke, *Die Reihen fast geschlossen.*

13 Klaus Wolbert, *Die Nackten und die Toten des "Dritten Reiches." Folgen einer politischen Geschichte des Körpers in der Plastik des deutschen Faschismus* (Giessen, 1982); W. F. Haug, *Faschisierung des Subjekts. Die Ideologie der gesunden Normalität und die Ausrottungspolitik im deutschen Faschismus* (Berlin, 1986); Hans-Dieter Schaefer, *Das gespaltene Bewusstsein. Deutsche Kultur und Lebenswirklichkeit 1933–1945* (Munich/Vienna, 1981); George L. Mosse, *Rassismus. Ein Krankheitssymptom der europäischen Geschichte des 19. und 20. Jahrhunderts* (Königstein, 1978); George L. Mosse, *Nationalismus und Sexualität. Bürgerliche Moral und sexuelle Normen* (Munich/Vienna, 1985).

14 The first comprehensive accounts of the different racist policies in their regional settings are given in Projektgruppe für die vergessenen Opfer des NS-Regimes (eds), *Verachtet–verfolgt–vernichtet. Zu den "vergessenen" Opfern des NS-Regimes* (Hamburg, 1986); Angelika Ebbinghaus *et al.* (eds), *Volksgemeinschaft und Volksfeinde. Kassel 1933–1945*, Vol. 1, *Dokumentation* (Fuldabruck, 1984); Vol. 2, *Studien* (Fuldabruck, 1987). The total history account by Norbert Frei, *Der Führerstaat. Nationalsozialistische Herrschaft 1933 bis 1945* (Munich, 1987), is the first adequate study of these complexities in the history of racism.

15 Detlev J. K. Peukert, *Grenzen der Sozialdisziplinierung. Aufstieg und Krise der deutschen Jugendfürsorge 1878 bis 1932* (Cologne, 1986).

16 Arthur E. Imhof, *Die gewonnenen Jahre. Von der Zunahme unserer Lebensspanne seit dreihundert Jahren oder die Notwendigkeit einer neuen Einstellung zu Leben und Sterben* (Munich, 1981).

17 George L. Mosse, *Nationalsozialismus und Sexualität. Bürgerliche Moral und Sexuelle Normen* (Munich/Vienna, 1985).

18 Thomas Koebner *et al.* (eds), *"Mit uns zieht die neue Zeit". Der Mythos Jugend* (Frankfurt, 1985).

19 Siegfried Kracauer, *Die Angestellten. Aus dem neuesten Deutschland* (Frankfurt, 1971; original edn 1929), p. 96. See also the stimulating essay by Erhard Lucas, *Vom Scheitern der deutschen Arbeiterbewegung* (Frankfurt, 1983).

20 Karl-Heinz Roth, "Schein-Alternativen im Gesundheitswesen: Alfred Grotjahn (1869–1931) – Integrationsfigur etablierter Sozialmedizin und nationalsozialistischer 'Rassenhygiene'" in Karl-Heinz Roth (ed.), *Erfassung zur Vernichtung. Von der Sozialhygiene zum "Gesetz über Sterbehilfe"* (Berlin, 1984), pp. 31–56.

21 See note 11 above.

22 See note 13 above.

23 See note 4 above.

24 See note 13 above.

25 Characteristically, a key role here was played by the Institute of Criminal Biology, directed by Dr Robert Ritter, at the Reich Security Head Office. The Institute was the scientific body responsible for

dealing with the persecution of the Gypsies, the Community Aliens Law and the Möringen and Uckermark experimental youth concentration camps.

26 Alexander Mitscherlich and Fred Mielke (eds), *Medizin ohne Menschlichkeit. Dokumente des Nürnberger Ärzteprozesses* (Frankfurt, 1962).

27 Heinrich Kranz, "Lebensvernichtung und Lebenswert" in Ludwig Lenhart (ed.), *Universitas. Dienst an Wahrheit und Leben* [Festschrift for Bishop Albert Stohr] (Mainz, 1960), Vol. 2, pp. 442–7; Bernhard Pauleikhoff, *Ideologie und Mord. Euthanasie bei "lebensunwerten" Menschen* (Hürtgenwald, 1986).

9

ONE DAY IN JOZEFOW
Initiation to mass murder

Christopher R. Browning

Peukert's essay expands the concept of the "Final Solution" to include the persecution and extermination of large numbers of non-Jews who were regarded by the Nazis as racially or biologically "inferior," as "lives unworthy of life." But the attempt to trace racism back to science and the welfare state could perhaps risk leaving us with a story of Auschwitz without the Jews. We must not lose sight of the unique position of anti-Semitism within the Nazi ideology of race or of the "special fate" of European Jewry in the years of the Third Reich. The Nazis constructed many racial "enemies," but they always attached an absolute priority to the "solution" of the "Jewish Problem."

Perhaps we too often visualize the "Final Solution" and the "Holocaust" in terms of the relentless, methodical, relatively anonymous, "industrialized" mass murder of millions of victims in the Nazi extermination camps. But large numbers of Jews were also murdered in bloody shootings, at close range, by men who had to look their victims, including women and children, directly in the face. How were the men who pulled the triggers able, psychologically and physically, to continue the killings after their uniforms were splattered with the blood and bone fragments of the people they had murdered? It is too easy to assume that only the fanatical anti-Semitism of Himmler's "Ideological Shock Troops" – the SS – could have motivated this kind of brutality. But as Christopher Browning shows in his chillingly concrete descrip-

This study is based entirely on the judicial records in the Staatsanwaltschaft Hamburg that resulted from two investigations of Reserve Police Battalion 101: 141 Js 1957/62 and 141 Js 128/65. German laws and regulations for the protection of privacy prohibit the revealing of names from such court records. Thus, with the exception of Major Trapp, who was tried, convicted, and executed in Poland after the war, I have chosen simply to refer to individuals generically by rank and unit rather than by pseudonyms.

tion of "One Day in Josefow," by no means all of of the mass shootings in occupied Poland and the Soviet Union were performed by the SS or the Gestapo. Otherwise quite "ordinary men" (in this instance, Hamburg police officers, some of them from working-class backgrounds) found themselves caught up in the "Final Solution" because the SS simply did not have enough manpower to murder the millions of Jews under German rule.

What made the men in this police unit hunt down and shoot thousands of Polish Jews? Certainly, it was not fear of punishment. Browning shows that some members of the unit were able to refuse from the outset to participate in the mass killings, or to stop killing once the mass murders had begun, without suffering serious consequences. Yet, these were the exceptions. The majority, who simply went ahead and did the "job" they had been given, appear to have been motivated by relatively mundane considerations. Some simply did not want to damage their future career prospects by showing that they were "unfit" for hard duty. Others, and these were probably the majority, submitted to a kind of perverse male peer group pressure which made refusing to murder defenseless Jews into an act of cowardice. Browning's article echoes important themes that have appeared in several of the earlier contributions to this volume; as both Alf Lüdtke and Adelheid von Saldern suggest, under Nazi rule, familiar values – such as pride in "quality work," "manliness" and "male comradeship" – might sanction barbarous behavior. And, as Bartov and also Mallmann and Paul argue, quite ordinary Germans made vital contributions to the construction of the Nazi system of terror and mass murder.

* * *

In mid-March of 1942, some 75 to 80 per cent of all victims of the Holocaust were still alive, while some 20 to 25 per cent had already perished. A mere eleven months later, in mid-February 1943, the situation was exactly the reverse. Some 75 to 80 per cent of all Holocaust victims were already dead, and a mere 20 to 25 per cent still clung to a precarious existence. At the core of the Holocaust was an intense eleven-month wave of mass murder. The center of gravity of this mass murder was Poland, where in March 1942, despite two and a half years of terrible hardship, deprivation, and persecution, every major Jewish community was still intact; eleven months later, only remnants of Polish Jewry survived in a few rump ghettos and labor camps.

In short, the German attack on the Polish ghettos was not a gradual or incremental program stretched over a long period of time, but a veritable *Blitzkrieg*, a massive offensive requiring the mobilization of large numbers of shock troops at the very period when the German war effort in Russia hung in the balance.

The first question I would like to pose, therefore, is what were the manpower sources the Germans tapped for their assault on Polish Jewry? Since the personnel of the death camps was quite minimal, the real question quite simply is who were the ghetto-clearers? On close examination one discovers that the Nazi regime diverted almost nothing in terms of real military resources for this offensive against the ghettos. The local German authorities in Poland, above all SS and Police Leader (SSPF) Odilo Globocnik, were given the task but not the men to carry it out. They had to improvise by creating *ad hoc* "private armies." Coordination and guidance of the ghetto-clearing was provided by the staffs of the SSPF and commander of the security police in each district in Poland. Security police and gendarmerie in the branch offices in each district provided local expertise.[1] But the bulk of the manpower had to be recruited from two sources. The first source was the Ukrainians, Lithuanians, and Latvians recruited out of the prisoner of war camps and trained at the SS camp in Trawniki. A few hundred of these men, among them Ivan Demjanjuk, were then sent to the death camps of Operation Reinhard, where they outnumbered the German staff roughly 4 to 1. The majority, however, were organized into mobile units and became itinerant ghetto-clearers, traveling out from Trawniki to one ghetto after another and returning to their base camp between operations.[2]

The second major source of manpower for the ghetto-clearing operations was the numerous battalions of Order Police (*Ordnungspolizei*) stationed in the General Government. In 1936, when Himmler gained centralized control over all German police, the Secret State Police (Gestapo) and Criminal Police (Kripo) were consolidated under the Security Police Main Office of Reinhard Heydrich. The German equivalent of the city police (*Schutzpolizei*) and county sheriffs (*Gendarmerie*) were consolidated under the Order Police Main Office of Kurt Daluege. The Order Police were far more numerous than the more notorious Security Police and encompassed not only the regular policemen distributed among various urban and rural police stations in

Germany, but also large battalion-size units, which were stationed in barracks and were given some military training. As with National Guard units in the United States, these battalions were organized regionally. As war approached in 1938–9, many young Germans volunteered for the Order Police in order to avoid being drafted into the regular army.

Beginning in September 1939, the Order Police battalions, each of approximately five hundred men, were rotated out from their home cities on tours of duty in the occupied territories. As the German empire expanded and the demand for occupation forces increased, the Order Police was vastly expanded by creating new reserve police battalions. The career police and prewar volunteers of the old battalions were distributed to become the noncommissioned officer cadres of these new reserve units, whose rank and file were now composed of civilian draftees considered too old by the Wehrmacht for frontline military service.

One such unit, Reserve Police Battalion 101 from Hamburg, was one of three police battalions stationed in the district of Lublin during the onslaught against the Polish ghettos. Because no fewer than 210 former members of this battalion were interrogated during more than a decade of judicial investigation and trials in the 1960s and early 1970s, we know a great deal about its composition. First let us examine the officer and noncommissioned officer (NCO) cadres.

The battalion was commanded by Major Wilhelm Trapp, a 53-year-old career policeman who had risen through the ranks and was affectionately referred to by his men as "Papa Trapp." Though he had joined the Nazi Party in December 1932, he had never been taken into the SS or even given an SS-equivalent rank. He was clearly not considered SS material. His two captains, in contrast, were young men in their late twenties, both party members and SS officers. Even in their testimony 25 years later they made no attempt to conceal their contempt for their commander as both weak and unmilitary. Little is known about the first lieutenant who was Trapp's adjutant, for he died in the spring of 1943. In addition, however, the battalion had seven reserve lieutenants, that is men who were not career policemen but who, after they were drafted into the Order Police, had been selected to receive officer training because of their middle-class status, education, and success in civilian life. Their ages ranged from 33 to 48; five were party members, but none belonged to the SS. Of the 32 NCOs on whom we have information, 22 were party members but only seven were in the SS. They ranged in age from 27 to 40 years old; their average was $33^1/_2$.

The vast majority of the rank and file had been born and reared in Hamburg and its environs. The Hamburg element was so dominant and the ethos of the battalion so provincial that contingents from nearby Wilhelmshaven and Schleswig-Holstein were considered outsiders. Over 60 per cent were of working-class background, but few of them were skilled laborers. The majority of them held typical Hamburg working-class jobs; dock workers and truck drivers were more numerous, but there were also many warehouse and construction workers, machine operators, seamen and waiters. About 35 per cent were lower-middle class, virtually all of whom were white-collar workers. Three-quarters of them were in sales of some sort; the other one-quarter peformed various office jobs, both in the government and private sectors. The number of independent artisans, such as tailors and watch makers, was small; and there were only three middle-class professionals – two druggists and one teacher. The average age of the men was 39; over half were between 37 and 42, the *Jahrgänge* most intensively drafted for police duty after September 1939.

The men in Reserve Police Battalion 101 were from the lower orders of German society. They had experienced neither social nor geographic mobility. Very few were economically independent. Except for apprenticeship or vocational training, virtually none had any education after leaving the *Volksschule* at age 14 or 15. About 25 per cent were Nazi Party members in 1942, most having joined in 1937 or later. Though not questioned about their pre-1933 political affiliation during their interrogations, presumably many had been Communists, Socialists, and labor union members before 1933. By virtue of their age, of course, all went through their formative period in the pre-Nazi era. These were men who had known political standards and moral norms other than those of the Nazis. Most came from Hamburg, one of the least Nazified cities in Germany, and the majority came from a social class that in its political culture had been anti-Nazi.

These men would not seem to have been a very promising group from which to recruit mass murderers of the Holocaust.

Yet this unit was to be extraordinarily active both in clearing ghettos and in massacring Jews outright during the *Blitzkrieg* against Polish Jewry. If these middle-aged reserve policemen became one major component of the murderers, the second question posed is how? Specifically, what happened when they were first assigned to kill Jews? What choices did they have, and how did they react?

Reserve Police Battalion 101 departed from Hamburg on June 20, 1942, and was initially stationed in the town of Bilgoraj, fifty miles south of Lublin. Around 11 July it received orders for its first major action, aimed against the approximately 1,800 Jews living in the village of Jozefow, about twenty miles slightly south and to the east of Bilgoraj. In the General Government a seventeen-day stoppage of Jewish transports due to a shortage of rolling stock had just ended, but the only such trains that had been resumed were several per week from the district of Krakau to Belzec. The railway line to Sobibor was down, and that camp had become practically inaccessible. In short the Final Solution in the Lublin district had been paralyzed, and Globocnik was obviously anxious to resume the killing. But Jozefow could not be a deportation action. Therefore the battalion was to select out the young male Jews in Jozefow and send them to a work camp in Lublin. The remaining Jews – about 1,500 women, children, and elderly – were simply to be shot on the spot.

On 12 July Major Trapp summoned his officers and explained the next day's assignment. One officer, a reserve lieutenant in 1st company and owner of a family lumber business in Hamburg, approached the major's adjutant, indicated his inability to take part in such an action in which unarmed women and children were to be shot, and asked for a different assignment. He was given the task of accompanying the work Jews to Lublin.[3] The men were not as yet informed of their imminent assignment, though the 1st company captain at least confided to some of his men that the battalion had an "extremely interesting task" (*hochinteressante Aufgabe*) the next day.[4]

Around 2 a.m. the men climbed aboard waiting trucks, and the battalion drove for about an hour and a half over an unpaved road to Jozefow. Just as daylight was breaking, the men arrived at the village and assembled in a half-circle around Major Trapp, who proceeded to give a short speech. With choking voice and tears in his eyes, he visibly fought to control himself as he informed his men that they had received orders to perform a very unpleasant task. These orders were not to his liking, either, but they came from above. It might perhaps make their task easier, he told the men, if they remembered that in Germany bombs were falling on the women and children. Two witnesses claimed that Trapp also mentioned that the Jews of this village had supported the partisans. Another witness recalled Trapp's mentioning that the Jews had instigated the boycott against Germany.[5] Trapp then explained to the men that the Jews in the village of Jozefow would have to be rounded up, whereupon the young males were to be selected out for labor and the others shot.

Trapp then made an extraordinary offer to his battalion: if any of the older men among them did not feel up to the task that lay before him, he could step out. Trapp paused, and after some moments, one man stepped forward. The captain of 3rd company, enraged that one of his men had broken ranks, began to berate the man. The major told the captain to hold his tongue. Then ten or twelve other men stepped forward as well. They turned in their rifles and were told to await a further assignment from the major.[6]

Trapp then summoned the company commanders and gave them their respective assignments. Two platoons of 3rd company were to surround the village; the men were explicitly ordered to shoot anyone trying to escape. The remaining men were to round up the Jews and take them to the market place. Those too sick or frail to walk to the market place, as well as infants and anyone offering resistance or attempting to hide, were to be shot on the spot. Thereafter, a few men of 1st company were to accompany the work Jews selected at the market place, while the rest were to proceed to the forest to form the firing squads. The Jews were to be loaded onto battalion trucks by 2nd company and shuttled from the market place to the forest.

Having given the company commanders their respective assignments, Trapp spent the rest of the day in town, mostly in a school room converted into his headquarters but also at the homes of the Polish mayor and the local priest. Witnesses who saw him at various times during the day described him as bitterly complaining about the orders he had been given and "weeping like a child." He nevertheless affirmed that "orders were orders" and had to be carried out.[7] Not a single witness recalled seeing him at the shooting site, a fact that was not lost upon the men, who felt some anger about it.[8] Trapp's driver remembers him saying later, "If this Jewish business is ever avenged on earth, then have mercy on us Germans." (*Wenn sich diese Judensache einmal auf Erden rächt, dann gnade uns Deutschen.*)[9]

After the company commanders had relayed orders to the men, those assigned to the village broke up into small groups and began to comb the Jewish quarter. The air was soon filled with cries, and shots rang out. The market place filled rapidly with Jews, including mothers and infants. While the men of Reserve Police Battalion 101 were apparently willing to shoot those Jews too weak or sick to move, they still shied for the most part from shooting infants, despite their orders.[10] No officer intervened, though subsequently one officer warned his men that in the future they would have to be more energetic.[11]

As the roundup neared completion, the men of 1st company were withdrawn from the search and given a quick lesson in the gruesome task that awaited them by the battalion doctor and the company's first sergeant. The doctor traced the outline of a human figure on the ground and showed the men how to use a fixed bayonet placed between and just above the shoulder blades as a guide for aiming their carbines.[12] Several men now approached the 1st company captain and asked to be given a different assignment; he curtly refused.[13] Several others who approached the first sergeant rather than the captain fared better. They were given guard duty along the route from the village to the forest.[14]

The first sergeant organized his men into two groups of about thirty-five men, which was roughly equivalent to the number of Jews who could be loaded into each truck. In turn each squad met an arriving truck at the unloading point on the edge of the forest. The individual squad members paired off face-to-face with the individual Jews they were to shoot, and marched their victims into the forest. The first sergeant remained in the forest to supervise the shooting. The Jews were forced to lie face down in a row. The policemen stepped up behind them, and on a signal from the first sergeant fired their carbines at point-blank range into the necks of their victims. The first sergeant then moved a few yards deeper into the forest to supervise the next execution. So-called "mercy shots" were given by a noncommissioned officer, as many of the men, some out of excitement and some intentionally, shot past their victims.[15] By mid-day alcohol had appeared from somewhere to "refresh" the shooters.[16] Also around mid-day the first sergeant relieved the older men, after several had come to him and asked to be let out.[17] The other men of 1st company, however, continued shooting throughout the day.

Meanwhile the Jews in the market place were being guarded by the men of 2nd company, who loaded the victims onto the trucks. When the first salvo was heard from the woods, a terrible cry swept the market place, as the collected Jews now knew their fate.[18] Thereafter, however, a quiet – indeed "unbelievable" – composure settled over the Jews, which the German policemen found equally unnerving. By mid-morning the officers in the market place became increasingly agitated. At the present rate, the executions would never be completed by nightfall. The 3rd company was called in from its outposts around the village to take over close guard of the market place. The men of 2nd company were informed that they too must now go to the woods to join the shooters.[19] At least one sergeant once again offered his men the opportunity to report if they did not feel up to it. No one took up his offer.[20] In another unit, one policeman confessed to his lieutenant that he was "very weak" and could not shoot. He was released.[21]

In the forest the 2nd company was divided into small groups of six to eight men rather than the larger squads of thirty-five as in 1st company. In the confusion of the small groups coming and going from the unloading point, several men managed to stay around the trucks looking busy and thus avoided shooting. One was noticed by his comrades, who swore at him for shirking, but he ignored them.[22] Among those who began shooting, some could not last long. One man shot an old woman on his first round, after which his nerves were finished and he could not continue.[23] Another discovered to his dismay that his second victim was a German Jew – a mother from Kassel with her daughter. He too then asked out.[24] This encounter with a German Jew was not exceptional. Several other men also remembered Hamburg and Bremen Jews in Jozefow.[25] It was a grotesque irony that some of the men of Reserve Police Battalion 101 had guarded the collection center in Hamburg, the confiscated freemason lodge house on the Moorweide next to the university library, from which the Hamburg Jews had been deported the previous fall. A few had even guarded the deportation transports to Lodz, Riga, and Minsk. These Hamburg policemen had now followed other Jews deported from northern Germany, in order to shoot them in southern Poland.

A third policeman was in such an agitated state that on his first shot he aimed too high. He shot off the top of the head of his victim, splattering brains into the face of his sergeant. His request to be relieved was granted.[26] One policeman made it to the fourth round, when his nerve gave way. He shot past his victim, then turned and ran deep into the forest and vomited. After several hours he returned to the trucks and rode back to the market place.[27]

As had happened with 1st company, bottles of vodka appeared at the unloading point and were passed around.[28] There was much demand, for among the 2nd company, shooting instructions had been less explicit and initially bayonets had not been fixed as an aiming guide. The result was that many of the men did not give neck shots but fired directly into the heads of their victims at point-black range. The victims' heads exploded, and in no time the policemen's uniforms were saturated with blood and splattered with brains and splinters of bone. When several officers noted that some of their men could no longer continue or had begun intentionally to fire past their victims, they excused them from the firing squads.[29]

Though a fairly significant number of men in Reserve Police Battalion 101 either did not shoot at all or started but could not continue shooting, most persevered to the end and lost all count of how many Jews they had killed that day. The forest was so filled with bodies that it became difficult to find places to make the Jews lie down. When the action was finally over at dusk, and some 1,500 Jews lay dead, the men climbed into their trucks and returned to Bilgoraj. Extra rations of alcohol were provided, and the men talked little, ate almost nothing, but drank a great deal. That night one of them awoke from a nightmare firing his gun into the ceiling of the barracks.[30]

Following the massacre of Jozefow, Reserve Police Battalion 101 was transferred to the northern part of the Lublin district. The various platoons of the battalion were stationed in different towns but brought together for company-size actions. Each company was engaged in at least one more shooting action, but more often the Jews were driven from the ghettos onto trains bound for the extermination camp of Treblinka. Usually one police company worked in conjunction with a Trawniki unit for each action. The "dirty work" – driving the Jews out of their dwellings with whips, clubs, and guns; shooting on the spot the frail, sick, elderly, and infants who could not march to the train station; and packing the train cars to the bursting point so that only with the greatest of effort could the doors even be closed – was usually left to the so-called "Hiwis" (*Hilfswilligen* or "volunteers") from Trawniki.

Once a ghetto had been entirely cleared, it was the responsibility of the men of Reserve Police Battalion 101 to keep the surrounding region "*judenfrei*." Through a network of Polish informers and frequent search patrols – casually referred to as *Judenjagden* or "Jew hunts" – the policemen remorselessly tracked down those Jews who had evaded the roundups and fled to the forests. Any Jew found in these circumstances was simply shot on the spot. By the end of the year there was scarcely a Jew alive in the northern Lublin district, and Reserve Police Battalion 101 increasingly turned its attention from murdering Jews to combatting partisans.

In looking at the half-year after Jozefow, one sees that this massacre drew an important dividing line. Those men who stayed with the assignment and shot all day found the subsequent actions much easier to perform. Most of the men were bitter about what they had been asked to do at Jozefow, and it became taboo even to speak of it. Even thirty years later they could not hide the horror of endlessly shooting Jews at pointblank range. In contrast, however, they spoke of surrounding ghettos and watching the Hiwis brutally drive the Jews onto the death trains with considerable detachment and a near-total absence of any sense of participation or responsibility. Such actions they routinely dismissed with a standard refrain: "I was *only* in the police cordon there." The shock treatment of Jozefow had created an effective and desensitized unit of ghetto-clearers and, when the occasion required, outright murderers. After Jozefow nothing else seemed so terrible. Heavy drinking also contributed to numbing the men's sensibilities. One nondrinking policeman noted that "most of the other men drank so much solely because of the many shootings of Jews, for such a life was quite intolerable sober" (*die meisten der anderen*

Kameraden lediglich auf Grund der vielen Judenerschiessungen soviel getrunken haben, da ein derartiges Leben nüchtern gar nicht zu ertragen war).[31]

Among those who either chose not to shoot at Jozefow or proved "too weak" to carry on and made no subsequent attempt to rectify this image of "weakness," a different trend developed. If they wished they were for the most part left alone and excluded from further killing actions, especially the frequent "Jew hunts." The consequences of their holding aloof from the mass murder were not grave. The reserve lieutenant of 1st company who had protested against being involved in the Jozefow shooting and had been allowed to accompany the work Jews to Lublin subsequently went to Major Trapp and declared that in the future he would not take part in any *Aktion* unless explicitly ordered. He made no attempt to hide his aversion to what the battalion was doing, and his attitude was known to almost everyone in the company.[32] He also wrote to Hamburg and requested that he be recalled from the General Government because he did not agree with the "non-police" functions being performed by the battalion there. Major Trapp not only avoided any confrontation but protected him. Orders involving actions against the Jews were simply passed from battalion or company headquarters to his deputy. He was, in current terminology, "left out of the loop." In November 1942 he was recalled to Hamburg, made adjutant to the Police President of that city, and subsequently promoted![33]

The man who had first stepped out at Jozefow was sent on almost every partisan action but not on the "Jew hunts." He suspected that this pattern resulted from his earlier behavior in Jozefow.[34] Another man who had not joined the shooters at Jozefow was given excess tours of guard duty and other unpleasant assignments and was not promoted. But he was not assigned to the "Jew hunts" and firing squads, because the officers wanted only "men" with them and in their eyes he was "no man." Others who felt as he did received the same treatment, he said.[35] Such men could not, however, always protect themselves against officers out to get them. One man was assigned to a firing squad by a vengeful officer precisely because he had not yet been involved in a shooting.[36]

The experience of Reserve Police Battalion 101 poses disturbing questions to those concerned with the lessons and legacies

311

of the Holocaust. Previous explanations for the behavior of the perpetrators, especially those at the lowest level who came face-to-face with the Jews they killed, seem inadequate. Above all the perpetrators themselves have constantly cited inescapable orders to account for their behavior. In Jozefow, however, the men had the opportunity both before and during the shooting to withdraw. The battalion in general was under orders to kill the Jews of Jozefow, but each individual man was not.

Special selection, indoctrination, and ideological motivation are equally unsatisfying as explanations. The men of Reserve Police Battalion 101 were certainly not a group carefully selected for their suitability as mass murderers, nor were they given special training and indoctrination for the task that awaited them. They were mainly apolitical, and even the officers were only partly hard-core Nazi. Major Trapp in particular made no secret of his disagreement with the battalion's orders, and by Nazi standards he displayed shameful weakness in the way he carried them out. Among the men who did the killing there was much bitterness about what they had been asked to do and sufficient discomfort that no one wished to talk about it thereafter. They certainly did not take pride in achieving some historic mission.

While many murderous contributions to the "Final Solution" – especially those of the desk murderers – can be explained as routinized, depersonalized, segmented, and incremental, thus vitiating any sense of personal responsibility, that was clearly not the case in Jozefow, where the killers confronted the reality of their actions in the starkest way. Finally, the men of Reserve Police Battalion 101 were not from a generation that had been reared and educated solely under the Nazi regime and thus had no other political norms or standards by which to measure their behavior. They were older; many were married family men; and many came from a social and political background that would have exposed them to anti-Nazi sentiments before 1933.

What lessons, then, can one draw from the testimony given by the perpetrators of the massacre of the Jews in Jozefow? Nothing is more elusive in this testimony than the consciousness of the men that morning of 13 July 1942, and above all their attitude toward Jews at the time. Most simply denied that they had had any choice. Faced with the testimony of others, they did not contest that Trapp had made the offer but repeatedly claimed that they had not heard that part of his speech or could not remember it. A few who admitted that they had been given the choice and yet failed to opt out were quite blunt. One said that he had not wanted to be considered a coward by his comrades.[37] Another – more aware of what truly required courage – said quite simply: "I was cowardly."[38] A few others also made the attempt to confront the question of choice but failed to find the words. It was a different time and place, as if they had been on another political planet, and the political vocabulary and values of the 1960s were helpless to explain the situation in which they had found themselves in 1942. As one man admitted, it was not until years later that he began to consider that what he had done had not been right. He had not given it a thought at the time.[39]

Several men who chose not to take part were more specific about their motives. One said that he accepted the possible disadvantages of his course of action "because I was not a career policeman and also did not want to become one, but rather an independent skilled craftsman, and I had my business back home. . . . thus it was of no consequence that my police career would not prosper" (*denn ich war kein aktiven Polizist und wollte auch keiner werden, sondern selbstständiger Handwerksmeister und ich hatte zu Hause meinen Betrieb. . . . deshalb macht es mir nichts aus, dass meine Karriere keinen Aufstieg haben würde*).[40] The reserve lieutenant of 1st company placed a similar emphasis on the importance of economic independence when explaining why his situation was not analogous to that of the two SS captains on trial. "I was somewhat older then and moreover a reserve officer, so it was not particularly important to me to be promoted or otherwise to advance, because I had my prosperous business back home. The company chiefs . . . on the other hand were young men and career policemen, who wanted to become something. Through my business experience, especially because it extended abroad, I had gained a better overview of things." He alone then broached the most taboo subject of all. "Moreover through my earlier business activities I already knew many Jews." (*Ich war damals etwas älter und ausserdem Reserveoffizier, mir kam es insbesondere nicht darauf an, befördert zu werden oder sonstwie weiterzukommen, denn ich hatte ja zuhause mein gutgehendes Geschäft. Die Kompaniechefs . . . dagegen waren junge Leute vom aktiven Dienst, die noch etwas werden wollten. Ich hatte durch meine kaufmännische Tätigkeit, die sich insbesondere auch auf das Ausland erstreckte, einen besseren Überlick über die Dinge. Ausserdem kannte ich schon durch meine geschäftliche Tätigkeit von frühen viele Juden).*[41]

Crushing conformity and blind, unthinking acceptance of the political norms of the time on the one hand, careerism on the other – these emerge as the factors that at least some of the men of Reserve Police Battalion 101 were able to discuss twenty-five years later. What remained virtually unexamined by the interrogators and unmentioned by the policemen was the role of antisemitism. Did they not speak of it because antisemitism had not been a motivating factor? Or were they unwilling and unable to confront this issue even after three decades, because it had been all too important, all too pervasive? One is tempted to wonder if the silence speaks louder than words, but in the end – as Claudia Koonz reminds us – the silence is still silence, and the question remains unanswered.

Was the incident at Jozefow typical? Certainly not. I know of no other case in which a commander so openly invited and sanctioned the nonparticipation of his men in a killing action. But in the end the most important fact is not that the experience of Reserve Police Battalion 101 was untypical, but rather that Trapp's extraordinary offer did not matter. Like any other unit, Reserve Police Battalion 101 killed the Jews they had been told to kill.

NOTES

Reprinted from Peter Hayes (ed.), *Lessons and Legacies. The Meaning of the Holocaust in a Changing World* (Evanston, Illinois: Northwestern University Press, 1991), pp. 196–209.

1 For ghetto-clearing in the various districts of the General Government, the following are the most important judicial sources. For Lublin: Staatsanwaltschaft Hamburg 147 Js 24/72 (indictment of Georg Michalson) and StA Wiesbaden 8 Js 1145/60 (indictment of Lothar Hoffmann and Hermann Worthoff); for Warsaw, StA Hamburg 147 Js 16/69 (indictment of Ludwig Hahn); for Krakau, Landgericht Kiel 2 Ks 6/63 (judgment against Martin Fellenz); for Radom StA Hamburg 147 Js 38/65 (indictment of Hermann Weinrauch and Paul Fuchs); for Bialystok, StA Dortmund 45 Js 1/61 (indictment of Herbert Zimmermann and Wilhelm Altenloh), and *Documents Concerning the Destruction of Grodno*, ed. Serge Klarsfeld (Publications of the Beate Klarsfeld Foundation); for Gali-

zia, LG Münster 5 Ks 4/65 (judgment against Hans Krüger), and LG Stuttgart Ks 5/65 (judgment against Rudolf Röder).

2 For the Trawniki units, see StA Hamburg 147 Js 43/69 (indictment of Karl Streibel).
3 StA Hamburg 141 Js 1957/62 gegen H. and W. *et al.* (hereafter cited as HW), 820–1, 2437, 4414–15.
4 HW, 2091.
5 HW, 1952, 2039, 2655–6.
6 HW, 1953–4, 2041–2, 3298, 4576–7, 4589.
7 HW, 1852, 2182; StA Hamburg 141 Js 128/65 gegen G. *et al.* (hereafter cited as G), 363, 383.
8 G, 645–52.
9 HW, 1741–3.
10 HW, 2618, 2717, 2742.
11 HW, 1947.
12 G, 504–14, 642, 647.
13 HW, 2092.
14 HW, 1648; G, 453.
15 G, 647.
16 G, 624, 659.
17 HW, 2093, 2236.
18 HW, 1686, 2659.
19 HW, 2717–18.
20 HW, 1640, 2505.
21 HW, 1336, 3542.
22 G, 168–9, 206–7.
23 G, 230.
24 HW, 2635.
25 HW, 1540, 2534, 2951, 4579.
26 G, 277.
27 HW, 2483.
28 HW, 2621, 2635, 2694.
29 HW, 1640, 2149, 2505, 2540, 2692, 2720.
30 HW, 2657.
31 HW, 2239.
32 HW, 2172, 2252, 3939; G, 582.
33 HW, 822–4, 2438–41, 4415.
34 HW, 4578.
35 G, 169–70.
36 G, 244.
37 HW, 2535.
38 HW, 4592.
39 HW, 1640, 2505, 4344.
40 G, 169–70.
41 HW, 2439–40.

SUGGESTIONS
FOR FURTHER READING

Burleigh, Michael and Wolfgang Wippermann, *The Racial State. Germany 1933–1945* (Cambridge: Cambridge University Press, 1991).

Childers, Thomas and Jane Caplan (eds), *Reevaluating the Third Reich* (New York/London: Holmes & Meier, 1993).

Frei, Norbert, *National Socialist Rule in Germany. The Führer State, 1933–1945* (Oxford: Blackwell, 1993).

Herbert, Ulrich, "Labour and extermination: Economic interest and the primacy of *Weltanschauung* in National Socialism," *Past and Present. A Journal of Historical Studies*, No. 138, February 1993, pp. 144–95.

Kershaw, Ian, *Popular Opinion and Political Dissent in the Third Reich. Bavaria 1933–1945* (Oxford: Clarendon Press, 1983).

Kershaw, Ian, *The Nazi Dictatorship. Problems and Perspectives of Interpretation* (London: Edward Arnold, 1985).

Mason, Timothy, *Social Policy in the Third Reich. The Working Class and the "National Community," 1918–1939* (Oxford: Berg Publishers, 1993).

Mommsen, Hans, *From Weimar to Auschwitz* (Princeton, N.J.: Princeton University Press, 1991).

Peukert, Detlev J. K., *Inside Nazi Germany. Conformity, Opposition and Racism in Everyday Life* (New Haven/London: Yale University Press, 1987).

"Resistance against the Third Reich," special issue of *The Journal of Modern History*, Vol. 64, December 1992.